M. Patrick Graham is Margaret A. Pitts Associate Professor of Theological Bibliography at Candler School of Theology, and Director of Pitts Theology Library, Emory University, Atlanta.
Rick R. Marrs is Chair and Professor, Religion Division, Pepperdine University.
Steven L. McKenzie is Associate Professor of Hebrew Bible at Rhodes College, Memphis, Tennessee.

JOURNAL FOR THE STUDY OF THE OLD TESTAMENT SUPPLEMENT SERIES
284

Sheffield Academic Press

John T. Willis

Worship and the Hebrew Bible

Essays in Honour of John T. Willis

edited by
M. Patrick Graham,
Rick R. Marrs and
Steven L. McKenzie

Journal for the Study of the Old Testament
Supplement Series 284

Copyright © 1999 Sheffield Academic Press

Published by
Sheffield Academic Press Ltd
Mansion House
19 Kingfield Road
Sheffield S11 9AS
England

Typeset by Sheffield Academic Press
and
Printed on acid-free paper in Great Britain
by Bookcraft Ltd
Midsomer Norton, Bath

British Library Cataloguing in Publication Data

A catalogue record for this book is available
from the British Library

ISBN 1-85075-924-3

CONTENTS

It is with appreciation and respect that this collection of essays by colleagues and former students is offered to Professor John T. Willis on the occasion of his 65th birthday. The essays deal in various ways with worship as it emerges in the Hebrew Bible, thus picking up on Willis's own attentiveness to the cultic relations of biblical texts. The volume celebrates the career of a man who has been a devoted scholar, teacher and man of faith.

John Willis's contributions to the investigation of the Old Testament began with his work on the structure of the book of Micah for a Vanderbilt dissertation under J. Philip Hyatt. Later publications would continue this analysis of Micah but then turn to examine 1 Samuel, Psalms and Isaiah. Willis's interest in Scandinavian Old Testament scholarship, with its emphasis on cult-functional and tradition-historical approaches to Scripture, is evident in his biblical researches, but it finds expression of another sort in Willis's translation of certain Swedish works by Ivan Engnell and in his elaboration of the latter's significance for Old Testament studies. These efforts made the work of this creative Scandinavian scholar available to a much wider audience and so have served scholarship well. Finally, Willis's publications in the areas of Old Testament theology and ethics should also be noted. In all these efforts one can detect a respect for the biblical text, a mastery of the secondary literature and a willingness to explore imaginatively new hypotheses for interpretation.

John Willis taught at David Lipscomb College before coming to Abilene Christian University, where he has served on the faculty since 1971. As a professor of Old Testament, he inspired a generation of students, typically already appreciative of the value of the New Testament but often less inclined to Old Testament study. Nevertheless, John Willis introduced his students to critical methodologies and new perspectives on Scripture, and he showed them that the study of the Old Testament could be enormously interesting and rewarding. His standards for work in his classes were demanding, and his own scholarship set an example of diligence and clarity not easily forgotten. It was essentially the force of his influence that inspired several of these students to pursue doctoral programs in Hebrew Bible, and his support and encouragement nourished their efforts in this direction.

It would be difficult to know John Willis for long and not be aware of what undergirded his scholarly activity: a vital faith in God and devotion to the community of faith. This was clear not only from what was said during class, but also from the prayers before class, the pastoral attention to students afterwards—including the hospitality that he and his wife Evelyn showed by inviting students into their home—and his enduring involvement in the life of the church, which included preaching, teaching and service as an elder.

Finally, the editors would like to express appreciation to Professors David J.A. Clines and Philip R. Davies of the Sheffield Academic Press for their inclusion of this collection of essays in the JSOT Supplement Series. Their creative and energetic leadership continues to yield great benefits for all interested in the interpretation of Scripture.

M. Patrick Graham
Rick R. Marrs
Steven L. McKenzie

ABBREVIATIONS

AASF	Annales Academiae Scientarum Fennicae
AB	Anchor Bible
ABD	*Anchor Bible Dictionary*
AJSL	*American Journal of Semitic Languages and Literatures*
AnBib	Analecta biblica
ANET	J.B. Pritchard (ed.), *Ancient Near Eastern Texts Relating to the Old Testament* (Princeton: Princeton University Press, 3rd edn, 1969)
Anton	*Antonianum*
AOAT	Alter Orient und Altes Testament
AOTS	Augsburg Old Testament Studies
ATD	Das Alte Testament Deutsch
ATR	*Anglican Theological Review*
BARev	*Biblical Archaeology Review*
BASOR	*Bulletin of the American Schools of Oriental Research*
BBB	Bonner biblische Beiträge
BDB	F. Brown, S.R. Driver and C.A. Briggs, *A Hebrew and English Lexicon of the Old Testament* (Oxford: Clarendon Press, 1907)
BEATAJ	Beiträge zur Erforschung des Alten Testaments und des antiken Judentums
BETL	Bibliotheca ephemeridum theologicarum lovaniensium
BHS	*Biblia hebraica stuttgartensia*
Bib	*Biblica*
BiBJS	Biblical and Judaic Studies
BJS	Brown Judaic Studies
BN	*Biblische Notizen*
BThSt	Biblisch-theologische Studien
BVC	*Bible et vie chrétienne*
BWANT	Beiträge zur Wissenschaft vom Alten und Neuen Testament
BZ	*Biblische Zeitschrift*
BZAW	Beihefte zur *Zeitschrift für die alttestamentliche Wissenschaft*
CAD	Ignace I. Gelb *et al.* (eds.), *The Assyrian Dictionary of the Oriental Institute of the University of Chicago* (Chicago: Oriental Institute, 1964–)
CahThéol	Cahiers Théologiques
CBQ	*Catholic Biblical Quarterly*
ConBOT	Coniectanea biblica, Old Testament

CRBR	*Critical Review of Books in Religion*
CR:BS	*Currents in Research: Biblical Studies*
DtrH	Deuteronomistic History
EJL	Early Judaism and Its Literature
ErFor	Erträge der Forschung
ETS	Erfurter theologische Studien
EvT	*Evangelische Theologie*
EVV	*English versions*
ExpTim	*Expository Times*
FAT	Forschungen zum Alten Testament
FOTL	Forms of Old Testament Literature
FRLANT	Forschungen zur Religion und Literatur des Alten und Neuen Testaments
FTS	Freiburger theologische Studien
FzB	Forschung zur Bibel
GBSOT	Guides to Biblical Scholarship, Old Testament
GTS	Gettysburg Theological Studies
HAR	*Hebrew Annual Review*
HAT	Handbuch zum Alten Testament
HBT	*Horizons in Biblical Theology*
HKAT	Handkommentar zum Alten Testament
HSM	Harvard Semitic Monographs
HTR	*Harvard Theological Review*
HUCA	*Hebrew Union College Annual*
ICC	International Critical Commentary
IEJ	*Israel Exploration Journal*
Int	*Interpretation*
JANESCU	*Journal of the Ancient Near Eastern Society of Columbia University*
JBL	*Journal of Biblical Literature*
JBQ	*Jewish Bible Quarterly* (formerly, *Dor le Dor*)
JEA	*Journal of Egyptian Archaeology*
JNES	*Journal of Near Eastern Studies*
JNSL	*Journal of Northwest Semitic Languages*
JSNTSup	*Journal for the Study of the New Testament*, Supplement Series
JPSTC	Jewish Publication Society Torah Commentary
JQR	*Jewish Quarterly Review*
JSOT	*Journal for the Study of the Old Testament*
JTS	*Journal of Theological Studies*
KAT	Kommentar zum Alten Testament
LCC	Library of Christian Classics
LD	Lectio divina
LWC	Living Word Commentary
LXX	Septuagint
MTZ	*Münchener theologische Zeitschrift*
NCB	New Century Bible

NCE	*New Catholic Encyclopedia* (18 vols.; New York: McGraw-Hill, 1967–)
NIB	L.E. Keck *et al.* (eds.), *New Interpreters Bible* (Nashville: Abingdon Press, 1994–)
NICOT	New International Commentary on the Old Testament
NIV	New International Version
NJB	New Jerusalem Bible
NJPSV	New Jewish Publication Society Version
NorTT	*Norsk Teologisk Tidsskrift*
NRSV	New Revised Standard Version
OBO	Orbis biblicus et orientalis
OBT	Overtures to Biblical Theology
OTE	*Old Testament Essays*
OTG	Old Testament Guides
OTL	Old Testament Library
OTM	Old Testament Message
OTS	Oudtestamentische Studiën
OTWSA	*Oud Testamentiese Werkgemeenschap in Suid-Afrika*
PSB	*Princeton Seminary Bulletin*
PTMS	Pittsburgh Theological Monograph Series
QD	Quaestiones disputatae
RA	*Revue d'assyriologie et d'archéologie orientale*
RefTR	*Reformed Theological Review*
ResQ	*Restoration Quarterly*
RHPR	*Revue d'histoire et de philosophie religieuses*
RivB	*Revista biblica*
RSR	*Recherches de science religieuse*
RSV	Revised Standard Version
SANT	Studien zum Alten und Neuen Testament
SBLDS	Society of Biblical Literature Dissertation Series
SBLMS	Society of Biblical Literature Monograph Series
SBLSP	Society of Biblical Literature Seminar Papers
SBLSS	Society of Biblical Literature Semeia Studies
SBS	Stuttgarter Bibelstudien
ScrB	*Scripture Bulletin*
SEÅ	*Svensk exegetisk årsbok*
SJLA	*Studies in Judaism in Late Antiquity*
SJOT	*Scandinavian Journal of the Old Testament*
ST	*Studia theologica*
TDOT	G.J. Botterweck and H. Ringgren (eds.), *Theological Dictionary of the Old Testament* (Grand Rapids: Eerdmans, rev. edn, 1977–)
TGUOS	*Transactions of the Glasgow University Oriental Society*
ThW	Theologische Wissenschaft
ThWAT	G.J. Botterweck and H. Ringgren (eds.), *Theologisches Wörterbuch zum Alten Testament* (Stuttgart: W. Kohlhammer, 1970–)
TJ	*Trinity Journal*

TLOT	E. Jenni and C. Westermann (eds.), *Theological Lexicon of the Old* Testament (3 vols.; Peabody, MA: Hendrickson, 1997)
TQ	*Theologische Quartalschrift*
TUMSR	Trinity University Monograph Series in Religion
TynBul	*Tyndale Bulletin*
TZ	*Theologische Zeitschrift*
UBSMS	United Bible Societies Monograph Series
VAT	Vorderasiatische Abteilung. Throntafelsammlung. Staatliche Musee zu Berlin
VoxTh	*Vox Theologica*
VT	*Vetus Testamentum*
VTSup	*Vetus Testamentum*, Supplements
WBC	Word Biblical Commentary
WMANT	Wissenschaftliche Monographien zum Alten und Neuen Testament
WTJ	*Westminster Theological Journal*
ZAW	*Zeitschrift für die alttestamentliche Wissenschaft*

LIST OF CONTRIBUTORS

Leslie C. Allen, Fuller Theological Seminary, Pasadena, CA

Christopher T. Begg, Catholic University of America, Washington, DC

Don C. Benjamin, Kino Institute, Phoenix, AZ

R.E. Clements, Cambridge University, UK

James L. Crenshaw, Duke University, Durham, NC

M. Patrick Graham, Emory University, Atlanta, GA

Walter Harrelson, Wake Forest University, Winston-Salem, NC

J. Kenneth Kuntz, University of Iowa, Iowa City, IA

Rick R. Marrs, Pepperdine University, Malibu, CA

Victor H. Matthews, Southwest Missouri State University, Springfield, MO

Steven L. McKenzie, Rhodes College, Memphis, TN

Phillip McMillion, Harding Graduate School of Religion, Memphis, TN

Roy F. Melugin, Austin College, Sherman, TX

J. J. M. Roberts, Princeton Theological Seminary, Princeton, NJ

Timothy M. Willis, Pepperdine University, Malibu, CA

'FOR HE IS GOOD...' WORSHIP IN EZRA–NEHEMIAH

Leslie C. Allen

I welcome the opportunity to contribute to this *Festschrift* in honor of John Willis. I was introduced to his work in the early 1970s, when I was writing a commentary on Micah. I discovered impressive periodical articles under his name and quickly obtained a copy of the doctoral dissertation from which they were derived. It proved to be a model of careful research on the book of Micah that left no bibliographical stone unturned and sought to do utmost justice to the evidence. This volume's accent on worship reminds me of the hymnic play on Micah's name in Mic. 7.18, 'Who is a God like you?' In my contribution I also pay tribute to the honoree's interest in literary structure by linking worship in Ezra–Nehemiah to the structure of the composite book.

Recent Discussion of Worship in Ezra–Nehemiah

In 1970 P.R. Ackroyd hinted at the crucial role of worship in Ezra–Nehemiah, in his discovery of a repeated pattern of a royal command from a Persian king, a narrative showing how that command was carried out and a culminating religious celebration.[1] He found that pattern occurring three times in the pre-redacted text, first in Ezra 1–6, then in a block consisting of Ezra 7–10 and Nehemiah 8–10, and finally in Nehemiah 1–7, 11–13, except that he regarded Neh. 13.4-31 as a later supplement because it did not fit his structure.

Since then other scholars, reflecting a more synchronic approach, have tended to concentrate on the structure of the redacted work. B.S. Childs detected a fourfold division: (1) the release of the exiles under Cyrus and the rebuilding of the temple in Ezra 1–6; (2) Ezra's arrival and initial reform in Ezra 7–10; (3) the rebuilding of the walls of

---

1. 'The Age of the Chronicler', an essay reprinted in *The Chronicler in his Age* (JSOTSup, 101; Sheffield: JSOT Press, 1991), pp. 27-28.

Jerusalem in Nehemiah 1–6; and (4) the reordering of communal life in Nehemiah 7–13, a climactic section in which Ezra's and Nehemiah's work was combined.[2] A.H.J. Gunneweg found in Ezra 1–Nehemiah 8 three 'acts', each made up of three similarly structured 'scenes' and reaching a climax related respectively to the completed temple, a pure community and right worship in the holy city protected by a wall.[3]

Subsequently T. Krüger analyzed the structure of Ezra 1–6 in conscious dependence on Gunneweg's work.[4] He noted the inclusion formed by 1.1 and 6.22. He found three parts: (1) the edict of Cyrus in 1.1-4; (2) the return of the exiles in 1.5-3.6, concluding in the festival of Tabernacles in 3.1-6; and (3) the rebuilding of the temple in 3.7–6.22, concluding in the Passover celebration at 6.19-22. The third part has two sections, consisting of a first attempt marked by opposition and failure in 3.7–4.22 and a second attempt marked by opposition and success in 5.1–6.22.

H.G.M. Williamson has built both on Childs's contribution and on Gunneweg's early work and found four 'chapters' marked by parallelism.[5] In the first three, Ezra 1–6, 7–10 and Nehemiah 1–7, Persian kings, who feature as divine agents, issue commands, and the execution of their commands entails opposition. The commands relate in turn to restoration of the temple, of the community and of Jerusalem. In Ezra 1–6 achievement is marked by specific celebration and by the Passover. However, the celebrations appropriate to the next two 'chapters' were held over until the last 'chapter', Nehemiah 8–13, which represents a suspended climax. Here the role of a Persian king's divinely instigated command is replaced by proclamation of the divine Torah. Opposition now gives way to confession and recommitment. The celebration of 11.21–12.26 honors the work of both Ezra and Nehemiah (cf. the

2. *Introduction to the Old Testament as Scripture* (Philadelphia: Fortress Press, 1979), pp. 632-33.

3. *Esra* (KAT, 19.1; Gütersloh: Gerd Mohn, 1985), pp. 30-31, repeated in *Nehemia* (KAT, 19.2; Gütersloh: Gerd Mohn, 1987), pp. 30-31; cf. his earlier attempt in 'Zur Interpretation der Bücher Esra-Nehemia', in J.A. Emerton (ed.), *Congress Volume: Vienna, 1980* (VTSup, 32; Leiden: E.J. Brill, 1981), pp. 146-61, esp. pp. 154-58.

4. 'Esra 1-6: Struktur und Konzept', *BN* 41 (1988), pp. 65-75.

5. *Ezra, Nehemiah* (WBC, 16; Waco, TX: Word Books, 1985), pp. xlviii-li; cf. his essay 'Post-exilic Historiography', in R.E. Friedman and H.G.M. Williamson (eds.), *The Future of Biblical Studies: The Hebrew Scriptures* (SBLSS; Atlanta: Scholars Press, 1987), pp. 189-207, esp. p. 203.

parallelism of Ezra 6.14 and Neh. 12.26). In Nehemiah 13 the rectifica-
tion of abuses relates to the temple, the community and use of the city
wall. It is noteworthy that in both Williamson's and Krüger's analyses
the element of religious celebration comes to the fore.

The same was true of R. Rendtorff's succinct description of structure,
which also followed in the wake of Gunneweg's early work.[6] He traced
three 'phases', Ezra 1–6, 7–10 and Nehemiah, evidently as a whole.
Each phase begins with God's help in inclining the heart of a Persian
king (Ezra 1.1; 7.6, 26-28; Neh. 1.11; 2.4-8). There is constant hostility,
always overcome by divine help. He actually located this hostility only
in the first and third phases: Ezra 3.3; 4.1–6.13; Neh. 2.10, 19-20; 3.33-
37; 4.1-2; 6.1-4, 17-19. Another constant theme is the purity of the new
community, evident in its separation from outsiders (Ezra 4.1-3; 9-10;
Neh. 2.20; 13.23-29) and in the emphasis on its members' separation
(Ezra 6.21; 10.11; Neh. 9.2; 10.29; 13.3). He found a cultic frame for
Ezra-Nehemiah in the two celebrations of Tabernacles, first at the
return (Ezra 3.4) and then, by deliberate literary placement, after the
building of the walls (Neh. 8.13-18), now preceded by the reading of
the Torah. Both celebrations are regulated by 'what is written' and by
'the ordinance' (Ezra 3.4; Neh. 8.14, 18).

T.C. Eskenazi re-opened the issue of structure in an insightful and
comprehensive study of the composite work.[7] In line with a literary
theory of narrative, she has found three sections concerned with poten-
tiality (or defining the objective), process of actualization and success,
in Ezra 1.1-4; 1.5–Nehemiah 7 and 8-13 respectively. The second section is largely made up of three 'movements', the first to build the altar
and temple (Ezra 1.7–6.22), the second to build up the community
(Ezra 7.1–10.44) and the third to build the wall (Neh. 1.1–7.5). In each
of the movements there is a parallel development: preparation and identification of characters and task (Ezra 1.7–2.67; 7.1-28; Neh. 1.1-28);
initial implementation of the task (Ezra 2.68–3.13; 8.1-36; Neh. 2.9–
3.32); conflict (Ezra 4.1-24; 9.1-15; Neh. 3.33–6.19); resolution (Ezra
5.1–6.13; 10.1-17; Neh. 6.1-15); and conclusion (Ezra 6.4-22; 10.18-
44; Neh. 7.1-5), in the first case including celebration at Ezra 6.19-22.

6. *The Old Testament: An Introduction* (Philadelphia: Fortress Press, 1986),
p. 282.
7. *In an Age of Prose: A Literary Approach to Ezra–Nehemiah* (SBLMS, 36;
Atlanta: Scholars Press, 1988); cf. her article 'The Structure of Ezra–Nehemiah and
the Integrity of the Book', *JBL* 107 (1988), pp. 641-56.

In the third section the community celebrates the accomplishment of its task in accord with the Torah, while Neh. 13.4-31 has the function of a coda. In this final section there is consolidation according to the Torah in Neh. 8.1–10.40, in which the Torah is read and implemented three times; religious celebration finds a role in 8.9-12, 16-18. A fresh reading and implementation of the Torah occurs in 13.1-3.

Eskenazi's analysis is similar in principle, though not in detail, to the 'three plus one' approaches we have already seen. A new feature is the singling out of Ezra 1.1-4 for a major structural role, which contrasts with Krüger's minor role and indeed with the way other structuralists have matched its royal authorization with that in Ezra 7 and Nehemiah 1–2. The impulse behind her highlighting of Ezra 1.1-4 is her expansive definition of 'the house of Yahweh/God' here and elsewhere in the work as a comprehensive entity that includes Jerusalem, rather than simply the temple. Accordingly, the rebuilding of the city wall marks the completion of the house of God and so the accomplishment of the initial task assigned by Cyrus. However, some uncertainty has been expressed by other scholars as to whether the phrase can bear the weight of Eskenazi's broad definition.[8]

Introduction to the Present Analysis

My own attempt to find a coherent structure for Ezra–Nehemiah preceded much of my investigation of previous efforts. This investigation has served partly to confirm my discovery of parallel elements and partly to challenge it by the detection of further elements that needed to be integrated and by confrontation with apparently contrary evidence. The topical structure I offer is not a definitive one but aims to build on earlier studies in order to advance discussion.[9] I agree with Rendtorff

---

8.   See J. Blenkinsopp's review in *CRBR* (1990), pp. 121-23, esp. p. 122; D.J.A. Clines, 'The Force of the Text', in J.C. Exum (ed.), *Signs and Wonders: Biblical Texts in Literary Focus* (SBLSS; Atlanta: Scholars Press, 1988), pp. 199-215, esp. pp. 203-206; J.C. VanderKam, 'Ezra–Nehemiah or Ezra and Nehemiah?', in E. Ulrich *et al.* (eds.), *Priests, Prophets and Scribes: Essays on the Formation and Heritage of Second Temple Judaism in Honour of Joseph Blenkinsopp* (JSOTSup, 149; Sheffield: JSOT Press, 1992), pp. 55-75, esp. pp. 71-74.

9.   Mention should also be made of the largely stylistic comments on structure made by S. Talmon in 'Ezra and Nehemiah', in R. Alter and F. Kermode (eds.), *The Literary Guide to the Bible* (Cambridge, MA: Belknap, 1987), pp. 357-64. Talmon's approach has been supported and developed by M.A. Throntveit, *Ezra–*

that there are basically three divisions: Ezra 1–6; 7–10 and Nehemiah 1–13. A pointer in this direction is the redactional superscription in Neh. 1.1, 'The words of Nehemiah ...' It seems not only to explain the first person narrative that immediately follows but also to imply a single block of Nehemiah 1–13, in the course of which the Nehemiah Memoir occurs. I sympathize with those who find in Ezra–Nehemiah a fourfold scheme that isolates Nehemiah (7 or) 8–13, but I suggest that the evidence may be explained in terms of a bifurcating development that applies not only to Nehemiah 1–13 but also to Ezra 1–6 and 7–10. I favor Ackroyd's basic thesis of a repeated pattern of a royal command (by divine agency, as others have noted), its execution and consequent religious celebration. However, it needs to be developed in terms of the present form of the book, if possible. The latter two elements appear to be repeated in each of the three sections of the work, with a bifurcating effect (ABCB′C′). In fact, there seems to be an extra, doubled element, relating to the establishment of standard guidelines for the cult or community, so that the full scheme is ABCDB′C′D′. Moreover, mention must be made of the factor of opposition, which has a widespread but evidently not total presence within the execution of the initial commands.

The royal, divinely instigated command of Ezra 1.1-4 for the exiles to return and build the temple (I.A) is carried out in two stages: in their return and rebuilding of the altar and temple foundation in the course of 1.5–3.13 (I.B) and in the rebuilding of the temple itself in 4.1–6.22 (I.B′). Similarly, Ezra's task to take exiles and temple supplies to Jerusalem and to implement the Torah in the community is commanded in 7.1-28 (II.A) and executed in two stages: the gathering of people, journey to Jerusalem and delivery of supplies to the temple in 8.1-36 (II.B) and the imposition of the Torah on the community in 9.1–10.44 (II.B′). Nehemiah's royal commission, set out in Neh. 1.1–2.8, is to travel to Judah and rebuild Jerusalem (III.A). This charge is duly executed in the wall building of 2.9–7.5a (III.B). Nehemiah proceeds in 11.1–12.26 to engage in the repopulation of Jerusalem as a separate fulfillment, in order to 'build' up the city in a different sense (2.5; cf. Jer. 24.6; Ps. 102.17 [16]) as a living nucleus of the community of faith (III.B′).

The opposition that has been observed above in the description of

Nehemiah (Interpretation; Atlanta: John Knox Press, 1992), pp. 4-8, and throughout the commentary.

Rendtorff's and Eskenazi's schemes occurs in my scheme at I.B, B′ and III.B. One may add the opposition encountered in Ezra 10.15 (II.B′) and also the hostility encountered on the journey in 8.31 (II.B). If so, only the section III.B′ omits this feature in the course of the various implementations, compensating perhaps for the multiple cases of opposition encountered in III.B.

Religious celebration occurs within Ezra 1-6 in two complex forms, the sacrificing when the altar is built, the festival of Tabernacles and the temple foundation ceremony in 3.3b-5, 10-13 (I.C) and the dedication of the temple and the festival of Passover and Unleavened Bread in 6.16-22 (I.C′). In Ezra 7-10 it occurs first in a brief but significant form, the offering of sacrifices when Ezra's party arrives, in 8.35 (II.C), and then in a lengthy series, Ezra's confession of infidelity in 9.1-15, the formal confession by the gathered community in 10.7-14 and the sacrifices of offenders in 10.19 (II.C′). In Nehemiah 1-13 this element appears first in a multiple form, the readings of the Torah and the festival of Tabernacles in Neh. 8.1-18 and the service of confession and Torah reading in 9.1-37 (III.C), and also in the ceremony to dedicate the city wall in 12.27-43 and the Torah reading of 13.1-3 (III.C′).

In Ezra 1–6 the establishment of permanent guidelines for the post-exilic community and cultic institutions occurs in the commencement of regular burnt offerings in line with the Torah (3.2) at 3.6a (I.D) and in the appointment of priests and Levites at 6.18 (I.D′), also in accord with the Torah. In Ezra 7–10 this element is presented less obviously, if at all. Its first occurrence may be the installation of donated vessels in the temple at 8.33 (cf. 7.19) (II.D). The second occurrence could be the ruling for the future as well as for the present that, in echo of Deut. 23.3, the community would 'never' enter into relations with the peoples of the lands: it is formulated at 9.12 (and endorsed at 10.5) (II.D′). In Nehemiah 1–13 we find communal and cultic guidelines established in two stages. In ch. 10 (9.38–10.39) the community took a pledge to purify itself in accordance with the Torah and to maintain the temple (III.D). In 12.44–13.31 the community did purify itself according to the Torah and duly provided for the temple staff as the Torah required, so that they could function properly in response to Nehemiah's strenuous efforts in these very areas (III.D′).

This analysis of the composition of Ezra–Nehemiah has served to clarify in detail what a number of scholars have observed in general terms, that worship in the wide sense of cultic engagement with God is a recurring element. I have attempted to delineate the precise structural role it plays in the work and thus to show its general importance. Of course, worship is also the focus of the cultic guidelines that feature in another element, but there the purpose is institutional rather than participatory, and cultic participation is the primary concern of this essay.

Analysis of Individual Texts

Ezra 3.3b-5, 10-13
The first passage is Ezra 3.3b-5 along with 3.10-13 (I.C). The former passage was doubtless extrapolated by the editorial narrator from later, Torah-based cultic practice. The inaugural burnt offerings of 3.3 are a translation of intention into satisfying fact, in the light of v. 2. Verse 2 also introduces a major theme of religious celebration in Ezra–Nehemiah, compliance with the Torah as the new community's cultic script. Here Num. 28.2-4 seems to be in view. The burnt offerings represent the consecration of the rebuilt altar or at least presuppose it (cf. Ezek. 43.27). From the perspective of v. 6 they stand for the resumption of regular worship. The chronology of vv. 1-6 is not easy to follow: the festival of Tabernacles that is featured in v. 4 takes the reader forward from the first day to the fifteenth day of the seventh month. If chronological consistency is required, vv. 2-3 (and 6) represent a flashback to the preparations made for the festival to which people came in v. 1.[10] In v. 4 the scriptural quality of the celebration is mentioned again. The specification of daily offerings at the week-long festival has Num. 29.12-38 in view. The reference encourages the narrator to enumerate in v. 5 the gamut of sacrifices covered in the adjacent Num. 28.1–29.11, to reinforce the fact that the event marked the re-establishment of regular worship in conformity with the Torah.[11] It is also no coincidence that the dedication of Solomon's temple took place at the time of the festival of Tabernacles (1 Kgs 8.2, 65). The echo of that event at the first stage of the rebuilding of the second temple makes a claim for continuity with the worship of the first.[12]

10. See B. Halpern, 'A Historiographic Commentary on Ezra 1–6: Achronological Narrative and Dual Chronology in Israelite Historiography', in W.H. Propp *et al.* (eds.), *The Hebrew Bible and its Interpreters* (BibJS, 1; Winona Lake, IN: Eisenbrauns, 1990), pp. 81-142, esp. p. 97.
11. M. Fishbane, *Biblical Interpretation in Ancient Israel* (Oxford: Clarendon Press, 1985), p. 112 n. 21.
12. W.J. Dumbrell, 'The Theological Intention of Ezra–Nehemiah', *Ref TR* 45

In 3.10-13 the temple foundation ceremony is described. In essence it corresponds to a traditional ancient Near Eastern practice, attested in the Mesopotamian *kalû* ritual, a ceremony of re-foundation of a ruined temple.[13] Using 5.16 as a historical basis, the narrator evidently reconstructed it from the standpoint of cultic celebrations in his own day, since the temple singers are identified with Levites, unlike the early postexilic perspective (contrast 2.40-41). The description of the service accords with those of temple worship in Chronicles; in both pieces of literature there is an imaginative reconstruction in terms of a later form of worship. From 2 Chron. 5.12 and 7.6 we learn that the priestly trumpeters stood in the temple court in front of the altar of burnt offering, opposite the Levitical musicians/singers who faced the altar. The trumpeters sounded a signal, here presumably to mark the beginning of the service, while the Levitical cymbalists clashed their instruments to announce the start of the hymn supplied in v. 11.[14] As in Chronicles, the institution of sacred music is traced back to David. There is an implicit contrast with the Pentateuchal authority underlying the priestly trumpeting (Num. 10.10). The Davidic emphasis nicely matches the explicit Mosaic one in vv. 2-5. The authenticity of second temple worship is firmly grounded in the traditions of the Torah and of the first temple. Another balance is achieved in ch. 3 by the accent on sacrifice earlier and on music and song here, both key elements in postexilic worship.

The narrator's enthusiastic description continues with a reference to the ensuing hymn, which is supplied as an epitome of vocal worship, as regularly in Chronicles in this form or an even shorter one (cf. 1 Chron. 16.41; 2 Chron. 5.13; 7.3, 6). In pre-exilic times it was a communal hymn specifically linked to the thanksgiving service, to which individuals brought their songs and offerings after deliverance from crisis (Jer. 33.11). In the postexilic era it developed into a standard expression of

(1986), pp. 65-72, esp. p. 66. In v. 5 the sabbath sacrifices are included in the sacred seasons (מועדי) and so need not be added with the LXX (D. Barthélemy *et al., Critique textuelle de l'Ancien Testament,* I [3 vols.; OBO, 50.1; Göttingen: Vandenhoeck & Ruprecht, 1982], pp. 531-32, who compare Isa. 1.14).

13. Cf. D.L. Petersen, *Haggai and Zechariah 1–8: A Commentary* (OTL; Philadelphia: Westminster Press, 1984), pp. 240-42.

14. Cf. 2 Chron. 5.13 and also 1 Chron. 15.28, 16.42. For the understanding of postexilic instrumental and vocal music we are indebted to J.W. Kleinig, *The Lord's Song: The Basis, Function and Significance of Choral Music in Chronicles* (JSOTSup, 156; Sheffield: JSOT Press, 1993), esp. chapter 3.

hymnic praise for what Yahweh had achieved by a new demonstration of power in Israel's return from exile (cf. the redacted Ps. 107).[15] So here it is appropriately used to celebrate the restoration of worship after the cultic silence of the exile, which is poignantly expressed in Ps. 137.2.

The ambivalence of vv. 12-13 was evidently based on Hag. 2.3, 9, where reference is made to dissatisfaction with the new temple's splendor on the part of the older generation. Some suggest the linguistic parallels with that passage in v. 12.[16] The dissatisfaction is here applied to the foundation or platform of the temple, though we are not told what aspect might have sparked the protest. In light of the upbeat nature of Hag. 2.1-9 it is probable that the narrator wanted to draw attention to the 'not yet' nature of the restoration, which will emerge later in the material. In terms of Psalm 126, the restored fortunes enjoyed thus far by the returned exiles fell short of their eschatological expectations. Far from surpassing the glory of Solomon's temple, the second temple promised to be decidedly inferior. A generation gap is expressed in terms of the vocal responses of the congregation, shouts of 'Hallelujah' or 'Amen' by one group and 'Alas' by the other (cf. Ezek. 9.9; 1 Chron. 16.36; Rev. 19.4). The narrator, while frankly admitting the mixed blessing represented by the new temple, stands firmly on the side of the younger generation, looking toward the future and patiently grateful for relatively unsatisfying mercies in the present.

Ezra 6.16-17, 19-22
The next passage is 6.16-17, 19-22 (I.C'). Now no murmur of dissatisfaction is allowed to intrude on a scene of celebration. Joy forms a tight framework for the passage in vv. 16 and 22. Verses 16-17 have their own inclusion: the references to Israel. In v. 16 'Israel' stands for all the returned exiles, who are then divided into religious and non-religious groups. Although this identification is qualified in v. 21, it is clear that continuity with pre-exilic Israel followed an exilic detour, as in 2.1-2. The returnees are regarded as successors to the pre-exilic

---

15. See my *Psalms 101–150* (WBC, 21; Waco, TX: Word Books, 1983), pp. 60-65.

16. The punctuation of the MT, which the NRSV makes an effort to keep, is historically impossible and has rightly been ignored in the NIV, NJPSV and REB. The phrase הבית זה is an exegetical gloss that accurately elucidates the text: 'this refers to the [present] temple' (Barthélemy, *Critique textuelle* I, pp. 531-32).

community. Historically they comprised only three tribes (Judah, Benjamin and Levi), but for the narrator they were the essential representatives of the traditional 12 tribes. Later on, the Chronicler was to express disagreement with this perspective and to call for a wider vision of the people of God.[17] The narrator has written his account with one eye on the narrative of the dedication of the first temple in 1 Kgs 8.62-63. The reference to 'all Israel' there doubtless prompted the claim here that the returned exiles were its current counterparts. The sin offering is presented not to decontaminate the temple of uncleanness contracted during its building,[18] but significantly as an offering 'for all Israel'. Taken with the reference to exile, this suggests that the temple required decontamination from the people's sin (cf. Lev. 16.19; 2 Chron. 29.24) and that their sin related to their uncleanness 'in an unclean land' (Amos 7.17; cf. Hos. 9.3; Ezek. 4.13). Now they could make a fresh start at worship, in a new and purified temple that represented their cultic continuity with the pre-exilic Israel of 12 tribes who had worshiped at Solomon's temple.

The resumption of worship is typified by the account of the celebration of the Passover and Unleavened Bread in the following month (vv. 19-22). Verse 20 was presumably reconstructed in terms familiar to the narrator from his own experience of temple worship, including the Levites' slaughtering the Passover lambs, which did not accord with the Pentateuch (Exod. 12.6; Deut. 16.2; cf. 2 Chron. 30.17; 35.11).[19] The account of the celebration in v. 22 is strongly flavored with the excitement of its being the first communal worship in the rebuilt temple. Ezra 1–6 is brought to a close with a sense that the double mission of temple building and return from exile announced in ch. 1 had been accomplished. A restored people could at last worship in a restored temple.

In v. 21 mention is made of converts who had joined the community of returned exiles, a phenomenon that occurs in Ezra–Nehemiah only here and in Neh. 10.29 (28). 'The acceptance of some from outside on

17. For a discussion of the extent of the people of God, see S. Japhet, *The Ideology of the Book of Chronicles and its Place in Biblical Thought* (BEATAJ, 9; Bern: Peter Lang, 1989), pp. 267-351.

18. D.J.A. Clines, *Ezra, Nehemiah, Esther* (NCB; Grand Rapids: Eerdmans, 1984), p. 96.

19. For the construal of v. 20, if the text is correct, see Williamson, *Ezra, Nehemiah*, pp. 69, 72.

limited terms implies... the rejection of the rest.'[20] Their inclusion implicitly echoes a provision in Exod. 12.48 (cf. Num. 9.14) that aliens who had been circumcised might celebrate the Passover.

Ezra 8.35

The next worship passage occurs in 8.35 (II.C). The third person references in vv. 35-36 probably indicate their editorial provenance.[21] As in much of the earlier material, sacrifice is the medium of worship. The sacrificing keys into the preceding context not only as a partial fulfillment of 7.17, but also as an act of thanksgiving for an arduous journey safely accomplished (cf. 8.21, 23). The '12'-ness of the sacrifices recalls the 12 offerings 'for all Israel' in 6.17.[22] Here, however, the new returnees seem to be the subject.[23] It is likely that Ezra viewed his leading a group of new immigrants as a partial fulfillment of prophecy relating to the return from exile of the people of God. The prayer for 'a straight way' in 8.21, the refusal to accept a bodyguard in 8.22 and the apparent necessity to include Levites to carry the religious vessels all seem to allude to Isa. 40.3; 52.11-12. The editor concurred in this interpretation and appropriately viewed the sacrifices of thanksgiving as tokens that the true Israel was being gathered to its homeland by 'the God of Israel'. Particular reference is made to an offering of 12 goats.[24] As suggested in the case of 6.17, here more obviously there is reference to the uncleanness of exile. The final clause draws attention to the quality of the other sacrifices as burnt offerings. There might have been an offering of שלמים, traditionally rendered 'peace offerings', in their role as thank offerings or votive offerings. As in Ps. 66.13-15, the more

20. Ackroyd, 'Some Religious Problems of the Persian Period', in *The Chronicler in his Age*, p. 138.

21. See Williamson, *Ezra, Nehemiah*, pp. 116, 122.

22. '72' is to be read for '77' on the evidence of 1 Esdr. 8.63 and Josephus, *Ant.* 11.137. See Barthélemy, *Critique textuelle*, I, p. 543.

23. It is less likely that the whole community is the subject, as claimed by D.R. Daniels, 'The Composition of the Ezra–Nehemiah Narrative', in D.R. Daniels *et al.* (eds.), *Ernten, was man sät: Festschrift für Klaus Koch zu seinem 65. Geburtstag* (Neukirchen–Vluyn: Neukirchener Verlag, 1991), pp. 320-21, and M.H. McEntire, *The Function of Sacrifice in Chronicles, Ezra and Nehemiah* (Lewiston, NY: Edwin Mellen Press, 1993), pp. 76, 104 n. 278. In v. 36 the new arrivals are clearly in view.

24. For the parenthetical nature of the phrase, see N.H. Snaith, 'A Note on Ezra viii. 35', *JTS* NS 22 (1971), pp. 150-52.

costly burnt offerings were brought as a measure of the returnees' high degree of gratitude and praise.

Ezra 9.5-15; 10.7-14, 19
The next reference to worship comes in a series of adjacent passages, which are to a large degree lament-related. In 3.10-13 we heard lamenting cries voiced by some in the community. Now Ezra prays an intercessory and hortatory prayer of confession of infidelity to God in 9.5-15, which is followed by a formal confession on the part of the gathered community in 10.7-14 and by mention of the sacrifices of individual offenders in 10.19 (II.C′).

In Ezra's prayer, which has been composed in harmony with the account of vv. 1-2, the introduction in vv. 6-7a moves from confession of the present guilt of the community to a statement of solidarity with former guilty generations. Ominously, that former guilt had resulted in deserved and dire punishment from God (v. 7b). Yet the postexilic community had seen evidence of divine grace overlaying the punishment (vv. 8-9). This account of punished guilt and grace functions as a double stimulus against continuing in present guilt. Verse 10 comes to the point of the prayer ('And now'). In vv. 10-12 the present guilt is specified in terms of mixed marriages and branded as forsaking the divinely revealed Torah, here represented by Deuteronomy 7 and 23. The history of divine punishment and grace is recapitulated in v. 13, before the fatal consequences of persisting in present guilt are spelled out in v. 14. The prayer concludes in v. 15 as it began, with general confession. No petition for forgiveness is included: the next logical step lay not with God but with the community, to identify themselves with the prayer's perspective as forsaking the Torah and guilty of infidelity, in the hope that God's fatal wrath might be averted. Even this human consequence is left for members of the community to draw for themselves and for its leaders to organize a religious service to this end (10.1-5, 7-8).[25] The narrative sequel to Ezra's prayer in ch. 10 seems to be a continuation of the so-called Ezra Memoir used earlier, now editorially adapted to third person references to Ezra. He is significantly labeled 'Ezra the priest' in vv. 9, 10, 16: he is engaging in the specifically priestly work of instructing the people about their uncleanness

25. In v. 5 the Hebrew is to be understood as referring to the leaders of the priests, of the Levites and of all the laity: see L.H. Brockington, *Ezra, Nehemiah and Esther* (NCB; London: Oliphants, 1969), p. 93.

and pointing to the remedy. His speech in vv. 10-11 begins with a virtual digest of his prayer, in terms of past and present guilt, and a definition of the latter. At last there comes a call to the community to make his perspective their own and to engage in reform, to which the assembly gives its enthusiastic 'Amen' in v. 12. The 'loud voice' recalls the earlier lamentation in 3.12. The assembly's pragmatic proposals in vv. 13-14 are rounded off by citing the theological goal of averting the divine wrath threatened in v. 14.

The list of the guilty in vv. 18-44 was probably already part of the Ezra Memoir and was reproduced here in a redactionally abbreviated form. It includes in v. 19 mention of the sacrifice of a guilt offering, a requirement that doubtless originally applied to members of each group of offenders.[26] As was customary, the guilt offering accompanied reparation on the human level, which in this case was equated with the resolution of the problem of mixed marriages by divorce.[27] There is an explicit echo of the earlier context in that the 'guilt" of the offenders repeats the term used in Ezra's prayer in 9.6-7, 13 and 15 and in his summary in 10.10. The concept of מעל, which also dominated chs. 9 and 10, is twofold. Here in v. 10 there is a cultic interpretation via an implicit intertextual reference to Lev. 5.15, where the term occurs in the sense of a trespass on holy things.[28] However, מעל was used in the sense of covenantal infidelity at 9.2, 4 and 10.2, 6, 10, where it was associated with confession. Such covenantal infidelity is also signified by the Hebrew term in Lev. 26.40 (cf. 26.15; Neh. 1.8-9), where it is linked with the need for confession. Now the covenantal offense is translated into a cultic one. This insured that the appropriate offering was brought to secure forgiveness, in line with the Torah's requirement at Lev. 5.14-16. By such means Ezra's mission to teach the Torah and to make it the basis of communal life (7.6, 25) found fulfillment in the context of prayer and sacrifice.

26. See Williamson, *Ezra, Nehemiah*, pp. 148-49, 159.

27. For the verb הוציא (bring out), cf. the Qal form in Deut. 24.2. The adjective אֲשֵׁמִים (guilty) in the MT is difficult to relate syntactically. The most natural solution is to revocalize as אַשְׁמָם (their guilt offering; *BHS*, which compares Lev. 5.15) and to make it the subject of the clause, as in the NJB and NRSV.

28. Cf. J. Milgrom, *Cult and Conscience: The Asham and the Priestly Doctrine of Repentance* (SJLA, 18; Leiden: E.J. Brill, 1976), pp. 71-73.

Nehemiah 8.1–9.36; 13.1-3

The account of Nehemiah's ministry is amplified with its first element of worship in the course of Neh. 8.1–9.37 and 13.1-3 (III.C), where successive readings of the Torah are associated with the celebration of Tabernacles and a service of confession. Apart from 13.1-3, the report of the Torah readings has evidently been redactionally transferred from the Ezra Memoir. At first sight the Torah seems irrelevant to Nehemiah's work. In fact, it serves to develop ch. 1, where Judah's current plight and Jerusalem's sorry state are traced back in Nehemiah's prayer to breaking the Torah. So Judah needed to be taught the Torah if its curses were to be averted and its promises enjoyed. Similarly Nehemiah's prayer of confession in the first chapter is virtually amplified in the later service, during which further prayer is offered, now in a communal setting. So the transferred material functions as a development of themes already brought to the fore in the Nehemiah Memoir.

As Eskenazi observed, there are three assemblies at which readings of the Torah are given, followed in each case by responses in terms of worship (8.1-2, 13-18; 9.1-37). Nehemiah 8 has probably been taken from an earlier position after Ezra 8. As in Ezra 10, the first person references of the Ezra Memoir were editorially changed to the third person. Ezra is again designated 'the priest' in Neh. 8.2, 9 to emphasize his religious role. 'Ezra the scribe' also occurs (8.1, 4, 9, 13), which for the editor specifically highlighted his teaching of the Torah, as in Ezra 7.6.

Ezra's reading of the Torah for six hours is summarized in 8.3 and then unfolded in detail in vv. 4-8. The preliminary liturgical acts, consisting of a benediction in praise of Yahweh and the people's response in word and act, provide a worshipful, appreciative setting for Ezra's reading and for its interpretation by trained Levites circulating among the assembly. Verses 9-11 are marked by a triple refrain concerning the holiness of 'this day' and the obligation not to mourn.[29] The reader is

29. In v. 9 'Nehemiah the governor and' appears to be a late gloss (*BHS*). There seems to be no role for this secular official in this cultic context. As Williamson, *Ezra, Nehemiah*, p. 279, has observed, while the accompanying singular verb is syntactically possible with a multiple subject, the singular verb in v. 10 refers naturally to Ezra. This in turn suggests that the other singular subject in v. 9 was not originally there. In fact, v. 9, minus the initial reference, has a summary role, which is subsequently explained by Ezra's statement in v. 10 and the Levites' in v. 11. Textual evidence suggests gradual accretion: the LXX only attests 'Nehemiah', and 1 Esdr. 9.49 only a transliteration of the Hebrew for 'the governor', while the MT seems to have conflated both readings.

reminded that the day was the first of the seventh month (v. 2). The monthly new moon festival and the regular longer festivals were to be days of rejoicing according to Num. 10.10. In Deuteronomy joyful celebration is a mark of the festivals (Deut. 12.7, 12, 18; 14.26; 16.11, 14). Of the new moon days, that of the seventh month had special significance as a festival of trumpets (Num. 29.1-6; Lev. 23.24-25). So this sacred day had to be respected by being celebrated in joy. The tension between the people's weeping and the service leaders' exhortations to rejoice is reminiscent of Ezra 3.12-13, where official rejoicing was shared with lamenting dissatisfaction. Here, however, the lamenting is due to the content of some of the reading, which prompted a recognition of falling short of its standards. The sacred nature of the day as devoted to the joyful nature of God rendered such lamentation inappropriate. Rejoicing in Yahweh is described as a source of protection (מעוז; cf. NJB 'stronghold'). Such a positive attitude supplied a stimulus to comply with the divine will thereafter, which in turn would give protection against the divine anger that had loomed in Ezra 9. Cultic joy is duly manifested in shared meals, at Ezra's behest (cf. 10, 12; cf. Deut. 12.7, 18; 14.26 and the generosity enjoined in Deut. 12.12, 19; 14.27). In a resumption of v. 8b, it is observed that the communal joy derived not simply from the holiday but from appreciation of the reading and interpretation of the Torah.

The community leaders and the clergy returned for a second day of Torah study. The festival of Tabernacles was due to be celebrated two weeks later in the month, and so attention was paid to its implementation in line with the Torah. It had been observed before, according to Ezra 3.4, and so the issue was not *whether* it should be celebrated but *how*. In Ezra 3.4 the focus had been on sacrifice, in line with Numbers 29. Here, Lev. 23.39-43 is evidently in view, particularly its prescription of living in booths (vv. 42-43). From this passage was extrapolated the practical steps involved in making booths. The fruit and branches mentioned in Lev. 23.40a, presumably to be carried as in later tradition, are reinterpreted as pointers to the materials for the booths, with necessary updating according to availability.[30] The eventual rejoicing of v. 17 also marks an implicit implementation of Lev. 23.40b. However, the stress on the placing of the booths near the houses of residents of

30. Cf. Williamson, 'History', in D.A. Carson and H.G.M. Williamson (eds.), *It Is Written: Scripture Citing Scripture: Essays in Honour of Barnabas Lindars, SSF* (Cambridge: Cambridge University Press, 1988), pp. 25-38, esp. pp. 29-31.

Jerusalem and in open areas of the city implicitly recalls the venue of worship prescribed in the course of Deut. 31.10-13, specifically at v. 11, though the phrase 'before Yahweh' in Lev. 23.40 also presupposes it.

Certainly it was the prescription in Deuteronomy 31 that motivated Ezra's reading of the Torah during the festival, in v. 18a. On the other hand, the duration of the festival for seven days, plus a closing ceremony on the eighth in v. 18b, reverts to Leviticus 23, primarily v. 39. Such a duration also occurs in Numbers 29, but the sacrificial emphasis of that passage, which finds no counterpart here, and the contextual dependence on Leviticus 23 suggest that the latter text is in view. Verse 17 brings again to the reader's attention the identification of the worshippers as returned exiles, as earlier in worship contexts (Ezra 6.21; 8.35). A typological parallel is drawn between this community and those Israelites who first entered the land under Joshua. There was a special bond between the contemporary generation and that first one, each brought home at last and celebrating a divine promise kept. In particular, the reader is invited to compare Moses' injunction in Deut. 31.10-13 for the reading of the Torah at Tabernacles every seven years. This injunction was given within the context of the appointment of Joshua as his successor (Deut. 31.7-8, 14-29), and it was assumed that Joshua carried out this injunction (cf. Josh. 1.8; 8.34-35). The Torah reading in v. 18a flows naturally from v. 17. As Rendtorff recognized, the double attestation that the Torah's prescriptions were honored (vv. 14 and 18, 'written', 'according to the ordinance') serves to recall Ezra 3.4.[31]

The joyful element of the two periods of worship in Nehemiah 8 gives way to a different mood in the next chapter. Nehemiah 9 seems to be of composite origin: vv. 1-5 fit best after Ezra 10.9-15, which is dated in 'the ninth month, on the twentieth day of the month' (v. 9), while the appended prayer was an independent reflection of contemporary worship.[32] The chapter functions as a third reading of the Torah followed by a response. As soon as the festivals of joy were over (8.12, 17), it was appropriate to give vent to the lamenting response to the Torah mentioned in 8.9. In a wider context, the prayer achieves the ideal expressed in Nehemiah's private prayer: the exiled community must confess its sins before taking up residence in Jerusalem (1.5-11).

---

31. *The Old Testament*, p. 282.
32. See the discussion in Williamson, *Ezra, Nehemiah*, pp. 308-309.

So it forms a necessary preliminary to 11.1-24. Verses 1-5 are no longer related to the specific sin of mixed marriages but take on a general flavor.

Verse 2 now serves as an inverse summary for the chapter, the confession of contemporary sins corresponding to vv. 33-37 in the prayer and that of ancestral sins to vv. 16-30. The details of the service commence in v. 3: a three-hour reading from the Torah, followed by three hours of confession and praise. Verses 4-5 specify first the Levites who engaged in confession on the people's behalf and then those who called them to concluding worship. The ensuing prayer reverts to confession, as detail for what the Levites uttered with 'a loud voice'. A parallel is here drawn with earlier material that featured 'a loud voice', the lamentation of Ezra 3.12 and the earlier confession of 10.12.

Apart from the theme of confession, what attracted this prayer to the present context, like iron filings to a magnet, was the host of references to the Torah, as given by God in vv. 13-14 and spurned by Israel in vv. 16, 26, 29 and 34. A similar factor was the span of Pentateuchal references covered in the prayer, from the Genesis account of creation in v. 6 to the eating, being filled and growing fat of Deut. 32.15 (cf. *BHS* there) in v. 25. The turning point of the prayer is v. 32 with its introductory 'And now'. It veers to a low-key petition and backs it with confession and a piteous description of distress. Williamson has observed that in the narrative of three past cycles of sin, confession and restoration in vv. 26-31 the third cycle is left incomplete. Its expected cry for help and divine response, parallel with vv. 22b and 28b, are replaced by the contemporary generation's petition, confession and lament.[33] Their pleas, explicit and implicit, are emboldened by the propositional theology of grace formulated in vv. 17 and 31 and by the 'great mercies' mentioned in vv. 19 and 31. There is an underlying hope that the covenant gift of the land (vv. 8, 22-25) might be restored in full.

At this point we may consider the final Torah reading and its implementation in 13.1-3. The interest of this editorial paragraph lies in the content of the reading from Deut. 23.4-7 and in the people's response, but a cultic setting is presupposed in the light of earlier passages. The III.C′ section is supplied by this passage and the earlier 12.27-43, a key worship element in Ezra–Nehemiah. It consists of the ceremony to dedicate the city wall in 12.27-43. As a service of dedication, it forms a

33. *Ezra, Nehemiah*, pp. 315, 317.

parallel to that of the temple in Ezra 6.16-17, but in its emphasis on sacred music and song it matches the temple foundation ceremony of Ezra 3.10-13. Indeed, the combined lamenting 'with a loud voice' and rejoicing in that passage has been resumed in the confessing 'with a loud voice' in Neh. 9.1-37 and the rejoicing of this final ceremony (12.27, 43). So a cultic framework is supplied for Ezra–Nehemiah. While this final ceremony marks the fulfillment of Nehemiah's mission to build Jerusalem literally and figuratively, it also represents a grand finale for the three missions recorded in Ezra–Nehemiah.

The ceremony appropriately takes the form of a double procession along the wall, which converged in the temple area. An extract from the Nehemiah Memoir (vv. 31, [part of] 32, 37-40, 43) appears to have been redactionally spliced into an alternative account, which summarized the ceremony in vv. 27-30. Lists of priests and Levites were incorporated in vv. 33-36 and 41-42.[34] While sacrifices of worship played an undeveloped role at the close of the ceremony, after the processions had reached the temple (v. 43), the focus of the passage is on the processional music and song of thanksgiving, especially that provided by the Levitical singers, whose pre-exilic continuity with David (proclaimed in v. 32) echoes that in Ezra 3.10. The two processions are represented as parallel in their composition: the choir, a leading layman (Nehemiah/Hoshaiah) with half the civil leaders, the seven priestly trumpeters and eight musicians led by a director.[35]

The account, with its liberal mention of gates in the wall, serves as a triumphant counterpoint of both Nehemiah's solitary walk around the ruined wall in Neh. 2.12-15, starting from the same point, the Valley Gate, and of the communal rebuilding of the wall in ch. 3. People, gates and wall (v. 30) are reunited in a grand celebration that culminates at the house of God (v. 40). The enthusiasm of the worship and its climactic role for the whole of Ezra–Nehemiah are indicated by the

---

34. See the discussion in Williamson, *Ezra, Nehemiah*, p. 370.

35. Verse 35a must go with v. 34: see *BHS* and NJB. Since in v. 36 'Ezra the scribe' does not accord with the symmetry of the processions, the reference must have been added at some stage; nor is his presence to be detected among the priestly trumpeters of vv. 33-34. In v. 38 'the people' refers to the group of officials in v. 40 (Barthélemy, *Critique textuelle*, I, p. 574). The processions to the sanctuary, with the singers in front and the musicians in the rear and incorporating civil leaders, precisely echoes the pre-exilic (at this juncture) order of Ps. 68.25-28 (24-27) (cf. Ps. 42.5 [4]).

fivefold reference to joy in v. 43. This service of dedication recalls the comprehensive perspective of the Songs of Zion, typified in Psalm 48 and reflected in Psalm 122, in which temple and city were the concentric focus of the people who came together to worship God.

Conclusion

The first part of this essay investigated the structure of Ezra–Nehemiah and attempted to establish that worship, in the broad sense of cultic engagement with God, is a regularly recurring element and so of fundamental importance for the composite work. The rest of the essay has looked in turn at each occurrence of this element to consider its features in detail. It is now possible to survey this material and detect its tendencies. Clearly Ezra–Nehemiah was intended to establish ideals of worship for the ongoing community, whose continuity with the divinely established pre-exilic Israel was emphasized. In contexts of worship this feature appears repeatedly with a literary emphasis in its claim to rely on the written Torah and so to reflect traditions associated with Moses, though postexilic developments are tacitly accepted. These traditions relate to observance of the calendar of sacred seasons and especially its cycle of sacrifices. This stress on the Torah is also manifested in the public practice of reading its text. Continuity with the first temple emerges too in the drawing of parallels with the dedication of Solomon's temple, to show that Israel's religious history was being faithfully echoed. And, as in Chronicles, the music of the postexilic temple is traced back to David, the inspired 'man of God' (Neh. 12.36). The combined worship of sacrifice and musical song are presented as the fulfillment of ancient, divinely endorsed patterns.

The tension of ardent lament ('with a loud voice', Ezra 3.12; 10.12; Neh. 9.4) and exuberant joy pervades Ezra–Nehemiah. Both are regarded as valid elements, whether they are combined in a single service or, more often, judiciously separated. Joy is demonstrated in music and song, in sacrifices and a party-like atmosphere of generous sharing. It revels in the worship of God and celebrates the community's role as the people of God. The lamentation is grounded in the recognition of two things: the partial fulfillment of divine promises relating to the land and temple, and the community's failure to match the standards of the Torah that called for change.

Mixed in with the regular, repeatable worship of sacrifice, music and prayer are accounts of dedicatory services relating to the new altar, the temple foundation, the temple itself and the wall of Jerusalem. These literary celebrations reinforced new beginnings that recreated old ideals: the resumption of worship as the norm for the new community and the re-establishment of the city of God as the symbolic focus of the whole community of faith.

The new community, essentially in definition, though not totally in fact, consisted of returned exiles who qualified by having undergone the prophetic pattern of communal judgment by deportation and (inaugurated) salvation. In returning to the land they functioned typologically as a counterpart to their ancestors' occupation of the land under Joshua. Such theological truths, taught through various aspects of worship, provided a solid and sustaining identity for the community that enabled it to survive during the critical period of restoration.

THE PEOPLES AND THE WORSHIP OF YAHWEH IN THE BOOK OF ISAIAH

Christopher T. Begg

Introduction

The last two decades have witnessed a surge of synchronically oriented studies of the book of Isaiah.[1] A prominent focus of these studies has been the extant book's overarching themes. One such theme is the worship of Yahweh, which surfaces already in ch. 1 (see vv. 10-20) and recurs in ch. 66 (see vv. 18-23). Equally pervasive is the theme of the non-Israelite nations; they are mentioned explicitly for the first time in 2.1-4 and make a final appearance in 66.18-23. In this paper I wish to look at the convergence of these two themes, that is, the book's statements concerning the relationship between the nations and the worship of Yahweh.[2] (For purposes of this paper I understand 'worship' as the

---

1. For surveys of recent scholarship—both diachronic and synchronic—on the book of Isaiah, see: R. Rendtorff, 'The Book of Isaiah: A Complex Unity, Synchronic and Diachronic Reading', in R.F. Melugin and M.A. Sweeney (eds.), *New Visions of Isaiah* (JSOTSup, 214; Sheffield: Sheffield Academic Press, 1996), pp. 32-49; M.E. Tate, 'The Book of Isaiah in Recent Study', in J.W. Watts and P.R. House (eds.), *Forming Prophetic Literature: Essays on Isaiah and the Twelve in Honor of John D.W. Watts* (JSOTSup, 235; Sheffield: Sheffield Academic Press, 1996), pp. 22-56.

2. Among more recent studies surveying the multiple roles of the nations in the book of Isaiah (and the Old Testament as a whole), including that of worshippers of Yahweh, see: A. Feuillet, 'La conversion et le salut des nations: chez le prophète Isaïe', *BVC* 22 (1958), pp. 3-22; R. Martin-Achard, *Israël et les nations: La perspective missionaire de l'Ancien Testament* (CahThéol, 42; Neuchâtel: Delachaux & Niestlé, 1959); H. Schmidt, *Israel, Zion und die Völker: Eine motivgeschichtliche Untersuchung zum Verständnis des Universalismus im Alten Testament* (Marburg: Görich & Weiershäuser, 1968); P.E. Dion, *Dieu universel et peuple élu: L'universalisme religieux en Israël depuis les origines jusqu'à la veille des luttes maccabéennes* (LD, 83; Paris: Cerf, 1975); H.F. van Rooy, 'The nations in

human response, both individual and communal, of recognition and submission to the deity, which characteristically involves specially designated objects, places, times, forms and persons.)[3] In conducting this investigation I shall take the book in its extant form and trace the unfolding of the above theme, following the book's own sequence.[4]

In view of space limitations, it will not be possible for me to provide a complete exegesis of the passages studied. Rather, I shall concentrate on trying to elucidate a series of questions about each text treated: Who is/are the non-Israelite(s) whose involvement with Yahweh's worship is being described here (an individual, a particular group, the peoples as a whole)? Is the nature of that involvement depicted as positive or negative (e.g. hostile, threatening, destructive, a kind of 'anti-worship')? What gives rise to the involvement? Where and on what occasions does/will it take place? Which forms of expression does it assume (and not assume)? Is anything said about Israel's role in the process? How

Isaiah: A synchronic survey', *OTWSA* 22–23 (1979–80), pp. 213-29; G.I. Davies, 'The Destiny of the Nations in the Book of Isaiah', in J. Vermeylen (ed.), *The Book of Isaiah/Le livre d'Isaïe* (BETL, 81; Leuven: Leuven University Press; Leuven: Peeters, 1989), pp. 93-120; W. Gross, 'YHWH und die Religionen der Nicht-Israeliten', *TQ* 169 (1989), pp. 34-44; *idem*, 'Israel und die Völker: Die Krise des YHWH-Volk-Konzepts im Jesajabuch', in E. Zenger (ed.), *Der Neue Bund: Studien zur Bundestheologie der beiden Testamente* (QD, 146; Freiburg: Herder, 1993), pp. 149-67; N. Lohfink, 'Bund und Tora bei der Völkerwallfahrt (Jesajabuch und Psalm 25)', in N. Lohfink and E. Zenger, *Der Gott Israels und die Völker: Untersuchungen zum Jesajabuch und zu den Psalmen* (SBS, 154; Stuttgart: Katholisches Bibelwerk, 1994), pp. 37-83 (37-58); H. Simian-Yofre, *Testi Isaiani dell'Avvento* (Studi Biblici, 29; Bologna: EDB, 1996); W. Fenske, 'Das Ringen des Volkes um die Stellung der Völker', *SJOT* 11 (1997), pp. 181-99.

3.   For a summary statement concerning the concept, see F. De Graeve, 'Worship', *NCE* 14 (1967), pp. 1030-34.

4.   My procedure here follows that employed in my earlier brief essay 'Babylon in the Book of Isaiah', in J. Vermeylen (ed.), *The Book of Isaiah/Le Livre d'Isaïe* (BETL, 81; Leuven: Leuven University Press; Leuven: Peeters, 1989), pp. 121-25. A similar approach is exemplified in the recent articles of R.E. Clements, 'A Light to the Nations: A Central Theme of the Book of Isaiah', in J.W. Watts and P.R. House (eds.), *Forming Prophetic Literature: Essays on Isaiah and the Twelve in Honor of John D.W. Watts* (JSOTSup, 235; Sheffield: Sheffield Academic Press, 1996), pp. 58-69; J.J. Schmitt, 'The City as a Woman in Isaiah 1–39', in C.C. Broyles and C.A. Evans (eds.), *Writing and Reading the Scroll of Isaiah: Studies of an Interpretative Tradition* (2 vols.; VTSup, 70.1; Leiden: E.J. Brill, 1997), I, pp. 95-119.

does Yahweh respond to the nations' involvement in his worship, and what sort of image(s) of Yahweh does his response suggest? (Of course, given the length and character of the relevant texts, answers to all these questions will not be forthcoming in every case.)

To facilitate my presentation of the material, I divide the book of Isaiah into the following, conventionally recognized segments, each with its own well-known peculiarities of content, focus, purpose, presupposed background, diction, and so on: chs. 1–12; 13–27; 28–39; 40–55; 56–66.[5]

Isaiah 1–12

Isaiah 1–12 focuses on Judah/Jerusalem, its present condition and coming fate that will encompass both judgment and subsequent restoration. Accordingly, it is not suprising to find relatively little attention being given to the topic of this paper in these chapters.[6] The one longer relevant passage occurs towards the opening of the complex, this being the famous *Völkerwallfahrt* oracle of 2.(1)2-4(5), which itself has a parallel in Mic. 4.1-3(4-5).[7]

The event the oracle announces for an unspecified future ('in the latter days', v. 2aα) is set in motion by the exaltation (v. 2aβbα) of the temple mount over all other heights. The metaphorical wording of this announcement leaves indeterminate—see, however, n. 8—wherein

5.   Since this is a synchronic study, my use of these divisions is purely for purposes of convenience and is not intended to make any diachronic claims about the five segments or their relationships to each other. Throughout this article all translations of Scripture are taken from the RSV.

6.   For (diachronically oriented) treatments of the role(s) of the nations in Isa. 1–12 (13–39), see F. Huber, *Jahwe, Juda und die anderen Völker beim Propheten Jesaja* (BZAW, 137; Berlin: W. de Gruyter, 1976), *passim*; W. Werner, *Eschatologische Texte in Jesaja 1–39: Messias, heiliger Rest, Völker* (FzB, 46; Würzburg: Echter Verlag, 1982), pp. 149-95.

7.   On Isa. 2.1-5 and its Micah parallel, see: H. Wildberger, 'Die Völkerwallfahrt zum Zion. Jes. ii 1-5', *VT* 7 (1957), pp. 62-81; Werner, *Texte*, pp. 151-63; L. Schwienhorst-Schönberger, 'Zion-Ort der Tora: Überlegungen zu Mic 4,1-3', in F. Hahn *et al.* (eds.), *Zion Ort der Begegnung: Festschrift für Laurentius Klein zur Vollendung des 65. Lebensjahr* (BBB, 90; Hain: Athenäum, 1993), pp. 107-25; J. Limburg, 'Swords to Plowshares: Text and Contexts', in Broyles and Evans (eds.), *Writing and Reading the Scroll of Isaiah*, pp. 279-93; J.T. Willis, 'Isaiah 2.2-5 and the Psalms of Zion', in Broyles and Evans (eds.), *Writing and Reading the Scroll of Isaiah*, pp. 295-316.

such exaltation will consist. In connection with or as a result of this event, there will be a movement of 'all the nations' and 'many peoples' (vv. 2bβ-3aα) towards Zion. In undertaking the journey, those nations exhort one another to approach Yahweh's mountain and house (v. 3aβ). Their doing this is, in turn, inspired by their expectation (v. 3bα) that there they will be 'taught' by the Lord to 'walk in his paths'. Such an expectation on their part is itself evoked (v. 3bβ) by the 'going forth' of Yahweh's law/word from Zion/Jerusalem. Verse 4 focuses on the consequences of the nations' initiative: Yahweh will referee their differences, doing this so efficaciously that they will rid themselves of their weapons and military training as things for which they no longer have any need. The oracle concludes (v. 5) with an appeal to 'Jacob' to 'walk' in Yahweh's 'light' (cf. v. 3bα, where the nations look forward to 'walking in his paths').

The nations' future worship of Yahweh is foretold in 2.1-5 and will be undertaken by them spontaneously, apart from any external pressure. It involves their pilgrimaging to Yahweh's temple on Zion with expectant readiness of learning from him how they are to conduct themselves, especially in their relationships with one another. On the other hand, the oracle does not speak of the nations' joining in the temple cult, nor of their putting aside their own deities in favor of Yahweh alone (although, of course, it does not exclude this either). The God portrayed by the oracle appears primarily as a universal teacher and resolver of the nations' disputes. Their worship of him will engender a universal benefit, that is, the definitive elimination of humanity's war-making capacities. In the entire process Jerusalem has a key role: word of the city's exemplary living by the light of the Lord's instruction (2.3bβ, cf. 1.26) is what will attract the nations' attention and stimulate them to make their pilgrimage there.[8]

The remaining references to an involvement by the nations with the worship of Yahweh in Isaiah 1–12 are both sporadic and very much *en passant*. As part of the judgment speech against Assyria in 10.5-19, v. 11b cites the personified empire's hubristic confidence that it will be able to dispose of Jerusalem's 'idols' (עצביה), just as it had the 'images' (אליליה) of Samaria (v. 11a) and the 'graven images' (פסיליהם) of other

---

8. On this point, see Schwienhorst-Schönberger, 'Zion', p. 125. I further suggest that this is what is concretely being referred to in v. 2, when it speaks of Zion's 'exaltation', that is, Jerusalem will acquire for itself a worldwide reputation as a pre-eminently righteous city.

'idolatrous' (הָאֱלִיל) kingdoms (v. 10). Here, the foreign nation's stance towards the worship of Yahweh is both radically mistaken and con-temptuous: Yahweh has his 'idols' just like the gods of other nations, which will no more be able to withstand Assyria's might than had theirs. Unsurprisingly, such an attitude calls forth Yahweh's judgment upon Assyria, announced in the continuation of the oracle. At the very end of the complex Isaiah 1–12, as part of the thanksgiving song(s) of 12.1-6 to be pronounced 'in that day', Yahweh's people are charged with making known his deeds 'among the nations' and proclaiming the exaltation of his name (v. 4b). Here, Jerusalem's future role in attract-ing the nations to Yahweh as portrayed in 2.1-5 finds an echo, though now without mention of the nations' response to the witness given them.

Isaiah 13–27

The segment Isaiah 13–27 shifts attention from the fate of Judah/ Jerusalem to that of the nations, with chs. 13–23 speaking of what awaits individual peoples, while chs. 24–27 (the [Great] 'Isaiah Apoca-lypse') looks to the destiny of the entire *Völkerwelt*. The bulk of this material evidences a negative outlook on the nations' present conduct and their resultant prospects. Here and there throughout it, however, the expectation of some sort of participation by a nation or the nations as a whole in Yahweh's worship keeps being voiced.

A first reference of this sort comes in 18.7, the conclusion to the Ethiopia ('Cush', v. 1) oracle of ch. 18, which announces a develop-ment beyond the overthrow of that nation (predicted in what precedes). In particular, v. 7 foresees a later time when 'gifts will be brought [יוּבַל־שַׁי]⁹ to the Lord of hosts' by the Ethiopians, their doing this at 'Mount Zion, the place [מְקוֹם] of the name of the Lord of Hosts'. The rare word שַׁי leaves indeterminate the nature and intended use of the Ethiopians' 'gifts'. The occasion for their initiative likewise remains unspecified, although the context might suggest that it is evoked by the catastrophe experienced by them as described in vv. 4-6, of which the

---

9. The above formulation has two close parallels in the Psalms, see 68.30 ('because of thy [God's] temple at Jerusalem kings bear gifts [יוֹבִילוּ...שַׁי] to thee') and 76.12b [EVV 11b] 'let all who are around him [God] bring gifts [יוֹבִילוּ שַׁי] to him who is to be feared'). With Isa. 18.7 these are the only occurrences of the word שַׁי in the Hebrew Bible.

Lord will be the serene onlooker. In any case, the mention in v. 7 of the Ethiopians' peaceful, voluntary approach to Yahweh on Mount Zion recalls 2.3. There, however, it is the nations *en bloc* who pilgrimage to Zion and do so 'empty-handed'. The brief allusion in Isa. 18.7 to the tribute brought to Yahweh by a foreign nation will be picked up and amplified in what follows.

The most elaborate treatment of our theme in the entire book of Isaiah comes in 19.16-25, which itself represents a positive sequel to and reversal of the word of doom for Egypt of 19.1-15.[10] The ten verses making up 19.16-25 are punctuated by a sixfold use of the formula 'in that day' (vv. 16, 18, 19, 21, 23, 24), this serving to indicate the successive increments in which the prediction unfolds. The first sub-unit (vv. 16-17) is transitional; it speaks of the Egyptians' 'fear' before Yahweh (v. 16) and the 'land of Judah' (v. 17), evoked by the devastation of their country depicted in 19.1-15. Such 'fear' is the basis for the developments described in what follows. Verse 18, the second sub-unit, announces a time when five Egyptian cities[11] will speak 'the language

10. On Isa. 19.16-25, see: A. Fcuillet, 'Un sommet religieux de l'Ancien Testament. L'oracle d'Isaïe, xix (16-25) sur la conversion d'Egypte', *RSR* 39 (1951), pp. 65-87; W. Vogels, 'L'Egypte mon peuple—L'Universalisme d'Is 19.16-25', *Bib* 57 (1976), pp. 494-514; L. Monsengwo-Pasinya, 'Isaïe XIX 16-25 et universalisme dans la LXX', in J.A. Emerton (ed.), *Congress Volume Salamanca 1983* (VTSup, 36; Leiden: E.J. Brill, 1985), pp. 192-207; J.F.A. Sawyer, '"Blessed Be my People Egypt" (Isaiah 19.25): The Context and Meaning of a Remarkable Passage', in J.D. Martin and P.R. Davies (eds.), *A Word in Season: Essays in Honour of William McKane* (JSOTSup, 42; Sheffield: Sheffield Academic Press, 1986), pp. 57-71; B. Renaud, 'La critique prophétique de l'attitude d'Israël face aux nations. Quelques jalons', *Concilium* 220 (1988), pp. 43-53 (49-53); Gross, 'Israel und die Völker', pp. 151-60; E. Haag, '"Gesegnet sei mein Volk Ägypten" (Jes 19,25). Ein Zeugnis alttestamentlicher Eschatologie', in M. Minas and J. Zeidler (eds.), *Aspkete spätägyptischer Kultur: Festschrift für Erich Winter zum 65. Geburtstag* (Aegyptiaca Treverensia, 7; Mainz: P. von Zabern, 1994), pp. 139-47; A. Schenker, 'La fine della storia d'Israele ricapitolera il suo inizio. Esegesi d'Is 19,16-25', *RivB* 43 (1995), pp. 320-29.

In contrast to Sawyer and Schenker among the above authors, I presume that all references to 'Egypt/the Egyptians' in 19.16-25, as in 19.1-15, are to persons who were by origin non-Israelites and non-Yahwists, rather than to Israelites living in Egypt. If the latter were, in fact, in view in 19.16-25, one would expect them to be more clearly identified as such and distinguished from the native Egyptians, who are clearly the object of the judgment oracle of 19.1-15.

11. On the question of the identity of these cities, particularly the one whose

of Canaan' (i.e. the Yahwistic *Kultsprache*, Hebrew) and 'swear allegiance to the Lord [נשבעות ליהוה] of hosts'. The passage's third sub-
unit, vv. 19-20, begins (v. 19) with mention of two cultic appurtenances
that are to figure in Egypt's future worship of Yahweh, that is, an 'altar
to the Lord' (מזבח ליהוה) in its midst and a 'pillar to the Lord' (מצבה
ליהוה...) at its frontier.[12] Verse 20 expatiates on the function of the
'pillar' as 'a sign and witness to the Lord of hosts' (לאות ולעד ליהוה)
which will prompt him to respond to the Egyptians' cry when they are
oppressed by sending them a 'savior' (מושיע) to 'defend and deliver'
them.[13] The sub-unit consisting of vv. 21-22 is intimately tied to
the preceding one. Yahweh's intervention on behalf of the afflicted
Egyptians (v. 20b) will cause them to 'know' (i.e. acknowledge) him
(v. 21a). That (ac)knowledge(ment), in turn, will find expression in a
series of particular actions, that is, 'and they will worship with sacrifice
and [burnt] offering' (ועבדו זבח ומנחה)[14] and 'make vows to the Lord
[נדרו־נדר ליהוה] and perform them'. Verse 22 then summarizes future
interaction between Yahweh and Egypt: when 'smitten' by him, the
Egyptians will 'return to the Lord' (שבו עד־יהוה), who will then himself
give heed to and 'heal' them.

The 'Egyptian perspective' of vv. 16-22 widens in the fifth sub-unit,
v. 23: the traditional enemies Egypt and Assyria are to be linked by a
'highway' that will allow each to enter the other's territory, this
exchange leading to their joint 'worship'.[15] Thereafter, the sixth and

'name' (MT עיר ההרס, LXX πόλις-ασεδεκ) is cited at the end of the verse, see the
works cited in n. 10.

12. Reference to Egypt's future possession of these two objects dedicated to the
Lord recalls the beginnings of Israel's own cult at Mount Sinai as recounted in
Exod. 24.4, where Moses builds 'an altar' (מזבח) and 'twelve pillars' (מצבה). As
the authors cited in n. 10 point out, what 19.16-25 announces with regard to
Egypt's future consistently recapitulates the past religious experience of Israel itself
in the periods of the Exodus, Conquest and Judges.

13. Cf. the function of the rainbow as a 'sign [לאות] of the covenant' in reminding Yahweh not to unleash another all-destroying flood upon the earth in Gen. 9.12-
16.

14. With this initiative the altar of v. 19 finds a use; such sacrificial worship
also seems to presuppose the existence of a Yahwistic Egyptian priesthood; so
Gross, 'Israel und die Völker', p. 52.

15. Given the theocentric focus of 19.16-25 as a whole, I take this as a more
likely understanding of the concluding words of v. 23 (ועבדו מצרים את־אשור, RSV
'and the Egyptians will worship with the Assyrians') than the alternative possibility, that is, 'the Egyptians will serve the Assyrians'. Note too the verbal echo of

final sub-unit, vv. 24-25, introduces Israel, the superpowers' long-time common victim, as co-beneficiary along with them of divine favor: Israel will stand together with Egypt and Assyria as a 'third' nation under divine 'blessing' (v. 24). Their equal sharing in Yahweh's blessing is signified by the titles awarded each of them by him: Egypt is 'my people', Assyria 'the work of my hands' and Israel 'my heritage' (v. 25).

Among the texts of the book of Isaiah that speak of a positive involvement by the nations in the worship of Yahweh, 19.16-25 stands out in several respects. First, it envisages two great nations of the biblical period, Egypt and Assyria, worshipping Yahweh in their own lands, rather than pilgrimaging to Zion to do so (cf. 2.3; 18.7); in the case of Egypt this is made possible by the provision of an 'altar' on its own soil (v. 19). Secondly, no other Isaiah text mentions so many forms of Yahweh worship undertaken by a foreign nation(s), that is, Egypt's 'fear' of Yahweh (v. 16), use of the Yahwistic *Kultsprache* and swearing allegiance to the Lord (v. 18), crying to him in affliction (v. 20), 'knowing/acknowledging' him (v. 21), sacrificing and making vows to him (v. 21), returning to him (v. 22) and joining another nation (Assyria) in its worship of Yahweh (v. 24). Conversely, the passage cites more beneficient acts of Yahweh in response to the worship offered him by Egypt (and Assyria) than do other related texts of the book: he sends Egypt a 'savior', defends and delivers it (v. 20), makes himself known to the Egyptians (v. 21), gives ear to them and heals them (v. 22) and 'blesses' both Egypt and Assyria (vv. 24-25). Finally, Isa. 19.16-25 goes beyond not only the rest of Isaiah, but the entire OT, in foreseeing other nations—and traditionally enemy ones at that—coming to participate in such a range of hitherto distinctively Israelite experiences and prerogatives (e.g. Egypt, in a reapplication of the *Bundesformel*, will be called 'my people', while Assyria will be invested with the title 'work of my [Yahweh's] hands' [v. 25], used of Israel itself in Isa. 60.21; 64.7 [8]) such that they will stand on a footing of full equality with Israel.[16] As such, the text well deserves the designation of 'a religious summit of the Old Testament', given it almost a half a century ago by A. Feuillet (see n. 10).

---

v. 21b announcing that the Egyptians will 'worship [ועבדו] with sacrifice and burnt offering'.

16. On this point, see Gross, 'Israel und die Völker', pp. 156-60.

A last relevant text occurs at the very end of the complex Isaiah 13–23. Verses 1-16 of ch. 23 feature a lament over the destruction of Tyre. Appended to this is an announcement of the city's eventual revival, vv. 17-18. When after 70 years the Lord 'visits' Tyre, she will resume her far-flung trading enterprises (metaphorically her 'harlotry', v. 17). The profits obtained thereby will, according to v. 18a, be 'dedicated to the Lord' (קֹדֶשׁ לַיהוה). So dedicated they will be used (v. 18b) to feed and clothe 'those who dwell before the Lord', that is, in first place, his priests and other ministers.[17] Like the Ethiopians in 18.7 then, the Tyrians of 23.18 will express their worship of Yahweh with material gifts. Whereas the former, however, seemingly do so under the impact of their misfortunes (see above), the latter appear to act out of gratitude for the Lord's restorative intervention on their behalf (see v. 17).

The first two chapters of the 'Isaiah Apocalypse' (chs. 24–27) contain several references to the nations' involvement in Yahweh's worship. A first allusion to this is likely to be found in 24.14-16, which speaks of various collectivities' response to the Lord's devastation of the earth portrayed in 24.1-13. The former sequence opens (v. 14) with mention of an unidentified 'they' who joyfully sing of the Lord's majesty. Next (v. 15), those 'in the east' and 'in the coastlands of the sea' are summoned to 'glorify' (the name of) the Lord. Thereafter, a 'we' declares that it has heard 'songs of praise' emanating 'from the ends of the earth' and addressed to the 'Righteous One'.[18] As in 18.7, the experience of catastrophe prompts non-Israelites to 'worship' Yahweh here, now, however, with their acclamations rather than with their goods.

In the context of the 'individual hymn' of 25.1-5, praising Yahweh for his definitive overthrow of the mysterious 'city' (see v. 2) that figures so prominently in the Isaiah Apocalypse, one meets a similar reference. At the center of this text stands the I-speaker's affirmation (v. 3) that, as a result of the divine initiative, 'many peoples will glorify thee

---

17. Cf. Num. 18.8, where Yahweh says to the Aaronides, 'I have given you whatever is kept of the offerings made to me, all the consecrated things [קֳדָשַׁי] of the people of Israel...'

18. Given the universal dimensions of the divine judgment announced in 24.1-13, as well as the reference to the 'nations' in v. 12, I take 24.14-16 as referring, in first place, to the nations' response to Yahweh's intervention. Cf. also the similar wording of 25.3 with its explicit mention of '[ruthless] nations' as those who 'fear' Yahweh. An alternative interpretation views the intended referent as rather the Diaspora Jews; see the commentaries.

[יכבדוך; cf. כבדו יהוה, 24.15]; cities of ruthless nations will fear thee' (ייראוך).

Another major text for our theme occurs in 25.5-8(9),[19] which itself picks up on the announcements of Yahweh's coming deeds in 24.21-23, following the hymnic interlude in 25.1-5 (see above). Isaiah 25.6 presupposes the nations' presence on 'this mountain', which in light of 24.23 is to be identified with Mount Zion; the link between these two verses likewise suggests that the nations' presence there is in response to Yahweh's future kingly rule and manifestation of his 'glory' on Zion (cited in 24.23). At the site Yahweh will confer a series of benefits on the assembled peoples. In first place, he will provide them with an opulent banquet (v. 6). He will likewise act to eliminate anything that hinders the peoples' joyful communion with himself and one another in this banquet. One such impediment is the mysterious 'covering/veil' hitherto suspended over the nations that Yahweh will 'destroy' (literally 'swallow up', בלע) according to v. 7.[20] He will do the same 'for ever' with 'death', at the same time removing the 'tears from all faces' (v. 8a). The enumeration of divine benefactions concludes in v. 8b with a shift of attention to Israel ('my people'), whose 'reproach' Yahweh will remove wherever it is found. Verse 9 then articulates the response by all those—Israel and the nations—who have experienced the blessings mentioned in vv. 6-8.[21] 'On that day' Yahweh's beneficiaries will acclaim him as 'our God', whose 'saving' of them (יושיענו, cf. מושיע,

---

19. On this text see: H. Wildberger, 'Das Freudenmahl auf dem Zion. Erwägungen zu Jes. 25,6-8', *TZ* 33 (1977), pp. 371-83; P. Welten, 'Die Vernichtung des Todes und die Königsherrschaft Gottes. Eine traditionsgeschichtliche Studie zu Jes. 25.6-8; 24.21-23 und Ex 24.9-11', *TZ* 38 (1982), pp. 129-46; B. Wodecki, 'The Religious Universalism of the Pericope Is 25.6-9', in K.-D. Schunck and Matthias Augustin (eds.), *Goldene Äpfel in silbernen Schalen* (BEATAJ, 20; Frankfurt am Main: Peter Lang, 1992), pp. 35-47.

20. On the proposed identifications—which need not be mutually exclusive—of the 'covering/veil' (e.g. mourning, spiritual blindness, blocked access to God's presence) in 25.7, see the articles cited in n. 19 and the commentaries.

21. The word cited in 25.9 is frequently understood as one that will be spoken by Israel alone, so, for example, R.E. Clements, *Isaiah 1–39* (NCB; Grand Rapids: Eerdmans, 1980), p. 209; M.A. Sweeney, *Isaiah 1–39* (FOTL, 16; Grand Rapids: Eerdmans, 1996), pp. 334-35. Given, however, the repeated references to all nations/peoples as the object of Yahweh's benefactions in vv. 6-8a, I take the reference to be universal, that is, to both Israel and the nations; so Wodecki, 'Universalism', p. 43.

19.20) they have awaited, and 'the Lord' in whose 'salvation' (יְשׁוּעָתוֹ) they exhort themselves to be 'glad and rejoice'.

Isa. (24.21-23) 25.6-9 recalls 2.2-4 in its localization of all peoples' worship of Yahweh on Mount Zion and its non-mention of tribute-bringing or sacrifice by them. With 19.16-25 it has in common its depiction of Yahweh as savior and deliverer also of non-Israelites. Unique to this text within the book of Isaiah (and the Old Testament as a whole) is its image of Yahweh as the universal banquet-giver.

Isaiah 28–39

After the 'nations' interlude' of chs. 13–27, Isaiah 28-39 reverts to a focus on Israel/Judah/Jerusalem. References to our theme are virtually absent in the latter segment. One might, however, make note of 36.10, where the king of Assyria, speaking through the Rabshakeh, claims to be acting on the Lord's behalf in assaulting Judah; cf. v. 7, where Rabshakeh charges that Hezekiah has provoked the Lord by removing all his extra-Jerusalem altars and high places. That claim is exposed as baseless in 37.28-29, where the Lord denounces by the voice of Isaiah the 'anti-worship' of the Assyrian king who has 'raged against' (הִתְרַגֶּזְךָ, *bis*) him and whose 'arrogance' (שַׁאֲנַנְךָ) has come to Yahweh's attention (cf. 10.10-11).

Isaiah 40–55

Expectations with regard to the nations' coming worship of Yahweh become prominent once again in the book's next main segment, chs. 40–55.[22] The theme is sounded already in the segment's opening unit (40.1-11), where v. 5 announces that 'all flesh' (כָל־בָּשָׂר) will jointly 'see' the manifestation of Yahweh's 'glory' (כָּבוֹד). It recurs in the context of the first Servant Song, 42.1-9, according to which the Servant's[23] God-given task includes 'bringing forth justice to the nations'

22. For a recent, diachronically oriented treatment of the topic in Isa. 40-55 and 56-66, see L. Ruppert, 'Das Heil der Völker (Heilsuniversalismus) in Deutero-und "Trito"- Jesaja', *MTZ* 45 (1994), pp. 137-54.

23. I cannot enter here into the controversy concerning the identity of the Servant. At any case on the level of the final text the Servant seems to be equated with Israel, see 49.3 ('you are my servant, *Israel...*') and cf. Lohfink, 'Bund und Tora', p. 48 n. 38.

(משפט לגוים יוציא), v. 1),[24] 'establishing justice in the earth' (משפט עד־ישים בארץ, v. 4) and a 'light to the nations' (לאור גוים, v. 6). For their part the 'coastlands' are said to be 'waiting for' the Servant's 'law' (לתורתו, v. 4; cf. 2.3 and n. 24).

Following the above intimations, the hymn appended to the first Servant Song (42.1-9) in 42.10-12 summons a whole range of sites and peoples (the end of the earth, the sea and its contents, the coastlands [cf. v. 4] and their inhabitants [v. 10], the desert and its cities, the villages of Kedar, the inhabitants of Sela, the top of the mountains [v. 11]) to sing a 'new Song to the Lord' (v. 10), thereby 'giving him glory' (ישימו ליהוה כבוד, v. 12).[25] In context, the occasion for this worldwide acclamation of the Lord is Yahweh's initiatives via the Servant, initiatives that are to affect the nations as well.

A next possible allusion to the nations' (positive) involvement with the worship of Yahweh comes in 44.5, at the climax of the salvation oracle in 44.1-5. In this verse unspecified individuals ('this one', 'another', 'another') responding to Yahweh's announced revival of Israel (see vv. 1-4) affirm that they belong to the Lord and lay claim to the names of 'Jacob' and 'Israel'. Recently, D.W. Van Winckle has argued, against the scholarly majority, that the speakers of 44.5 are not representatives of the nations, but rather previously apostate Jews or children of mixed marriages.[26] I would suggest, however, that just as in 25.9 (see n. 21), the two possibilities are not mutually exclusive.

In any event, non-Israelites are clearly the focus of the 'Cyrus oracle' (44.24–45.7). As Yahweh's designated 'shepherd' and fulfiller of the divine purposes (44.28a), the pagan king is the implied subject of the rebuilding of Jerusalem and the laying of the temple foundations announced in 44.28b. The military successes he will achieve with Yahweh's support (45.1-3a) and that will accrue to Israel's benefit (v. 4a) are to occur, initially, without Cyrus's 'knowing' (vv. 4b-5) the

24. Cf. 2.2-4, where the Torah 'goes forth' (תצא) from Zion (v. 3), prompting 'all the nations' (כל־הגוים, v. 2) to repair there where the Lord will 'judge' (שפט) between them (v. 4). The role of Zion as imparter of the Lord's (legal) guidance for the nations is now assumed by the Servant.

25. This last reference echoes links made between the nations and Yahweh's 'glory' earlier in the book; see 24.15 ('in the east give glory to the Lord [כבדו יהוה]'); 25.3 ('strong peoples will glorify thee [יכבדוך]'); 40.5 ('the glory of the Lord [כבוד יהוה] shall be revealed and all flesh shall see it together').

26. 'Proselytes in Isaiah XL–LV?: A Study of Isaiah XLIV', *VT* 47 (1997), pp. 341-59.

Lord. The ultimate divine purpose behind Cyrus's triumphs is, however, that he himself will come to 'know' that the Lord is the one who
has 'called him by name' (v. 3b), just as from east to west 'they [the
nations] will know' (i.e. acknowledge; see 19.21) thereby that the only
deity is Yahweh. Here for the first time in the book of Isaiah, one hears
of the nations adopting a Yahwistic 'monotheism'.

The nations' monotheistic realization resurfaces throughout the
continuation of Isaiah 45. Verse 14 announces that three nations—
Egypt (cf. 19.16-25), Ethiopia (Cush, 18.7) and the Sabeans—will pay
tribute and offer their submission to Israel. In so doing, they will make
supplication of Israel, prompted by the recognition that Yahweh, the
only God (v. 6), is with Israel alone. The chapter's concluding segment
(vv. 20-25) constitutes a 'trial speech'. It opens with a summons to the
'survivors of the nations' (v. 20a), who are challenged to vindicate the
divine status of their gods in the face of Yahweh's own claims for himself (vv. 20b-21). Challenge turns to appeal in v. 22, where Yahweh
urges 'all the ends of the earth' to turn to him as the sole God and 'be
saved'. Verse 23 then proclaims the Lord's sworn, irrevocable decision:
'to me every knee shall bow and every tongue shall swear' (cf. 19.18).
In consequence of this decision, the Lord will be recognized ('it shall
be said of me', that is, by 'every tongue', v. 23; cf. 25.9) as the exclusive source of 'righteousness and strength' (v. 24a). Furthermore,
everyone who previously resisted him will be shamed (v. 24b), whereas
all Israelites will find their honor in the Lord (v. 25). This last
announcement indicates that the nations' future worship of Yahweh
will involve regret over their previous stance towards him.

The Servant's task in the spiritual illumination also of the nations,
emphasized already in the First Song (see 42.3–4, 6), is reiterated in the
Second Song (49.1-6) at the opening of the second main division within
Isaiah 40–55, that is chs. 49–55. Addressing the Servant directly in
49.6, the Lord makes clear that the Servant's mission is not to be
limited to Israel alone. Rather, 'I will give you as a light to the nations
[לאור גוים; see 42.6] that my salvation [ישועתי] may reach to the end of
the earth'; see 45.22, where 'all the ends of the earth' are urged by
Yahweh to turn to him and 'be saved' (הושעו). Yahweh's salvific plans
for the nations as expressed in the appeal of 45.22 will then be realized
through the Servant's acting as 'light' to them.

Yahweh's intentions vis-à-vis the nations are synthesized in 51.4b-5,
as the content of what Israel is summoned by him to 'hear' (v. 4a), that

is, 'a law will go forth from me [תורה מאתי תצא; cf. תורה תצא מציון,
2.3], and my justice for a light to the peoples [ומשפטי לאור עמים; cf.
לאור גוים of the Servant in 42.6; 49.6]. My deliverance draws near
speedily, my salvation [ישעי; cf. ישועתי, 49.6] has gone forth, and my
arms will rule the peoples; the coastlands wait for me and for my arm
they hope' (אלי איים יקוו ואל־זרעי ייחלון; cf. לתורתו איים ייחילו of the
Servant in 42.4). Here, terminology used elsewhere in the book of Zion
for the Servant/Israel's role in bringing the nations to acknowledge
Yahweh is applied to Yahweh in person, thereby underscoring the
divine origin of the process.

Within the series of promises for the nations and their participation in
Yahweh's worship running through Isaiah (1–39) 40–55, 52.1b sounds
a somewhat different note. This verse motivates the preceding summons
to Zion/ Jerusalem, 'the holy city' (עיר הקדש) to adorn herself with the
assurance 'for there shall no more come into you the uncircumcised and
the unclean' (טמא).[27] Such a word does not exclude a participation in
Jerusalem's cult by those foreigners who are willing to undergo cir-
cumcision and purification. It does, however, make clear that there are
conditions attached to their participation—just as there are for the
Israelites themselves. As such, it looks forward to what will be said
concerning 'the foreigner' in 56.1-8 (see below).

The nations were cited as recipients of the Servant's mission in the
first two Songs. The fourth Song (52.13–53.12) accords them (and their
'kings') a role as well, that is, as the astounded, awestruck witnesses to
the Servant's humiliation and exaltation, which they will in time both
'see' and 'understand' (52.15).[28]

Isaiah 56–66

The nations' future worship of Yahweh continues to be a significant
concern in the final segment of Isaiah, chs. 56–66. Already the

27. Cf. Ezek. 47.9, 'No foreigner, uncircumcised in heart and flesh, of all the
foreigners who are among the people of Israel, shall enter my sanctuary.' Cf. also
Isa. 52.11 with its exhortation to the Israelites, 'Depart, depart, go out thence, touch
no unclean thing [טמא]; go out of the midst of her [Babylon?], purify yourselves,
you who bear the vessels of the Lord.'

28. It is unclear (and so controverted) whether the nations/kings of 52.15 are to
be regarded as (also) the speakers of the collective confession quoted in 53.1-10.
Accordingly, I leave the latter verses out of consideration here.

segment's first unit, 56.1-8, focuses attention on the question.[29] The core of this unit (vv. 3-8) comprises Yahweh's word of assurance for two groups of persons who seem to have their doubts whether the Lord will allow them to remain part of his people, that is, 'the foreigner' (הנכר) and the eunuch (v. 3). Yahweh first addresses the plight of the latter in vv. 4-5. Thereafter, he takes up the case of 'the foreigners' (בני הנכר) in vv. 6-7(8). These persons are first (v. 6) circumscribed with a whole series of qualifications that make clear the extent of their commitment to Yahweh. They are, first of all, those who have 'joined themselves [הנלוים] to the Lord' so as to 'minister to him [לשרתו], to love [ולאהבה] the name of the Lord, and to be his servants' (לעבדים).[30] More specifically, they are all those who keep the sabbath and do not profane it[31] and who hold fast to 'my covenant' (מחזיקים בבריתי; this same phrase is used of the eunuchs in v. 4). To foreigners meeting these conditions, the Lord makes a triple promise in v. 7a: 'these I will bring to my holy mountain [והביאותים אל־הר קדשׁי],[32] and make them joyful in my house of prayer [בבית תפלתי], and their burnt offerings and their sacrifices [עולתיהם וזבחיהם, cf. זבח ומנחה, 19.21] will be accepted [לרצון] on my altar' (מזבחי; cf. מזבח ליהוה, 19.19). Verse 7b then states

29. On Isa. 56.1-8, see: M.A. Beek, 'De vreemdeling krijgt toegang (Jesaja 56.1-8)', in H.H. Grosheide *et al.* (eds.), *De knecht: Studies rondom Deutero-Jesaja aangeboden aan Prof. Dr. J.L. Koole* (Kampen: Kok, 1978), pp. 17-22; H. Donner, 'Jesaja LVI 1-7: Ein Abrogationsfall innerhalb des Kanons—Implikationen und Konsequenzen', in J.A. Emerton (ed.), *Salamanca 1983*, pp. 81-95; R.D. Wells, Jr, '"Isaiah" as an Exponent of Torah: Isaiah 56.1-8', in R.F. Melugin and M.A. Sweeney (eds.), *New Visions of Isaiah* (JSOTSup, 214; Sheffield: Sheffield Academic Press, 1996), pp. 140-55.

30. This last indication concerning the 'foreigners' applies to them the title used of Israel throughout Isa. 40-55, notably in the 'Servant Songs' (see n. 23). Here then one would have another instance, as in 19.25, of the book's application to non-Israelites of titles elsewhere characteristic of Israel itself. On the plural use of the term 'servant' as a *Leitwort* of Isa. 56–66 as against the singular usage of Isaiah 40–55, see W.A.M. Beuken, 'The Main Theme of Trito-Isaiah: "The Servants of Yahweh"', *JSOT* 47 (1990), pp. 67-87; J. Blenkinsopp, 'The Servant and the Servants in Isaiah and the Formation of the Book', in C.C. Broyles and C.A. Evans (eds.), *Writing and Reading the Scroll of Isaiah*, pp. 155-75.

31. Emphasis on sabbath-keeping runs all through 56.1-8; see vv. 2 ('blessed is the one who keeps the sabbath, not profaning it') and 4 (the eunuchs 'who keep my sabbath').

32. Contrast 52.1, where Jerusalem, 'the holy city' (עיר הקדשׁ), is assured that 'the uncircumcised and the unclean' will henceforth not 'come [יבא] into you'.

Yahweh's reason for making these promises, this echoing the wording of his initial promise: 'for my house shall be called a house of prayer for all peoples' (בית תפלה...לכל־העמים). Finally, v. 8 summarizes the Lord's assurances for both eunuchs (vv. 4-5) and foreigners (vv. 6-7) with the statement that Yahweh intends to gather 'yet others' (i.e. the two groups just cited) to the 'outcasts of Israel' already gathered by him. The benefits hitherto conferred on the newly re-assembled Israelites will not be restricted to them, but will be extended to other groups as well.

Isaiah 56.(1-2)3-8 evidences similarities with but also distinctive features vis-à-vis the book's preceding texts concerning our theme. In its focus on the temple as the site of the encounter between God and the foreigners (and eunuchs), it recalls the Zion-centered passages 2.2-4, 18.7 and 25.5-9. Like 19.16-25 it makes explicit mention of the non-Israelites' Yahwistic sacrifices. At the same time, the text is set apart by, for example, its emphasis on the prior conditions—sabbath observance in particular—demanded of foreigners who would participate in Yahweh's worship. Again, whereas the previous texts spoke of the nations' *en bloc* participation in Yahweh's worship, Isa. 56.3-8 is directed to individual 'foreigners'. No other text speaks, as does v. 6, of non-Israelites having part in Yahweh's 'covenant'. Lastly, Isa. 56.1-8 is unique in its starting point, that is, the existence of questions/controversy concerning the right of foreigners (and eunuchs) to be considered part of Yahweh's people.[33]

The long segment of Isa. 60.1-22 revolves around the nations' future homage to the divinely exalted Jerusalem. At the same time, the chapter also makes clear that their homage is ultimately meant for Yahweh himself. Thus v. 6 states that the nations will bring their gold and frankincense and 'proclaim the praise of the Lord' (ותהלת יהוה יבשרו).[34] Similarly, v. 7 announces that the sheep of Kedar and Nebaioth, which Jerusalem is to receive, 'shall come up with acceptance upon my altar' (יעלו על־רצון מזבחי).[35] Likewise according to v. 9 'the coastlands shall

---

33. On the law of Deut. 23.2-9 regulating access to the Israelite 'assembly' by non-Israelites as the/a likely background to this controversy, see Donner, 'Jesaja LVI 1-7'.

34. This announcement echoes the hymnic summons addressed to various peoples in 42.10-12; see vv. 10 ('sing to the Lord [שירו ליהוה] a new song') and 12 ('let them declare his praise [תהלתו] in the coastlands').

35. Note the echo of 56.7, where Yahweh promises the foreigners that their

wait for' the Lord (יְקַוּוּ אִיִּים לִי; cf. 51.5 אֵלַי אִיִּים יְקַוּוּ). Among the things that these distant places 'wait' to do is to bring 'their silver and gold with them'. The one for whom these treasures are meant, in turn, is 'the name of the Lord your God, and for the Holy One of Israel', this in recognition of his having 'glorified' Jerusalem. This same 'dupli-cation' regarding the recipient of the nations' tribute surfaces in v. 13, where the purpose of the coming of the woods of Lebanon to 'you' (i.e. Jerusalem) is 'to beautify the place of my sanctuary and I will make the place of my feet glorious' (אֲכַבֵּד; cf. v. 7bβ, where Yahweh announces 'and I will glorify my glorious house' [וּבֵית תִּפְאַרְתִּי אֲפָאֵר]). The nations' acknowledgment of Jerusalem as 'the city of the Lord, the Zion of the Holy One of Israel' (v. 14b), for its part, implies their acknowledgment of Yahweh himself as well. Throughout Isaiah 60 then one finds allusions to the nations' worship of Yahweh being super-imposed on descriptions of their homage to Jerusalem.

The promises of Isa. 61.5-7 for Jerusalem prolong those of ch. 60 with v. 6b, stating 'you shall be called the priests of the Lord, men shall speak of you as the ministers of our God'. In context (see vv. 5, 6b) this promise points in the first place to Jerusalem's inhabitants being pro-vided for by the nations, the way Israel itself saw to the upkeep of its priests and Levites. This primary meaning does not, however, exclude the nations also looking to the Israelites—their clergy in particular—to perform priestly services on their behalf, for example, offering sacrifice (see n. 35) and making supplication to Yahweh for them (see 45.14). Here, as in ch. 60, the nations' worship of Yahweh is mediated through Israel.

Following the divine promises for Israel's future making up Isaiah 60–62 (63.1-6)—these including a (mediated) worship of Yahweh by the nations—the lengthy national lament of 63.7–64.11 introduces both a dramatic change of tone and a different outlook on the nations. According to the retrospective complaint of 63.18 'our adversaries [צָרֵינוּ] have trodden down' the Lord's sanctuary, while in 64.10 the Lord is reminded that 'our holy and beautiful house [בֵּית קָדְשֵׁנוּ וְתִפְאַרְתֵּנוּ] has been burned by fire.'[36] Such memories inspire the

---

burnt offerings and sacrifices 'will be accepted on my altar' (לְרָצוֹן עַל־מִזְבְּחִי). In both cases, it would appear that while the non-Israelites provide the victims, it is the legitimate Israelite priesthood that will actually offer these; see on 61.6.

36. Cf. 60.7, where Yahweh announces 'I will glorify my glorious house'

speakers in 63.19-64.1 to implore Yahweh to 'come down' and thereby 'make thy name known [להודיע] to thy adversaries [לצריך, cf. צרינו, 63.18] and the nations [note the parallelism made here between the divine "adversaries" and the nations] tremble [ירגזו] at thy presence'. The anticipated outcome of Yahweh's intervention as spoken of here recalls the indications concerning the Lord's dealings with Egypt in 19.16-25; see vv. 16 (Egypt will 'tremble with fear' [פחד] before the divine hand) and 21 (the Lord will 'make himself known' [נודע] to the Egyptians). In both instances the Lord's (punishing) self-manifestation is designed to bring non-Israelites to an awe-filled acknowledgment of himself.

The nations and their future worship of Yahweh make a final, major appearance in the penultimate unit of the book of Isaiah, that is, 66.18-23.[37] The unit begins with Yahweh announcing (v. 18a) his intention of coming 'to gather [לקבץ] all nations and tongues'.[38] The result of this divine initiative is that they, in turn, will 'come and see my glory' ובאו וראו את־כבודי.[39]

The enumeration of Yahweh's coming initiatives with regard to the nations continues in v. 19. This verse commences with mention of the 'sign [אות]' Yawheh proposes to 'set among them' (i.e. the nations and tongues of v. 18a). Commentators acknowledge that the text fails to supply sufficient data to allow for the determination of the nature/-content of this 'sign'. In any event, however, the 'sign for the nations' puts one in mind of the designation of the 'pillar' at the border of Egypt that will function as 'a sign [לאות] and a witness to the Lord of hosts' (19.21). This intratextual link might suggest that also in 66.19 the 'sign' is to function as a reminder for Yahweh concerning his commitments towards the nations.

Having gathered the nations, let them see his 'glory' and endowed them with a 'sign' (vv. 18-19a), Yahweh in v. 19b confers a 'mission-

(ובית תפארתי אפאר), thus undoing the work of Israel's adversaries alluded to in 64.10.

37. On this passage, see: G. Rinaldi, 'Gli "scampati" di Is. LXVI, 18-22', in A. Barucq *et al.* (eds.), *A la rencontre de Dieu: Mémorial Albert Gelin* (Paris: Mapus, 1961), pp. 109-18; Gross, 'Israel und die Völker', pp. 160-67; Ruppert, 'Heil der Völker', pp. 155-56.

38. This statement echoes the divine announcement in 56.8b, 'I will gather [אקבץ] yet others to him [Israel] besides those already gathered.'

39. This announcement picks up on that of 40.5, 'The glory of the Lord [כבוד יהוה] will be revealed and all flesh shall see [ראו] it together.'

ary' task upon 'their survivors'.[40] Those survivors will be dispatched to distant regions (Tarshish, Püt [MT Pul], Lüd, Tübal, Javan), summarily designated as 'the coastlands afar off' (הָאִיִּם הָרְחֹקִים)[41] who had not hitherto heard of Yahweh's 'fame' (שֵׁמַע) or 'seen his glory' (וְלֹא־רָאוּ אֶת־כְּבוֹדִי). There, Yahweh's 'missionaries' 'shall declare my glory [כְּבוֹדִי] among the nations'; in so doing they tell others of what they themselves have experienced (see v. 18b). The hearers will respond (v. 20) to the missionaries' proclamation of Yahweh's 'glory' by bringing an 'offering to the Lord' (מִנְחָה לַיהוה; cf. 19.21), the Egyptians 'will worship with sacrifice [וּמִנְחָה] to my holy mountain [עַל הַר קָדְשִׁי, cf. אֶל־הַר־יְהוה, 2.3], Jerusalem'. That 'offering' will consist, not of sacrificial victims (so, e.g., 56.7; 60.7) or of precious metals (so 60.9), but rather of the Jews ('your brethren') who have been living among them (so 60.4, 9); this will be the nations' equivalent ('just as...') to the acceptable 'cereal offering' (הַמִּנְחָה) that the Israelites themselves present 'in a clean [טָהוֹר] vessel' at the 'house of the Lord' (בֵּית יהוה, see 2.2). So acceptable will this 'offering' prove to Yahweh that he will select from among the nations 'priests and Levites' (literally 'Levitical priests', לְכֹהֲנִים לַלְוִיִּם).[42]

---

40. Use of this term indicates that the 'all nations' of v. 18a is to be taken in the sense of those members of the nations who survived the divine judgment on 'all flesh' described in 66.15-16. The continuation of v. 19 further suggests that 'all nations' there designates, in fact, those living in proximity to Israel, who will themselves be sent to 'nations' living further afield; see above.

41. With this initiative Yahweh responds to the expectations voiced in 42.4, 'The coastlands [אִיִּים] wait for his [the Servant's] law,' and 51.5, 'The coastlands [אִיִּים] wait for me.' Strikingly, the ones through whom those expectations are ultimately to be met are, it now turns out, the nations themselves acting as 'missionaries' to other nations. Cf. the conferral of Israel's title 'Servant(s)' on the foreigners in 56.6.

42. This is the generally accepted understanding of the ambiguous wording of v. 21, where the referent of the 'them' from whom Yahweh chooses his clergy might also be identified as the 'your brethren' in v. 20; see Ruppert, 'Heil der Völker', pp. 155-56, who holds that whereas v. 21 did originally refer to Yahweh's choice of non-Israelite clergy, the secondary v. 20 is intended to indicate that it is rather Israelites who are in view. Given the emphasis throughout 66.18-20 on Yahweh's initiatives with regard to the nations (who, in turn, act on behalf of diaspora Israelites in v. 20) and the very ambiguity of the formulation in v. 21, I suggest that the—biblically unprecedented—thought that Yahweh indeed might choose clergy also from among non-Israelites (cf., e.g., 61.5) is, at least, not excluded by that verse.

The unit 66.18-23 ends up with two additional divine promises/ announcements. The first of these (v. 22) concerns Israel itself whose descendants and 'name' are to 'remain' before the Lord like/as long as the 'new heavens and the new earth' (see 65.17) that he is going to make. By contrast, the second (v. 23) encompasses the entirety of humanity and its participation in the cycle of Israel's holy days: 'from new moon to new moon, and from sabbath to sabbath [see 56.6], all flesh [כל־בשר, see 40.5] will come to worship before me [להשתחות לפני], says the Lord'.

As the foregoing discussion indicates, Isa. 66.18-24 recapitulates many formulations used in previous texts concerning our theme. At the same time, it assigns two noteworthy new roles to the nations in their worship of Yawheh, that is, as divinely appointed 'missionaries' to each other (v. 19) and Yahwistic clergy (v. 21). New too is the notion of the diaspora Jews as the nations' 'offering' to the Lord (v. 20).

Conclusion

The theme of the nations' involvement with the worship of Yahweh has indeed emerged as a significant one throughout the book of Isaiah, with increasing attention being devoted to it as one moves from chs. 1–39 to 40–66. To an overwhelming degree the texts speak in positive terms of the nations' relation to Yahweh's worship. Only rarely is there mention of the nations as a threat to that worship (see, e.g., 10.10-11; 63.8; 64.12) or of their exclusion from this (see 52.1b). While particular peoples (Egypt, Cush, the Sabeans, see 45.14) are mentioned by name as those who will worship Yahweh, and there is likewise allusion to individual foreigners who are to do so (see 56.6-7), it is more often the nations *en bloc* who are cited as Yahweh's future worshippers (so, e.g., 2.2-4; 25.6-9; 66.18-23). The dominant perspective in the material surveyed is that the nations' worshipping of Yahweh will take place at the temple on Zion, just as does Israel's own. Isaiah 19.16-25, however, reckons with Egypt conducting its own local Yahwistic cult. The nations' offerings to Yahweh likewise vary: monetary gifts (60.9), sacrificial victims (60.7) and Jews living in the diaspora whom distant peoples will present to the Lord in his temple (66.20).

In the process of the nations coming to participate in Yahweh's worship, Israel itself has a consistently significant role, it being, for example, Israel's manner of life, God-given prosperity and teaching of them that inspire the nations to approach the Lord. A number of texts as well envisage Israel as exercising a mediatorial role in the worship of the nations for whom it is to make intercession (45.14) or perform the sacrifices for which they supply the victims (60.7; 61.6). Similarly, the nations' worship of Yahweh himself is intimately tied to their homage to Israel in various texts, for example, Isaiah 60. At the same time, it is especially striking to observe how the texts foresee the nations as Yahweh's worshippers, entering fully and equally into the privileges of Israel. Thus, titles used elsewhere of Israel ('my people', 'the work of my hands', 19.25; 'servant[s]', 56.6) will be predicated of them. They will function too as Yahweh's 'missionaries' (66.19) and clergy (66.21). Non-Israelites are to have an altar of their own (19.20), will present acceptable sacifices to the Lord (19.21; 56.7), participate in his feasts (56.6; 66.23) and have a part in his 'covenant' (56.6). Yahweh for his part will 'teach' the nations (2.3), feed them (25.6), abolish all that causes them grief (25.7-8) and make himself/his 'glory' known to them (19.22; 66.18). In sum, the nations' worship of Yahweh constitutes a key, insistently underscored component of the future hopes that occupy so large a part of the extant book of Isaiah.

It is a privilege for me to offer this modest contribution to John T. Willis whom I have long admired as a scholar and even more as a Christian gentleman.

MOURNERS AND THE PSALMS

Don C. Benjamin and Victor H. Matthews

Given John Willis's long-standing interest in the Psalms and in cultic ritual, it seemed appropriate to dedicate an article to him dealing with the activities of midwives and mourners in the Psalms. Although rulers and their priests led their people in the singing of psalms during worship in ancient Israel and other cultures, many of these psalms, marking times of both celebration and mourning, may have originally been sung by women who functioned as both midwives and mourners.[1] These women were the guardians of the threshold that newborns crossed to enter the human plane and that the dead traversed as they left this life.

In the world of the Bible, midwives and mourners used rites of passage to conduct the newly born and the newly dead from death to life and from life to death. Rites of passage have three phases: separation, isolation and reintegration.[2] Separation detaches passengers from their current status in their households. During isolation or liminality passengers are without status. They enjoy rights and privileges neither in the households from which they have been detached nor in the households

---

1. The national cult of YHWH in Jerusalem made very slow progress against the family shrines. Whereas the care and feeding of the dead could only be done by the family, the national religion served historical and political needs of the monarchy. Yahwism had to desacralize and demythologize death radically in order to check the popularity of the family cults. B. Levine, 'Silence, Sound, and the Phenomenology of Mourning in Biblical Israel', *JANESCU* 22 (1993), pp. 92-93, cites an Ebla text from the reign of Ibbi-Zikar that provides a list of sacrifices prescribed for use during the Ishtar festival. Among the rituals to be performed by the king of Ebla and his family are the 'laments for the kings'. Although this is tied to the political structure, it clearly goes back to a purely family and clan ritual form of mourning and ancestor cult.

2. V.W. Turner, *The Ritual Process: Structure and Anti-Structure* (New York: Aldine, 1969), pp. 94-95. See also A. van Gennep, *The Rites of Passage* (London: Routledge & Kegan Paul, 1909).

into which they will be integrated. Reintegration then concludes a rite by endowing passengers with a new status. Midwives facilitated the transference of the unnamed, statusless newborn into the living world, where it may be named and welcomed to the community of the living. Mourners used funeral rites to separate the dead from the living and the cult of the dead to reintegrate the dead with the living.[3]

In the world of the Bible, midwives provided legal as well as clinical services to their households. Hymns were part of their legal responsibilities in conducting the adoption of a newborn into the household. After the midwife delivered the child, she aspirated the newborn to allow it to fill its lungs with air. The cry of the newborn was not only the clinical symptom of air rushing from its lungs, but a legal petition for admission into a household in the clan. In support of the infant's primal scream, the midwife held up the child asking, 'Who will accept this child into its household?' Only a father of a household could adopt the child, with such formulas as, 'This is my beloved son!' or, 'His name is "John"!' The midwife then cut and tied off the umbilical cord; washed, anointed and swaddled the child; and then placed it on the lap of the mother of the adopting household for her to begin nursing it. As the mother accepted the newborn, the midwife affirmed her actions by intoning a hymn inviting the household to praise Yahweh, who created the earth, who delivered the Hebrews from slavery and who had now endowed this household with children.

Mourners were the midwives for the dead.[4] Like midwives, who opened the eyes and cleared the airways of the newborn, mourners closed the eyes and mouths of the dead. Like midwives, mourners then washed and anointed their bodies. Like midwives, who swaddled the

3. For E.M. Bloch-Smith, 'The Cult of the Dead in Judah: Interpreting the Material Remains', *JBL* 111 (1992), p. 213: '...the belief in the empowered dead, with the attendant practices stemming from that belief, is interpreted as a cult of the dead.' For C.A. Kennedy, 'Dead, Cult of the', *ABD* 2 (1992), pp. 106-107: 'Funerals ritualize the process of separation of the dead from the living. By contrast, the cult of the dead stressed the continuity of kinship and family status. In the words of the Arabic proverb, "Were it not for the living, the dead would have died long ago."'

4. A.M. Roth, 'Fingers, Stars, and the "Opening of the Mouth": The Nature and Function of the NṮRWJ-Blade', *JEA* 79 (1993), pp. 58-66. This study of the opening of the mouth ritual also concludes, on the basis that Isis and Nephthys both mourn Osiris and assist with his rebirth, that mourners in Egypt could also be midwives.

newborn, mourners shrouded the dead. Like midwives, who nursed the newborn, mourners placed food on the graves and in the tombs of the dead.[5] Like midwives, who celebrated the birth of the newborn with hymns, mourners announced the passage of the dead with laments. Therefore the lamenting or keening of mourners was not simply a clinical symptom of pain, but a legal petition for admittance into the world of the dead. As the legal representatives of the dead, mourners used laments to petition the long-dead to accept the newly-deceased as members of their household. Just as the primal scream of the newborn was understood as a legal petition to enter a household in the clan, the lament of mourners was considered to be a legal petition for admittance to the world of the dead.

An Anthropology of Mourners

Mesopotamia

Traditions in southern Mesopotamia during the Bronze Age (3000–1250 BCE) identify two important groups of mourners. One group of mourners were transvestite males (Akkadian: *gala*) or 'lamentation priests'. The other were women past menopause (Akkadian: *dam-ab-ba*, *um-ma-er*) or 'old wives'. Since many of the Sumerian lamentation texts use the *emesal* dialect, a form of speech once thought to be exclusively used by females,[6] there was some consternation about males speaking in this dialect.[7] However, both of these groups of mourners

---

5. For Kennedy, 'Dead', pp. 105-107, the deceased was the host of the meal celebrated on the occasion of a death for those attending the funeral: '…food offerings to the dead are specifically condemned (Deut. 26.14; Ps. 106.28) and yet there are biblical narratives describing family shrines and yearly sacrifices…for all the family (1 Sam. 20:6).'

6. S.N. Kramer, *The Sumerians: Their History, Culture, and Character* (Chicago: University of Chicago Press, 1963), p. 223.

7. M. Cohen, 'Analysis of *balag*-Composition to the God Enlil Copied During the Seleucid Period' (PhD Dissertation, University of Pennsylvania, 1979), p. 39, suggests that the mention of 'him of tears' (*mu-lu-ir-ri*) in the 'Lament over the Destruction of Ur' is merely a 'literary device' and does not indicate a change in gender for the speaker. It seems more likely, however, as P.W. Ferris, Jr, *The Genre of Communal Lament in the Bible and the Ancient Near East* (SBLDS, 127; Atlanta: Scholars Press, 1992), pp. 27-28, argues that the *gala*-priests were male. This would mean that they either had taken over the *emesal* dialect or that they shared it with female mourners.

would have been considered liminal, since neither the *gala* mourners nor the *dam-ab-ba* mourners were childbearing.[8] In the traditions of ancient Sumer both birth and death put all childbearing adults present at risk. Therefore, mourners and midwives were almost always members of the village who were not (or who were no longer) childbearing.

Both *gala* mourners and *dam-ab-ba* mourners held a recognized status within Sumerian society and were paid in rations for their service to the clan. An inscription on the Gudea Statue B describes *gala* mourners playing instruments to accompany the laments that they lead the congregation in singing.[9] A group similar to these priests is ordered by Gilgamesh to mourn for Enkidu (Gilgamesh 7.3.45).[10]

Egypt
In the Old Kingdom (2575–2134 BCE) and Middle Kingdom (2040–1640 BCE) traditions for the opening of the mouth ritual in Egypt portray Isis and Nephthys as both mourners and midwives. The two godmothers first lament the death of Osiris, and then, as midwives, assist in his re-birth.[11] Paintings also portray mourners (Egyptian: *dryt*) as Isis and Nephthys. The inscriptions that accompany the paintings do not usually give the proper names of the mourners. Even when their names are given, the *dryt*-mourners do not seem to be members of the household of the dead. Members of the household of the dead who join the mourners in lamenting the dead are also usually anonymous in the inscriptions.

8. Ferris, *The Genre of Communal Lament*, p. 27, notes that 'there is ample evidence to support the conclusion that females did play a major role in the cultural phenomenon of communal laments—both as a speaker in certain literary texts (primary speaker) and as performers of the lament rituals'.

9. G.A. Barton, *The Royal Inscriptions of Sumer and Akkad* (New Haven: Yale University Press, 1929), p. 181.

10. *CAD*, 'D', pp. 60-61. See also Levine, 'Silence', p. 92. The women, [*samhati*], instructed to mourn here are translated as 'courtesans' in the *CAD*. It is possible that this additional liminal category for women also functioned at times as both midwives and mourners.

11. Roth, 'Fingers', pp. 66. In a personal communication she further suggests that such a connection between Isis and Nephthys argues that one woman might be both a mourner and a midwife in a single social setting. It seems to us, however, that the functions of midwives and mourners are better regarded as comparable. They may be the same women, but the two activities would have been kept separate and different psalms and rituals would have been used to keep them distinct.

In the New Kingdom (1550–1070 BCE), paintings portray the mourners as the wives and daughters of the dead rather than as Isis and Nephthys. On a coffin for Ahmose at Thebes, one mourner appears near his shoulder as his wife Hapu, and another as his daughter Ahmose. Each is mourning him by striking their foreheads with the palms of their right hands.[12] A painting in a tomb for Nebamen at Thebes portrays mourners as his wife, Henutnofret, and as his daughters.[13] They appear several times in the funeral procession. In one of these, Henutnofret appears crouched before her husband's coffin with tears streaming down her face, one hand touching the foot of the coffin and the other rubbing dust into her hair.[14] These classic poses follow prescribed ritual and set the proper tone for the family's public expressions of grief and loss.

Syria–Palestine
Burials along the southern coast of Syria-Palestine between 1250 and 1000 BCE included grave goods like bowls, jars, pilgrim flasks, pyxides and craters manufactured in Syria–Palestine, Mycenea and Cyprus. There were also amulets like beads, pendants, bangles, rings, earrings, eyes of Horus, scarabs and small statues of Bes.[15] The Bes statues, particularly, stress the connection between birth and death. Bes was the divine patron of midwives and apparently the divine patron of mourners as well. His power in escorting the newborn into the life of the village was parallel to his power to escort the newly dead into the afterlife.[16]

Households in both Egypt and along the coast highway in Syria-Palestine had great devotion to both Bes and Taweret.[17] They regarded

12. C.H. Roehrig, 'Women's Work: Some Occupations of Nonroyal Women as Depicted in Ancient Egyptian Art', in A.K. Capel and G.E. Markoe (eds.), *Mistress of the House, Mistress of Heaven: Women in Ancient Egypt* (New York: Hudson Hills, 1996), p. 14, cites this as 'Fig. 1, The Metropolitan Museum of Art, 14.10.2, gift of the Earl of Carnarvon, 1914'.
13. Roehrig, 'Women's Work', p. 14, cites this as 'Fig. 2, TT 181'.
14. Roehrig, 'Women's Work', p. 14.
15. Bloch-Smith, 'Cult of the Dead in Judah', p. 214.
16. M. Lurker, *The Gods and Symbols of Ancient Egypt: An Illustrated Dictionary* (London: Thames & Hudson, 1980), p. 33, points to Bes's role as a guardian deity. He is often carved into columns or as a bas-relief in Mammisi, 'the subsidiary buildings of temples in the Late Period, in which the annual mysteries of birth of the divine son were celebrated'.
17. A. Erman, *A Handbook of Egyptian Religion* (Boston: Longwood Press,

them as important members of the divine assembly to be present during childbirth. They are the divine midwives whose images are a key to the responsibilities of those women who assisted birth mothers in the world of Egypt. Sometimes Bes wears a feather crown or wings of hawk feathers over his shoulders and arms, like the Horus of Behdet.[18] He often carries the glyph *sa*, which means, 'protection'. Taweret is a hippopotamus–crocodile creature with human breasts and a distended uterus.[19]

The connection between celebration and mourning is once again demonstrated in Bes's association with musical instruments. He is often depicted with a lute, whose music was expected to drive away evil or predatory spirits.[20] Similar use of musical instruments is also found in the *Testament of Job* (52.4). Knowing he is about to die, Job distributes a lyre, a censer and a drum to his daughters, who will mourn him and summon the long-dead who will welcome him into the afterlife.[21] The music and incense used by mourners both summoned those who would accompany the dead across the threshold from life to death and protected the dead from those who would obstruct their passage from life into the afterlife.

Israel

Excavations in private houses and in burials in the foothills of Judah often contain pillar statues of the godmother Asherah.[22] Like the statues of Bes in graves found along the coastal plains, these statues of Asherah emphasize the connection between birth and death. The body of Asherah is a solid or hollow cone. Her head is cast in a mold or shaped by hand, and her arms support the full breasts of a nursing mother. The presence of statues of the godmother Asherah and the

---

1988), p. 161, reproduces a protective stela from the Berlin Museum (no. 4434) that depicts Bes's head and serves as protection against serpents.

18. G. Hart, *A Dictionary of Egyptian Gods and Goddesses* (New York: Routledge & Kegan Paul, 1986), pp. 58-60.

19. J. Baines and J. Malek, *Atlas of Ancient Egypt* (New York: Facts on File, 1980), p. 217.

20. A. Erman, *Handbook*, p. 76, reproduces a picture of Bes with a lute (Berlin Museum 5666).

21. R.P. Spittler, 'Testament of Job', in J.H. Charlesworth (ed.), *The Old Testament Pseudepigrapha* (2 vols.; Garden City, NY: Doubleday, 1983), I, p. 867.

22. R. Hestrin, 'Understanding Asherah: Exploring Semitic Iconography', *BARev* 17.5 (1991), p. 57.

divine midwives Bes and Taweret in the tombs of the dead demonstrates the relationship that the world of the Bible established between birth and death. The artifacts also relate the midwives who assisted and celebrated the arrival of newborns into the household with the mourners who escorted them into the afterlife.[23]

Mourners in Syria–Palestine dressed the bodies of the dead with the clothes and jewelry reflecting their status in the clan. In the world of the Bible, clothes and jewelry were not simply personal accessories, they identified the social status of the wearer. It was typical for mourners, whether professionals or family members, to tear their clothing and wear sackcloth (2 Sam. 3.31; Est. 4.3; Jer. 6.26). Some grievers also shaved their heads (Isa. 22.12; Ezek. 27.31) and fasted during the period of mourning (Deut. 26.14; Ps. 35.14; Joel 2.12).[24] This altered appearance allowed mourners to be separated temporarily from the world of the living and join the dead during their journeys to the underworld.[25]

When the dead were dressed, mourners wrapped them in a cloak. Toggle pins and fibulae clips that mourners used to close the cloak over the body are a familiar artifact in burials.[26] When the woman of En-dor (בעלת־אוב) summons Samuel (cf. Gen. 28.22; Isa. 8.19) to meet with Saul in the books of Samuel–Kings (1 Sam. 28.1-25), Samuel is still wrapped in his cloak (מעיל, 1 Sam. 28.14). This is not the cloak (מעילו) whose hem Saul tore during their meeting on Gilgal (1 Sam. 15.27;

23. G.A. Anderson, *A Time to Mourn, a Time to Dance: The Expression of Grief and Joy in Israelite Religion* (University Park, PA: Pennsylvania State University Press, 1991), p. 97, notes that the mourner does not just express grief, but symbolically 'descends to the underworld'. Following the period of mourning, usually seven days, movement is then possible back to life and a restoration of normal affairs.

24. It seems unlikely that many families would have had the resources to employ professional mourners to wail continuously throughout the period of mourning (see Gen. 50.10 and Deut. 34.8 for a range of between 7 and 30 days). Thus the family would have modelled their dress (dark clothing), their appearance, and their manner of walking (a sort of shuffle in Mal. 3.14) after that of persons 'skilled in lamentation' (Amos 5.16).

25. Anderson, *A Time to Mourn*, pp. 74-75, cites Gilgamesh 12.10-46 where the hero engages in a 'ritual dishevelment' as a rite of passage during the period of mourning.

26. Bloch-Smith, 'Cult of the Dead', p. 218.

1 Sam. 2.19; Exod. 28.4).[27] This cloak is his burial shroud, which functions as a ritual placenta placed over the body to prepare it for the period of gestation in the tomb before the dead person is resurrected into the afterlife.[28]

Israelite creation stories use three important metaphors to indicate the connection between birth and death: a womb, a tomb and a dungeon. The womb is the primary metaphor. Both the grave or tomb and the dungeon are regarded as wombs from which new life emerges. All three are dark and wet, which are also the two most common ways in which the Bible describes the chaos from which Yahweh builds a new world. These metaphors characterize Yahweh as a midwife, who pulls back the placenta covering the newborn.

> And Yahweh will destroy on this mountain the shroud that is cast over all people, the sheet that is spread over all nations; Yahweh will swallow up death forever. Then Yahweh Elohim will wipe away the tears from all faces, and the disgrace of the people of Yahweh; Yahweh will take away from all the earth, for Yahweh has spoken (Isa. 25.7-8, authors' translation).

Just as midwives pulled back the placenta from the body of the new-born so that it could breathe, mourners shrouded the body of the newly dead in a cloak and closed it with toggle pins or fibulae clips so that it could gestate in the womb of its earth mother before being resurrected into the afterlife.

Throughout the Bible, but particularly in the book of Psalms, rejoicing (שׂמח) and mourning (אבל) are corollaries.[29] The customs are inversely related to one another, and the metaphors used to describe them are all related by color.[30] The words create a type/antitype relationship with one another.[31] Rejoicing is light, mourning is dark (קדר).

27. Pace P.K. McCarter, *I Samuel* (AB, 8; Garden City, NY: Doubleday, 1980), p. 421.

28. Roth, 'Fingers', p. 77, points to a similar process of 'rebirth' for the dead into the world of the afterlife, involving the rituals similar to those associated with the midwife's separating the child from its mother. Thus cult statues are formed from a clay placenta and repeatedly called to life by worshippers or priests.

29. The Hebrew word אבל has a cuneiform cognate, *abalu*, which has the usual meaning of 'to carry or transport', but also means 'to die' in contexts where it takes on the sense of 'to be carried off or swept away'. In 2 Sam. 14.2 and Ps. 35.14 it refers to a person knowledgeable of the rituals of mourning.

30. Anderson, *A Time to Mourn*, p. 49.

31. Anderson, *A Time to Mourn*, p. 51. These connotations in Hebrew also

Rejoicing is dawn, mourning is dusk. Rejoicing is a plant blooming, mourning is a plant withering.

Mourners in the Book of Psalms

The Psalms reflect all of the major traditions that developed in ancient Israel. Some psalms summarize creation stories, some the stories of the exodus. Some psalms retell the hero stories in the books of Joshua and Judges, others the stories of David's rise to power.[32] There are psalms that teach, like the book of Proverbs,[33] and there are psalms that revisit the verdicts announced by the prophets. Finally, there are apocalyptic psalms that describe the death of the old world and the creation of a new one.

Most psalms are laments. Standard laments have five components: complaint, petition, vow, declaration of innocence and confession of faith.[34] The core of most laments is a complaint describing the suffering of the clan. Complaints express the anger of a clan at Yahweh for breaking the covenant by which Yahweh promised to protect it from its enemies. This anger is not simply an internal emotion, but a legal protest filed in a public forum. Complaints do not simply help the clans vent their feelings and get something off their chests, they are a form of judicial outrage. The clan has suffered a loss, and it is demanding that Yahweh compensate it for its loss.

A lament in part two of the book of Psalms (Ps. 44.1-26) complains that Yahweh has allowed the enemies of a clan to defeat its warriors in battle, plunder its land and sell its women and children as slaves for virtually nothing. Mourners blame Yahweh for allowing the people who had been delivered from slavery to be sold back into slavery. Such a tragic reversal leaves the clan without honor, hunted and hated, not just by their enemies, but by everyone. No one grants them status. No

appear in Akkadian (*samahu*), Aramaic (*s-m-h*) and Arabic *(samaha)*. These words, which originally simply described a plant's growth, acquired the connotations of blooming, then of prospering and finally of proudly celebrating life.

32. Pss. 2; 18; 20; 21; 45-48; 72; 76; 84; 87; 93; 97-99; 101; 110; 122 and 132.11-18 are the 'songs of Zion' and the 'enthronement psalms'. See S. Mowinckel, *Psalms in Israel's Worship* (New York: Abingdon Press, 1962).

33. Pss. 1.1-6; 15; 24; 34; 37.

34. G.S. Ogden, 'Psalm 60: Its Rhetoric, Form, and Function', *JSOT* 31 (1985), p. 89.

one allows them to participate in daily life.[35] Everyone considers the clan to be such an object of scorn that they taunt the people with jokes and stories.

Complaint (Ps. 44.10-17):

You disown us and shame us,
    You do not march into battle with our soldiers.
You let our enemies drive us back;
    Our foes plunder us without opposition from you.
You mark us as sheep to be slaughtered;
    Among strangers you scatter us.
You sell your people at a loss;
    You make no profit.
You make us fools in the eyes of our enemies,
    Our foes laugh at us.
You make us a proverb among strangers.
    Outsiders tell jokes about us.
All the day my shame is before me,
    Everyday shame covers my face.
When my foes taunt me,
    When my enemies make fun of me.

(Authors' translation)

Complaints in most laments are not only painfully outspoken, but shockingly frank in blaming Yahweh for suffering. Few Muslims, Christians or Jews today pray with such unrestrained anger at God. Nonetheless, these ancient people were not heretics who had lost their faith; they simply expressed their faith differently than most people in biblical religions today. They considered themselves to be full partners with Yahweh in determining what happened, and how it happened. Believers today are much more passive, and, in some ways, more fatalistic than their ancestors in the Bible. They more often pray with resignation rather than with anger or outrage. They pray to accept the will of God. The laments in the book of Psalms pray to change it.

Laments are the traditions of a people in process, not a fully defined theology of suffering. Therefore, petitions for help from Yahweh that appear in many laments can represent both healthy and unhealthy

---

35. Anderson, *A Time to Mourn*, p. 88, citing Pss. 9.14-15; 71.20; 86.13, suggests that the depths of despair found in the psalms of lament are a means of comparing the psalmist's experience to the 'descent into Sheol, and the act of deliverance as a raising up from Sheol'.

reactions in a clan to its loss of land and children.[36] Petitions reflect a healthy human participation in developing the will of God when they remind Yahweh to protect and provide for a clan whose land and children are threatened. Petitions reflect an unhealthy denial when they treat suffering as an unreal or only temporary aspect of human life.

Petition (Ps. 3.7 [Heb. v. 8]):

> Awake from your sleep, Yahweh!
>   Deliver me, my divine patron!
> Land a blow with your fist right on the jaw of my enemies,
>   Hit them in the mouth and break their teeth.

(Authors' translation)

Petitions are a form of denial when they are prayed without passion or pain or anger. The denial in unhealthy petitions pretends that loss has not occurred at all, or that the loss is only temporary. Denial not only postpones the beginning of recovery, it also prolongs the time during which unconfronted loss continues to drain the resources of a victim. In contrast, the acceptance in healthy petitions that angrily call upon Yahweh to come to the aid of a clan in crisis allows victims of loss to begin recovery.

The petition in a lament from part one of the book of Psalms (Ps. 3.1-8) is a healthy petition that wakes up Yahweh and angrily orders Yahweh to attack the enemies of the clan. Mourners in ancient Israel assumed that in times of peace Yahweh rested or slept. Yahweh had not fallen asleep like an irresponsible sentry.[37] Sleep was the normal state of a divine patron whose people were secure. Sleep was a sign of peace. At a moment of crisis, the people went to wake up their divine patron. This petition also asks Yahweh to attack the enemies of Israel like a boxer. The lament pleads: '…land a blow with your fist right on the jaw of my enemies. Hit them in the mouth and break their teeth.' The lament wants Yahweh to wake up and come out fighting.

There is a lament in part five of the book of Psalms (Ps. 137.1-9) whose last two lines contain one of the most painful petitions in the entire Bible. 'You are a monster, Babylon. Blessed are they who do to

---

36. See Ps. 35.13-14, which provides the full ritual of mourning by a righteous person, even for his enemies.

37. Cf. Elijah's charge against Ba'al in 1 Kgs 18.27. On this theme, see B.F. Batto, 'The Sleeping God: An Ancient Near Eastern Motif of Divine Sovereignty', *Bib* 68 (1987), pp. 153-77.

you what you did to us. Blessed are they who grab your children by the ankles. Blessed are they who smash their skulls against a rock' (Ps. 137.8-9). Nothing in the opening lines of the lament prepares today's audiences to hear such scandalizing words spoken by the people of God.

> *Complaint* (Ps. 137.1-3):
> We mourned by the Rivers of Babylon,
>> We prostrated to remember Zion.
> Our enemies told us to sing hymns,
>> Our conquerors ordered us: 'Sing the songs of Zion!'

> *Vow* (Ps. 137.4-6):
> We hung our harps in the weeping willows.
>> How could we sing hymns to Yahweh in a strange land?
> If I forget you, Jerusalem,
>> Paralyze the hand with which I play.
> Let my tongue stick to the roof of my mouth,
>> If I do not remember Jerusalem above everything else.

> *Petition* (Ps. 137.7-9):
> Remember, Yahweh, how the people of Edom sang when Jerusalem fell:
>> 'Pull down its walls.
>> Raze the city to its foundations.'
> You are a monster, Babylon.
>> Blessed are they who do to you what you did to us.
> Blessed are they who grab your children by the ankles,
>> Blessed are they who smash their skulls against a rock.
>>>> (Author's translation)

The lament opens with a complaint in which the mourners indict the Babylonians for not only destroying Jerusalem, but also ordering their prisoners of war from Judah to celebrate the Babylonian victory by singing hymns celebrating Yahweh as the builder and the protector of Jerusalem (Pss. 46; 48; 76; 84). The more exalted and heroic the descriptions of Yahweh in these hymns, the more exalted and heroic the victory of Babylon over the people of Yahweh. Raping the culture of captives was a common practice in the world of the Bible. War was not simply a matter of victory on the field of battle, but the victory of one way of life over the other.[38]

---

38. B. Oded, *War, Peace, and Empire: Justification for War in Assyrian Royal Inscriptions* (Wiesbaden: Reichert, 1992), p. 41, in describing Assyrian warfare

The mourners then describe the vow of the people of Judah not to sing and not to forget Jerusalem. 'We hung our harps in the weeping willows. How could we sing hymns to Yahweh in a strange land? If I forget you, Jerusalem, paralyze the hand with which I play. Let my tongue stick to the roof of my mouth, if I do not remember Jerusalem above everything else' (Ps. 137.4-6). The people of Judah would not betray Jerusalem as the people of Edom had done (Obad. 8-14; Ezek. 25.12-14; 35.2-9). The mourners then recall with bitterness how this Semitic people from southern Jordan betrayed their covenant with the people of Judah and joined wholeheartedly in the Babylonian campaign against Jerusalem and then sang enthusiastically to celebrate its destruction.

The complaint and the vow in the lament elicit respect for clans that reflect such grace under fire. The petition that follows, however, completely destroys the sympathy of most audiences today, who hold Jews, Christians, Muslims and their biblical ancestors to an ethic of forgiveness rather than vengeance. The words were strong in the world of the Bible as well, but not as outrageous as they sound now. The petition is an unvarnished description of one of the cruel and common practices of war in the world of the Bible.

In the world of the Bible, war was waged on four fronts. Warriors from one tribe confronted warriors from another first on the field of battle. Victory here, however, was only a prelude to three other confrontations. A battlefield victory was only a victory over the present generation. Warriors were expected to go on to the second front by raping childbearing women, disemboweling pregnant women and massacring newborn infants.[39] When this future generation had been destroyed, warriors laid siege to the past generation by desecrating graves and sanctuaries.[40] The dead and the divine were the third and fourth fronts in a war. Human remains were exhumed and burned or scattered to

---

practices, notes that the Assyrian king is the 'agent whose mission is to enforce the divine decree and conduct the punitive war'.

39. The annals of Tiglath-Pileser I (1115–1077 BCE) contain a parable in which the king is portrayed as a hunter who includes in his battlefield targets the pregnant women of his enemies. He rips open their bellies as a military tactic of psychological terrorism (VAT 13833). This practice is also mentioned in 2 Kgs 8.11-12 and 15.16.

40. See Josiah's action of desecrating the graves of the priests of Bethel in 2 Kgs 23.16.

prevent the ancestors of a village from coming to its defense from the land of the dead. Then sacred furniture from sanctuaries was smashed and burned, and sacred images were decapitated or taken into exile to prevent the divine patrons of a tribe from restoring its clans to life either in the land of the living or the land of the dead.[41] The petition in this lament reflects the simple and harsh reality that war in the world of the Bible was always total war.

The petition is not lawless. It carefully asks that the punishment of Babylon fit its crime. The law of *talion*, an eye for an eye and a tooth for a tooth, exercised a civilizing control against unrestrained vengeance of one tribe against another. Even today the golden rule of doing unto others as others have done unto us is considered an exercise of divine conduct by human beings.

Admittedly believers today can pray the petition only with contrition for this dark side that lurks in every culture, and never as a justification for violence, even against oppressors. Nevertheless, even today parents cannot witness the murder of their children with serenity. The petition voices the pain of all those who watch the innocent suffer, and it cries out to believers to be their companions in suffering the loss.

A Hymn and a Lament (Psalm 66.1-20)

In some laments clans vow to acknowledge Yahweh as their divine patron if their losses are restored (Pss. 22.22-31; 50.14; 61.4-8; 66.13-17; 116.14-18). Vows reflect the efforts of clans to bargain with Yahweh to relieve suffering. Complaints, petitions and bargaining with Yahweh by making a vow all reflect the respect that traditional cultures have for the responsibility of humans in determining the course of events. Admittedly, bargaining is an anthropomorphic way to describe Yahweh. Nonetheless, it does not intend to reduce Yahweh to a merchant haggling over the price of a sale. The Hebrews considered what happened in the world of the Bible to have been the result, not simply of divine action, but also of human reaction. Yahweh did not act unilaterally, but interacted with humans. Bargaining reflects the understanding that different human reactions to divine initiatives produce different results. Few who pray today are so confident.

Some laments in the book of Psalms lack a complaint or a petition

---

41. See this practice by the kings of Mari in V.H. Matthews, 'Government Involvement in the Religion of the Mari Kingdom', *RA* 72 (1978), pp. 151-56. This is also clearly the policy of the Chaldean kings, as described in the Cyrus Cylinder.

and have only a vow. These laments have been labelled 'songs of thanksgiving'.[42] One psalm with a vow is preserved in part two of the book of Psalms. This numbered psalm in the Bible today actually combines two psalms: a hymn (Ps. 66.1-12) and a lament (Ps. 66.13-20).

Hymn (Psalm 66.1-12).

> *Call to worship* (Ps. 66.1-5):
> Make a joyful noise to Yahweh, all the earth.
>> Sing the glory of the name of Yahweh.
> Give to Yahweh glorious praise.
>> Say to Yahweh, 'How awesome are your great works.
> Because of your great power, your enemies prostrate before you.
>> All the earth worships you;
> They sing praises to you,
>> They sing praises to your name.'
> Come and see what Yahweh has done:
>> Come and see the great works Yahweh does for the powerless.

> *Creation story* (Ps. 66.6a):
> Yahweh turned the sea into dry land;
>> They passed through the river on foot.

> *Call to worship* (Ps. 66.6b-7a):
> Let us rejoice in Yahweh,
>> Let us rejoice in Yahweh, who rules by might forever,

> *Creation story* (Ps. 66.7b):
> Who watches over the nations
>> Who humbles the rebellious.

> *Call to worship* (Ps. 66.8):
> Bless Yahweh, O peoples,
>> Let the sound of praise be heard,

> *Creation story* (Ps. 66.7-12):
> Who kept us alive,
>> Who did not let our feet slip.

42. C. Westermann, *The Praise of God in the Psalms* (Richmond, VA: John Knox Press, 1965), pp. 82-83.

Who tested us;
    Who tried us as silver is tried.
Who brought us into the net;
    Who laid burdens on our backs;
Who let strangers rule over us;
    Who led us through fire and through water;
Who, finally, brought us into this fertile land.

Lament (Psalm 66.13-20).

Vow (Ps. 66.13-17):
I will come into your house with burnt offerings;
    I will pay you my vows,
The vows that my lips uttered
    The vows that my mouth promised when I was in trouble.
I will offer you burnt offerings of fatlings,
    I will offer you the smoke of the sacrifice of rams;
    I will offer you bulls and goats.
Come and hear, all you who fear Yahweh,
    I will tell what Yahweh has done for me.
I cried aloud to Yahweh,
    Yahweh was extolled with my tongue.

Declaration of innocence (Ps. 66.18-19):
If I had cherished iniquity in my heart,
    Yahweh would not have listened.
But Yahweh has listened;
    Yahweh has given heed to the words of my prayer.

Confession of faith (Ps. 66.20):
Bless Yahweh, who has not ignored my prayer.
    Bless Yahweh, who has not stopped loving me.

                    (Authors' translation)

    The hymn alternates three calls to worship with three creation stories. The initial call to worship and the final creation story are long, while the calls to worship and creation stories in the middle of the hymn are short. The initial call to worship summons the community ten times to acknowledge Yahweh as its divine patron. 'Make a joyful noise! Sing! Praise! Say! Prostrate! Worship! Praise! Praise! Come! See!' (Ps. 66. 1-5).
    The first creation story reminds the clans in the community that Yahweh delivered them from slavery in Egypt. 'Yahweh turned the sea

into dry land' (Ps. 66.6). The second creation story reminds them that Yahweh delivered them from slavery in Syria–Palestine. Yahweh 'watches over the nations' (Ps. 66.7). The third creation story reminds them that Yahweh delivered them from slavery in Babylon. Yahweh 'tested us...tried us as silver is tried' (Ps. 66.10).

The lament is made up of a vow (Ps. 66.13-17), a declaration of innocence (Ps. 66.18-19) and a confession of faith (Ps. 66.20). In the vow mourners promise that the shamed clan will do something and will say something. It will offer sacrifice to Yahweh: 'I will come into your house with burnt offerings...' (Ps. 66.13). And it will tell all those from the clan who are eating the sacrifice how Yahweh delivered it from its enemies: 'I will tell what he has done for me' (Ps. 66.16).

The vows that appear in laments are not promises made by unbelievers to become converts. Vows are the promises of believers to assemble the community, to eat a sacrifice and to tell the story.[43] Those whom Yahweh delivers will not forget to celebrate their salvation from their enemies.

Lament (Psalm 22.1-31)

Some laments have declarations of innocence that explain why a clan should not suffer. These declarations can express both healthy and unhealthy reactions of a clan to loss. As a healthy reaction, declarations of innocence place in evidence the public record of a clan that has fulfilled the stipulations of its covenant with Yahweh in order to argue that it has kept its part of the covenant and that it expects Yahweh to do the same. As an unhealthy reaction, declarations of innocence can reflect the depression of a clan that acknowledges its loss but cannot express its anger over the loss. Therefore, the clan simply represses the anger as if the loss of its land and children were without consequences for the honor or survival of the clan, which the declaration of innocence describes as if it were still intact.

A lament in part one of the book of Psalms (Ps. 22.1-31) contains each of the five standard components of a lament. There is a complaint, a petition, a declaration of innocence, a vow and a confession of faith.

> *Complaint* (Ps. 22.1-2):
> My God, my God, why have you forsaken me?

43. In this way, they resemble the covenant renewal ceremonies found in Exod. 24.3-8 and Josh. 24.1-28.

Why are you not helping me?
Why are you not listening to the words of my lament?
My God, I cry out during the day, but you do not answer;
    I cry out at night, but I find no peace.

Confession of faith (Ps. 22.3-5):
You are holy.
    The hymns of Israel rise up to your throne.
Our ancestors had faith in you.
    They had faith, and you delivered them from their enemies.
They cried out to you, and were saved.
    They had faith in you, and were not shamed.

Complaint (Ps. 22.6-8):
I am a maggot, not a man.
    Scorned by animals, despised by humans.
All who see me mock me,
    They make faces at me,
    They shake their heads.
'What good is your faith in Yahweh?
    Why cannot Yahweh deliver you?
    Why cannot Yahweh rescue a beloved heir?'

Declaration of innocence (Ps. 22.9-10):
You were my midwife,
    You showed me to my mother's breast.
I have depended upon you since I was born,
    Since my mother bore me you have been my divine patron.

Petition (Ps. 22.11):
Do not be far from me.
    Trouble is near.
    No one else can help me.

Complaint (Ps. 22.12-18):
Herds of bulls encircle me.
    Powerful bulls from Bashan surround me.
They roar at me like hungry lions,
    They bawl like lions on the prowl.
I am poured out like water,
    All my bones are out of joint.
My heart is like wax;
    My heart melts within my breast.
My mouth is as dry as clay,

My tongue sticks to my cheek.
You let death return me to clay,
    Dogs are all around me.
Evildoers encircle me.
    My hands and feet have shriveled.
I can count all my bones,
    They stare and gloat over me.
They divide my clothes among themselves,
    They gamble for my clothing.

Petition (Ps. 22.19-21):
Yahweh, do not stay so far away.
    My helper (עזר), come quickly.
Deliver me from the sword,
    Save me from powerful dogs.
Protect me from the mouths of lions,
    Rescue me from the horns of wild oxen.

Vow (Ps. 22.22-31):
I will praise your name in my clan.
    At the sanctuary I will sing hymns to you…
I will praise Yahweh in the assembly,
    My vows I will pay before the people of Yahweh,
    I will feed the hungry until they are satisfied…
Our descendants will serve Yahweh.
    Future generations will hear of Yahweh.
They will hand on the stories of the great works of Yahweh to a people
    yet unborn.
    They will tell future generations everything Yahweh has done.
                                            (Authors' translation).

The complaint is divided into three parts (Ps. 22.1-2, 6-8, 12-18). Mourners grieve that both humans and animals, and even Yahweh, shun the clan as if it were a maggot (Ps. 22. 6; Isa. 41.8-13). The clan is not only excommunicated from all divine, human and animal companionship, but it is also attacked by bulls, lions, dogs and oxen. The array of creatures in the lament is striking. Its enemies knock the members of the clan to the ground. They lie there dying like water soaking into the land as it runs out of a jar or like wax cooling on the earth as it runs out of a mold.[44] They are so helpless that their enemies loot even the clothes they are wearing.

44. See J.T. Willis's comment on these verses in 'Alternating (ABA´B´) Parallelism in the Old Testament Psalms and Prophetic Literature', in E.R. Follis (ed.),

The petition is divided into two parts (Ps. 22.11, 19-21). In the first petition mourners cry out to Yahweh to stay close, so that Yahweh can come quickly to the aid of the clan when its enemies attack. Many Muslims, Christians and Jews today consider suffering as a sign that God has abandoned them or is far away from those who suffer. This petition, however, reflects the standard biblical belief that Yahweh is always close at hand. In good times or in bad, in sickness or in health, in poverty or in riches, Yahweh is Emmanuel (Isa. 7.14), the 'divine patron [אל], who is with us [עמנו]'. In the world of the Bible, suffering did not separate divine patrons from their people.

In the second petition, the mourners address Yahweh with the same title that the stories of Adam and Eve use for the woman in the book of Genesis (Gen. 2.20): both are 'helpers' or 'helpmates' (עזר). In neither tradition do the titles carry connotations of inferiority or subordination. They are the titles of the mothers on whom clans depend for food and protection.

The mourners not only address Yahweh as the mother of a clan, but as its midwife as well. The declaration of innocence in the lament affirms: 'You were my midwife [אתה גחי מבטן]. You showed me to my mother's breast. I have depended upon you since I was born, since my mother bore me you have been my divine patron' (Ps. 22.9-10). The declaration certifies that at no time in its life has the clan ever forgotten who feeds it and who protects it. It has always known and publicly acknowledged Yahweh as its mother and midwife (Jer. 1.5). Like all declarations, this one puts Yahweh on notice that Yahweh's reputation as a divine patron is completely dependent upon the fate of the clan. If it falls victim to its enemies, everyone in the clan will know that Yahweh was either powerless or unwilling to save it.

As in other laments, the vow promises that when the clan gathers at the sanctuary, the clan will sacrifice enough to feed everyone, and, while they are eating, it will retell the stories of the great works that Yahweh used to deliver it from its enemies. The clan also promises that these stories will be told not only during the lifetimes of those whom Yahweh actually saved, but also by the future generations of the clan as well: 'Our descendants will serve Yahweh. Future generations will hear of Yahweh. They will hand on the stories of the great works of Yahweh

Directions in Biblical Hebrew Poetry (JSOTSup, 40; Sheffield: JSOT Press, 1987), p. 51. He notes how the similes here are designed to express fully how 'distraught' the psalmist truly is. See Pss. 68.2 and 97.5 for similar use of this simile.

to a people yet unborn. They will tell future generations everything Yahweh has done' (Ps. 22.30-31). The entire Bible, not just this lament, is the fulfilment of these vows not to forget what Yahweh has done. Storytelling transcends the boundaries of time and endows divine works with immortality.

Confessions of faith are spoken by the mourners singing a lament (Ps. 22.3-5). Words of assurance are spoken by someone else in the clan on behalf of Yahweh. The intention of both confessions of faith and words of assurance is to express a clan's acceptance of its loss without losing its faith in Yahweh as its creator and deliverer. Mourners affirm that suffering is real, and that land and children have been lost, but they also affirm that the loss does not prove that 'Yahweh is not Lord'.

The confession of faith here affirms, first of all, that Yahweh is 'holy' (קָדֹשׁ). Holiness is the distinguishing characteristic of Yahweh, which describes Yahweh as a mystery that human beings must learn to respect, and not a problem that human beings can solve. There are no metaphors that can accurately and completely explain Yahweh to Israel. Every tradition in the Bible is only a limited reflection on the Yahweh whom the Hebrews encounter. Suffering is the experience of human limitations. The greatest limitation for human beings—and consequently their greatest suffering—is their inability to understand God. Therefore, this confession of faith reminds the clan that it suffers, ultimately, because it can never fully understand Yahweh, who is holy.

Secondly, the confession of faith reminds the clan that its ancestors cried out to Yahweh in laments and that they survived their suffering: 'Our ancestors had faith in you. They had faith, and you delivered them from their enemies. They cried out to you, and were saved. They had faith in you, and were not shamed' (Ps. 22.4-5). Today, people in western European cultures look forward to find the answers to their problems. Research and development define their lifestyles and their worldviews. In contrast, the Hebrews looked backward to find the answers to their problems. In the worldview of the Bible, there was nothing new to discover, nothing new to find. Problems resulted when a people overlooked or forgot something. For them, the world came with a complete set of instructions. Problem-solving was simply taking the time to reread them. To a large extent, the Bible today is the legacy of the kind of remembering the past that this confession of faith reflects. The ancestors suffered, and so we suffer. The ancestors cried out to

Yahweh, and so we cry out to Yahweh. The ancestors survived, and so we will survive.

The emphasis in the confession of faith is not that the ancestors cried out to Yahweh and the suffering stopped. The ancestors cried out to Yahweh, and they survived the suffering, which, in due time, ran its course. Laments were not intended to help the Hebrews avoid pain, but to survive it.

Today, it is common enough for people to embrace a faith tradition as an insurance policy against suffering. Believers often think that they cannot, or at least that they should not, suffer. When they do suffer, some Muslims, Christians and Jews revoke their faith. Suffering in ancient Israel was no different than suffering today, but, in the world of the Bible, suffering was not an argument against the existence of God. The Hebrews did not expect to lead a life without suffering, but, unlike many today who suffer alone, they suffered as a community and with their divine patron at their side. Laments did not create a pain-free world, but rather assembled the clan and Yahweh to support the clan whose land and children were at risk. Like the mourners themselves, Yahweh and the clan did not take away the pain of the clan, they simply stood with it, in its pain, and that made it so much easier for the clan to survive.

WORSHIP AND ETHICS: A RE-EXAMINATION OF PSALM 15

R.E. Clements

In an essay published in 1974 John Willis examined the general subject
of 'ethics in a cultic setting' with particular regard to Psalms 15 and
24.[1] In this he raised a number of pertinent questions respecting these
psalms that have a bearing on wider issues of methodology in Psalm
studies. Moreover, once serious question marks are raised regarding the
widely accepted view that these psalms provide evidence that there
once existed 'entrance liturgies' for worshippers and pilgrims entering
the Jerusalem temple, a number of further issues are raised regarding
the manner in which psalmody was related to the cultus as well as to
social ethics. With many of the observations and questions raised by
John Willis, I am in agreement, especially regarding the necessity for a
re-examination of the form and purpose of these two psalms. In the
present essay, in addition to reconsidering these questions, I should like
to propose some further suggestions concerning the relationship
between psalmody, the cult and the moral structuring of society.

Although there is a close relationship between the two psalms
referred to, several further issues are raised by Psalm 24 that fall
outside the scope of this essay. These particularly concern the question
whether the psalm is a unity or has been constructed from more than
one element.[2] We can therefore concentrate on Psalm 15 alone and
begin by considering what the psalm actually says.

---

1.   J.T. Willis, 'Ethics in a Cultic Setting', in J.L. Crenshaw and J.T. Willis
(eds.), *Essays in Old Testament Ethics* (New York: Ktav, 1974), pp. 145-70.
2.   H. Gunkel, *Die Psalmen* (HKAT, 14; Göttingen: Vandenhoeck & Ruprecht,
5th edn, 1968), pp. 101-105, distinguished no less than three psalm elements (vv. 1-
2, 3-6, 7-10).

Psalm 15

1. O LORD, who may reside in your tent?
   Who may dwell on your holy mountain?
2. The one who walks in integrity and does what is right
   and wholeheartedly means what he says.
3. The one who does not spread slander with his tongue;
   Who does no harm to a fellow human being
   and speaks no lies against his neighbor.
4. Who holds those whom God rejects in contempt,
   but those who fear the LORD he respects.
   Who stands by his oath even to his own disadvantage;
5. Who does not lend money at exorbitant interest,
   and does not take a bribe against the innocent.
   Those who act like this will always be secure.

A number of minor problems are raised by the translation, but they do not seriously impair an understanding of the text. Only in v. 4 does the textual transmission appear sufficiently disturbed to leave the meaning in doubt. Comparable admonitions in the legal and wisdom traditions might lead us to expect that the misconduct referred to would be that of committing perjury under oath in a lawsuit. However, the translation given has reasonable support and is that followed in the major modern English versions. The conduct approved is that of speaking the truth under oath even when to do so would have been to the disadvantage of the person taking the oath.

The situation envisaged in the law of Exod. 22.10-13 provides a useful illustration concerning such action. In this ruling contained in the Book of the Covenant (Exod. 20.22–23.19), when property or livestock placed under another's custody went missing, the negligent custodian was held responsible, unless he could claim, under oath, that he had not laid hands on the animal. If it had been stolen, he was required to make appropriate restitution. In such a situation telling the truth under oath could be to the custodian's disadvantage, since it could render him liable to pay compensation.

The Subject Matter of the Psalm

If we leave aside for the moment the issue of the interrogation formula in v. 1, with which the psalm begins, the subject matter is clear. It concerns compassionate, responsible and truthful conduct in regard to a number of social issues. These are set out in the form of firmly implied demands for the avoidance of bad and devious conduct. All told, 10 areas of attitude and conduct are listed, which set out in a short summary form what may be expected of the person who worships in the LORD's sanctuary.

The individual descriptions indicate dishonorable and disruptive behavior, the avoidance of which is more usually made the subject for moral education, particularly in the wisdom tradition. They do, however, include actions that could subvert the processes of justice in lawsuits. More broadly they look beyond the range of operation of the law to questions of attitude and personal integrity. That of acting as talebearer and slanderer (v. 3) is widely condemned in comparable wisdom admonitions.[3] Such behavior could prove extremely disruptive of social order but was obviously outside the competence of the available legal processes to punish. Similarly the practice of usury (v. 5) could prove ruinous to what were in any case likely to be economically vulnerable communities. It was evidently not easily prevented and is prohibited in Exod. 22.25 and Deut. 23.19-20. In spite of such prohibitions, the presence of such a warning as that of Prov. 28.8 suggests that the practice was rife. It was undoubtedly a factor leading to the evils of debt-slavery and would have had an influence on fundamental aspects of economy and social order.

The broad admonition set out in v. 4 to conform to the accepted standards of religious and social behavior establishes a fundamental summons to form judgments in accordance with religious commitment and scruple. It calls for adherence to the emotional and psychological patterns of thinking that the community as a whole had embraced in accepting its religious foundation. The overlap with admonitions contained in the book of Proverbs is noteworthy.[4] However, this overlap need not be regarded as indicating an influence from wisdom circles upon the Psalter,[5] nor an influence from the strictures of the prophets,

---

3.   Cf. Prov. 18.8; 20.19; 24.28; 26.22, 23, 24, 25.

4.   Bribery is condemned in Prov. 17.23; 21.14 and 28.21, and the general call to respect the administration of justice is called for in Prov. 17.26; 19.28; 21.15; 24.23; 25.7-8. The evil of giving false evidence is condemned in Prov. 14.5.

5.   Cf. W. Beyerlin, *Weisheitlich-kultische Heilsordnung: Studien zum 15. Psalm* (BThSt, 9; Neukirchen–Vluyn: Neukirchener Verlag, 1985).

as H. Gunkel thought.[6] Rather it simply reflects the fact that certain kinds of problems were endemic to most ancient societies, once the limitations of legal procedures and a weakening of the moral authority of the extended family became evident. Worship provided a medium of instruction and moral sanction, as did education within the family circle and the threat of legal punishment and redress. It is not surprising therefore that the priesthood and the commonplace patterns of worship were called upon to help discourage and prevent abuses of behavior that would have undermined the quality of life experienced within a community.[7]

The descriptions of particular offenses given in the psalm declare categorically that belonging to the worshipping congregation of the LORD God of Israel imposes ethical restraints that must be observed. Overall the point that is significant is that, once the issue of the interrogation formula for entry into the sanctuary of God (v. 1) is left aside, the contents of the psalm very satisfactorily disclose its purpose. It is an admonition, closely comparable to many similar wisdom admonitions, concerned with advocating conduct that reinforced respect for the law, while at the same time recognizing its inevitable limitations. It deals with issues affecting the conduct of lawsuits (perjury, malicious accusations and bribery) and with general regard for the well being of the community as a whole. It is the kind of admonition that could quite properly be impressed on every adult citizen and inculcates a general attitude of honesty, integrity and social responsibility. In the standard of conduct it demands, it stands close to a wide range of declaratory statements regarding what constitutes good and bad behavior, which are to be found in the sentence instruction of Proverbs.[8]

The question of the mismatch between the apparent form of the psalm as a liturgy for entrance to a sanctuary and the evident purpose of its content to serve as a didactic admonition concerning 'the good life'

---

6. Gunkel, *Die Psalmen,* pp. 47-50.

7. Cf. my essay 'Wisdom, Virtue and the Human Condition', in M.D. Carroll R., D.J.A. Clines and P.R. Davies (eds.), *The Bible in Human Society: Essays in Honour of John Rogerson* (JSOTSup, 200; Sheffield: Sheffield Academic Press, 1995), pp. 139-57.

8. Cf. my book *Wisdom in Theology* (Carlisle: Paternoster Press, 1992), pp. 123-50; and J.L. Crenshaw, *Old Testament Wisdom: An Introduction* (London: SCM Press, 1982), pp. 82-91.

is noted by John Willis[9] and was earlier discussed at some length in a note by S. Mowinckel.[10] The question arises therefore whether we should give as much weight to the apparent form of the psalm as an antiphonal liturgy, as many scholars have been inclined to do.[11] As a didactic admonition its purpose is clear, and it is the question and answer formula that calls for more explanation.

In assessing the psalm's significance and the conclusions that may be deduced about its original setting from its content, we may rule out the suggestion that it could have been composed as a liturgy for a piece of royal public ceremonial, as proposed by J.L. Koole.[12] Not only are there no indications that the office of the king is involved in any of the activities that are condemned, but the problems covered are of a widely experienced social nature, virtually endemic to communities with relatively limited systems of legal administration and practice. They reflect 'small town' wrongdoing and anti-social behavior, rather than the abuse of high office. Though it was the responsibility of the king to uphold the law, it is highly improbable that he could have been singled out (in such fashion as this psalm describes) as a person likely to flout it!

When we form a broad assessment of the psalm, its content leaves us in no doubt that it was essentially admonitory in its purpose and designed to reinforce socially and legally acceptable conduct. It fastens on issues where the intervention of the law was vulnerable or ineffective.

The Formal Structure of the Psalm

However, in spite of the evident didactic function of its ethical descriptions, Psalm 15 has attracted attention as an example of the form of a cult liturgy. Its unexpected distinguishing feature is found in the fact that a fixed question and response formula concerning the conditions of entry into a sanctuary has been adapted to provide a medium of ethical

9. Willis, 'Ethics in a Cultic Setting', p. 156.

10. S. Mowinckel, *Psalmenstudien V* (Oslo: Kristiania, 1923; Amsterdam: P. Schippers, repr., 1961), pp. 123-25.

11. K. Koch, 'Tempeleinlassliturgien und Dekaloge', in R. Rendtorff and K. Koch (eds.), *Studien zur Theologie der alttestamentliche Überlieferungen* (Neukirchen–Vluyn: Neukirchener Verlag, 1961), pp. 45-60. Koch describes the psalm as 'the clearest example of a temple entrance liturgy', p. 46.

12. J.L. Koole, 'Psalm XV—eine königliche Einzugsliturgie', in *Studies on Psalms* (OTS, 13; Leiden: E.J. Brill, 1963), pp. 98-111.

instruction. The presumed original setting of the form is generally regarded as still applicable to the psalm as we now have it. The surprising feature is then to be found in the major shift that is assumed to have occurred in the nature of the 'conditions of entry' that are listed. Whereas we should have expected from comparative evidence that such conditions would be of a formal and predominantly physical nature, here they are personal, highly ethical and of such a kind that only the worshipper would actually know whether they had been met!

It is certainly not to be doubted that conditions of entry into a sanctuary were an important feature of cultic life in the ancient Near East, and it is noteworthy that the legislative rules of Deut. 23.1-9 are expressed in terms of admission to the 'assembly [Heb. קהל] of the LORD'. K. Koch,[13] like S. Mowinckel,[14] draws attention to the ruling cited in 2 Sam. 5.8b, and the existence of comparable conditions for entering the 'holy space' of a sanctuary in ancient Egypt are noted by E. Otto.[15] Yet the existence of conditions of this kind, which at a later period could be given visible expression by a written notice at the sanctuary entrance, falls far short of demonstrating that an established liturgical form existed involving an antiphonal chant between the worshippers and a priestly gatekeeper. John Willis points out that

> there is no way that the priests could know whether pilgrims or worshippers kept some of the conditions specified in Pss. 15.2-5 and 24.4-5, and thus there was no legitimate reason for them to keep them from entering the temple grounds for worship.[16]

At the very least a substantial transformation is evident in Psalm 15 between a list of entry conditions regarding sanctuary admission and an ethical list of instructions concerning the type of conduct that the LORD God of Israel expects from worshippers.

---

13. 'Tempeleinlassliturgien', p. 48.

14. *Psalmenstudien II* (Oslo: Kristiania, 1921; Amsterdam: P. Schippers, repr., 1961), p. 119.

15. E. Otto, *Theologische Ethik des Alten Testaments* (ThW, 3.2; Stuttgart: W. Kohlhammer, 1994), pp. 94-99, 101, 105-106; *idem*, 'Die Geburt des moralischen Bewusstseins: Die Ethik der Hebräischen Bibel. Bibel und Christentum im Orient', in E. Otto and S. Uhlig (eds.), *Bibel und Christentum im Orient: Studien zur Einführung der Reihe 'Orientalia biblica et Christiana'* (Orientalia Biblica et Christiana, 1; Glückstadt: J.J. Augustin, 1991), pp. 63-87; cf. also the same author's 'Kultus und Ethos in Jerusalemer Theologie: Ein Beitrag zur theologischen Begründung der Ethik im Alten Testament', *ZAW* 98 (1986), pp. 161-79.

16. Willis, 'Ethics in a Cultic Setting', p. 157.

Ethics and Cultus

A further point of significance has a bearing on this so-called entrance liturgy form. It concerns the fact that, as a point of critical study of the relationship between the psalms and the cult and the rise of a distinctive tradition of law in ancient Israel, S. Mowinckel regarded such entrance liturgies as having played a significant role in the developments that led to the Decalogue of Deut. 5.6-21 (= Exod. 20.2-17).[17] This is followed closely by K. Koch.[18] However, the major factor in questioning the widely adopted cultic understanding of Psalm 15 is that it presupposes that a radical shift had occurred in early Israel respecting the concept of cultic holiness: away from ritual and quasi-physical factors towards broader ethical and non-cultic activities.

So far as the larger development of written *torah* is concerned, there is no doubt that eventually such a shift occurred. Yet it appears as the consequence of a long and only imperfectly completed process, even by the time the Hebrew canon was finished. Even as late as the time of the origin of Deuteronomy in its final form, it is evident that a rather uneasy balance had been achieved between the formal requirements of the cultus and the social needs of a system of public law, which was predominantly secular in its assumptions and application. Much of the unique interest of the Decalogue of Exod. 20.2-17 lies in its marriage between cultic duty and moral demand. The entire development of *torah* in the postexilic period maintained this uneasy balance between ethic and cultus. The law could never be wholly secular as a purely civil concern in a society in which its structural foundations were deeply religious. At the same time the enforcement of purely cultic and ritual obligations by the sanctions of the law could become cruel, and even barbaric, as a number of rulings illustrate. Prominent among these are the capital punishments laid down for the offering of sacrifice to a deity other than the LORD (cf. Exod. 22.20), breach of sabbath observance (cf. Num. 15.32-36) and the practice of non-Yahwistic worship (cf. Deut. 13.1-18). If law and cultus stood in an uneasy relationship to each other, then the question of the moralizing of entrance requirements to a sanctuary belonged within this uneasy relationship.

17. Cf. n. 13 above.

18. Koch, 'Tempeleinlassliturgien', pp. 45-60; cf. also H.-J. Kraus, *The Psalms 1–59: A Commentary* (Minneapolis: Augsburg Fortress, 1988), pp. 225-32.

Even in respect to its form it must be seriously questioned whether Psalm 15 displays so transparently a liturgical response formula as has often been claimed. The two questions of v. 1 are addressed directly to God, and the response in vv. 2-5 cannot have provided a genuine and effective means for excluding any would-be worshipper from entering the sanctuary. The interrogation formula appears as little more than a rhetorical device, so that in fact all of the psalm was probably intended to be voiced by a congregation, rather than being divided for antiphonal use. In it the people identify themselves as a group of loyal worshippers of the LORD God and declare their solidarity in embracing a conscientious and socially responsible standard of conduct. The form is rhetorically shaped and may be regarded as akin to the Amen-formula used in the dodecalogue of curses of Deut. 27.15-26. Just as this formalized list of curses outlaws behavior with which the law found it difficult to deal effectively, so the same can be seen to be true of Psalm 15. It serves as an endorsement of the standards of the law, but seeks to bolster these standards where their implementation was either weak or nonexistent.

Moreover, if Mowinckel's assumption is correct that the liturgical form progressed from covering purely formal and physical restrictions to those concerning ethical behavior, then it is this progression that is the morally and spiritually significant shift. The point has been noted by E. Otto.[19] Yet such a shift lies wholly submerged in the psalm's presumed prehistory. Even more significantly, we have emphasized already that what is especially noteworthy in the psalm is its focusing on areas concerning personal attitude and a willingness to act responsibly so as to enable the processes of law to function effectively. Its very appeal rests on its moral inwardness and power to require an individual to engage in an exercise of heart-searching. It calls for integrity and probity in social behavior and asks the question, 'Is my life pleasing to God?'

So far as the claim that the reconstruction of the form of such entrance liturgies provides us with a guide towards understanding the distinctive nature and form of the Decalogue, it cannot be said to offer much. The primary overlap between the two lies in the conjunction between moral and ethical duties and the fact that the Decalogue, like the psalm, pays close attention to issues where the effectiveness of the law had shown itself to be vulnerable. There also appears to be a

19. Cf. n. 14 above.

connection between the two in the use of the number 10 as a teaching aid. Both Psalm 15 and the Decalogue show an awareness that if the law was to work as an effective instrument of social order and justice, it required a right attitude and personal commitment on the part of every member of the community. Similarly, the admonition of Lev. 19.18 urged every member of the community to follow the rule: 'You shall love your neighbor as yourself.' This was a way of generating a proper respect for the law so that it would be an effective instrument of social justice and moral order. In those areas of social activity and legal administration where the processes of judicial administration could not be trusted to work effectively, it was necessary that goodwill, lack of malice and truthfulness should prevail. If they did not, the law itself quickly forfeited the confidence of those people it was intended to protect.

Morality, Cultus and the Law

Questions of the moralizing of the cult, of the infusing of ideas of holiness with ethical content and of imbuing all religious activity with a high level of ethical commitment are widely evident in psalmody, prophecy and the wisdom tradition.[20] Taken as a whole they require to be understood in their social context, as varied expressions of the need for a community to employ all its resources of education, religious commitment and traditional authority in order to promote good social order and justice. They must be studied in relation to the many and varied forces that operated to shape the concept of *torah* in early Judaism and in the formation of a written canon of scripture with *torah* at its center. In many ways it was the incompleteness and untidiness of the various attempts to integrate purely cultic with ethical concerns that provided a continuing problem for the Judaism of late antiquity and a major point of departure for the Christian break with it. To arrive at the conclusion that Psalm 15 can be regarded as a straightforward instance of the moralizing of cultus by adapting sanctuary entrance liturgies to serve as an example of ethical admonition appears too simple a conclusion to draw from the evidence. As it is now preserved, the simple list of religious standards and duties as set out in vv. 2-5 makes excellent sense. They focus attention, as do other admonitory parts of the

---

20. Cf. especially, J.G. Gammie, *Holiness in Israel* (OBT; Minneapolis: Fortress Press, 1989), pp. 125-49.

Hebrew Bible, upon those areas of life that were of great importance for social harmony and wellbeing but where the processes of law were of limited effectiveness.

We have already noted that the two questions of v. 1, which are addressed directly to God, do not fit as easily as has been supposed into a reconstructed liturgy in which pilgrims seek to enter the sanctuary of the LORD. They are set as the psalm's opening in order to provide opportunity, with appropriate rhetorical coloring, for the admonition that follows. Although they come first, they are from a structural perspective the secondary and dependent literary feature of the psalm. We must question, therefore, whether they contain some larger meaning than simply asking for permission to enter the sanctuary of God.

Admittedly this does not altogether preclude that the form of seeking and receiving permission to enter the LORD's sanctuary through a responsive dialogue may at one time have been a well-established one. Yet this conclusion appears unlikely, and it is certain that such liturgical responses restricting admission to a place of worship cannot readily have been expressed in the terms now preserved in Psalm 15. The most that we can reasonably deduce is that we find here a relic of a liturgical form that, by the time Psalm 15 was composed, had been completely transformed into a convenient didactic device. It draws attention to the high ethical demands of God in much the same manner as various prophetic strictures declare.[21] The hypothetical 'entrance liturgy' form has become simply an ornament to other more pressing concerns.

Once these considerations are born in mind, it would certainly appear that the question and answer formula used in this psalm is likely to be little more than a rhetorical device aimed at lending color and fresh vigor to social issues that were the subject of deep moral concern.

Worship and the Forms of Legal Administration

When we inquire into the early history of the relationship between Israelite cultus and the administration of law, we discover that a number of significant practices shed informative light upon the psalm. Most to the fore here is the importance of oaths to support claims to

---

21. The dependence of Isa. 33.14-16 and Mic. 6.6-8 upon the supposed 'entrance liturgy' form has been widely argued. Cf. H. Gunkel, 'Js. 33, eine prophetische Liturgie', *ZAW* 42 (1924), pp. 177-208.

truthfulness in the giving of evidence (cf. Exod. 22.8, 9, 11). The potential threat of incurring divine anger and punishment by deceiving the deity is reckoned to provide a serious deterrent against lying and prevarication. This was undoubtedly a major aspect of the prohibition against invoking the divine name 'to what is false' (Heb. לשוא, Deut. 5.11 = Exod. 20.7) in the Decalogue.

Consistently the sophisticated and well-documented prescriptions of the ancient Israelite legal system made use of the authority of the cult to strengthen its procedures and to supplement them when lack of sufficient proof meant that the situation could not be dealt with by a simple decision based on precedent (cf. esp. Deut. 17.8-13).[22] It is evident from the emphasis upon truthfulness and integrity as characteristics of the good citizen in wisdom instruction, and from the many warnings against abuse of the legal system,[23] that recognition of the potential for mishandling legal procedures was widespread and persistent.[24] The law could be flouted if respect for the divine foundations of its authority was not maintained. This weakness in judicial procedures was prevalent for a variety of reasons and seldom because the wrongfulness of certain types of conduct was not recognized. Problems arose because the system could be cheated, the laws of evidence were in a relatively rudimentary state, officials who administered the law could be bribed, and in many instances it appears that substantial sections of the population were without adequate representation in the legal processes that were available.

Consequently the law had its limitations and could even be used by unscrupulous citizens to achieve evil ends by obtaining wrongful punishments through the framing of knowingly false accusations. Where such behavior prevailed, the entire system of law was undermined. Ancient Judaism found it necessary to build a protective fence around the law, not in the sense of multiplying its demands, but by doing whatever was possible to safeguard its administration.

If the taking of oaths was one prominent way in which the resources of the cult were employed to reinforce and supplement the limitations

22. Cf. J.C. Gertz, *Die Gerichtsorganisation Israels im deuteronomischen Gesetz* (FRLANT, 165; Göttingen: Vandenhoeck & Ruprecht, 1994), pp. 72-81.

23. Cf. Prov. 17.26; 19.28; 21.15; 24.23; 25.7-8

24. Cf. my essay 'The Concept of Abomination in the Book of Proverbs', in M.V. Fox *et al.* (eds.), *Texts, Temples, and Traditions: A Tribute to Menahem Haran* (Winona Lake, IN: Eisenbrauns, 1996), pp. 211-26.

of the law, then other means also were available. Most familiar in this regard is the granting of a right of asylum at a sanctuary in order to provide protection against premature vengeance upon a suspected killer.[25] The claim that many psalms were originally composed as pleas for asylum at a sanctuary has been strongly and extensively argued by L. Delekat,[26] and this represents a development of the earlier recognition of a close link between certain psalms and accusations of criminal conduct.[27]

If it is the case that psalmody itself, in the language of several extant compositions, directly reflects cases where individual citizens found themselves falsely accused and anxious to vindicate themselves, then Psalm 15 may be seen to represent a recognizable development of such a tradition. It calls for conduct in which respect for the law, respect for the rights and privacy of a neighbor, and a wholehearted desire to share the community's concern for a compassionate social solidarity were upheld. At the same time the opening questions convey strong echoes of the privilege of asylum provided by a sanctuary in which the innocent could be protected, but from which the guilty would be removed and punished (Exod. 21.14). It supplements the resources of whatever legal administration was in operation by calling for integrity, honesty and a right attitude towards a neighbor.

From a formal perspective the admonitory listing of good behavior in the psalm serves to fill the gap between the rigorous taking of oaths at a sanctuary to establish lack of malice and truthfulness in giving evidence and education to good citizenship, which occurred in the home. The link between ethics and the cult was a logical extension of the use of the sanctuary to provide a powerful sanction where the law was vulnerable. Moreover, if the earlier systems of legal administration left many citizens feeling that they had no access to justice except to plead directly to God, as the study of many psalms has advocated, then Psalm 15 endeavors to demonstrate what the demands of divine justice truly require.

Once the link between the origins of psalmody in the ancient Near

25. Cf. esp. Exod. 21.12-14 and J.C. Gertz, *Gerichtsorganisation*, pp. 117-27.

26. L. Delekat, *Asylie und Schutzorakel am Zionheiligtum: Eine Untersuchung zu den privaten Feindpsalmen* (Leiden: E.J. Brill, 1967).

27. For the whole subject cf. especially, W. Beyerlin, *Die Rettung der Bedrängten, in den Feindpsalmen der Einzelnen auf institutionelle Zusammenhänge untersucht* (FRLANT, 99; Göttingen: Vandenhoeck & Ruprecht, 1970).

East and the development of a system of law in which the cultus played a significant role is recognized, then this fact has a bearing on the origins and background of the psalm. In form it is a piece of ethical admonition aimed at reinforcing and supplementing legal practice, as its contents amply confirm. The echo of a form of interrogation for entry into a sanctuary uses it as a rhetorical device to establish a basis of community identity and soldarity. It does so in part by recalling earlier situations in which the seeking of asylum at a sanctuary was a step towards establishing one's innocence if falsely accused. The questions are there to provide a peg on which the response can be hung. In this responsive affirmation the community of loyal Jews declare their own individual commitment to the way of life that shows a whole-hearted respect for the *torah* of the LORD God. It is a catechism that makes explicit reference to entry into a sanctuary because it is worship of the LORD in the temple, or in the prayerful assembly that served as an extension of the temple, that defines the most effective and workable category by which the community of loyal Jews could be identified.

The Holy Mountain and the Holy Community

We have already urged that the beginning of the psalm with the posing of two parallel questions is not a simulated 'entrance liturgy', but rather a rhetorical device that provides a context for the religious and ethical admonition that follows. It is nevertheless striking that those who are encouraged to question God concerning the nature and privilege of worship are encouraged to do so in terms of asking, 'Who may reside in your tent?' It could be supposed that the use of the term 'tent' to describe the sanctuary is a conscious archaism for the temple. It has either been retained because a tent was a widely used form of sanctuary in the traditions of worship of the ancient Near East from which psalmody sprang, or because the precursor of the Jerusalem temple was itself quite specifically envisaged as a 'Tent of Meeting' (Exod. 33.7-11). At the same time the notion of God's 'tent' could be employed as a metaphor indicating hospitality and protection, as Ps. 27.5 shows. The use of the term in Ps. 15.1 may therefore occasion less surprise than at first appears to be the case. Nor can we rule out of consideration the observation that the openness of such a term may have helped to retain its meaningfulness.

The use of psalms among Jews of the dispersion served as an

important extension of the Jerusalem temple, and this was a factor in the development of forms of non-ritual worship. The Psalter itself became a primary medium of extension and eventual displacement of the earlier ritual practices that they had at one time accompanied. In this process the necessity for retaining a close sense of identity with the Jerusalem temple, while recognizing its inaccessibility for an increasing number of loyal Jews, became an important aspect of post-587 BCE Jewish life. When this occurred, then the definition of the scattered communities of faithful Jews became a far from obvious one. The abstraction of a 'covenant community' and the concreteness of 'those who dwelt, or worshipped, in the LORD's house' became ways of indicating categories of loyalty and commitment that could not otherwise be easily defined.

Certainly there can be no question but that the temple cultus was the formative base from which Israelite psalmody grew and that it possessed much older roots in a poetic tradition reaching far back in the ancient Near East. So it is not surprising, for instance, that the conventional expression of 'seeing the face of God' has been retained in biblical psalmody, and elsewhere in the Hebrew Bible, without any continuing sense of its incompatibility with the prohibition of an image of God set up in a sanctuary.[28] It is a poetic archaism, which was widely understood, and which ceased to conjure up thoughts of divine images in a tradition of worship where no such images were present. It eventually took on an eschatological dimension.

Much the same literary phenomenon can be observed in modern hymnody, which uses many biblical images of sacrifice and the divine presence that are no longer strictly compatible with an inquiring theological and ethical sensitivity. In ancient Judaism the language of the 'face' (= image) of God could readily be understood in a manner that rendered it acceptable and helped to retain a strong sense of the directness and intimacy with which worship made the presence of God real.

Certainly, of the many possible areas of visual and poetic imagery used in psalmody, those pertaining to ideas of the presence of God have needed to be most flexible and open. They have been required to retain their significance when transplanted into a wide variety of intellectual traditions. Ultimately they have been employed in promoting forms of mysticism, and, more popularly, in strengthening an eschatological

---

28. Cf. now especially J. Reindl, *Das Angesicht Gottes im Sprachgebrauch des Alten Testaments* (ETS, 25; Leipzig: St. Benno, 1970), esp. pp. 227-38.

hope. Even Psalm 15 can be read in an eschatological sense.[29] One of the most significant theological developments of early Judaism in retaining and reinterpreting the psalmody of the old Israelite cult lay precisely in this direction. Rhetorical devices, such as the addressing of God directly, the preservation of the prophetic convention in which God speaks directly to the worshipper, and the many metaphors, associations and ideas of divine presence and heavenly actuality, have all been preserved in the Psalter. Verbal imagery related to the temple cultus has proved to be adaptable to a large number of worship situations far outside those that belonged to the Jerusalem temple in which they originated. Only when its originating contexts and the literal understanding of much of its phraseology were more closely explored could the cultic roots of psalmody be fully and frankly recognized.

However, the process of adapting and reinterpreting the language of temple and cultus begins within the Psalter itself. We have already noted that psalmody was undoubtedly a primary medium of continuity and adaptation that enabled the post-587 Judaism of the dispersion to hold fast to a claim of authority and reality in its worship.[30] In the process old images and concepts were subjected to a strangely dual pattern of requirements. First of all they had to retain their authenticity by preserving as much as possible of the language and traditions of the temple rituals from which they had sprung. Yet, rather conflictingly, they needed to be adapted and reinterpreted to fit them for the needs and circumstances of a number of very diverse worshipping communities.We may claim that the shaping and growth of the worship of the synagogue was directly based on the versatility and adaptability of the Psalter as a primary adjunct to structuring life around the precepts of a written *torah*.

When seen against this larger background of use and adaptation, we can see that the two questions with which Psalm 15 commences were conscious archaisms designed to express membership and strong emotional identity with the loyal communities of Judaism. The extent to which actual entry into a sanctuary was consciously carried in the mind of a worshipper must have varied greatly with individual circumstances. It seems unlikely that a psalm such as this could properly have been intended exclusively for the moment of entering the House of the

29. Cf. Willis, 'Ethics in a Cultic Setting', p. 158.

30. Cf. W.L. Holladay, *The Psalms through Three Thousand Years: Prayerbook of a Cloud of Witnesses* (Minneapolis: Fortress Press, 1993), pp. 63-65.

LORD, whether that was the Jerusalem temple or a much simpler assembly of Jewish worshippers. First and foremost, the questions posed to the LORD God were rhetorical questions aimed at expressing identity with Judaism and all its traditions.

We may note that many of the same issues concerning the flexibility and extended use of concepts and imagery of the presence of God appear in other psalms. My own very first published academic paper was on the interpretation of the idea of 'dwelling' in the house of the LORD as expressed in Pss. 23.6 and 27.4.[31] A.R. Johnson subsequently suggested in an essay that the concept of the 'house of the LORD' may have received an extended interpretation as indicative of 'the household of faith', that is, the company of all loyal worshippers of the LORD as God.[32] All such claims have a relative usefulness in showing how cultic language, which can be traced back to specific and quite limited situations, may afterwards be given a much wider range of meaning. Language is flexible, and most especially the poetry of the biblical psalms has shown itself to be susceptible of wide adaptation and reinterpretation. The Christian use of the Psalter through two thousand years is a rich illustration of this.

At what historical point in the processes of psalm composition and revision the imagery of dwelling in the 'tent of the LORD' and on God's 'holy hill' reached beyond a literal understanding of entering the Jerusalem temple on Mount Zion cannot now be recovered. Yet it was the wider understanding of such terminology that made it lastingly meaningful and that brought to mind a variety of mental images of a spiritual, and sometimes mystical, nature. The importance of the archaic phraseology is evident. It reflects awareness that entering a sanctuary was a privileged and solemn entry into a 'different' world of wholeness and holiness that required the worshipper to look deep into his or her own heart to see if what lay there was compatible with so great a passage into the realm of God. The questions given to the worshipper to speak are themselves both a cry of identity and a confession of unworthiness.

We may therefore venture to summarize our conclusions regarding

31. R.E. Clements 'Temple and Land: A Significant Aspect of Israel's Worship', *TGUOS* 19 (1963), pp. 16-28.

32. Cf. A.R. Johnson, 'Psalm 23 and the Household of Faith', in J.I. Durham and J.R. Porter (eds.), *Proclamation and Presence: Old Testament Essays in Honour of Gwynne Henton Davies* (London: SCM Press, 1970), pp. 255-71.

this memorable psalm. Foremost is the primary point that, when we look aside from its question and answer form, it is evident that its content shows it to be a piece of ethical admonition. Even the form, when it is re-examined, reveals that the frequently assumed claim that it originated as an antiphonal liturgical structure based on a concern with admission to a sanctuary can only have been a very stylized and marginal aspect of it. Moreover, the degree of divergence from the known conditions that could enforce a person's exclusion from a sanctuary are so marked that the extent to which these conditions are recalled at all becomes questionable.

When, however, we re-examine the areas of social behavior dealt with in the psalm, we find that they are very closely linked to demands for truthfulness and integrity in legal procedures, and with a responsible social attitude. The concern to uphold such integrity was related to early Israelite cultus through the employment of solemn oaths and careful priestly examination 'before God'. So the cult was used to provide a means of testing the truthfulness, or otherwise, of a person's claim to innocence when accused of wrongdoing. It therefore became a natural extension of this that psalmody should promote more generally a lifestyle of integrity and moral decency.

Seen in this light the content of Psalm 15 is wholly in line with a long-standing tradition of psalmody in which the justice of the law and the righteousness of the cult were linked. If anything, it is the introduction of a token interest in the conditions for entering a sanctuary that represents the more novel feature. Finally, we have noted that the questions posed in the opening verse are themselves indicative of a complex understanding of the presence of God. The way in which this presence was understood and was thought to be related to a visible sanctuary changed considerably as the circumstances in which the psalm was used altered.

It is a privilege to offer these reflections on a memorable psalm to a scholar whose own spiritual warmth and published contributions have been greatly admired and valued.

'FROM WHERE WILL MY HELP COME?':
WOMEN AND PRAYER IN THE APOCRYPHAL/
DEUTEROCANONICAL BOOKS

Toni Craven

Introduction

John T. Willis's contributions to our understanding of the psalmist's query and response, 'From where will my help come? My help comes from the LORD, who made heaven and earth' (Ps. 121.1b-2) has served as a springboard for this present study.[1] While Willis has persuasively argued that 'Psalm 121 was originally composed by a wisdom teacher for the purpose of instructing and exhorting his pupils',[2] I have questioned what kind of access there is for women in the Psalms and the Scriptures. How does a woman—a wise woman—answer the question, 'From where will my help come?' In the spirit of John Willis's dedicated pursuit of questions related to the academy and church, I offer the following reflection on biblical testimony to God's help for women.

Hebrew Bible

My concern—to rephrase Miriam's question, 'Has the LORD spoken only through Moses?' (Num. 12.2)—is, 'Has the LORD spoken only to the likes of Moses?' Evidence in Psalms in general, and Psalm 121 in particular, offers little explicit indication of God's listening to women's voices, which, given the androcentric content and context of the Bible, is not particularly surprising. Even in a psalm like 131, in which the mother's role in taking her child in her arms serves as the point of connection for the metaphor (vv. 1-2), it is not certain that the psalm is

1. See J.T. Willis, 'An Attempt to Decipher Psalm 121.1B', *CBQ* 52 (1990), pp. 241-51; and 'Psalm 121 as a Wisdom Poem', *HAR* 11 (1987), pp. 435-51.
2. Willis, 'An Attempt to Decipher Psalm 121.1B', p. 251.

a woman's prayer. With J.C. McCann Jr, I would hold that 'it is diffi-cult to be too confident' that Psalm 131 was uttered originally by a woman.[3]

Such reservation, however, is not reflected in the NRSV translation of Psalm 131, particularly of the last phrase of v. 2c, which makes it sound as if a mother holding her weaned child prays:

> O LORD, my heart is not lifted up,
>   my eyes are not raised too high;
> I do not occupy myself with things
>   too great and too marvelous for me.
> But I have calmed and quieted my soul,
>   like a weaned child with its mother;
>   my soul is like the weaned child that is with me (Ps. 131.1-2).

In a note, the NRSV offers an alternate translation, 'my soul within me is like a weaned child', and in such case the voice that speaks is the weaned child—which, of course, could be female or male. Female imagery is not necessarily evidence of female authorship or voice.

Who can forget Moses' exchange with God in Numbers with its striking female imagery: 'Did I conceive all this people? Did I give birth to them, that you should say to me, "Carry them in your bosom, as a nurse carries a suckling child"' (Num. 11.12). If Moses' name were not attached to this passage, would we argue these are a woman's words? Context, of course, attributes these words to a male and 70 male elders are appointed on account of this complaint to assist Moses. In this instance female metaphors and female voice are clearly differ-entiated (Num. 11.16-25).

Indeed it is 'difficult to be confident', to borrow McCann's phrase, about concrete evidence for real women's voices in biblical texts, most particularly where metaphorical language is employed. What evidence is there, then, for God hearing women's prayers? At best, the words attributed to women are fragments in a Bible that is thoroughly andro-centric in its perspective, authorship and cultural background. With Carol Meyers and Ross Kraemer, I am gathering these fragments and compiling a comprehensive listing of all the named and unnamed

---

3.   J.C. McCann, Jr, 'The Book of Psalms', in *NIB* 4 (1996), p. 1208. For defense of the poem as written by a woman, see G. Quell, 'Strucktur und Sinn des Psalms 131', in F. Maas (ed.), *Das Ferne und nahe Wort: Festschrift Leonard Rost* (BZAW, 105; Berlin: Alfred Töpelmann, 1967), pp. 173-85.

women and female representations in the Bible.[4] In what follows, I offer some of the highlights of this research in the area for which I have had editorial responsibility, the Apocrypha/Deuterocanonical Books.

Apocryphal/Deuterocanonical Books

The Apocryphal/Deuterocanonical Books are Jewish religious books or parts of books not found in the Hebrew Bible.[5] The NRSV includes 18 such books, which various Christian expressions regard as part of the Bible. All of the works, with the exception of 2 Esdras (which is found in Old Latin translations), are included in the Greek version of the Old Testament (Septuagint or LXX).

> The evaluation of the deuterocanonical Old Testament writings in the Orthodox Church is based on a complicated series of official statements and resolutions, agreed, partly explicitly and partly implicitly, by local synods and leading Church Fathers, and confirmed, even before the schism between the eastern and western churches, by resolutions of general councils: the Trullan Synod of 692 and the 7th Ecumenical Council of 787.[6]

In the sixteenth century they were excluded from the canon by the Protestant reformers[7] but formally accepted by the Roman church (Council of Trent, 1546). Though the Protestant Old Testament does not include these books, all Orthodox and Catholic Old Testaments include Tobit, Judith, Additions to Esther, Wisdom of Solomon, Ecclesiasticus or the Wisdom of Jesus Son of Sirach, Baruch, Letter of Jeremiah, three Additions to Daniel (Prayer of Azariah and the Song of

4. *Women in Scripture: Hebrew Bible, Apocryphal/Deuterocanonical Books, and New Testament* (Boston: Houghton Mifflin, forthcoming).

5. For consideration of the significance of the Apocryphal/Deuterocanonical Books in eastern and western church traditions and for the 1987 revision of the agreement between the Bible societies and the Catholic Church's Secretariat for Christian Unity, 'Guidelines for Interconfessional Cooperation in Translating the Bible', which provided the necessary presuppositions for publication of common editions of the Bible, see S. Meurer (ed.), *The Apocrypha in Ecumenical Perspective* (UBSMS, 6; New York: United Bible Societies, n.d.).

6. E. Oikonomos, 'The Significance of the Deuterocanonical Writings in the Orthodox Church', in Meurer (ed.), *The Apocrypha in Ecumenical Perspective*, p. 16.

7. A.R. Bodenstein von Karlstadt, *De canonicis scripturis libellus* (Wittenberg: Ioannem Viridi Montanum, 1520).

the Three Jews, Susanna, Bel and the Dragon) and 1–2 Maccabees. The Greek Orthodox Bible also includes Prayer of Manasseh, Psalm 151, 1 Esdras, *3 Maccabees*, with *4 Maccabees* in an appendix. The Slavonic Orthodox Bible includes 3 Esdras (= 2 Esdras in NRSV).

In all, 16 women are mentioned by name in the Apocryphal/Deutero-canonical Books: Agia, 1 Esd. 5.38; Anna, Tob. 1.20–2.14; Antiochis, 2 Macc. 4.30; Apame, 1 Esd. 4.29-31; Arsinoë, *3 Macc.* 1.1, 4; Cleopatra, Add. Est. 11.1, 1 Macc. 10.54-58, 11.9-12; Deborah, Tob. 1.8; Edna, Tob. 7.2–8.21; Esther, esp. Add C, 14.1-19; Eve in Tob. 8.6; Hagar in Bar. 3.23; Judith, Jdt. 8–16; Sarah, Tob. 3.7-17; Susanna, Sus vv. 2-63; Vashti, Add. Est. 1.9-22; and Zosara, Add. Est. 5.10-14. Women figure as unnamed characters (variously as servants, community members, brides, widows, wives, mothers, daughters, nurses, prostitutes, worshippers) in all but the three books that are men's prayers— Prayer of Azariah and the Song of the Three Jews, Prayer of Manasseh and Psalm 151. Female representations appear in five of the books. Wisdom is personified as a woman (Wis. 6.12–11.4; Sir. 4.11; 6.18; 14.20-21; 15.2-4; 51.13-22; Bar. 3.9–4.4). God is personified as a mother (2 Esd. 1.28; 2.2), nurse (2 Esd. 1.28) and hen (2 Esd. 1.30). Earth (2 Esd. 7.54, 62), Zion (2 Esd. 9.38-10.54), Babylon and Asia (2 Esd. 15.46-63), righteousness and iniquity (2 Esd. 16.49-52) are personified as females. One goddess, Nanea, is cited, and it is in her Persian temple that Antiochus IV (Epiphanes) is stoned and decapitated (2 Macc. 1.13-16).

Important for our consideration is the fact that women's prayers and women's relationships with God are significant narrative components in Tobit, 2 and *4 Maccabees*, as well as in Esther, Susanna and Judith—the three Apocryphal/Deuterocanonical Books titled by the names of women.[8] When troubles threaten from without or within the covenant community, women in these narratives turn to relationship with God for survival. Each actively participates in the resolution of the difficulty she or her community faces in ways that suggest freedom to

8. In the Hebrew Bible two books, Ruth and Esther, are titled by women's names, but women's prayers are not conspicuous in either. In fact, God's name is not mentioned in the Hebrew Esther. In the New Testament, no book is titled by the name of a woman. Women's prayers are, of course, significant in both the MT and New Testament. In the Apocryphal/Deuterocanonical Books, special prominence is given to women's prayers, perhaps on account of the critical nature of the times (roughly 200 BCE–100 CE).

lament, praise, or instruct equal to that of men as reflected in most of the Psalms. Prayer often undergirds female actions that are courageous, unconventional and subversive. All the narratives evince experiential disruptions for Jewish daughters, mothers, wives or widows that were rectified through right covenant relationship. These narratives demonstrate how covenant faithfulness entitled women to voice their concerns to God and others.

Tobit

Five women are named in the book of Tobit: Deborah, mother of Tobiel (Hananiel), the grandmother who raised the orphaned Tobit and instructed him concerning the law of Moses (Tob. 1.8); Anna, the outspoken wife of Tobit and devoted mother of Tobias, who earned money at women's work after her husband was blinded by bird droppings (Tob. 1.9–2.14); Sarah, daughter of Edna and Raguel, wife of seven husbands who have died on their wedding night and eventual wife of Tobias (Tob. 3.7-17); Eve, of Genesis, mentioned in Tobias's prayer with Sarah on their wedding night as created by God to help and support Adam (Tob. 8.6); Edna, the wife of Raguel and the encouraging mother of Sarah (Tob. 7.2–8.21), who blesses Tobias and entrusts her daughter to him (Tob. 10.12). Three of these five named women are associated with prayer: Eve, by way of reference in a prayer; Edna, for blessing Tobias and Sarah; and, most significantly, Sarah, whose prayer illustrates God's disregard of gender differences in answering prayers.

Sarah speaks in the first person only twice in the book, in her own prayer (Tob. 3.10-15) and her 'Amen' to her husband's prayer (Tob. 8.8). Sarah speaks only to God to whom she expresses her grief over her maid's accusation that she has killed her seven husbands. Alone in an upper room where she intended to hang herself (Tob. 3.10), she— her father's only child—prays for death 'with hands outstretched toward the window' (Tob. 3.11), protesting her innocence and disgrace. In this same chapter, immediately before Sarah's exchange with her maids, Tobit—blinded by bird droppings—had also prayed for death on account of his argument with his wife Anna about her extra wages (Tob. 3.1-6). The prayers of both Tobit, the elder male, and Sarah, the young female, are heard in heaven simultaneously (Tob. 3.16-17).

> Raphael was sent to heal both of them: Tobit, by removing the white
> films from his eyes, so that he might see God's light with his eyes; and

> Sarah, daughter of Raguel, by giving her in marriage to Tobias son of
> Tobit, and by setting her free from the wicked demon Asmodeus (Tob.
> 3.17a).

Sarah is not active in the story after her scene with her maid, but her
prayer and plight are important to the plot of the tale. In the end she
does not die but prospers as a faithful—albeit silent—daughter, wife
and mother of seven sons (see Tob. 14.3, 12).

Only in prayer is Sarah allowed a fully articulated voice. In the end
when Tobias's father and mother are buried, Sarah and her husband and
their children return to her homeland, where 'he treated his parents-in-
law with great respect in their old age and buried them in Ecbatana'
(Tob. 14.13). Tobias inherits the property of Raguel, maintaining patri-
linear, patrilocal customs without challenge. Nevertheless, no reproach
accrues to Raguel on account of his 'beloved daughter' (3.10), whose
lament was 'heard in the glorious presence of God' (Tob. 3.16). In the
book of Tobit, help comes from God, who hears and answers a young
woman's prayer.

2 and 4 Maccabees
In 2 and *4 Maccabees*, an unnamed mother of seven sons lifts life itself
to God through her words to her sons. She offers to each son in turn
pious instruction not unlike that found in wisdom psalms, as they are
sentenced and subjected to hideous mutilation by Antiochus Epiphanes
on account of their refusal to eat swine flesh. She encourages each to
die nobly, saying,

> The Lord God is watching over us and in truth has compassion on us, as
> Moses declared in his song that bore witness against the people to their
> faces, when he said, 'And he will have compassion on his servants'
> (2 Macc. 7.6).

When six of her sons had been scalped, dismembered and burned, the
text says of this brave woman:

> The mother was especially admirable and worthy of honorable memory.
> Although she saw seven sons perish within a single day, she bore it with
> good courage because of her hope in the Lord. She encouraged each of
> them in the language of their ancestors. Filled with a noble spirit, she
> reinforced her woman's reasoning with a man's courage and said to
> them, 'I do not know how you came into being in my womb. It was not I
> who gave you life and breath, nor I who set in order the elements within
> each of you. Therefore the Creator of the world, who shaped the

beginning of humankind and devised the origin of all things, will in his mercy give life and breath back to you again, since you now forget yourselves for the sake of his laws' (2 Macc. 7.20-23).

Her privately spoken encouragement in her own language (2 Macc. 7.21)—likely Aramaic or Hebrew—to her sons is taken as a reproach by Antiochus, who appeals to her youngest son with promises of riches. The young man does not listen to the king but rather heeds his mother's counsel:

> My son, have pity on me. I carried you nine months in my womb, and nursed you for three years, and have reared you and brought you up to this point in your life, and have taken care of you. I beg you, my child, to look at the heaven and the earth and see everything that is in them, and recognize that God did not make them out of things that existed. And in the same way the human race came into being. Do not fear this butcher, but prove worthy of your brothers. Accept death, so that in God's mercy I may get you back again along with your brothers (2 Macc. 7.27-29).

Details of this courageous mother's death are not recorded, only the fact that she dies after her sons (2 Macc. 7.41). She dies without a word. In fact, as Young notes, she never once speaks publicly in 2 Maccabees 7, offering instead private encouragement to her sons (2 Macc. 7.21, 27).[9] For this martyr-mother, the natural world as well as personal and interpersonal experience mediated the presence of God. Notable in this passage is belief in bodily resurrection (2 Macc. 7.9, 11, 22-23, 29) for the righteous (2 Macc. 7.14) and hope in compassion that defies even death (2 Macc. 7.6, 11, 14, 20, 37). Faithfulness to God's laws and the ways of the ancestors (2 Macc. 7.2, 23, 24, 30, 37) result in death that is itself life. In 2 Maccabees, the mother is praised for her manly courage (7.21), which, according to Moore and Capel Anderson, is a widespread literary and philosophical *topos* in which female anatomy, negatively valued in itself, is subsumed in superior masculine morality.[10]

The story of this martyr-mother and her seven sons is elaborated in *4 Maccabees* 8-18, written perhaps a century later, with expansive

---

9. R.D. Young, 'The "Woman with the Soul of Abraham": Traditions about the Mother of the Maccabean Martyrs', in A.-J. Levine (ed.), *'Women Like This': New Perspectives on Jewish Women in the Greco-Roman World* (EJL, 1; Atlanta: Scholars Press, 1991), p. 70.

10. S.D. Moore and J. Capel Anderson, 'Taking It Like a Man: Masculinity in 4 Maccabees', *JBL* 117 (1998), pp. 266-69.

details of how the seven sons and their mother 'take it like a man', demonstrating great self-mastery and courage—essential Stoic masculine virtues. In *4 Maccabees*, the mother does not affront the king by speaking in her own language to her sons. She is hailed for following the course of religion (*4 Macc.* 15.1-3). 'Devout reason, giving her heart a man's courage in the very midst of her emotions, strengthened her to disregard, for the time, her parental love' (*4 Macc.* 15.23). Lauded as 'mother of the nation, vindicator of the law and champion of religion' (*4 Macc.* 15.29), 'guardian of the law' (*4 Macc.* 15.32), 'soldier of God in the cause of religion' (*4 Macc.* 16.14), this mother is 'the prime exemplar of masculinity in *4 Maccabees*'.[11] She, 'the weaker sex' (*4 Macc.* 15.5), heroically displays devout reason, endurance and self-control. In the end the mother upholds the four cardinal virtues of the Greco-Roman world: prudence, temperance, justice and courage on account of her 'devout reason' and service of the religious laws of her ancestors.[12] Unnamed in *2* and *4 Maccabees*, the martyr-mother became known as Hannah or Miriam bat Tanhum in Jewish tradition, Solomone in the Greek Christian tradition and Mart Simouni in the Syriac.[13]

Additions to Esther

Four women are named in Greek Esther: Vashti, the Persian queen who refused her husband's summons to be crowned queen and display her beauty (Add. Est. 1.9-22); Zosara (= Zeresh in the Hebrew Esther), Haman's wife who recommends that Mordecai be hanged (Add. Est. 5.10-14); Cleopatra, mentioned in a postscript date reference to 'the fourth year of the reign of Ptolemy and Cleopatra', likely a reference to c. 114 BCE (Add. Est. 11.1); and Esther, who, in the Greek version of the story, is portrayed as not only replacing Vashti as queen but as praying for eloquence and deliverance for her people and herself before

11. Moore and Capel Anderson, 'Taking It Like a Man', p. 252.

12. For additional information on gender roles in *4 Maccabees* and the story's support of masculine superiority, see Moore and Capel Anderson ('Taking It Like a Man', p. 273), who point out that the mother's closing speech in 18.6-19 'returns the woman to her proper place on the continuum in relation to her husband. She may be more masculine than a Gentile tyrant, but not unfeminine in relation to her Jewish husband. She may have mastered the tyrant, but her own master is her husband.'

13. See Young, 'Woman with the Soul of Abraham', p. 67; and Moore and Capel Anderson, 'Taking It Like a Man', pp. 270-71.

her audience with Artaxerxes (= Ahasuerus in MT; Add. Est. 14.1-19), invoking God's aid, fainting and falling before the king (Add. Est. 15.1-16).

Greek Esther expands upon the canonical tale of a beautiful young Jewish exile in Persia chosen queen to Ahasuerus (Artaxerxes in Greek) with six additions that smooth out some of the disturbing features of the Hebrew story: God is named from start to finish, with Mordecai's dream of what God determined to do (Addition A) and remembrance of the dream at the story's conclusion (Addition F); decrees written in the king's name (Additions B and E) vilify Haman, legitimate the Jews defending themselves and attribute salvation to 'the living God' (Add. Est. 16.16); prayers offered by Mordecai and Esther (Addition C) assert God's power to deliver; and additions to the scene of Esther's unbidden audience with the king (Addition D) include her prayer and personal preparation for the audience with the king, as well as specific mention that 'God changed the spirit of the king' (Add. Est. 15.8) and that Esther 'fainted and fell' as she approached the king (Add. Est. 15.15). Help in Greek Esther comes through praise, petition and demise of the enemy. Esther has 'no helper' but God (14.3), and it is to God that she turns, 'save us by your hand, and help me, who am alone and have no helper but you, O Lord' (Add. Est. 14.14). She prays, 'O God, whose might is over all, hear the voice of the despairing, and save us from the hands of evildoers. And save me from my fear!' (Add. Est. 14.19). Victory for the Jews comes with the destruction of Haman and his ten sons, which is memorialized in annual celebration of the festival of Purim.[14]

Susanna, Bel and the Dragon

In Susanna (a Greek addition to Daniel), a God-fearing beautiful wife and exile in Babylon stands against the corruption of two Jewish judges who try to force sexual intimacy with her, choosing death over submission to their lust, and is saved by the boy Daniel's interrogation and condemnation of the judges. Denied a voice in the narrative except in her refusal of the judges' advances and prayers to God, this woman finds help not from her righteous parents who 'had trained their daughter according to the law of Moses' (Sus. v. 3) nor from any

---

14. For a review of literature on the Book of Esther, see L.R. Klein, 'Esther's Lot', *CRBS* 5 (1997), pp. 111-45.

character in the story, save the little boy Daniel. 'A subversive piece of literature, Susanna satirizes the Jewish "establishment". It contrasts the virtuous Jewess Susanna with lecherous elders, and wise children with aged scoundrels.'[15]

Susanna is a narrative about God raising up a champion of faith who triumphs over adversity. The story celebrates the courage and loyalty of a woman who protests her innocence (vv. 42-43) so that 'the Lord heard her cry' (v. 44) and 'stirred up the holy spirit of a young lad named Daniel' (v. 45). The champions in the story are both the woman who says, 'I will fall into your hands, rather than sin in the sight of the Lord' (v. 23) and the young boy named Daniel who speaks out in her defense (vv. 45-46).

Before the judges, 'Susanna groaned and said, "I am completely trapped. For if I do this, it will mean death for me; if I do not, I cannot escape your hands. I choose not to do it; I will fall into your hands, rather than sin in the sight of the Lord." Then Susanna cried out with a loud voice' (vv. 22-24a). Condemned to death, 'Susanna cried out with a loud voice, and said, "O eternal God, you know what is secret and are aware of all things before they come to be; you know that these men have given false evidence against me. And now I am to die, though I have done none of the wicked things that they have charged against me!" (vv. 42-43). So it happened that, 'The Lord heard her cry. Just as she was being led off to execution, God stirred up the holy spirit of a young lad named Daniel' (vv. 44-45).

Prayer is Susanna's only recourse in the story. 'Through her tears she looked up toward Heaven, for her heart trusted in the Lord' (v. 35). Help came for this woman when God heard and delivered. Susanna is the only named woman in the story that bears her name and in the entire book of Daniel to which her story is attached, sometimes appearing before ch. 1, since Daniel is a young boy, and sometimes appearing as Daniel 13. In an otherwise male-dominated world, 'she champions prayer and the finding of one's own voice in refusing evil and choosing good. Good triumphs because of God's attention to her cry.'[16]

---

15. A. LaCocque, *The Feminine Unconventional: Four Subversive Figures in Israel's Tradition* (OBT; Minneapolis: Fortress Press, 1990), p. 28.

16. T. Craven, 'Daniel and its Additions', in C.A. Newsom and S.H. Ringe (eds.), *The Women's Bible Commentary* (Louisville, KY: Westminster/John Knox Press, 1992), p. 194.

Judith

Judith, the last of the women whose prayers we will consider, is a God-fearing, beautiful widow, who delivers Israel from Assyrian aggression that threatens both the religious and political well-being of her community. She first urges the town leaders of Bethulia to join her in calling to God for help while waiting for God's deliverance (Jdt. 8.17) and in setting an example for the townspeople (Jdt. 8.24) who are waiting five days before surrendering to the Assyrian enemy. Judith then goes into the enemy camp with only her maid to deliver Israel by her own hand (Jdt. 8.33).

Prayer is important throughout the 16 chapters of the book of Judith. Part I (Jdt. 1.1-7.32) is like a communal lament gone awry. Faced with the political and religious threat of Assyrian aggression under the leadership of Nebuchadnezzar and his general Holofernes, the fearful Israelites nearly surrender. At the instruction of their high priest Joakim, the Israelites fortified the passes that led to the hilltop towns blocking Holofernes' advance to Jerusalem (Jdt. 4.7-8), and then they cried out to God with fasting, sprinkling ashes on their heads and putting sackcloth everywhere (Jdt. 4.10-11). They petitioned God to 'look with favor on the whole house of Israel' (Jdt. 4.15).

The narrative records that God 'heard their prayers and had regard for their distress' (Jdt. 4.13), but the Israelites, not knowing this, lost heart. Concluding that God had abandoned them (Jdt. 7.28) and wishing to surrender to the Assyrian army after 34 days without water, the people in Bethulia cried, 'We have no one to help us; God has sold us into their hands' (Jdt. 7.25). The town leader Uzziah urged courage but vowed to surrender to the Assyrians if God did not rescue them within five days (Jdt. 7.30-31).

Part II (Jdt. 8.1-16.25) details how a childless, wealthy widow (Jdt. 8.2; 16.22), Judith, a woman of habitual and daily prayer (see Jdt. 8.5-6), delivered the Israelites from their own fears and the Assyrian enemy. 'No one spoke ill of her, for she feared God with great devotion' (Jdt. 8.8). As Judith told Holofernes, the enemy general, she 'serves the God of heaven night and day' (Jdt. 11.17). Indeed, it is her nightly practice of going outside the enemy camp to bathe and pray that provides the ruse for her escape after she beheads the enemy general (see Jdt. 11.17-19; 12.6-9; 13.10).

Judith's personal lament in Judith 9 is embedded in a narrative unit detailing Judith's plan to save Israel (Jdt. 8.9–10.8). Concatenated uses of the verb 'hear' underscore the importance of hearing and being heard. Judith, who has 'heard' of the five-day compromise (Jdt. 8.9), insisted that the leaders of Bethulia, Uzziah, Chabris and Charmis 'hear' her judgment (Jdt. 8.11, 32) that they had put themselves in the place of God, who is not like a 'human being, to be threatened, or like a mere mortal to be won over by pleading' (Jdt. 8.18). Declaring that God is free to deliver or destroy (Jdt. 8.17) and that God will 'hear', if God so pleases (Jdt. 8.15), Judith challenged the leaders, 'let us set an example' (Jdt. 8.24), 'let us give thanks to the Lord our God, who is putting us to the test' (Jdt. 8.25). She argued that God's chastisement is pedagogical, not punitive.

When the leaders leave her house, Judith prays her longest prayer in the book (Jdt. 9.1-14). She asks that God's fury crush the foreigners who have threatened the safety of the Jerusalem temple (Jdt. 9.1, 8). Judith invokes God, the one who empowered Simeon to annihilate those who defiled Dinah by means of a sword given into his hand by God (Jdt. 9.2-4a), to 'hear' (Jdt. 9.4, 12) her. Like Simeon, Judith prays to carry out heaven-sent vengeance against Israel's enemies. Crediting God with control of past, present and future events (Jdt. 9.5-6) and quoting Exod 15.3, Judith implores 'the Lord who crushes wars; the Lord is your name' to destroy the Assyrians (Jdt. 9.7-8) by giving her—a widow and a female[17]—a 'strong hand' and 'deceitful words'[18] (Jdt. 9.9-10). She declares that God's 'strength does not depend on numbers', nor God's 'might on the powerful' (Jdt. 9.11).

A litany of 10 titles for God summarizes her personal theology: 'God of the lowly, helper of the oppressed, upholder of the weak, protector of the forsaken, savior of those without hope, God of my father [unclear whether Judith's own father or her ancestor Simeon], God of the heritage of Israel, Lord of heaven and earth, Creator of the waters, King of all your creation' (Jdt. 9.11b-12). Reiteration of her petition that God hear her prayer and grant her success in deceiving the enemy closes her prayer (Jdt. 9.13-14).

---

17. In patriarchal societies, there was no greater dishonor than that a man be brought down by a female's hand (see Judg. 9.53-54). The Greek word θήλεια (female) is used rather than the more common γυνή (woman).

18. On lying, see O. Horn Prouser, 'The Truth about Women and Lying', *JSOT* 61 (1944), pp. 5-28, and Toni Craven, 'Women Who Lied for the Faith', in P. Paris and D.A. Knight (eds.), *Justice and the Holy: Essays in Honor of Walter Harrelson* (Atlanta: Scholars Press, 1989), pp. 49-60.

Judith's prayer and her understanding of God stand in sharp contrast to the community's near-despair (see Jdt. 7.32). Having defended the radical freedom and foreknowledge of God to the town leaders, she asks three things of God: that God hear her prayer (Jdt. 9.4, 12), that God destroy the Assyrians (Jdt. 9.8) and that God use the deceit of her lips and the hand of a female (θήλεια) to crush the enemy (Jdt. 9.10, 13). Her petition that God arm her with the unusual weapon of deceit is fitting given the circumstances (cf. Ps. 149.7-8). The story is not critical of her deception, as are some readers who are offended that Judith intentionally lies and murders.

As it turns out, the petitions of ch. 9 are fundamental to the plot and success of the entire narrative. Judith trusts God, prays to deceive and successfully deceives and destroys her enemy. By her hand, the enemy general is beheaded because God grants her prayer. It is not for herself that Judith prays, as the final words of her prayer in ch. 9 make clear: 'Let your whole nation and every tribe know and understand that you are God, the God of all power and might, and that there is no other who protects the people of Israel but you alone!' (Jdt. 9.14). In her prayers and in the book as a whole, Judith serves an example that faithfulness to the covenant with God, not deliverance, counts most.[19]

Judith's prayers in the remainder of the book play out the fulfillment of the petitions of ch. 9. As she stands at the bed of Holofernes, she prays, 'O Lord God of all might, look in this hour on the work of my hands for the exaltation of Jerusalem. Now indeed is the time to help your heritage and to carry out my design to destroy the enemies who have risen up against us' (Jdt. 13.4b-5). Taking hold of the hair of Holofernes' head, she prays again, 'Give me strength today, O Lord God of Israel!' (Jdt. 13.7) before striking his neck twice with all her might and cutting off his head (Jdt. 13.8).

As she returns to Bethulia, she calls out to the sentries, 'Open, open the gate! God, our God, is with us, still showing his power in Israel and his strength against our enemies, as he has done today!' (Jdt. 13.11). As the townspeople gather unbelieving, she says with a loud voice, "Praise God, O praise him! Praise God, who has not withdrawn his mercy from the house of Israel, but has destroyed our enemies by my hand this very night!"' (Jdt. 13.14).

---

19. See T. Craven, 'Judith 9: Strength and Deceit', in M.C. Kiley (ed.), *Prayer from Alexander to Constantine: A Critical Anthology* (London: Routledge, 1997), pp. 59-64.

Judith inspires her community, which worships God itself, saying, 'Blessed are you our God, who have this day humiliated the enemies of your people' (Jdt. 13.17). Uzziah says to her,

> O daughter, you are blessed by the Most High God above all other women on earth; and blessed be the Lord God, who created the heavens and the earth, who has guided you to cut off the head of the leader of our enemies. Your praise will never depart from the hearts of those who remember the power of God. May God grant this to be a perpetual honor to you, and may he reward you with blessings, because you risked your own life when our nation was brought low, and you averted our ruin, walking in the straight path before our God.'

And all the people said, 'Amen. Amen' (Jdt. 13.18-19).

After the enemy has been destroyed, Joakim, the high priest of Jerusalem, and the elders of Israel add words of blessing, saying to Judith,

> 'You are the glory of Jerusalem, you are the great boast of Israel, you are the great pride of our nation! You have done all this with your own hand; you have done great good to Israel, and God is well pleased with it. May the Almighty Lord bless you forever!' And all the people said, 'Amen!' (Jdt. 15.9-10)

Judith, like Miriam and Moses in Exodus 15, sings a song of praise as she leads a triumphant procession to Jerusalem, in which she calls the people to worship and proclaims God victor and deliverer (Jdt. 15.14-16.17). After three months of feasting in Jerusalem, all return to their homes. 'Many desired to marry her, but she gave herself to no man all the days of her life after her husband Manasseh died and was gathered to his people' (Jdt. 16.22). On her account, 'no one ever again spread terror among the Israelites during the lifetime of Judith, or for a long time after her death' (Jdt. 16.25).

Conclusion

The Apocryphal/Deuterocanonical Books contain memorable narratives about God's hearing and answering the prayers of women. Relationship with God is of greater value than death or life. In prayer, Sarah gives up her desire for death if it is not pleasing to God (Tob. 3.15). In 2 and *4 Maccabees*, the martyr-mother counsels seven sons to die rather than break God's law. After sending the message to Mordecai that she would go to the king, contrary to the law, even should she die (Add. Est. 4.16), Esther prays acknowledging 'no helper' but God (Add. Est.

14.3, 14). Susanna chooses death over falling into the wicked judges' hands (Sus. vv. 22-24a). Judith declares that faithfulness matters more than deliverance or destruction (Jdt. 8.15). All together, these women's prayers in the Apocryphal/Deutero-Canonical Books proclaim the help that 'comes from the LORD, who made heaven and earth' (Ps. 121.2).

FLIRTING WITH THE LANGUAGE OF PRAYER (JOB 14.13-17)

James L. Crenshaw

In her stimulating commentary on Job 14.13-17, Carol Newsom writes that 'Job starts to be drawn into the language of prayer', only to turn away in 14.18-22 because this mode of discourse 'is still too powerful and too seductive for Job to trust himself to speak in its accents'.[1] Job's momentary shift from attack to imagined refuge, from angry talking about the deity to plaintive addressing of that sovereign one,[2] reveals the lingering power of an intimate relationship with the divine, despite the total collapse of Job's belief system. His hasty abandonment of a renewed effort to sustain direct discourse with God indicates the extraordinary force at work aimed at driving a permanent wedge between him and the deity. The next few centuries witnessed several such stabs in the dark brought on by horrific personal circumstances and energized

1. 'The Book of Job', *The New Interpreter's Bible* (Nashville: Abingdon Press, 1996), IV, p. 439. On the language of prayer in wisdom literature, see J.L. Crenshaw, 'The Restraint of Reason, the Humility of Prayer', in *idem, Urgent Advice and Probing Questions: Collected Writings on Old Testament Wisdom* (Macon: Mercer University Press, 1995), pp. 206-21. Job's reluctance to adopt the stance of prayer occasions little surprise in the light of the sages' virtual silence in this regard. Only three prayers appear in canonical wisdom: Prov. 30.7-9; Sir. 22.27-23.6; and 36.1-22. The subject of prayer in ancient Israel has been examined in some detail by S.E. Balentine, *Prayer in the Hebrew Bible: The Drama of Divine–Human Dialogue* (OBT; Minneapolis: Fortress Press, 1993). See also M. Greenberg, *Biblical Prose Prayer as a Window to the Popular Religion of Ancient Israel* (Taubman Lectures in Jewish Studies, 6; Berkeley: University of California Press, 1983). Identifying texts that can legitimately be classified as prayers is difficult (cf. Job 13.20-22; Prov. 30.7).

2. Each of Job's speeches in the first cycle ends with an address to the deity (7.7-21; 10.2-22; 13.20–14.22). After that, only 17.3-4 (and possibly 16.7-8); 30.20-23; 40.3-5 and 42.1-6 do so. The dominant concept now appears to be forensic; Job increasingly voices a concern to face the deity in a 'courtroom'. Vindication has replaced reconciliation as Job's goal.

by an undying love for the sacred.[3] The persistence of an undying hope, now generalized to embrace everyone born of woman, invites closer scrutiny of Job's bold ruminations.

14.13   Oh that you would hide me in Sheol,
            you would conceal me until your anger abates,
            you would fix a statute of limitations, and remember me.
14.14   If mortals[4] die, will they live again?
            All the days of my service I would wait
            until my release arrived.
14.15   You would call and I would answer[5] you;
            you would long for[6] the work of your hands.
14.16   For now you number my steps,
            you do not watch over my sins.
14.17   My transgressions are sealed in a bag;
            and you cover over my iniquity.

The translation requires comment at two points: חק (statute) in 14.13 and כי־עתה (for now) in 14.16. The former may signify nothing more than temporality, hence a set date on which the deity will remember Job, hidden in the underworld, just as the avenging YHWH remembered

3.   The harsh treatment of faithful Jews by the Seleucid authorities during the Maccabean revolt gave rise to the anticipation of divine redress for some, punishment for others (Dan. 12.2). The martyrology surrounding 2 Macc. 7.9 was precipitated by the same calamity. The exact circumstances evoking a similar belief in resurrection expressed in Isa. 26.19 cannot be established, but the allusion to the power of dew to bestow life on the dead reappears in the story about Isaac's resuscitation in the garden of Eden following Abraham's actual sacrifice of his son. One can make a strong case for viewing Ps. 73.24 as an expression of the conviction that profound intimacy with God will survive death's ravages.

4.   The translation avoids gender-specific renderings when the Hebrew text implies both male and female—hence the plural 'mortals'. In other instances, it omits a notable feature of Hebrew style, the frequent use of 'and' to connect lines in parallelism.

5.   In 13.20-22 Job pleads for the deity to enable him to enter into litigation with his frightening opponent. Only when God removes the oppression and Job's terror can he stand a chance in a trial. Then the deity can call and Job will respond. He desperately needs an arbiter, a champion of his cause (9.32-34), but he has discarded such a possibility as unlikely. He returns to this idea in 19.25-27, but the terrible state of the text renders its meaning uncertain.

6.   Job has already accused the deity of loathing the work of divine hands (10.3); now Job imagines a different emotion, an instinctual affection for one's progeny. The verb כסף (long for) denotes powerful inner feelings of both animals and humans.

Noah and the animals shut up in the ark, according to ancient legend (Gen. 8.1). The forensic language permeating Job's complaints, however, invites another interpretation, one facilitated by the legal concept of a statute of limitations, a precise date at which criminal culpability becomes null and void.[7] This translation permits one to retain the usual sense of חק as statute.

The temporal force of כי־עתה poses difficulty. Ordinarily, it connotes the present in contrast with what has preceded. The translation adopted above implies a change in point of view; Job imagines that the deity conceals him[8] in Sheol until the divine fury passes, which brings about a decisive change toward a wronged Job. Then he places himself in that sheltered situation, at least in his imagination, and encounters a different sovereign, one who solicitously counts every step Job takes and no longer spies on him to catch every misstep. In such an altered context, Job need not worry, for the deity has sealed the evidence against him, whitewashing his offenses the way the Chronicler covered up David's villainy.

The absence of a negative particle in 14.16a may favor an alternative rendering, 'Whereas now you count my steps...' The final two verses of this imaginary meditation would then harbor an ominous thought, one that has already abandoned the optimism of the initial three verses. This interpretation accords with the usual meaning of language about the deity's numbering of an individual's steps; however, the unique concept envisioned by Job may also imply a rare understanding of divine surveillance as well.[9]

---

7. The modern idea that time's passage alters the conception of justice was not entirely unknown in ancient Israel. This willingness to pardon debtors after the lapse of a specified number of years may have more to do with compassion for the needy than with the Jubilee year, which had as its primary purpose the preservation of family land holdings.

8. Here he shifts from posing a universal question, 'If mortals die, will they live again?' to asking a purely personal one. The injustice surrounding his own case prompts this way of putting the question. Job thinks that the cruel circumstances of his own life merit exceptional treatment, if not in this life then beyond the grave. This depiction of existence in Sheol differs sharply from his earlier account (3.17-19). In N.C. Habel's view, vv. 13-17 function as a pivotal text, a radically new dream that synthesizes earlier speeches (*The Book of Job: A Commentary* [OTL; Philadelphia: Westminster Press, 1985], p. 238).

9. The expression for observing one's steps seems always to carry a hostile meaning. The author may have Job reverse this use as part of his wholesale attack

Even when the translation lacks problematics, its meaning remains obscure at some points. What imagery is conjured up by the words צבא and חליפתי in v. 14 and חתם בצרור in v. 17? Does Job refer to arduous labor as a slave and to the relief at day's end,[10] or to conscription in the military and release from service when a replacement arrives?[11] Use of גבר, which frequently has the sense of a warrior, may tilt the evidence in the direction of military language. The conscious effort to include the whole human race in the larger context, where three other words designating mortals occur (אדם in v. 1; גבר and אדם in v. 10; איש in v. 12; אנוש in v. 19; אשה in v. 1) encourages caution, as does the apparent synonymous use of גבר and אדם.

The allusion to sealing transgressions in a bundle likewise evokes two possible practices. According to an obscure reference in 1 Sam. 25.29, it was thought that YHWH kept certain favored persons secure by placing their life in a bundle of the living.[12] Scholars have explained this image as a reflection of a practice in accounting whereby shepherds entrusted with animals would keep pebbles in a bag to indicate the precise number under their care.[13] The problem with this interpretation

on traditional belief. The book teems with irony, on which see above all Y. Hoffman, *A Blemished Perfection: The Book of Job in Context* (JSOTSup, 213; Sheffield: Sheffield Academic Press, 1996).

10. The primary sense of צבא is enforced service (A.S. van der Woude, 'צבא army', *TLOT* [1997], II, p. 1041). That involuntary service may take the form of corvée labor on administrative projects or on any one of many lesser tasks. L.G. Perdue, *Wisdom in Revolt: Metaphorical Theology in the Book of Job* (JSOTSup, 112; Bible and Literature Series, 29; Sheffield: Almond Press, 1991) understands the term in 14.14 as slavery. He finds a comparable use in Isa. 40.2 with reference to the exile in Babylon.

11. Referring to 7.1, where Job compares daily existence to service in the military, Habel writes that Job now finds such service endurable under the new rules he has just outlined (*Book of Job*, p. 243). In the end such speculation proves unproductive, for Job does not believe that the deity will act in this kindly manner toward him.

12. This conviction that YHWH preserved the life of the faithful, even gathering every tear, finds expression in the concept of a heavenly scroll in which were inscribed the names of those designated for life (cf. Exod. 32.33; Ps. 139.16; Dan. 12.1). On this belief in the ancient Near East, see S.M. Paul, 'Heavenly Tablets and the Book of Life', *JANESCU* 5 (1973), pp. 345-53.

13. A.L. Oppenheim, 'On an Operational Device in Mesopotamian Bureaucracy', *JNES* 18 (1959), pp. 121-28. For an account of the earliest form of keeping records, see D. Schmandt-Besserat, 'Record Keeping Before Writing', in J.M.

of Job's imagery is the word חתם, for such bundles would have been closed by means of a drawstring. Therefore, some interpreters view the expression in terms of official written documents, papyri containing important data and sealed in a bundle by means of hot wax.[14] These documents provided decisive evidence in judicial proceedings once the seal was broken and the contents were examined. The two images convey opposite dispositions when applied to the deity. The former suggests providential care, whereas the latter points to an exact, but fair, judgment, an idea that seems at odds with what follows immediately: a divine pardon for all offenses.

The belief that a transgressor could hide from YHWH in Sheol was dealt a death blow by the prophet Amos, who denied that anyone could escape divine punishment.

> If they hide in Sheol,
>   from there my hand will take them;
> if they ascend to heaven,
>   from there I will bring them down;
> if they conceal themselves on top of Carmel,
>   from there I will search and capture them;
> if they hide from my sight in the bottom of the sea,
>   from there I will command the Serpent[15] and it will bite them;
> if they go into captivity before their enemies,
>   from there I will command the Sword[16] and it will slay them.
> I will fix my eyes on them for evil and not for good (Amos 9.2-4).

Sasson (ed.), *Civilizations of the Ancient Near East* (4 vols.; New York: Charles Scribner's Sons, 1995), IV, pp. 2097-2106. She traces a development from clay tokens to envelopes for holding them and ultimately to written tablets.

14. N.H. Tur-Sinai (Torczyner), *The Book of Job: A New Commentary* (Jerusalem: Kiryath Sepher, 1957), adopts this explanation and reproduces an illustration from E.G. Kraeling, *The Brooklyn Museum Aramaic Papyri: New Documents of the Fifth Century B.C. from the Jewish Colony at Elephantine* (New Haven: Yale University Press, 1953), pl. 21. The picture shows a bundle of written documents with the wax seal intact.

15. The Hebrew word for serpent, הנחש, is otherwise used of ordinary snakes, but in Amos's mind it functions in an extraordinary way as an agent of divine punishment. The usual designations for the chaos-monster (Leviathan, Tannin, Rahab) belong to poetic texts in Isaiah, Psalms and Job. In them, the fearful creature is either conquered and destroyed, like its prototype Tiamat, or its activity is severely restricted.

16. The personification of the sword as an agent ready to perform YHWH's command occurs also in prophetic texts (e.g. Jer. 15.3; along with dogs, birds and beasts).

Similarly, the psalmist who composed the following meditation believed that YHWH's dominion extended to Sheol.

> Where can I go from your spirit,
>> where can I flee from your presence?
> If I ascend to heaven, you are there;
>> if I make my bed in Sheol, you are there.
> If I take the wings of dawn
>> and dwell at the outermost region of the sea,
> Even there your hand guides me,
>> your right hand holds me.
> If I say, 'Surely darkness will conceal me
>> and light around me will become dark,'
> Even darkness is not dark to you
>> and night is bright as day,
>> for darkness is like light to you (Ps. 139.7-12).

Such boundless confidence about the extent of the deity's domain does not translate into a perfect society, for the psalmist complains mightily about evildoers.[17]

Job's incisive question, 'If mortals die, will they live again?' evoked different answers in the ancient world. In the absence of firsthand knowledge about what happens after death,[18] one was left to speculation. The gradual decomposition of the body could be observed, as Gilgamesh discovered following the demise of his companion Enkidu. In mythic lore, the gods possessed the capacity to rise from the dead, waxing and waning like the processes of nature itself in its seasonal

---

17. The vindictive spirit at the end of this exquisite psalm troubles those who believe one should have compassion on all, even enemies. For an effort to understand the religious dynamic of such psalms, see E. Zenger, *A God of Vengeance?: Understanding the Psalms of Divine Wrath* (Louisville, KY: Westminster/John Knox Press, 1996).

18. N. Gillman, *The Death of Death: Resurrection and Immortality in Jewish Thought* (Woodstock, VT: Jewish Lights, 1997), shows how competing views about the future life—resurrection and immortality of the soul—have fared through the centuries in Jewish circles. His discussion ranges widely, beginning with biblical and rabbinic sources and tracing the canonization of a doctrine. His insights on Maimonides' teachings and those of mystic Jews provide a useful background for his analysis of modern prayer books compiled by the four branches of Judaism in the United States. Gillman does not belong to those persons excoriated in E. Becker's *The Denial of Death* (Glencoe: Free Press, 1973), but neither does he believe that death has the final word.

unfolding. Do mortals have the same power?

According to the myth in Genesis 2–3, the tree of life became permanently inaccessible to mortals, who joined the hapless serpent in transgressing divine limits and provoked the deity to declare the tree off limits. In the Gilgamesh epic the snake snatches a branch from the tree of life, sheds its skin and rejuvenates itself, leaving the hero to face his mortality. In ancient Egypt this pessimistic view did not prevail, for these people believed that their soul (*ba*) survived death. Not surprisingly, the Hellenistic author of Wisdom of Solomon assumes that people possess souls that make them immortal.[19]

The larger context of Job's question comprises three distinct units.[20] The first, 14.1-6, reflects on life's brevity and unwelcome limitations. The finality of death is the subject of the second unit, the eternal sleep into which mortals fall (14.7-12). The third unit, 14.18-22, graphically describes the deity's destruction of human hope. All three units contrast certain aspects of nature with the experience of mortals. The motivating thought seems to rise from the kinship between humankind and the natural world, proclaimed in the YHWHistic creation story, where the אדם is fashioned from the dust of the earth, אדמה, and receives the divine animating breath. Have the mythic discussions of nature's periodic resuscitation spilled over into reflections on the destiny of humankind? The commingling of earthly body and divine breath corresponds to the two prevailing concepts regarding human destiny: the largely Mesopotamian and Canaanite notion of dying and rising gods

---

19. M. Kolarcik, *The Ambiguity of Death in the Book of Wisdom 1–6: A Study of Literary Structure and Interpretation* (AnBib, 127; Rome: Pontificio Istituto Biblico, 1991), pp. 163, 174, recognizes the complexity of death in this book. He argues that three distinct yet related perceptions of death occur here: mortality, physical death as punishment and ultimate death.

20. P. van der Lugt, *Rhetorical Criticism and the Poetry of the Book of Job* (OTS, 32; Leiden: E.J. Brill, 1995), p. 171, identifies two cantos (vv. 1-12, 13-22) and four canticles (vv. 1-6, 7-12, 13-17, 18-22). Because the first word begins with א and the last with ת, and because the canticle has 22 lines, he labels it alphabetic. According to Habel, the elegy on the human condition moves from proverbial to formulaic tradition in question form to probing question to blunt accusation (vv. 1, 10, 14, 19; *Book of Job*, p. 237). E.M. Good, *In Turns of Tempest* (Stanford: Stanford University Press, 1990) connects 14.1-6 with what immediately precedes, 13.23-28, and considers this section cross-examination. He then links 14.7-22 together and calls it Job's pondering of life and death, permanence and ephemerality, hypothetical hope and actual decay (p. 237).

representing nature's transformation and the Egyptian belief in an immortal soul (*ba*).

Job 14.1-6

The fragility of flowers in the searing heat of the Near East must have been obvious to any observer. How much truer if the author thinks of cut flowers before the days of air-conditioned houses. The poet who composed Deutero-Isaiah used a similar analogy to describe the fleeting nature of all flesh. Here grass stands alongside flower as a metaphor for the human condition; in contrast to both of these elements of nature, the divine word endures. The repetitive language gives the impression that the poet has hit upon an apt analogy and does not want to give it up before exhausting its emotive range.

> A voice says, 'Proclaim.'
> And I said, 'What shall I proclaim?'
> All flesh is grass
> and all its loyalty is like the flower of the field.
> Grass withers, flowers fade
> when YHWH's breath blows on them.
> Surely the people is grass.
> Grass withers, flowers fade;
> but the word of our God stands forever (Isa. 40.6-8).

Something more is at play here than the composition of humankind from elements of nature. Deutero-Isaiah characterizes the bonds uniting mortals with one another and with the sacred as short-lived and therefore unreliable. In his view, all that humans constitute, together with whatever they produce in the affective realm, resemble the most transitory of things, grass and flowers. Both that which exposes human fragility and whatever affirms divine permanency come from God's mouth, a scorching wind in one instance, an utterance in the other case. The specification, 'flower of the field', goes beyond Job's simple 'flower', indicating, like grass, something that grew without human cultivation. Springing up hither and yon, such grass and flowers were entirely subject to the whims of nature.

In characterizing humankind, the unknown author of Ps. 144.4 combines the notions of breath and passing shadow, an astonishing shift from what takes place in Psalm 8, which 144.3 echoes. Instead of remarking on human grandeur and expressing amazement over divine attentiveness, this text likens mortals to a breath and a fleeting shadow.

> Humanity [אדם] resembles breath [הבל];
>> its duration is like a moving shadow [כצל עובר].

The resemblances between this assessment of mortal existence and Qoheleth leap to mind, for not only does the latter frequently characterize human existence as הבל, by which he means transitory, futile and absurd,[21] but he also uses the comparison between life under the sun and a shadow, a natural accompaniment of sunshine (Qoh. 6.12). Here, too, Qoheleth associates this simile with that penetrating question attributed to Job concerning the future, now formulated in different language: 'For who can inform a mortal as to what will take place afterwards under the sun?' In this teacher's view, death brings about the original state of things: dust returns to earth and the divine breath goes back to its source. Neither departure brings a modicum of comfort to Qoheleth.

Job's assessment of the human condition in 14.1 comes close to Qoheleth's dismal picture.

> A mortal [אדם], born of woman,
>> short in duration and sated with trouble,
> emerges like a flower and withers,
>> flees like a shadow and does not tarry (14.1).

The expression ילוד אשה functions comprehensively; it includes everyone and in no way suggests a flawed nature[22] resulting from association with woman, who was thought to be impure at certain times. The description of human existence as brief and painful gathers force from its variation on a traditional formula for a good life (old and full of days; cf. Gen. 35.29; 1 Chron. 29.28; Job 42.17).

Having established the incontrovertible nature of human existence as

21. J.L. Crenshaw, *Ecclesiastes: A Commentary* (OTL; Philadelphia: Westminster Press, 1987) opts for 'ephemeral' and 'futile' as the usual meanings, whereas M.V. Fox, *Qohelet and his Contradictions* (JSOTSup, 71; Bible and Literature Series, 18; Sheffield: Almond Press, 1989) prefers 'absurdity'. C.L. Seow, *Ecclesiastes* (AB, 18c; Garden City, NY: Doubleday, 1997) retains the traditional translation, 'vanity'.

22. In the Hebrew Bible the phrase ילוד אשה occurs only in Job (15.14; 25.4 besides 14.1), but it also appears outside the canon in Sir. 10.18; 1QS 11.21; 1QH 13.17; 16.23-24; 18.12-13. 'A person born of woman' includes everybody (A. de Wilde, *Das Buch Hiob* [OTS, 22; Leiden: E.J. Brill, 1981], pp. 172-73). If v. 4 represents a cultic rather than a forensic view, it may comprise a gloss on a misunderstanding of v. 1 as a reference to the impurity of women during specific periods.

transitory and onerous, possibly by generalizing from his own case, Job proceeds to argue against anything that would increase life's burden. It seems that the deity has fixed a gaze on miserable Job, and by extension on everyone, for the purpose of catching them in a misstep. Such extraordinary surveillance strikes Job as excessive, given the severe restrictions on mortals and divine foreknowledge. Job has no quarrel with the deity's placing restrictions on the mythological chaos monster, for those limits are essential to cosmic order.[23] Neither Job nor his fellows pose a threat to society. Why, therefore, does the deity hedge them in and limit their days?

This line of thinking leads Job to utter a plea on behalf of beleaguered mortals.

> Look away and desist
> so that, like laborers, they may take pleasure in their sojourn (14.6).

In asking for some relief, Job stops short of petitioning for radical measures, for example, the immediate removal of the causes for trouble unrelated to the deity's steady gaze. He continues to assume that life will resemble hard labor, which the darkness of night alone brings to an end.

Job 14.7-12

It occurs to Job that nature also offers an analogy for permanence, a longevity occasioned by dormancy and resuscitation. In contrast with ephemeral flowers and grass, a tree has the capacity to renew itself under certain conditions. For emphasis, Job personifies a tree, ascribing to it hope when circumstances seem to imply otherwise. Not without cause does mythic lore point to a tree of life and do genealogies depict family trees.[24] In Job's imagination, the mere scent of water activates

23. J.D. Levenson, *Creation and the Persistence of Evil: The Jewish Drama of Divine Omnipotence* (San Francisco: Harper & Row, 1988) examines the motif of a chaos monster in the Hebrew Bible and the ancient Near East, tracing the development of the traditions relating to this mythical figure in ancient cosmologies. G. Fuchs, *Mythos und Hiobdichtung: Aufnahme und Umdeutung altorientalischer Vorstellungen* (Stuttgart: W. Kohlhammer, 1993), although more comprehensive, throws considerable light on the myth as employed in the book of Job.

24. The author of Ps. 1 restricts the comparison of mortals to a tree, limiting its applicability to the righteous and likening the wicked to wind-driven chaff. The sages viewed wisdom as a tree of life; in contrast to the other tree of mythic lore,

the process of rejuvenation for a felled tree. Pressing beyond the conviction expressed in Isa. 11.1 that the Davidic monarchy will rise from its stump to former glory, Job broadens the thought to universal dimensions. The idea of vibrant growth utilizes the same verb (חדל with negative particle) that conveyed the notion of ceasing when applied to the deity's close scrutiny.

In v. 8 Job concedes that trees resemble humans in the aging process; their roots grow old in the ground and their stumps decay. That process of rotting comes to an abrupt halt with the arrival of water. Perhaps in the case of מות (death) the difference indicates degree, for according to ancient mentality a person became enmeshed in death to a greater or lesser extent.[25]

Water, the rejuvenating agent in v. 9, cannot boast a similar staying power, according to v. 11. Large bodies of water disappear, either from shifts in terrain or from absorption and seepage. This vanishing agent of renewed life ironically mirrors the permanent disappearance of women and men.[26]

> Mortals die and are weakened,
>> human beings expire and where are they?...
> So people lie down and do not rise;
>> until heavens cease they will not awake
>>> or rouse from slumber (14.10, 12).[27]

The unexpected use of the verb חלש (be weak) in v. 10 may have arisen as a compelling contrast to the noun גבר (mortal). Whatever intimations of strength individuals may entertain are quickly negated. The process of death drains away every pretence of might, leaving individuals

this one had no guardian cherubim and no flaming sword to prevent access. Within Jewish apocalyptic, a mighty king can be symbolized by a majestic tree, and its stump represents the survival of the dynasty (Dan. 4).

25. Laments within the Bible frequently picture the speaker as already sinking into Sheol, its raging waters engulfing the helpless supplicant. Sickness was understood as transporting its victim into the realm of the dead. Since the rhetoric easily lends itself to misunderstanding, the modern interpreter needs to exercise caution.

26. Some critics interpret this comment about disappearing streams as an ironic statement of the impossible (e.g. E. Dhorme, *A Commentary on the Book of Job* [London: Thomas Nelson, 1967], p. 200).

27. The expansive vocabulary (awake, rise, rouse from slumber) echoes that found in Isa. 26.19 (rise) and Dan. 12.2 (awake). J.E. Hartley thinks the choice of several verbs reflects a period devoid of technical language for resurrection (*The Book of Job* [NICOT; Grand Rapids: Eerdmans, 1988], p. 235).

unable to lift themselves from earthly graves. Now Job asks a variant of the deity's first address to Adam and Eve: 'Where are you?' has become 'Where are they?' (cf. Gen. 3.9). Unlike the eternal heavens, mortals are no more.

Job 14.18-22

The images chosen to symbolize human existence have gone from a fragile flower and a fleeting shadow in the first unit to a stately tree and substantial streams and beds of water in the second one. In this final unit they become even more durable: a mountain, a rocky crag, a stone and dirt. Now, however, the same quality that has demonstrated its evanescence shows yet another face. The enormous velocity of cascading water wears away mountains, dislodges rocky crags, smoothes out small stones, erodes soil. Nature's caprice thus comes to expression in the opposing descriptions of water, first as a disappearing entity and later as a force at work, altering the most durable surface as the years go by.

The logic of the argument from first to last demands one conclusion: so mortals succumb to the erosive power of time. Just as water alters mountains, the succession of days and nights wears down the body. That anticipated conclusion does not appear; instead, Job accuses the deity of destroying human hope. Whereas a tree possessed that positive attribute, hope, mortals were denied its fruition. For them, hope constituted a delusion. No one saw this fact with more clarity than Qoheleth, who ironically identified the advantage of the living over the dead as a hope defined by certainty of death (Qoh. 9.4-5).

The depiction of the deity as an inexorable flow of energy gradually demolishing human hope demonstrates the short-lived nature of Job's fanciful thinking in vv. 13-17, for he relentlessly pursues the attack against the destroyer of hope.

> You always triumph over them and they die;
>> you change their appearance and dispatch them (14.20).

Job harbors no illusion that mortals could prevail in combat with the deity; the natural outcome of such futile endeavor is death. The verb הלך in this verse is elliptical for the traditional formula announcing one's journey to dwell in Sheol with ancestors (cf. Qoh. 3.20; Ps. 39.14 [EVV 13]). The irrepressible force distorts human visage, leaving the telltale signs of age, until at last sending mortals on their way. In this new state, they do not participate in reality as we know it, either the swelling of pride and joy over positive social feedback or the shrinking in dismay resulting from negative sentiment. A deep abyss separates residents of Sheol from family members left behind, and no one has access to knowledge about things on the other side of the divide. The bane of sickness, its utter isolation,[28] has replaced the social being; the threat to existence has focused thoughts inward. All that remains is physical pain and psychic grief.[29] Every vestige of hope has vanished forever.

Conclusion

To expose Job's personal struggle in the face of utter vulnerability, the poet grounds his fantasy on an intimacy that refuses to surrender before perceived breach of trust. For him, survival beyond death, if it happens, springs from profound love rather than from belief in either divine justice or power.[30] Ultimately, however, Job abandons this hope as unrealistic; the enemy has triumphed, as Job's name implies.[31] Nature's extraordinary capacity to renew itself may have generated myths about dying and rising deities,[32] but the flimsy analogy that Job entertains,

28. Note the structure of the verse, specifically the centering of the personal reference in each colon (עליו). He feels only *his own* flesh; he mourns *his own* self (14.22). On suffering as a theological problem, see J.L. Crenshaw, 'Suffering', in B.M. Metzger and M.D. Coogan (eds.), *The Oxford Companion to the Bible* (New York: Oxford University Press, 1993), pp. 718-19. J. Lamb, *The Rhetoric of Suffering: Reading the Book of Job in the Eighteenth Century* (Oxford: Clarendon Press, 1995), treats the manner in which the literati read the book of Job in the eighteenth century, and D. Kraemer, *Responses to Suffering in Classical Rabbinic Literature* (New York: Oxford University Press, 1995), looks at a much earlier time.

29. The location of v. 22 presents a problem. Unlike Uralu in Mesopotamian lore, Sheol was not a place of punishment, with a single canonical exception (Isa. 66.24; cf. Jdt. 16.17). Newsom solves this difficulty by projecting the time of v. 22 to the experience of death rather than viewing it as postmortem pain (*The Book of Job*, p. 443).

30. On various responses to the problem of perceived injustice by the deity, see Crenshaw, *Urgent Advice and Probing Questions*, pp. 141-221.

31. 'איוב' has definitely become 'אויב' (Good, *In Turns of Tempest*, p. 241). In this unit, the order of references to water, dust and hope is the reverse of the sequence in vv. 7-9.

32. Perdue, *Wisdom in Revolt*, pp. 157-62 examines the two trajectories represented by (1) 'The Death of Gilgamesh' and 'Gilgamesh, Enkidu and the

that of a tree's trunk sprouting at the scent of water, cannot offset the crushing weight of widespread decay. In the end, he sees his own destiny symbolized by the wilting of grass and flowers, the sinking of ponds and wadis into the voracious earth and the wearing away of mountains, crags, stones and soil.

Netherworld', and (2) 'Gilgamesh, Inanna, and the Bull of Heaven' and 'Gilgamesh, Enkidu and the Netherworld', as well as their combination in 'The Gilgamesh Epic'. The two traditions celebrate a hero who marries and appropriates the powers of fertility and a powerful king who conquers all enemies.

SETTING THE HEART TO SEEK GOD:
WORSHIP IN 2 CHRONICLES 30.1–31.1*

M. Patrick Graham

Introduction

While it is commonly recognized that worship is an important topic in
Chronicles, this is one of the last places that many Protestants would go
for instruction on the topic. Chronicles' location in the Hebrew canon—
well after the parallel material in Samuel–Kings—and the traditional
characterization of the work as a supplement[1] to Genesis—2 Kings
have led historically to its devaluation. The extraordinarily creative
work of Julius Wellhausen and other German Protestant scholars in the
latter half of the nineteenth century gave further justification for the low
regard that many had for Chronicles. Since the books derive from a
later period than Samuel–Kings and are heavily dependent on the latter,
it has often held little interest for scholars with primarily historical
concerns (it is too far from the 'font' of the historical events reported).
As for (especially Protestant) scholars interested in theological matters
or the development of ancient Israelite religion, Chronicles was similarly devalued. It was seen as representative of late Jewish legalism—
precisely the sort of religion that Jesus of Nazareth attacked so vigorously[2]—and the priestly concerns of Chronicles sounded a bit too

---

* It is indeed a pleasure to dedicate this essay to Prof. John Willis, the teacher
at Abilene Christian University who introduced me to the Old Testament and
inspired me to pursue graduate studies in this field. The title chosen for my contribution is intended not only to identify a critical element in the Chronicler's
theology of worship but also to take up a theme in Professor Willis's own teaching-
—the spirit with which worship is offered to God—a theme that can be traced to
his 1956 M.A. thesis at Abilene Christian College, 'A Study of the Usages and
Meanings of the Word "Heart" in the Old Testament'.

1. In the LXX, παραλειπομένων (omitted things).

2. This is often expressed in terms of law versus gospel, and the Chronicler is

Roman Catholic for their tastes.[3] Couched in more popular, religious terms, Chronicles promotes a religion based on outward, cultic observance and shows little concern for the orientation of the inner person to God.[4] It comes as no surprise then to find that there is little place for Chronicles in Protestant liturgy and preaching.[5] Therefore, it seems appropriate to ask, 'For Protestant reflection on worship, can anything good come out of Chronicles?'

It is the thesis of this paper that the concern for worship in Chronicles is accompanied by a sincere appreciation for the grace of God and a profoundly spiritual perspective,[6] whose balance has something to

accused of 'judaizing' the past. See the analysis of J. Wellhausen in *Prolegomena to the History of Ancient Israel* (Gloucester, MA: Peter Smith, repr., 1973), pp. 171-227, and the analysis of Wellhausen's treatment of Chronicles by L.H. Silberman, 'Wellhausen and Judaism', in D.A. Knight (ed.), *Julius Wellhausen and his Prolegomena to the History of Israel* (Semeia, 25; Chico, CA: Scholars Press, for the Society of Biblical Literature, 1983), pp. 75-82. See also the scant treatment accorded Chronicles in G. von Rad's influential *Old Testament Theology* (New York: Harper & Row, 1962), I, pp. 347-54 (esp. pp. 352-53 on the Chronicler [author of Chronicles and Ezra–Nehemiah] on the law). Ascribing the tenor of the religion of the Pharisees to the Chronicler is evident in the statement by W. Rudolph (*Chronikbücher* [HAT, 21; Tübingen: J.C.B. Mohr (Paul Siebeck), 1955], p. 300) that Hezekiah's letter (2 Chron. 30.6-9) does not have the 'pharisaic tone' that one finds in Abijah's address to Israel (2 Chron. 13.4b-12); both compositions derive from the Chronicler.

3.   On some of the anti-Catholic and anti-Jewish aspects of nineteenth-century New Testament scholarship, see J.C. O'Neill, 'The Study of the New Testament', in N. Smart, *Religious Thought in the West* (3 vols.; Cambridge: Cambridge University Press, 1985), III, pp. 143-78.

4.   Nevertheless, some maintained that the value of such a religious faith is that it served to distinguish the Jews from their Gentile neighbors and so to preserve the Jewish Scriptures and religion, and it prepared for the appearance of Christ and the Christian church. See E.L. Curtis and A.A. Madsen, *A Critical and Exegetical Commentary on the Books of Chronicles* (ICC; Edinburgh: T. & T. Clark, 1910), pp. 16-17.

5.   The New Common Lectionary, for example, offers only a single text from the 52 chapters of Chronicles (2 Chron. 36.14-23 in Year B, Lent, Holy Week, Easter section) in its three-year cycle of readings from Scripture. While this text may help fill a historical narrative—evidently the purpose of the selection—it assists little in exposing audiences to the rich theology of Chronicles.

6.   In the preface to his commentary on Chronicles, S.J. De Vries writes, 'Having now devoted a number of years to the research and writing for this volume, I regard Chronicles as one of the richest mines of spirituality in all of

offer the Christian church. An attempt will be made to illustrate this by an examination of 2 Chron. 30.1–31.1, an important text in Chronicles that deals with worship. The investigation will begin with comments on the structure and function of the text chosen, proceed to an elaboration of the chapter's role within the Chronicler's[7] historiography and then offer some observations about what this text has to reveal about its author's theology of worship. A summary of findings and some reflections on the implications of this study for Christian worship will conclude the article.[8]

Scripture' (*1 and 2 Chronicles* [FOTL, 11; Grand Rapids: Eerdmans, 1989], p. xiv).

7. 'Chronicler' will be used in this paper to designate the anonymous author of the books of Chronicles. The work was composed in Jerusalem in the last half of the fourth century. Ezra–Nehemiah was produced at an earlier time and does not derive from the Chronicler's hand. For a concise treatment on these matters, see R.W. Klein, 'Chronicles, Book of 1–2', *ABD* 1 (1992), pp. 992-1002.

8. Since the purpose of this paper is to elaborate the theological message of Chronicles as it relates to the topic of worship, there will be no attempt to examine the historicity of the events described in 2 Chron. 30.1–31.1 or to relate this text to the historical development of the festivals of Passover and Mazzoth. The sources of information for the Chronicler's description of the events in this text remain unknown, with some arguing that the author invented the account, others that it is largely an adaptation of Josiah's Passover (2 Chron. 35.1-19) and still others that reliable sources of information underlie the description. For discussions of these issues, see M. Delcor, 'Le récit de la célébration de la Pâque au temps d'Ezéchias d'après 2 Chr 30 et ses problèmes', in A. Schenker, *Studien zu Opfer und Kult im Alten Testament* (FAT, 3; Tübingen: J.C.B. Mohr [Paul Siebeck], 1992), pp. 93-106; T.L. Eves, 'The Role of Passover in the Book of Chronicles: A Study of 2 Chronicles 30 and 35' (PhD dissertation, Annenberg Research Institute [formerly Dropsie College], 1992); H. Haag, 'Das Mazzenfest des Hiskia', in H. Gese and H.P. Rüger (eds.), *Wort und Geschichte: Festschrift für Karl Elliger zum 70. Geburtstag* (AOAT, 18; Neukirchen–Vluyn: Neukirchener Verlag, 1973), pp. 87-94; S. Levin, 'Hezekiah's Second Passover', *JBQ* 19 (1991), pp. 195-98; M. Nobile, 'La Pasqua del Re Ezechia (2 Cr 30)', *Anton* 67 (1992), pp. 177-97; J.R. Shaver, *Torah and the Chronicler's History Work: An Inquiry into the Chronicler's Reference to Laws, Festivals, and Cultic Institutions in Relationship to Pentateuchal Legislation* (BJS, 196; Atlanta: Scholars Press, 1989), pp. 110-14; S. Talmon, 'Divergences in Calendar-Reckoning in Ephraim and Judah', *VT* 8 (1958), pp. 48-74; A.G. Vaughn, 'The Chronicler's Account of Hezekiah: Relationship of Historical Data to a Theological Interpretation of 2. Chronicles 29-32' (PhD dissertation, Princeton Theological Seminary, 1996); and the summaries in H.G.M. Williamson, *1 and 2 Chronicles* (NCB; Grand Rapids: Eerdmans, 1982), pp. 361-65; and S. Japhet, *I and II*

Comments on the Structure and Function of 2 Chronicles 30.1–31.1

The Chronicler describes Hezekiah's reign in 117 verses (2 Chron. 29–32), more space than given to any other king after Solomon. He describes Hezekiah's sanctification of the temple and cultic officials (ch. 29), the celebration of Passover/Mazzoth (ch. 30),[9] the destruction of idols and their altars and certain provisions made for the support of the Jerusalem cult (ch. 31). While these descriptions do not appear to have been drawn from 2 Kings, it does appear that 2 Kings 20 is the primary source for 2 Chronicles 32 (Sennacherib's attack on Jerusalem, Hezekiah's illness and wealth and the concluding summary). Consequently, it is clear that the Chronicler has sharply departed from the emphases of the Deuteronomistic Historian in order to focus his attention on Hezekiah's religious reforms, all of which occurred within a seven-month period that began in the first year of his reign.[10] Therefore, Hezekiah is presented as pursuing a decisive policy of religious reform, of which the Passover of ch. 30 is only one part.

2 Chronicles 30.1–31.1 may be generally classified as a 'report'[11]

_____

Chronicles: A Commentary (OTL; Louisville, KY: Westminster / John Knox Press, 1993), pp. 932-34.

9. The use of the terms 'Passover' and 'Mazzoth' in 2 Chron. 30 seem to indicate that the two have become completely merged in the Chronicler's thinking. 'This verse represents the most advanced stage of the liturgical calendar in the Bible' (Japhet, *I and II Chronicles*, p. 948). It is also interesting that while vv. 1-5 refer to Hezekiah's decision to send letters to Israel and Judah to invite the people to observe Passover in Jerusalem, Passover is nowhere mentioned in the text of the letter that follows. Finally, the perspective of Deuteronomy (16.5-6) is assumed: Passover is to be celebrated at the Jerusalem temple ('the place which Yahweh your God will choose').

10. Hezekiah was 25 years old when he began to reign, and he initiated the restoration of the temple in his first year (2 Chron. 29.1, 3). The priests and Levites began to restore the temple on the first day of the first month, finishing their work on the sixteenth day of Nisan, two days after the prescribed date of Passover (29.17). Then Hezekiah summoned the peoples of Israel and Judah to come to Jerusalem to celebrate the Passover on the fourteenth day of the second month (30.1-2). Many responded to this invitation and the Passover lamb was slain on schedule (30.15); Mazzoth was celebrated for the next seven days (30.21-22); and the people decided to extend the festivities for an additional week (30.23). Finally, it was in the third month that the people began to pile up their tithes for the temple in heaps, and they finished this in the seventh month (31.7).

11. Cf. De Vries, *1 and 2 Chronicles*, pp. 370, 434. K. Galling's view (*Die*

and—as far as content is concerned—sets Hezekiah in good company with David and Solomon, two kings who launched significant initiatives involving the temple. While it is possible to understand this text as essentially falling into two parts—preparations for Passover/Mazzoth and celebration of the festival[12]—the function of the story is better apprehended by a tripartite arrangement:

1. Composition and sending of Hezekiah's letter to Israel and Judah (30.1-9).
2. Reception of the letters (30.10-12).
3. Results of the positive reception by most Judeans and some Northerners (30.13–31.1).

This narrative scheme reminds one of the report of a prophetic word, a genre that appears fairly often in Chronicles[13] and typically has a prophet or Levite rise to proclaim the word of God to a king. This is followed by a description of the king's response, and then there is an indication of the consequences of this response—blessing for a receptive king but destruction for the willful ruler. The crux of such a narrative is the nature of the decision made by the one(s) receiving the prophetic word. In the report from Hezekiah's reign, though, it is the king himself who issues the prophetic word,[14] thus indicating his role as a bearer of the word of God to the people (cf. 2 Chron. 30.12b). The response to Hezekiah's message is mixed: most Israelites reject the

Bücher der Chronik, Esra, Nehemia [ATD, 12; Göttingen: Vandenhoeck & Ruprecht, 1954], pp. 8-12, 159), of the entire chapter as the work of a second Chronicler (the work of his 'Chron**', who supplemented an earlier writing) has failed to win scholarly support. See, e.g., Japhet, *I and II Chronicles*, pp. 6-7.

12. E.g. Japhet, *I and II Chronicles*, p. 936.

13. Cf. De Vries, *1 and 2 Chronicles*, p. 434, where the following texts are offered as examples of the report of a prophetic word: 1 Chron. 17.3-15; 21.10-12; 2 Chron. 11.2-4a; 12.5; 16.7-10; 19.1-3; 20.13-19; 21.12-15; 24.20; 25.7-8, 15-16; 28.9-11; 34.22-28.

14. 'Hezekiah's summons for a united Passover contains all the elements normally found in the Chronicler's orations. A specific audience is addressed...four imperatives...and two jussives...provide access to the main points of the address; an historical retrospect is found...and the people respond to the imperatives in vv. 10-12 of the narrative framework' (M.A. Throntveit, *When Kings Speak: Royal Speech and Royal Prayer in Chronicles* [SBLDS, 93; Atlanta: Scholars Press, 1987], p. 41). See also the analysis of Hezekiah's letter as an 'address' with roots in postexilic preaching in R. Mason, *Preaching the Tradition: Homily and Hermeneutics after the Exile* (Cambridge: Cambridge University Press, 1990), pp. 102-107.

king's summons, though some respond positively, but all of Judah responds obediently to the king. The account ends with a magnificent description of the reconciliation, blessing and vigorous reform that ensued for those who had humbled themselves[15] before Hezekiah's word.

This suggestion regarding the function of the narrative is reinforced by an analysis of the roles played by the figures in it. God is presented as one who extends grace, forgiveness and healing, and, as the recipient of his people's worship, he is benevolent and generous (30.9b, 12, 20, 27). Hezekiah is appropriately portrayed in royal terms, issuing a decree (30.6b-9), generously lending support to his people and cult (30.24aα), and then (in a more religious/priestly function, by no means unknown to kings of the day; cf. 2 Chron. 6.12-42) offering intercessory prayer for his people (30.18b-19) and encouragement for the Levites who served well (30.22). The princes and the assembly are portrayed in somewhat similar terms, participating in the issuance of the decree (30.2, 5-9) and generously supporting the festivities (30.24aβ).[16] The priests and Levites are shown simply fulfilling their roles in the cult, though sometimes shamed by their own negligence (30.15-17).[17] Most Northerners reject Hezekiah's invitation to repentance (30.10; cf. 2 Chron. 10.19), and, as a group that mocks Hezekiah's entreaty, they resemble the later generation, who would at first plead to be included in the program to rebuild the temple but, after being rejected, plot to overthrow the work of the Restoration community (Ezra 4). Some Northerners, and all of Judah, though, humbled themselves and joined in the joyous celebration of Passover with the king, other leaders of the people and the cultic officials (30.11-12).

The loyalty of certain groups to God during Hezekiah's reign was

15. Typical of Chronicles is the use of כנע in the niphal with the reflexive meaning (cf. 2 Chron. 30.11; 13 occurrences in Chronicles; 17 in the entire Hebrew Bible). This usage belongs to the 'theology of repentance' (p. 207), and in Chronicles it often occurs in cultic contexts (p. 209) (S. Wagner, 'כנע', *TDOT* 7 [1995], pp. 204-10). The term is also used of Hezekiah's humbling himself because of his pride (2 Chron. 32.26). See also S. Japhet, *The Ideology of the Book of Chronicles and its Place in Biblical Thought* (BEATAJ, 9; Frankfurt: Peter Lang, 1989), pp. 260-61.

16. Cf. the role of Israel's leaders in the preparations for the building of the temple (1 Chron. 29.6-9).

17. There is a pronounced anti-priestly theme in the Chronicler's description of Hezekiah's reign (cf. also 2 Chron. 29.3-11, 34).

determined earlier in ch. 29—Hezekiah, cultic personnel and Jerusalem officials, for example, indicated their commitment to God by means of their participation in the reform of the Jerusalem temple. However, the burden and suspense of ch. 30 concern the peoples outside Jerusalem—in both Judah and Israel—and whether they would be willing to return[18] to God after Ahaz' idolatry and that of the Northern kingdom. Those whose commitment to God had already been determined in ch. 29 simply play the roles appropriate for their functions. Hence, the response by Judah and Israel to the invitation to Passover becomes tantamount to their response to God. While historians have been careful to delineate the economic and political aspects to the king's invitation,[19] the Chronicler presents it solely in terms of one religious issue: Will the people return to God so that he may bless and heal them?

Role within the Historiography of Chronicles

Recovery of the Promise of David and Solomon
A considerable body of scholarship has been devoted to the way that the Chronicler describes the reigns of the kings, who are treated in his work in terms that would lead the reader to recall other figures in Israel's history.[20] In the case of Hezekiah the debate has usually been about whether the king is represented in terms more reminiscent of David[21] or Solomon.[22] A mediating position that seems to do greater

18. The term שוב offers exceptionally rich possibilities for theology in the Old Testament (on its usage in Chronicles, see A. Graupner, 'שׁוּב', *ThWAT* 7 [1993], cols. 1158-59). It plays an important role in Hezekiah's appeal for Judah and Israel to 'return' to God so that he may 'turn' to them with favor and deliverance (2 Chron. 30.6-9).

19. See, for example, J.M. Miller and J.H. Hayes, *A History of Ancient Israel and Judah* (Philadelphia: Westminster Press, 1986), p. 357; J. Bright, *A History of Israel* (Philadelphia: Westminster Press, 3rd edn, 1981), pp. 283-84.

20. R. Mosis in particular (*Untersuchungen zur Theologie des chronistischen Geschichtswerkes* [FTS, 92; Freiburg: Herder, 1973]) has developed a schema in which Saul, David and Solomon provide the prototypes for all later kings. Those who are faithless are reminiscent of Saul; the faithful call to mind David; and Solomon provides the model for the king to come. Cf. also R.B. Dillard, 'The Chronicler's Jehoshaphat', *TJ* NS (1986), pp. 17-22, and the literature cited there.

21. Mosis, *Untersuchungen*, p. 189.

22. H.G.M. Williamson, *Israel in the Books of Chronicles* (Cambridge: Cambridge University Press, 1977), pp. 119-25. Also, see the more recent summary of

justice to the evidence and avoids forcing the Chronicler to unnec-
essarily precise distinctions holds that the reigns of David and Solomon
are seen to form a single period—a united Israel—and so the Chronicler portrays Hezekiah with images reminiscent of both of these rulers
in order to point to Hezekiah as the one who recovered that unity for
Israel.[23] More specifically related to Hezekiah's celebration of Pass-
over/Mazzoth, it appears that the Chronicler is intending his account of
these festivities to remind the reader of David's move to bring the ark
of the covenant to Jerusalem[24] and of Solomon's dedication of the
temple.[25]

In the case of the David's actions with regard to the ark (1 Chron. 13
and 15), David consulted (יעץ)[26] with the leaders (שׂר) of the people and
'all the assembly (קהל) of Israel' (13.1-4; without parallel in 2 Sam. 6),
just as Hezekiah had consulted (יעץ) with his princes (שׂר) and the
assembly (קהל) in Jerusalem (2 Chron. 30.2-4), and the Chronicler
concludes in both instances that the decision seemed right to all
involved (כי־ישר הדבר בעיני, 1 Chron. 13.4; וייׁשר הדבר בעיני, 2 Chron.
30.4). People in the land of Israel, as well as priests and Levites, are
invited to assemble to accompany the ark to Jerusalem (1 Chron. 13.2,
5), just as Hezekiah sent messages to Israel and Judah to join him with
the priests, Levites and populace of Jerusalem (2 Chron. 30.1). In both
cases the king intended to correct former cultic negligence; in the case
of David, it was that the ark had been neglected ('we did not seek
[דרׁש][27] it') in the days of Saul (1 Chron. 13.3), and in the case of

this evidence by Eves, 'The Role of Passover in the Book of Chronicles', pp. 128-
33.

23. Throntveit, *When Kings Speak*, pp. 109-25; *idem*, 'Hezekiah in the Books of
Chronicles', in D.J. Lull (ed.), *Society of Biblical Literature 1988 Seminar Papers*
(SBLSP, 27; Atlanta: Scholars Press, 1988), pp. 302-11.

24. There is a suggestion of this parallel in J. Becker, *2 Chronik* (Neue Echter
Bible: Kommentar zum Alten Testament, 20; Würzburg: Echter Verlag, 1988),
p. 99; Japhet, *I and II Chronicles*, p. 940; Mason, *Preaching the Tradition*, p. 106;
Williamson, *1 and 2 Chronicles*, p. 366.

25. Cf. R.B. Dillard, *2 Chronicles* (WBC, 15; Waco, TX: Word Books, 1987),
pp. 242-43.

26. On the use of the term in Chronicles, see L. Ruppert, 'יעץ', *TDOT* 6 (1990),
pp. 162, 181-82. Japhet (*I and II Chronicles*, p. 940) refers to this as a 'democra-
tizing tendency' in Chronicles.

27. On the use of the term in Chronicles, see S. Wagner, 'דרׁש', *TDOT* 3 (1978),
pp. 298-306; and on the larger significance of this term for understanding the aim

Hezekiah, it was part of the recovery from the idolatrous reign of Ahaz (2 Chron. 28.1-4; 29.5-11), when those who set their hearts to seek (דרש) God (2 Chron. 30.19) assembled for Passover in Jerusalem. Both occasions were characterized by joy[28] and accompanied by music/-singing (1 Chron. 13.8; 2 Chron. 30.21-23, 26). It is notable that, in the case of David's first, abortive attempt to bring the ark to Jerusalem, there was no effort by the cultic personnel to sanctify themselves for the occasion, and there were no sacrifices to accompany the transport (2 Sam. 6.1-11; 1 Chron. 13.1-14). Later, however, when David and the people successfully transported the ark into the city, there was at the behest of David the sanctification of the priests and Levites (1 Chron. 15.12-14; without parallel in 2 Sam. 6), proper carriage for the ark on poles held by Levites (1 Chron. 15.15; without parallel in 2 Sam. 6) and sacrifices ('they sacrificed seven bulls and seven rams', 1 Chron. 15.26; 'And it came to pass that when those carrying the ark of Yahweh had advanced six steps, he sacrificed an ox and a fatling', 2 Sam. 6.13). Similarly, Hezekiah attended to the sanctification of the priests and Levites (2 Chron. 29.4-15; 30.15)—as well as attending to unsanctified lay participants in the Passover celebration through prayer (2 Chron. 30.18-19)—and many sacrifices were offered (2 Chron. 30.15-17, 22, 24). Therefore, it appears that Hezekiah showed proper respect for God and so avoided David's disaster with Uzzah.

As for connections between Hezekiah and Solomon, there is, first of all, the explicit statement in 2 Chron. 30.26 that the observance of Passover/Mazzoth under Hezekiah had not been equaled since the time of Solomon.[29] In addition, just as Solomon built the temple and presided

of the Chronicler, see C.T. Begg, '"Seeking Yahweh" and the Purpose of Chronicles', *Louvain Studies* 9 (1982), pp. 128-41.

28. The Chronicler uses שׂחק in 1 Chron. 13.8 to refer to the merriment that accompanied the transfer of the ark toward Jerusalem, simply reproducing the usage of his source (2 Sam. 6.5). (This term is also used in 2 Chron. 30.10 to designate the mocking reception that Hezekiah's messengers received from most Israelites.) Later, after this attempt to bring the ark to Jerusalem had been thwarted by Uzzah's violation of holiness (1 Chron. 13.9-14; 2 Sam. 6.6-11), David successfully conducted the ark into Jerusalem with rejoicing (שׂמחה, 1 Chron. 15.16, 25; 2 Sam. 6.12). In the case of Hezekiah's Passover, it is this noun שׂמחה that is used (2 Chron. 30.21, 23, 26; cf. also 29.30). On the relatively frequent appearance of שׂמחה in Chronicles, see G. Vanoni, 'שׂמח', *ThWAT* 7 (1993), col. 819.

29. Whether the Chronicler is saying that the joy of this celebration had not been equaled since Solomon (Rudolph, *Chronikbücher*, pp. 303-305) or (more

at its dedication, which lasted for two weeks and brought together members of all the tribes of Israel (2 Chron. 2–7), so Hezekiah sanctified the temple (2 Chron. 29) and held a two-week observance of Passover/Mazzoth there for the peoples of Israel and Judah (2 Chron. 30). Thirdly, the promises of divine mercy and salvation that Hezekiah made to those he summoned to the festival in Jerusalem (2 Chron. 30.6-9) are reminiscent of the words of Solomon at the dedication of the temple (2 Chron. 6.24-25; cf. vv. 36-39) and the affirmation of God to Solomon in a night that followed (2 Chron. 7.12b-15).[30] There is also the concern for foreign worshippers in both Solomon's remarks at the dedication of the temple (2 Chron. 6.32-33) and in the Chronicler's description of the assembly that came to Jerusalem to celebrate Passover (2 Chron. 30.25). Fifthly, there are the intercessory prayers that Solomon (2 Chron. 6) and Hezekiah (2 Chron. 30.18b-19) offered for their peoples, and it is affirmed that God accepted their entreaties (2 Chron. 7.1-3, 12; 30.20). Sixthly, great joy and praise of God characterized both occasions (2 Chron. 5.13; 7.6, 10; 30.21-23, 26). Finally, there were enormous sacrifices and provisions made for the people by Solomon and Hezekiah (2 Chron. 5.6; 7.1, 4-5; 30.15-16, 22, 24).

The consequence of the foregoing is that Hezekiah's reign and actions at Passover/Mazzoth are highlighted and receive some of the lustre of Solomon's reign and his achievement with the construction and dedication of the temple. In addition, this linkage points to the significance of Hezekiah's actions as they relate to the reunion of Israel and Judah.

Reversal of the Dissolution of the Kingdom under Rehoboam
The attention shown to Hezekiah as a second David or Solomon and as the one under whom Israel was reunited through his Passover celebration has already been treated. Such a connection between Hezekiah and these two earlier kings does not *de facto* exclude the possibility of parallels between Hezekiah and other figures, since such comparisons

---

likely) that the magnitude/length of the celebration had not been seen since Solomon (Japhet, *I and II Chronicles*, p. 956) is uncertain.

30. Several verbal links between 2 Chron. 7.14 and 2 Chron. 30 are striking: 'And if my people...humble themselves [כנע; 30.11]...then I will hear [שמע; 30.20, 27] from heaven [השמים; 30.27], and I will forgive their sin, and I will heal [ארפא; 30.20] their land' (2 Chron. 7.14).

were seen as valuable by the Chronicler.[31]

For example, Hezekiah's reunion of Judah with some of the tribes of Israel for Passover leads one to examine an earlier period when the tribes divided into two kingdoms under Rehoboam and Jeroboam I. In this case, Hezekiah's reign may be seen as reversing some of the effects of Rehoboam's and may be comparable to his reign in other aspects. For example, Rehoboam leaves Jerusalem to go north to Shechem to confer with the Northern tribes to become their king (2 Chron. 10.1), while Hezekiah invites Israel to come south to Jerusalem to acknowledge God's sovereignty by the observance of Passover (2 Chron. 30.5-9). Rehoboam harshly rejects Israel's demands for leniency in his rule (2 Chron. 10.13-14), while Israel harshly rejects Hezekiah's invitation to celebrate Passover in Jerusalem (2 Chron. 30.10). While the division of the kingdom and the establishment of Jeroboam I's reign promoted idolatry (2 Chron. 10.16; 11.15), Hezekiah's reunion of Israel and Judah leads to a suppression of idolatry (31.1). Both the revolt of Israel (2 Chron. 10.15) and the favorable response of Judah to Hezekiah's invitation (2 Chron. 30.12) are claimed to be the work of God. Because of Rehoboam's failure, the nation divides, though some Levites and priests in Israel, as well as others 'who had given/set [נתן] their heart to seek [בקש] Yahweh, God of Israel', migrate south to Judah (2 Chron. 11.13-16); conversely, because of Hezekiah's success, some Israelites unite with Judah for Passover and the reform spreads to the North (2 Chron. 30.11; 31.1). Jeroboam evicted many priests and Levites from their property in order to suppress their service in the cult (2 Chron. 11.14); Hezekiah established the Jerusalem cult so that priests and Levites were supported for their work in the temple (2 Chron. 31.2-19). The foregoing should not be taken to mean that the Chronicler took pains to portray Hezekiah systematically as an antitype to Rehoboam,[32]

31. See n. 21 above. Sometimes such comparisons were made explicit by the Chronicler, who followed the Deuteronomistic Historian in this regard: 2 Chron. 17.3 (Jehoshaphat 'walked in the earlier ways of David his father'); 21.6 (Jehoram 'walked in the way of the kings of Israel'); 22.3 (Ahaziah 'also walked in the ways of the house of Ahab'); 29.2 (Hezekiah 'did what was right in the eyes of Yahweh, according to all that David his father had done').

32. If anything, Hezekiah is presented as the antitype of Ahaz, whose religious and political policies he reverses. Ahaz' idolatry is chronicled repeatedly (2 Chron. 28.2-4, 19, 22-25) and contrasts sharply with the faithfulness of his son Hezekiah, whose restoration of the temple (2 Chron. 29), summons to Judah and Israel to signal their turn to God by the celebration of Passover (2 Chron. 30) and promotion

but it does suggest that Hezekiah's reign is sketched in such a way to lead the reader to recall the experiences of Rehoboam and then appreciate the significance of Hezekiah's achievements and the degree to which his reign signaled a reversal of the dissolution of the kingdom that occurred during Rehoboam's reign.

Geography of Holiness

The Chronicler makes use of geographical indications in his description of Hezekiah's reign in order to portray the Jerusalem temple as the center of holiness and blessing and to show that, as people are brought into respectful and obedient proximity to it, they are blessed.[33] Holiness spreads from the temple in Jerusalem outward. The process began with Hezekiah's purification of the Jerusalem temple and its personnel (2 Chron. 29) and proceeded to the next stage—a cleansing of Jerusalem of idols (2 Chron. 30.14)—with the invitation for Israel and Judah to celebrate Passover in Jerusalem (30.6-9; cf. the message of Isa. 2.1-4 regarding the word of the Lord going forth from Mt Zion). Those who are stubborn and disobedient resist the invitation and remain outside Jerusalem, but those who humble themselves and determine to return to God travel to Jerusalem, and, while there, join in the efforts to remove the offending altars and cast them into the Kidron Valley (30.13-14). In this way, a physical journey/return to Jerusalem parallels a spiritual return to God, and, conversely, refusal to return to Jerusalem represents a refusal to return to God. It is at Jerusalem and in worship at the temple that the people are reconciled to God, and then, as the pilgrims return to their homes outside Jerusalem, they spread the reform and extend the holiness of Jerusalem to the rest of the land by

of cultic reform (2 Chron. 30.14; 31.1) must be interpreted as a reversal of his father's religious policies. Similarly, Ahaz is faulted for appealing to the Assyrians for aid in his war with Syria, it being duly noted that the Assyrians served only to afflict Judah further (2 Chron. 28.16-21), while Hezekiah's resistance against Assyria was blessed with success by God (2 Chron. 32.1-22). Among the consequences of all this was the depletion of Ahaz' treasury (2 Chron. 28.21) and the augmentation of Hezekiah's (2 Chron. 32.23).

33. On the Chronicler's development of this theme in the genealogies, see M. Oeming, *Das wahre Israel: Die 'genealogische Vorhalle' 1 Chronik 1–9* (BWANT, 128; Stuttgart: W. Kohlhammer, 1990), pp. 73-205; on the importance of Jerusalem in Chronicles, see P.C. Beentjes, 'Jerusalem in the Book of Chronicles', in M. Poorthuis and C. Safrai (eds.), *The Centrality of Jerusalem: Historical Perspectives* (Kampen: Kok, 1996), pp. 15-28.

destroying sacred pillars, Asherim, high places and altars in both
Judah-Benjamin and in Ephraim and Manasseh (31.1). In this way, the
land is rid of the idolatry promoted by Ahaz and the kings of Israel. The
impact of this movement out from Jerusalem will extend even to those
exiled by Assyria, if their countrymen in the North will turn to God (if
the Northerners will *return* to Jerusalem [i.e. God], then God will
return their exiled countrymen to their homeland [2 Chron. 30.9]).
Finally, there is suggested a parallel between God's holy dwelling place
on earth, the temple, and his dwelling place in heaven (cf. 2 Chron.
30.8, 27), though the Chronicler acknowledges that God cannot be
confined to either (2 Chron. 6.18-22).[34]

Aspects of a Theology of Worship

The God Who Is Worshipped
Worship is not the glorious work of a perfect people, but the humble
offering of flawed humans to God. It is God who calls the people into
being (30.6b), gives law and prescriptions for religious observance
(30.2-3, 18-19), summons the assembly to worship (30.12b), makes
possible their humble response (30.12; cf. 29.36) and then forgives the
inevitable failings and inadequacies of their response (30.20). This is
hardly the image of God as the harsh, arbitrary and distant tyrant of
popular imagination. God is indeed just, punishing the faithlessness[35] of
his people (30.7-8), and he is portrayed as a holy God, who resides in a
holy place (30.27) and seeks a holy people (30.17-18) to offer him holy
gifts (30.17b) in a holy place (30.13-14).[36] When his people are
responsive, holiness spreads to distant places (31.1). Along the way, the

34. On the Chronicler's view of God's presence in the temple and in heaven,
see Japhet, *Ideology*, pp. 59-85.
35. The Chronicler often uses the term מעל (to be faithless) to designate the
infidelity (typically idolatary or some offense against the temple or cult) of God's
people (1 Chron. 2.7; 5.25; 10.13; 2 Chron. 12.2; 26.16, 18; 28.19, 22; 29.6; 30.7;
36.14). See H. Ringgren, 'מעל', *TDOT* 8 (1997), pp. 460-63; W. Johnstone, *1 and 2
Chronicles* (JSOTSup, 253; Sheffield: Sheffield Academic Press, 1997), I, pp. 13-
14.
36. On the use of קדשׁ in Chronicles, see H. Ringgren, 'קדשׁ', *ThWAT* 6 (1989),
cols. 1192-93. It is used often in the Chronicler's account of Hezekiah's reign and
designates action with God as the subject, the preparation of priests for cultic
activity or the people for participation in Passover/Mazzoth, and heaven as a holy
dwelling for God (2 Chron. 29.5, 15, 17, 19, 34; 30.3, 8, 15, 17, 24; 31.6, 18).

Chronicler also shows God to be gracious, merciful, forgiving and eager to heal (30.9, 19-20). These qualities coexist in the God of Israel, sometimes expressing themselves in surprising ways, and the consequence is that God continues to elude human understanding and control. And so the experience of worship leaves the community of faith to wonder at the majesty of the God it serves.

The People Who Worship

The worshipping community is not circumscribed narrowly by the Chronicler and restricted to the faithful of Judah and Jerusalem. On the contrary, assembly for worship is made possible for the faithless of Israel and Judah, negligent priests and Levites, and resident aliens who have turned to God (30.25)[37]—in fact, it is their own former faithlessness that contrasts with their worship and sets in relief the bold contours of their present obedience (30.6-8).[38] And so, true to human experience, the worship that ensues takes place in circumstances of ambiguity, unevenness and mystery: while Judah accepts God's summons eagerly, as do some in the North and sojourners in both the North and the South, there are the multitudes in the North that greet God's proffer of mercy and grace with derisive laughter and scorn

---

37. These sojourners were Gentiles who resided in Israel/Judah and adopted the worship of Yahweh. According to Exod 12.48-49, they were allowed to participate in Passover, provided the males had been circumcised (cf. also Num. 9.14). Cf. D. Kellermann, 'גור', *TDOT* 2 (1977), pp. 439-49. W. Meier ('"...Fremdlinge, die aus Israel gekommen waren..." Eine Notiz in 2 Chronik 30, 25f. aus der Sicht der Ausgrabungen im jüdischen Viertel der Altstadt von Jerusalem', *BN* 15 [1981], pp. 40-43) suggests that 1970 excavations in Jerusalem may be interpreted to indicate that Hezekiah enlarged Jerusalem in order to provide room for these sojourners who came out of Israel to Jerusalem, seeking asylum.

38. A major trend in Chronicles scholarship since the time of de Wette has been to assert that the Chronicler favored Judah but maintained a strong antipathy for Israel, explained by some as an anti-Samaritan *Tendenz* and often linked with the view that the same author wrote Chronicles and Ezra–Nehemiah. This view has, in turn, contributed to the widespread perception of the Chronicler as a narrow sectarian. In fact, however, 2 Chron. 30.1–31.1 exhibits a great openness to Israel, as well as to Gentiles who reside in the land. This inclusive spirit and understanding of 'all Israel' to encompass all these peoples has been documented thoroughly by Japhet (*Ideology*, pp. 267-351) and Williamson (*Israel in the Books of Chronicles*, pp. 87-140). Cf. M. Cogan 'For We, Like You, Worship your God: Three Biblical Portrayals of Samaritan Origins', *VT* 38 (1988), pp. 289-91.

(30.10). Observers are left to puzzle at the variety of responses to God's summons.

What the worshipping community does is indeed rooted in their experience as the people of God, the recipients of his instruction and heirs of the traditions of their ancestors. It is the memory of this story and the knowledge of the present generation's relation to their ancestors who served God that nourishes them (30.6). There is concern for cultic detail (30.3, 18), because such detail is rooted in the story and is rich in significance. Yet, in the story of Hezekiah's Passover there seems to be little loss of vision regarding the aim of worship; the plea is for a return to God, not simply for participation in barren ritual (30.6-9).

As indicated earlier, the account of Hezekiah's Passover does not cast worship and the turning to God that it represents as a wholly human endeavor: while there is great emphasis on the accountability of people to God (e.g. Hezekiah's call for them to 'return' to God in 30.6-9), there is also a confession that God's grace enables a people to turn to him (v. 12; cf. also 1 Chron. 29.18). Their worship becomes a liturgical drama that demonstrates their turning from faithlessness to set their hearts to seek God, and in fact it is the turning of the heart to God that is requisite for worship (30.19a; cf. also 1 Chron. 29.17).[39] Nevertheless, it is also clear that even when a people turn to worship God, complete purity/holiness is elusive. In the present account, the intercession of Hezekiah is required for their worship to be acceptable to God (30.18-19), and his words articulate the prayer for successive generations of worshippers, 'O God, accept the intent of your people to offer you their adoration in spite of their imperfections—it is you who are holy, not your people nor their worship, unless you make them such.' Such intense focus on the heart and internal orientation of the worshipper is a far cry from the hollow legalism and ritualism that so many associate with the books of Chronicles.[40] While worship may

39. On the use of 'heart' (לב/לבב) in the Hebrew Bible, see H.W. Wolff, *Anthropology of the Old Testament* (Philadelphia: Fortress Press, 1974), pp. 40-58, who designates this 'the most important word in the vocabulary of Old Testament anthropology' (p. 40). More recently: H.-J. Fabry, 'לבב/לב', *TDOT* 7 (1995), pp. 399-437. While the research indicated above certainly notes an emotive or affective element in some instances of the usage of לב/לבב in the Hebrew Bible, it is the rational or volitional aspects that dominate, a pattern that has been turned upside down in contemporary American secular (and even religious) usage in which 'head' (i.e. mind) is set in opposition to 'heart' (i.e. emotions/feelings).

40. Williamson (*1 and 2 Chronicles*, pp. 30-31) asserts three arguments against

arise at the behest of a community's leaders and be nourished by their gifts and support, its health depends on the orientation of the people's heart and their decision about God (cf. 1 Chron. 29.18).

The effects of worship are widespread. It grows out of community but further establishes community. In the case at hand, Hezekiah's invitation to Passover arises as a consequence of his reforms of the Jerusalem temple (cf. 2 Chron. 29.35b–30.1). A community of faith was established, and then the invitation is issued for others to join them. Those who accept the summons enlarge the community, influence its celebrations (30.14, 23) and initiate further programs to extend its influence (31.1). From the standpoint of Chronicles, one can see in the activities surrounding Hezekiah's Passover a sort of reunion of the nation of Israel, thus reversing the effects of the rebellion of the Northern tribes against Rehoboam.

In addition, it is clear that the behavior of those who responded wholeheartedly and suffered the hardships of pilgrimage to offer their worship to God shamed the negligent and privileged leaders of the cult (30.15), inspiring them to enthusiastic praise of God (30.21b); move the entire assembly to joy (30.21) and further devotion (30.23); and elicit generosity from their leaders (30.24). In addition, while worship is a consequence of reform and devotion, it inspires further reforms and greater devotion (31.1), and the blessings that the worshippers receive as a consequence of their engagement with God are expected to have consequences for others, who are far removed and suffering in distress (30.9). It is clear that worship is powerful and seldom ends with the last prayer and the dismissal of the assembly. In this way, worship affirms linkages with other, distant parts of the community and so gives hope to all for deliverance and restoration of community.

As for the widespread misperception that the Chronicler understands ancient Israel's worship to be immutable and unaffected by the circumstances of the worshippers, the description of Hezekiah's Passover suggests the opposite. Worship not only arises from community tradition, but it sometimes departs from those traditions as well (30.2-3, 28). It may be set for certain times, but it cannot be restricted by those

those who portray the Chronicler as an extreme ritualist: (1) the Chronicler typically stresses the joy of religious celebration; (2) in the Levitical sermons of Chronicles the focus is on faith in God—not perfect ritual—as the means of blessing; and (3) the Chronicler shows that genuine religion is possible in settings outside the temple and apart from its rituals.

boundaries (30.2-3, 23).[41] It may be prescribed for observance at certain places, but its results will spread and resist confinement to a single place (30.9, 20, 27; 31.1). In short, worship has the illusion of order, predictability and changelessness, but the Chronicler shows it to be alive, vigorous and capable of breaking boundaries of time, place and expectation—not in ways that are chaotic, but in ways that attest the sovereignty and majesty and mercy of God. In the case of Hezekiah, what began as a king and his assembly's decree, an invitation for others to join them in an act of confession and sacred observance to God, endured the disappointment of harsh and mocking rejection by many to spread to lands beyond that king's control and inspire effects beyond those of the immediate celebration.

Summary and Reflections

Summary

2 Chronicles 30.1–31.1 offers a corrective to the misperceptions of Chronicles as a work that promotes a narrow, legalistic and ritualistic view of worship. This text shows that the Chronicler did not view worship as essentially a mechanical and ritualistic human enterprise, that he did not construe it in essentially legalistic terms and that his view of the worshipping community was more inclusive than some have maintained. God is portrayed as the holy one who makes worship possible and who receives it with grace and mercy. The worshippers, on the other hand, emerge as sinful and essentially flawed humans, who nevertheless have oriented their hearts toward God. In worship they find joy, community, inspiration for religious reform and devotion and hope. In addition, the rich texture of 2 Chron. 30.1–31.1 becomes more

41. It seems most likely that Hezekiah's celebration of a belated Passover on the fourteenth day of the second month, instead of on the fourteenth day of the first month, represents an extension of the practice sanctioned in Num. 9.1-14 (persons who were ritually unclean because of contact with corpses or who were away on journeys and so were unable to participate in Passover may celebrate the feast on the fourteenth day of the second month). M. Fishbane, 'Revelation and Tradition: Aspects of Inner-biblical Exegesis', *JBL* 99 (1980), pp. 344-47; J. Milgrom, *Numbers* (JPSTC; Philadelphia: Jewish Publication Society, 1990), pp. 67-70; B. Levine, *Numbers 1–20* (AB, 4; Garden City, NY: Doubleday, 1993), pp. 293-98; R.B. Dillard, *2 Chronicles* (WBC, 15; Waco, TX: Word Books, 1987), pp. 243-44. Counter arguments are offered by Talmon, 'Divergences in Calendar-Reckoning', pp. 48-74; and Japhet, *I and II Chronicles*, pp. 938-40.

apparent as one locates its place in the Chronicler's historiography. It illustrates the role of Hezekiah in the recovery of the promise of David and Solomon and his role in reversing the disintegration of the monarchy under Rehoboam, and it offers a narrative representation of the centrality of the temple and Jerusalem in the Chronicler's geography of holiness.

Reflections

What has been offered above as aspects of the Chronicler's theology of worship suggests a certain balance and flexibility, all maintained and articulated in the devoted service of God. Such an image of worship often stands in tension with what one finds in American churches. Popular culture has a way of corrupting and perverting religion so as to shift the object of worship from God to the self, thus creating a perverse sort of idolatry. Flexibility becomes worship without rules or principles; the internal aspect of worship becomes an excuse for worship without regard for the communities in which one's life is placed for service and nurturing; joy and praise become ubiquitous, pushing out remorse for sin, repentance and confession, lament over disaster and tragedy that defy human understanding; the inclusiveness of worship creates a pseudo-fellowship that is often more illusion than reality—a gathering for a brief time of people from similar socio-economic backgrounds who agree on little of religious significance—and worship is fashioned on the basis of market research to appeal to current human aesthetics, ideology and convenience—by, to and for oneself.

The books of Chronicles have something to offer the contemporary American church on the topic of worship. Rather than advancing a perspective on worship conceived as essentially rigid, a matter of external forms, without joy or spirit, an occasion for hostility and separation, a human enterprise, and offered to God grudgingly, Chronicles presents a vision of worship as a matter of the heart as much as of the hands, an occasion for joy, thankfulness, generosity, healing, reconciliation and a time for God to empower and enthuse his people. In short, it is a time for the reorientation of the human heart—to remember what God has done in the past and to infuse the present with hope for a future life of well-being and communion with God.

PSALM 19: A MEDITATION ON GOD'S GLORY IN THE HEAVENS AND IN GOD'S LAW*

Walter Harrelson

The distinction between the two parts of Psalm 19 has been observed through the centuries. Many attempts have been made to show how the two parts relate to one another, or at least how they can have been understood in ancient times to relate to one another. My view of the relation of the two parts, spelled out below, is that the author of the second part made use of an existing hymn in praise of Shemesh (Sun) in order to register two related points about God's gifts to humankind. The first point is that the mystery and glory of the sun, the dominant heavenly body, is matched by the mystery and glory of God's Torah. Psalm 19, then, is from first to last a meditation on the mystery and glory of Torah, to which the mystery and glory of the sun closely correspond.

The second point is that both parts of the Psalm are at heart a meditation on how human beings ought rightly to acknowledge the mystery and glory of both sun and Torah and ought rightly to live in relation to the splendor of both. The psalm, that is to say, is a meditation on God's beauty, God's glory, God's splendor, discernible (as Kant observed) in 'the starry sky above and the moral law within'. While the psalmist is not bent on affirming a religious position within the limits of reason alone—far from it—this poet is, I believe, arguing for something much more powerful and much more impressive than the 'order' of the universe or the 'order' provided by a commitment to Torah. Esthetic and moral considerations are closely woven together in both parts of the psalm.

I begin with a translation of the psalm.

---

* Much of the work of Professor John T. Willis has been devoted to the book of Psalms. This brief study is offered as a tribute to him and to that work.

| 1. | To the leader of worship: A song in the tradition of David. |

1. To the leader of worship: A song in the tradition of David.
2. The heavens themselves declare the glory of God;
   the sky-dome announces the works of God's hands.
3. Day pours out speech to the next day;
   night passes on knowledge to the next night.
4. There is no utterance, no word at all;
   not a single voice is heard.
5. Even so, their strong word goes out to all the earth,
   their words to the ends of the universe.

In the heavens God has pitched a tent for the sun.
6. It, like a bridegroom striding out from his bridal hut,
   shouts for joy, like a runner who has won a race.
7. Its rising is from the very extremity of the heavens,
   and its circuit reaches to heaven's end;
   nothing is hidden from the sun's ardor.

8. The Torah of the LORD is perfect,
   renewing the inner self.
The testimony of the LORD is faithful,
   bringing the young to maturity.
9. The precepts of the LORD are elegant,
   rejoicing the heart.
The commands of the LORD are clear,
   brightening the eyes.
10. The fear of the LORD is clean,
   standing firm for all time.
The ordinances of the LORD are sound,
   righteous in every way.
11. They are more desirable than gold,
   even fine gold, much of it.
They are even sweeter than honey,
   than drippings from the honeycomb.
12. Your servant, too, is enlightened by them;
   the keeping of them brings great gain.

13. But who indeed can discern their faults?
   Clear me, I pray, from hidden failings.
14. Hold your servant back from proud thoughts;
   let them not rule over me!
Then I will be free of blame,
   innocent of great transgression.
15. Let the words of my mouth
   and the meditations of my heart
be pleasing in your sight,
   O LORD, my rock and my redeemer!

The Poem to Shemesh and its Transformation

We look first at the (hypothetical) hymn to Shemesh and its transformation at the poet's hands. The nearest equivalent that has been preserved from the ancient Near Eastern world may be the Egyptian 'Hymn to the Sun-Disc' which has survived in several versions.[1] There we read the following lines:

> Thou appearest beautifully on the horizon of heaven,
> Thou living Aton, the beginning of life!
> When thou art risen on the eastern horizon,
> Thou hast filled every land with thy beauty.
> Thou art gracious, great, glistening, and high over every land;
> Thy rays encompass the lands to the limit of all that thou hast made:
> …
> Thy rays suckle every meadow.
> When thou risest, they live, they grow for thee.
> Thou makest the seasons in order to rear all that thou hast made,
> The winter to cool them,
> And the heat that *they* may taste thee.
> Thou hast made the distant sky in order to rise therein,
> In order to see all that thou dost make.
> …
> Eyes are (fixed) on beauty until thou settest.
> All work is laid aside when thou settest in the west.

The Hymn to the Aten is of course much closer in language and pattern to Psalm 104 than it is to our psalm. The purpose of the hypothetical hymn to Shemesh, or Shapash, the West Semitic sun-deity known from Ugaritic literature as well, would have been identical with that found in the Egyptian hymn: to praise the deity for its beauty and splendor and also to participate in the ritual acts through which human beings were able to assist the sun-disc in its journey across the heavens and (especially) its perilous trek through the underworld until it rose again in the east the following day. In our poem the transformation is complete. All of the heavenly bodies render their own praise to the one God, the LORD, sovereign of the universe. Shamash/Shapash in West Semitic religious understanding embodied the high God or ranked among the highest gods. The demotion is complete in Psalm 19: God has built a tent in the eastern horizon to house the sun. It makes no

---

1. See the translation by J.A. Wilson in *ANET*, pp. 370-71.

perilous journey through the underworld when night falls; rather, it goes quickly to rest in its tent/home, while moon and stars fulfill their appointed nightly tasks. We are not told how the sun makes its journey back to its eastern home.

But the poet of Psalm 19 has added much as well. The sun is much more than a giver of heat and fertility to earth, an aid to mark the seasons. While clearly a creature of God and no deity at all, the sun like Wisdom at the creation (Prov. 8.30-31) is overwhelmed with joy and delight at God's creation. Other heavenly bodies make their appointed rounds, and the order is witness to the God who created them and appointed them to serve. They praise God with their silent fulfillment of the task. But the sun does more: its delight in God cannot be contained, for it races across the heavens, now fast and now slow, now providing fierce heat and now mitigating that heat, bursting with energy, scattering its treasures much as God does, as the Spirit does in Psalm 104, and as Wisdom does in Proverbs 8. Nothing is hidden from its heat (Heb. חמה), just as Wisdom touches all that God has created (Ps. 104.24) and was present with God at the creation of all things (Prov. 8.22-31).

Moreover, the delight and uncontrollable energy of the sun as it dances and races across the heavens mirror Wisdom's delight in all the variety of God's universe (Prov. 8.30-31). Our poet has taken a West Semitic hymn, or the theme of such a hymn, and brought it into close association with two other themes: the presence of God's spirit at the creation (Ps. 104.24; Gen. 1.1-3) and the presence of Wisdom at the creation (Prov. 8.22-31).

The Poem on the Splendor of Torah

The other part of the psalm also owes a good deal to the theme of Wisdom in the Hebrew Bible and in the Deuterocanonical literature. This poem recounting the beauty and splendor of the Torah is clearly intended to complement the delight that the sun finds in its coursing through the universe, rejoicing like a bridegroom coming forth from the bridal chamber. The Torah is good and useful, offering sane and sage counsel for the human community. But the Torah is more: it is clear, clean, wholesome, full of wisdom, marked by beauty, delighting all who will come to its feast. Psalm 119, of course, carries forward the same theme, in architechtonic splendor. But much is found here, as well, to relate the gift of Torah to God's gift of Wisdom and the Spirit. Sirach 24 will make the explicit identification of Wisdom with Torah, and our psalm probably assisted in the making of that identification. Baruch 3.9-4.4 completes the identification, also underscoring the mystery and the hiddenness of Wisdom, bringing into play the marvelous poem on Wisdom found in Job 28. Psalm 19 powerfully juxtaposes the praise rendered to God by the heavenly bodies and the praise of God that arises from the study of Torah and meditation on its mysteries. And in the poem on Torah, the psalmist may be the first to bring into association the Torah as a delight to humankind that is comparable with Wisdom's delight in all that God has created. If so, we can see that the two parts of the psalm may have as their connecting link the biblical theme of Wisdom present at the creation, related first to the sun in the first part of the poem and to Torah in the second part. Sirach and Baruch will then have filled out the picture.

The Psalmist's Meditation on the Psalm's Two Parts

Estimates by scholars of the place of Torah in the life of biblical Israel have changed radically in recent decades. Norms for the guidance of the life of the community are now recognized to have been in place long before the prophets of Israel spoke. Such norms guided them, in fact, in their judgments. These norms were also much more than norms. In the life of the worshipping community, Torah was understood to share in the very life of the Giver of Torah, just as Wisdom partook of the Giver of Wisdom and the presence of the Spirit meant an even more intimate sharing in the divine life. The author of Psalm 19 must surely have understood Torah in this way. In the closing section of the psalm (vv. 13-15; EVV 12-14), the author prays for guidance in the claiming of God's revelations through the heavenly bodies and through the Torah. Who is in position to detect those times when we misinterpret the order of the universe and misinterpret the requirements and blessings of Torah? Neither the order of the heavens nor the guidance of Torah can assure that we will not pervert that order, misread it, twist it to our own ends. Our doing so is often an impenetrable mystery, deeply hidden in the mysterious recesses of the self. No completely reliable safeguards exist for a proper appreciation of God's beauty and order in the universe or for a right reading and meditation upon God's Torah. Even though Wisdom and the Spirit bring the divine presence ever so near, through both the universe and the Torah, there remains the mystery of human selfhood that can spurn the very gifts given for its health and delight.

The psalmist therefore closes with a word of petition to the one God: make my words and my thoughts (and of course, my deeds) acceptable to You, who are Rock and Redeemer. But the psalmist has, we believe, started a process of thought and imagination in Israel that will go on to bear much fruit: the relating of the glories of heaven to the (almost) divine gift of Wisdom, and the relating of (almost) divine Torah to the same Wisdom. Even so, the psalmist closes with a prayer to the one God, and the monotheism of biblical Israel is soundly reaffirmed.

GROUNDS FOR PRAISE:
THE NATURE AND FUNCTION OF THE MOTIVE CLAUSE
IN THE HYMNS OF THE HEBREW PSALTER

J. Kenneth Kuntz

Through the medium of both the printed and spoken word, I have often been instructed by the scholarly insights of John Willis. His steady flow of publications on the Hebrew Bible and presentations at the Society of Biblical Literature meetings across the years have helped many in their quest to approach Jewish and Christian scripture with greater sensitivity. Since John and I have both tarried with the book of Psalms, I offer this essay on a specific characteristic of Israelite psalmography in the hope that it will cast some light on the practice of ancient Israelite worship and betoken my appreciation of John's scholarship and our friendship.

Initial Reflections about Israelite Hymnody

If it would be entirely presumptuous to maintain that only the book of Psalms matters in serious discussions of our theme, 'Worship in the Hebrew Bible', it would likewise be presumptuous to maintain that among diverse psalmic forms (*Gattungen*), only the hymn yields data that instruct us about ancient Israelite worship. Nevertheless, if we may assume that praise is an undeniably foundational element in worship of the deity, then the centrality of hymns impresses itself upon us. James Mays rightly asserts,

> The function of praise in the Psalter belongs first of all to the hymn. There are elements of praise in the prayers. Songs of thanksgiving praise the LORD for a specific experience of deliverance. But the primary genre of praise is the hymn.[1]

1. J.L. Mays, *Psalms* (Interpretation; Louisville, KY: John Knox Press, 1994), p. 26.

As a song of praise (תהלה), the hymn ever fixes its attention on God. Both the poet to whom it owes its origin and the gathered congregation that voices its lines within a cultic setting are well aware that 'Great is Yahweh and worthy of high praise' (Ps. 145.3a). As reverent Israelite worshipers prepare to meet the august deity in the sanctuary, they come with awe and trembling. At the same time, it is the *adoration* of the Holy One that truly propels them. The discourse of their praise is one of exuberant joy as they give expression to their understanding of who God is, what he has done and will continue to do for them, and what he expects from them as the people of his choice. In their pilgrimage, the people of ancient Israel had ample opportunity to witness signs of Yahweh's benevolence. Such praiseworthy divine actions evoked their heartfelt response in the context of seasonal festive assemblies and on other recurring occasions of corporate worship. Accordingly, the hymn presented itself as a most felicitous medium for expressing grateful praise of their benevolent Lord. Also, as Erhard Gerstenberger reminds us, 'Yahwistic hymnology turned out to be a vigorous vehicle *sui generis* of Israel's faith. To this day it has not lost its contagious force, providing ever new songs of praise all over the world.'[2]

As it extols Yahweh's grandeur and goodness manifest in deeds of creation and history, the hymn evolves from intentions not unlike those evident in the thanksgiving psalm. As is often noted, Claus Westermann argues that with respect to the canonical Psalter, it is neither desirable nor possible to isolate a separate genre of thanksgiving psalm (תודה) that is fully distinct from what hitherto have been known as hymns. Claiming that *both* are psalms of praise, he attaches the label 'descriptive praise' to the so-called hymn (תהלה) that 'praises God for his actions and his being as a whole' and the label 'declarative praise' to the so-called thanksgiving song (תודה) that 'praises God for a specific deed which the one who has been delivered recounts or reports in his song'.[3]

Since all verbal expressions of thanksgiving to God can readily be construed as praise, and much praise of God conveys human gratitude, Westermann's determination to retain those two psalm types in close juxtaposition has its appeal. Both fall within the comprehensive

2. E.S. Gerstenberger, *Psalms: Part I with an Introduction to Cultic Poetry* (FOTL, 14; Grand Rapids: Eerdmans, 1987), p. 17.

3. C. Westermann, *Praise and Lament in the Psalms* (Richmond, VA: John Knox Press, 1981), p. 31.

category of praise to God. Surely those psalms that Hermann Gunkel in his pioneering form-critical analysis named thanksgiving songs (*Dank-lieder*) are no less stingy in exalting and glorifying Yahweh than are those that he named hymns (*Hymnen*).[4] Even so, Westermann's twofold terminology is itself an admission that some kind of bona fide distinction should be drawn between praise and thanksgiving, one that mainly turns on the issue of degree of specificity. Since in contrast to the thanksgiving song, the hymn distinguishes itself as a superb poetic medium for ascribing praise to the deity in a more summarizing manner that takes fuller account of the range of Yahweh's attributes and actions in both history and creation, we affirm it as a significant form-critical category in this essay.

A related issue beckons our attention. Today few scholars are comfortable endorsing Gunkel's judgment that among the numerous form-critical categories hosted by the Psalter, the hymn is the most easily recognized and identified.[5] Whereas Gunkel's discussion of the hymn is often perceptive, this assessment assumes a degree of homogeneity within psalmic hymnody that the evidence time and again belies. Thus Gerstenberger's succinct appraisal of the Psalter's hymns of praise as 'a diversified group of sacred poems'[6] is assuredly more accurate. A bolder response issues from H. Spieckermann, who submits that the Hebrew Bible actually lacks a hymn *genre* consisting of texts governed by such constraints as recognizable arrangement, formation and intention. Aware that the Psalter preserves 'hymns' that are resolute in their praise of the deity, Spieckermann prefers the designation *Textgruppe* to that of *Gattung*.[7]

In his attempt to introduce definite nuances into the form-critical classification of hymn, Frank Crüsemann distinguishes hymns of imperative provenance from participial hymns.[8] Whereas the pronounced use

4.   H. Gunkel and J. Begrich, *Einleitung in die Psalmen: Die Gattungen der religiösen Lyrik Israels* (HKAT, 2; Göttingen: Vandenhoeck & Ruprecht, 1933), pp. 32-94, 265-92.

5.   Gunkel and Begrich, *Einleitung in die Psalmen*, p. 32.

6.   E.S. Gerstenberger, 'The Lyric Literature', in D.A. Knight and G.M. Tucker (eds.), *The Hebrew Bible and its Modern Interpreters* (Philadelphia: Fortress Press, 1985), p. 429.

7.   H. Spieckermann, 'Alttestamentliche "Hymnen"', in W. Burkert und F. Stolz (eds.), *Hymnen der alten Welt im Kulturvergleich* (OBO, 131; Göttingen: Vandenhoeck & Ruprecht, 1994), pp. 97-108.

8.   F. Crüsemann, *Studien zur Formgeschichte von Hymnus und Danklied in*

of plural imperatives in hymns of praise has long been recognized as characteristically Israelite, Crüsemann argues for the independent existence of the 'imperative hymn' as the basic and most important form of hymn in Israel. The exhortation *to* praise and the ensuing recitation *of* praise are its two most characteristic elements. He theorizes that in due course, especially under the influence of Babylonian practice, a style dominated by hymnic participles evolved that was remarkably adept in enumerating the deity's glorious attributes. He aptly observes that such participial predications are prominent in the hymnic poetry of Deutero–Isaiah. During the postexilic era, claims Crüsemann, the standard imperative hymn form came to adopt the use of participial predication for its own purpose. Whereas Hans-Joachim Kraus generously credits Crüsemann for having 'placed the study of hymns on completely new foundations',[9] Roland Murphy rests uneasy with Crüsemann's form-critical proposals that entail 'highly inferential' argumentation. Above all, he questions whether those imperatives and participles that lie at the very center of Crüsemann's analysis 'can carry the weight placed upon them (such as making them constitutive elements of literary types—imperative and participial hymns)'. Moreover, Martin Buss rightly complains that Crüsemann's hypothesis of a participial hymn genre is much too speculative since 'no examples have survived except in fragments and mixtures'.[10]

On this issue, Gerstenberger brings to psalms studies a perspective that I find especially cogent. On the one hand, he admits that all hymns of the Psalter project 'a certain common mood'. On the other, he urges that we take into account the 'specific situation to which each [hymn] owes its existence instead of dealing with one group only'.[11] Faulting form critics for overreaching themselves in their attempts to isolate several hymn types solely on formal grounds, Gerstenberger argues that the different hymnic styles that are discernible in the Psalter 'never

Israel (WMANT, 32; Neukirchen–Vluyn: Neukirchener Verlag, 1969), pp. 19-154.

9. H.-J. Kraus, *Psalms 1–59: A Commentary* (Minneapolis: Augsburg, 1988), p. 43. W. Zimmerli, *Old Testament Theology in Outline* (Richmond, VA: John Knox Press, 1978), p. 154, is likewise enthusiastic about Crüsemann's discernment of 'various groups of [hymn] forms differing in origin and genesis'.

10. R.E. Murphy, book review of Crüsemann, *Formgeschichte von Hymnus und Danklied*, in *CBQ* 33 (1971), p. 251; M.J. Buss's review of the same volume, in *JBL* 89 (1970), p. 468.

11. E.S. Gerstenberger, 'Psalms', in J.H. Hayes (ed.), *Old Testament Form Criticism* (TUMSR, 2; San Antonio, TX: Trinity University Press, 1974), p. 209.

formed distinct genres'.[12] Notwithstanding their stylistic diversity and
adherence to more than one structural pattern, we shall follow the lead
of Gunkel in understanding the hymn of praise as a single form-critical
category. On occasion, we may find it instructive to name those psalms
that closely adhere to the pattern of summons plus proclamation as
imperative hymns of praise—the succinct Psalm 117 is a parade example. In this essay, however, the adjective 'imperative' will be invoked
not to speak for the existence of a distinct genre but simply to highlight
a crucial characteristic of the hymn form.

The Motive Clause as a Legitimate Feature of Israelite Hymnody

We begin by referring not to a hymnic text in the Psalter but to the
poetic couplet attributed to Miriam in Exod. 15.21a:

> Sing to Yahweh, for [כִּי] he has triumphed gloriously;
> Horse and rider he has hurled into the sea.

With its genesis independent from the narrative Exodus tradition, this
exceedingly brief hymn opens with a summons invoking the assembled
worshippers to praise the deity. At once it anchors that praise in
Yahweh's marvelous deed at the Sea of Reeds. Assessed by Westermann as 'an integral part of descriptive praise',[13] an imperative call to
praise, 'Sing to Yahweh!' initiates the hymn. From that point on we
encounter the ground for praise that is introduced by the Hebrew
particle (כִּי), which in its causative function means 'for', 'because'. In
the present instance, says Martin Noth, the reference is confined 'to the
miracle at the sea, and we may imagine that wherever the Exodus was
recalled in the oldest Israelite worship this hymn had a principal
place'.[14] If the plural imperative clarifies at the outset that Yahweh is
the subject of the hymn, what follows forthrightly provides the reason
why praise is due. The statement of motivation that buttresses the introductory exhortation in Exod. 15.21a invites the label 'motive clause'.

Widely attested in Pentateuchal legislation, motive clauses were first
seriously examined by B. Gemser.[15] After defining them as 'the

12. Gerstenberger, *Psalms*, p. 17.

13. Westermann, *Praise and Lament in the Psalms*, p. 123.

14. M. Noth, *Exodus: A Commentary* (OTL; Philadelphia: Westminster Press,
1962), pp. 121-22.

15. B. Gemser, 'The Importance of the Motive Clause in Old Testament Law',

grammatically subordinate sentences in which the motivation for the commandment is given' and recommending that their German equivalent be *Begründungssätze*,[16] Gemser takes account of both their form and content. Among his most convincing examples is Deut. 24.6, 'No man shall take a mill or an upper millstone in pledge; for [כִּי] he would be taking a life in pledge.' Prone to defend their originality, Gemser claims that motive clauses lack any counterparts in known ancient Near Eastern legal codes. Mindful that Pentateuchal motive clauses open with a diverse range of particles, he rightly observes that the 'motivating or causal conjunction *kî*' was the favored way of linking commandment and motivation.[17] And when no particle separates the motive clause from the legislative item to which it is attached, he identifies the connection as asyndetic.[18] On the basis of their content, Gemser assigns motive clauses in biblical law to four rather imprecisely conceived categories—explanatory, ethical, religious and historico-religious.[19] Aware that his handling of the topic is more suggestive than comprehensive, he concludes by speaking for the coherence between legal and wisdom discourse.

In reflecting on the significance of Hexateuchal legislation, von Rad affirms Gemser's contribution as he sets forth his own stipulation of the motive clause as that which grants a given law to which it is appended a high degree of authority or renders it comprehensible to those charged with obeying it. Above all, attending to legislation in Deuteronomy and the Holiness Code, von Rad reasons, 'Jahweh wants obedience, admittedly; but he also wants men who understand his commandments and ordinances, that is, men who assent inwardly as well. The obedience which Jahweh wants is the obedience of men who have come of age.'[20]

Gemser's pioneering endeavor was appreciably sharpened and supplemented by Rifat Sonsino, whose revised 1975 University of Pennsylvania dissertation was published five years later.[21] He holds that

Congress Volume: Copenhagen, 1953 (VTSup, 1; Leiden: E.J. Brill, 1953), pp. 50-66.

16. Gemser, 'The Importance of the Motive Clause', p. 50.
17. Gemser, 'The Importance of the Motive Clause', p. 53.
18. Gemser, 'The Importance of the Motive Clause', p. 55.
19. Gemser, 'The Importance of the Motive Clause', pp. 55-61.
20. G. von Rad, *Old Testament Theology* (2 vols.; New York: Harper & Row, 1962), I, p. 198.
21. R. Sonsino, *Motive Clauses in Hebrew Law: Biblical Forms and Near Eastern Parallels* (SBLDS, 45; Chico, CA: Scholars Press, 1980).

Pentateuchal commandments and prohibitions are interspersed with explicative notes, parenetic statements and motive clauses, each of which must be perceived on its own terms. In particular, he objects that Gemser does not differentiate between parenesis and motive clauses, but regards both as motive clauses. Sonsino argues that direct appeals of general import that are characteristic of the hortatory discourse of parenesis and explicative notes designed to clarify certain phraseology within Hebrew legislation must be distinguished from motive clauses. Only the latter have as their main purpose 'to provide a *raison d'être* for the law, to justify the appropriateness of the particular legal prescription, to show that the law is just because of the specific reason or purpose formulated therein'.[22] Sonsino states that in most cases, a conjunction or preposition serves as the grammatical particle that opens the motive clause. Otherwise, the legal prescription as the main clause and the motive clause as the subordinate element are linked asyndetically. Whatever the format, all motive clauses 'provide a rationale for the law at hand'.[23]

Sonsino supplements Gemser in two important respects: he attends to relevant data within extra-biblical texts, and he discusses legal motive clauses in relation to their counterparts in other biblical literary genres. Given our topic, we have no reason to consider Sonsino's detection of motive clauses in the Code of Hammurabi and in Middle Assyrian legal tradition, which effectively falsifies Gemser's assertion that biblical legal motive clauses existed without parallel in ancient Near Eastern culture.[24] We should take seriously, however, Sonsino's convincing demonstration that 'motivation is a normal part of speech and is used, whenever needed, in a number of genres throughout the Bible'.[25] Within non-legal biblical literary genres, motive clauses are most often encountered in wisdom texts. Sonsino's appreciation of the role that motive clauses play in wisdom instruction is paralleled, for example, in Wolfgang Richter's analysis of admonition speech in sapiential

22. Sonsino, *Motive Clauses*, p. 68.

23. Sonsino, *Motive Clauses*, p. 105. Also deserving mention is P. Doron's essay, 'Motive Clauses in the Laws of Deuteronomy: Their Forms, Functions and Contexts', *HAR* 2 (1978), pp. 61-77, where he argues against Gemser that the juxtaposition between commandment and buttressing motive clause entails *logical* rather than grammatical subordination (p. 61).

24. Sonsino, *Motive Clauses*, pp. 156-72.

25. Sonsino, *Motive Clauses*, pp. 119-20.

contexts, in William McKane's commentary on Proverbs and in James Crenshaw's discussions about biblical wisdom.[26] Beyond question, no item in Sonsino's monograph has greater bearing on the present paper than his well-informed assertion that motive clauses are at home in various forms of biblical Hebrew poetry, including certain laments, songs of thanksgiving, and *hymns* in the canonical Psalter.[27] To illustrate hymnic use of motive clauses, he cites Pss. 33.4; 96.4 and 147.1, observing that each is introduced by the כִּי particle.[28]

Motive clauses may be discerned in quite varied types of canonical psalms. Psalms of lamentation, songs of thanksgiving, wisdom psalms and hymns all resort to this literary device. Though our focus falls on the last-mentioned of these four form-critical categories, one specific demonstration of motive clause usage in the other three should enhance our sensitivity to this phenomenon.

It is quite conceivable that, in the context of lamentation, the suppliant might voice imperative appeals to the deity that from his own troubled perspective would appear more compelling if they were

---

26. See W. Richter, *Recht und Ethos: Versuch einer Ortung des weisheitlichen Mahnspruches* (SANT; Munich: Kösel, 1966), pp. 37-39, 68-78; W. McKane, *Proverbs: A New Approach* (OTL; Philadelphia: Westminster Press, 1970), pp. 3, 121-22, 155-56, 370, and *passim*; and J.L. Crenshaw, *Urgent Advice and Probing Questions: Collected Writings on Old Testament Wisdom* (Macon, GA: Mercer University Press, 1995), pp. 421-22, where his essay on 'Prohibitions in Proverbs and Qoheleth' identifies the use of motive clauses in various sapiential texts and briefly notes their highly varied formulations.

27. Sonsino, *Motive Clauses*, pp. 114, 118 nn. 178-80.

28. Whereas few scholars have isolated specific lines in psalmic poetry and named them 'motive clauses', Gerstenberger (*Psalms*, p. 144) refers to the presence of 'motive clauses' in Ps. 33.4, and J. Day (*Psalms* [OTG, 14; Sheffield: Sheffield Academic Press, 1990], p. 40), in his discussion of Israelite hymnody, takes account of 'motivation clauses'. In his analysis of the literary structure of the hymn, L. Sabourin (*The Psalms: Their Origin and Meaning* [New York: Alba House, 1970], p. 177) focuses on 'the motives of the praise', and P.D. Miller (*Interpreting the Psalms* [Philadelphia: Fortress Press, 1986], p. 71) speaks of 'motivations' within hymnic discourse. In his description of the hymn form, A. Bentzen (*Introduction to the Old Testament* [2 vols.; Copenhagen: G.E.C. Gad, 1948], I, p. 149) directs attention to 'the cause of the exhortation to praise God'. Studies in psalmic hymnody often refer to the 'reason' or 'basis' or 'ground' for praise. Such terminology accords well with H. Gunkel's mention of the *Begründung* in his form-critical discussion of hymns (*Einleitung in die Psalmen*, p. 43).

accompanied by poignant motivations.[29] Presumably cogent answers
would then emerge, which might adequately cover in advance the
question that God himself might pose, namely, 'Why *should* I come to
your aid?' Opening verses in Psalm 5 yield an outstanding example of
how a motive clause may enhance discourse within an individual
lament. Surely this poem would serve well the need of a faithful Israelite entering the temple in order to offer a sacrifice in the hope that his
distress might be alleviated. As one who has been wrongly accused, he
appeals to the deity to guide him through his torment, demonstrate his
saving help and establish his right. In the opening strophe (vv. 2-4)[30]
urgent words of address assume the form of impassioned imperatives:
'Give ear to my words, O Yahweh; Heed my cry for help.' In its
entirety, the second strophe (vv. 5-7) offers the motivation:

> For [כי] you are not a god who delights in wickedness;
>> Evil cannot abide with you.
>> The boastful cannot stand before you.
> You hate all evildoers;
>> You destroy those who speak lies.
> Murderers and deceivers Yahweh abhors.

By specifically declaring that the evil person cannot be a guest in
Yahweh's house, that the deity delights in goodness and detests treach-
ery, the psalmist gives shape to an elaborate motivation that reminds
Yahweh that he is in fact the arch opponent of evil. Artur Weiser aptly
remarks, 'What is at stake here is the nature of God, more particularly,
his unapproachable holiness which is opposed to anything evil.'[31] This
is at once the psalmist's vision of the deity and his motivational appeal
that for the suppliant's sake, let God be God. If one of the main functions of Torah motive clauses is to make Yahweh's commandments

29. For perceptive reflections bearing upon motivational discourse in lament
psalms, see Gunkel, *Einleitung in die Psalmen*, pp. 130-32, 231-39; E.S. Gerstenberger, *Die bittende Mensch: Bittritual und Klagelied d. Einzelnen im Alten Testament* (WMANT, 51; Neukirchen–Vluyn: Neukirchener Verlag, 1980), pp. 40-42;
and two studies by A. Aejmelaeus: *The Traditional Prayer in the Psalms* (BZAW,
167; Berlin: W. de Gruyter, 1986), p. 77, and 'Function and Interpretation of כי in
Biblical Hebrew', *JBL* 105 (1986), p. 204.

30. In citing psalmic references in this essay, I follow the Hebrew verse numbering, which here and in many instances is one numeral higher than its equivalent
in many English translations.

31. A. Weiser, *The Psalms: A Commentary* (OTL; Philadelphia: Westminster
Press, 1962), p. 126.

more comprehensible to his covenant people, then, conversely, motive clauses advanced in psalms of individual lament might, from a human perspective, be viewed as most useful in making human plight more comprehensible to the deity.

Motive clauses likewise play a vital role in the poetic discourse of thanksgiving psalms. It is not difficult to assume that, in the context of congregational worship, the one who has recently been delivered from severe affliction might invite his companions to join him in thanking Yahweh and, in the process, provide apt motivations for doing so. Such motive clauses are intended for human rather than for divine hearing.[32]

Typically they play an integral role in calls to worship that invite the temple congregation to engage in heartfelt adoration of the deity. Commencing with obvious doxological overtones, Ps. 9.12-13 presents itself as a clear example. In the first bicolon (v. 12) two imperatives (זמרו and הגידו) are assigned strategic positions:

> Sing praises to Yahweh enthroned on Zion!
> Proclaim among the people his deeds!

A bicolon of motivation (v. 13) immediately follows, reminding the worshippers that Yahweh does in fact address the needs of those who suffer affliction:

> For [כי] the avenger of blood has remembered them;
> he does not forget the cry of the afflicted.[33]

In the temple the psalmist relates in celebratory fashion Yahweh's saving help that he has received. His summons to the faithful assembled there is grounded in his own personal awareness that the deity is inclined in a special way toward the underprivileged. As is also the case in thanksgiving contexts reflected in Pss. 22.25 and 30.6, well-framed motive clauses make the summons for congregational praise all the

---

32. To be sure, some motive clauses in psalms of individual thanksgiving are addressed to the deity. For example, in Book I of the Psalter (Pss. 1–41), such poems in roughly equal measure yield motive clauses addressed to Yahweh and to the assembled congregation. Psalms 9.14-15; 31.2-5, 10-11, 17-19 and 41.11 host motive clauses intended for divine hearing, whereas Pss. 9.12-13; 22.24-25; 30.5-6; and 31.24 host motive clauses intended for human hearing. In the former category, the motivations accompany petitions for favorable divine intervention that strongly resemble those voiced in psalms of individual lament.

33. To achieve clarity, the Hebrew ordering of the cola in v. 13 is transposed in the Jewish Publication Society translation.

more compelling. And, as we shall soon discover, they honor a similar purpose in psalmic hymns.

Moreover, since the motive clause fulfills a crucial function in various admonitory couplets in the book of Proverbs, it comes as no surprise that it surfaces with some regularity in the wisdom poetry of the Psalter. For a specific instance, we turn to Psalm 1, which is frequently identified as a wisdom composition.[34] Opening confidently with an אשרי formulation (v. 1) declaring whose life is blessed, Psalm 1 concludes with a forthright bicolon (v. 6) that buttresses its fundamental message. In the process of proclaiming who is divinely favored and who is not, the psalmist enlists in v. 6 a motive clause on which he rests his testimony:

> For [כי] Yahweh watches over the way of the righteous,
> but the way of the wicked will perish.

As Walther Zimmerli has shown,[35] the אשרי formulation stands midway between sentence (*Aussagewort*) and admonition (*Mahnwort*). Here third-person assertion claims the emphatic force of a second-person admonition. It instructs how an individual should act. Thus Psalm 1 recommends with all seriousness that Torah be embraced. Through its motivation in v. 6, an appeal to the efficacy of divine justice is confidently sounded. As further examples in Psalms 34 and 37 make clear,[36] in their direct address to seekers of wisdom, motive clauses in sapiential psalms have a penchant for highlighting a manifestly cherished retribution motif that is heavily invested in the temporality of evildoers, the well-being that awaits the godly and the efficacy of divine justice.

Whereas motive clauses are a readily identifiable element of poetic discourse in individual laments, thanksgiving compositions and wisdom poems in the canonical Psalter, they are no less a legitimate feature of Israelite hymnody. There is no better way to discern their presence than to take account of the way in which many psalmic hymns are structured.

Ordinarily the hymn is set in motion by a summons to praise. The

34. For my own defense of Psalm 1 as a wisdom psalm, see J.K. Kuntz, 'The Canonical Wisdom Psalms of Ancient Israel: Their Rhetorical, Thematic, and Formal Dimensions', in J.J. Jackson and M. Kessler (eds.), *Rhetorical Criticism: Essays in Honor of James Muilenburg* (PTMS, 1; Pittsburgh: Pickwick Press, 1974), p. 206.

35. W. Zimmerli, 'Zur Studien der alttestamentlichen Weisheit', *ZAW* 51 (1933), p. 185.

36. See Pss. 34.10-11; 37.1-2, 4, 5-6, 8-9, 27-28a, 34 and 37-38.

words 'Rejoice in Yahweh', 'Sing to Yahweh', 'Raise a shout to Yahweh' and 'Praise Yahweh' respectively initiate Psalms 33, 98, 100 and 117. Such calls to worship tend to be framed in a plural imperative form of address to an audience whose identity is disclosed by a vocative (e.g. 'you righteous' in 33.1; 'all the earth' in 100.1; 'all you nations' in 117.1). Then comes a section that offers the ground (*Begründung*) for praise. This is commonly introduced by the Hebrew particle כִּי, which, as we previously noted, means 'for', 'because' in its causal function. Motive clauses tend to cluster in this main portion of the hymn, which advances various characteristics and actions of Yahweh as the *reason* for praise. The basic structuring of Miriam's famous couplet (Exod. 15.21a), which we have already noted, is hereby replicated. A summons *to* praise ('Sing to Yahweh') is fused with a reason *for* praise ('for [כִּי] he has triumphed gloriously'). In some instances a hymn will enlist as its final component a renewed summons to praise. Such recapitulation completes the circle, as it deftly echoes the note that was struck at the outset.

In the briefest manner possible, Psalm 117, widely acknowledged as the Psalter's shortest composition, illustrates the fundamental structure of the Israelite hymn of praise. This independent unit is rightly assessed by Walter Brueggemann as 'almost a pure form waiting to be claimed for more substantive and specific content'.[37] In the bicolon of v. 1 we meet the introductory summons to praise:

> Praise Yahweh, all you nations!
> Extol him, all you peoples!

As the main section, the bicolon in v. 2ab presents the motive for praise:

> For [כִּי] great is his steadfast love toward us;
> and the faithfulness of Yahweh is everlasting.

As the concluding element, the monocolon in v. 2c repeats the summons to praise:

> Praise Yah(weh)!

The definitive fusion of the summons *to* praise and reason *for* praise that is foundational in the biblical paradigm of the hymn likewise

37. W. Brueggemann, *The Message of the Psalms: A Theological Commentary* (AOTS; Minneapolis: Augsburg, 1984), p. 199.

appears in bold relief in Psalm 136. As a fixed liturgical antiphon, the hymn opens with a summons to the congregation to render thankful praise to the deity: 'Give thanks [הודו] to Yahweh!' This initial colon achieves closure in the phrase, 'for he is good' (כי טוב). With extraordinary brevity, a reason is advanced to account for the praise of God. Indeed, to announce that the deity is good is 'to affirm that the Lord of Israel is the source of all that makes life possible and worthwhile'.[38] Solely consisting of a crucial particle and predicate adjective, that motivation is amplified by the colon that immediately follows: 'For [כי] his steadfast love is everlasting.' As a stereotypical formula, this second member of the hymn's opening bicolon is appropriated as the second member of all 25 bicola that follow, until the entire composition comes to rest in a renewed summons to render thankful praise:

> Give thanks to the God of heaven,
> For [כי] his steadfast love is everlasting (v. 26).

As a recapitulation of the theme struck at the beginning, this terminating bicolon effectively completes the circle. When Psalm 136 is viewed in its entirety, it appears that its first three bicola (vv. 1-3) constitute a summons to divine praise that so characteristically initiates Israelite hymns. In the main body of the psalm (vv. 4-25), splendid deeds of Yahweh in behalf of his covenant people become the ground—indeed, the very motivation—for praise. Finally, as a forceful recapitulation, the concluding bicolon rounds off the whole. Clearly, Psalm 136 yields an effective fusion of the summons *to* praise and motivating reason *for* praise that is basic to Israelite hymnody.

Admittedly, the basic hymn form that is particularly evident in Psalms 117 and 136 is not lacking in variation as it makes itself known in the Psalter. As we shall have occasion to observe in some detail, the introductory summons to praise may incorporate a sweeping array of plural imperatives; the motive or reason for praise may span several verses that enlist both finite verbs and participial ascriptions; the introductory summons may be renewed and extended in the body of the hymn; and a new section enumerating additional motives for praise may present itself.

If a careful analysis of hymnic structure promises to heighten our sensitivity to the presence of motive clauses in Israel's songs of praise,

---

38. P.D. Miller, '"Enthroned on the Praises of Israel": The Praise of God in Old Testament Theology', *Int* 39 (1985), p. 12.

it will also call our attention to the specific ways whereby motive clauses are set in motion. Gemser was mindful that 'formally the motive clauses are not all of one and the same type' and that the type commencing with 'the motivating or causative conjunction' כִּי (for, because) is especially well attested.[39] Of course, other options were available for introducing motive clauses in the Torah. Those most worthy of mention are the ו conjunction as *Waw explicativum*, the dissuasive conjunction פֶּן (lest), the conjunction לְמַעַן (for the sake of, so that) with occasional promissory thrust and asyndetic constructions.

Each of these four options is likewise discernible within diverse *Gattungen* in the Psalter. In Ps. 37.4, 6, 27 and 34, the *Waw explicativum* effectively initiates motive clauses within a wisdom psalm. Thus, in 37.27 the first member of the bicolon offers an admonition and the second a motivation. The poet advises the one who searches for wisdom, 'Turn from evil and do good, *and* you shall abide forever.' As an individual lament, Psalm 13 attests a twofold usage of פֶּן as the agent chosen to introduce motive clauses that might induce the deity to act favorably toward the suppliant. It is not enough for him to address Yahweh with two imperatives, 'look upon me, answer me' (v. 4a). He will also attempt to motivate the deity by insisting that now is the time to manifest his saving presence *lest* (פֶּן) he 'sleep the sleep of death' (v. 4b), *lest* (פֶּן) his enemy say, 'I have prevailed' (v. 5a). And as it resolutely focuses on purpose, the conjunction לְמַעַן initiates the brief motive element in Ps. 6.5 that accompanies the suppliant's urgent request of the deity. In this individual lament, the imperative 'deliver me' is buttressed by the motivation, 'for the sake of your steadfast love' (לְמַעַן חַסְדֶּךָ). Finally, Psalm 31 yields an asyndetic motive clause that lacks any distinctive marker. As this composition modulates from an individual lament into an individual song of thanksgiving for divine help already rendered, the worshipping congregation as Yahweh's faithful is urged to 'love Yahweh' (v. 24a). That plural imperative is fused to the asyndetic motivation, 'Yahweh preserves the loyal, but repays the arrogant in full' (v. 24bc). We thereby confront a motive clause rooted in the notion of retributive justice.

It is noteworthy that, whereas motive clauses play a vital role in hymns of praise as they do in other psalmic *Gattungen*, they are introduced with truly minimal variation. Of the four options enumerated in the preceding paragraph, three are entirely lacking in hymnic

39. Gemser, 'The Importance of the Motive Clause', p. 53.

motive clauses. Not once does one encounter a *Waw explicativum*, the dissuasive conjunction פֶּן or the purpose-oriented conjunction לְמַעַן. When the hymnists of the Psalter set about framing motive clauses, they seemed content to open them in merely two distinct ways. In many instances they resorted to the causal conjunction כִּי. Otherwise they depended on asyndetic constructions of two types—participial and non-participial.

After setting aside the bicola of Ps. 136.2-26, whose second member ever replicates its counterpart in the opening bicolon of this impressive litany, I would with some confidence submit that 20 verses in the hymns of the Psalter offer motive clauses that commence with the כִּי particle. They appear in Pss. 33.4, 9; 47.3, 8; 95.3, 7; 96.4, 5, 13 (twice); 98.1; 99.9; 100.5; 117.2; 135.3 (twice), 4; 136.1 (twice); 147.13; 148.5, 13 and 149.4.

Though asyndetic hymnic motive clauses are less abundant than those initiated by the causal conjunction כִּי, they are not rare. We turn first to the participial type. At five junctures these hymnic motivations, lacking a distinctive marker, open with a masculine singular participle whose subject is always the deity. Three attest a prefixed ה article in its role as a relative pronoun and two do not. The latter appear in Pss. 33.5 and 66.5. The motive clause in Ps. 33.5 commences with the Qal participle אֹהֵב ('He [Yahweh] loves righteousness and justice') and that in Ps. 66.5 commences with the Niphal participle נוֹרָא ('He [God] is held in awe by humankind for his deeds'). The former, bearing the ה article, appear in Ps. 66.9; 103.3 and 147.8. In Ps. 66.9 the motivation is initiated by הַשָּׂם, a Qal participle referring to the deity 'who has kept' his people 'among the living' by virtue of protecting them. In Ps. 103.3 the motivation opens with the Qal participle הַסֹּלֵחַ, denoting Yahweh 'who forgives' humanity's iniquity, and in Ps. 147.8 the motivation commences with the Piel participle הַמְכַסֶּה, portraying the creator deity 'who covers the heaven with clouds'.

Moreover, the asyndetically constructed motive clauses in Psalms 103 and 147 display one other important feature. In contrast to the asyndetic motivation in Ps. 66.9, whose opening word offers a solitary participial ascription for deity in its bicolon, the motivations initiated in Pss. 103.3 and 147.8 yield an entire series of ascriptions. In Psalm 103, the basis for the imperative 'to bless' Yahweh spans three bicola (vv. 3-5) that host a generous total of five masculine singular participles. The beneficent God whom this psalm celebrates 'forgives' (סֹלֵחַ), 'heals'

(רפא), 'redeems' (גואל), 'crowns' (מעטר) and 'satisfies' (משביע). And in Psalm 147 the motivation spanning five cola (a tricolon in v. 8 and a bicolon in v. 9) yields three participles (מצמיח, מכין and נותן) that collectively enrich the motivation that was engaged by the initial participle המכסה in v. 8a. In this motivation, the deity who merits a thankful song of praise (v. 7) is fully celebrated as the one who 'provides rain', 'makes grass grow on the mountains' and 'gives the beasts their food'.

Asyndetic hymnic motive clauses of the non-participial type are infrequent. Three present themselves in Pss. 33.1, 99.5 and 100.3. In Ps. 33.1 the initial imperative that the righteous 'rejoice' in Yahweh is accompanied by an asyndetic motivation, commencing with לישרים— 'praise befits the upright'. In Ps. 99.5 the command to exalt Yahweh and render obeisance is grounded in the highly succinct motivation, 'holy is he!' (קדוש הוא). This compelling attribute of the deity is thought sufficient to warrant the praise of humankind. Finally, Ps. 100.3 features a non-participial asyndetic motive clause that is initiated by the subject personal pronoun הוא—'He made us and his we are.'[40] Belonging to the creator deity becomes the ground for praise.

We have already noted that once the hymn has issued an initial summons to praise, it moves forward with the expression of praise itself by means of a causal clause. Intended to advance a reason for praise, it customarily commences with the כי particle. Since it plays such a central role in the introductory formulary of hymnic motive clauses, it is imperative that we reflect more fully on this critical word. In his pioneering study, James Muilenburg celebrates this morpheme as one among several Hebrew particles that function as 'the signals and sign-posts of language…guides to the progress of words, arrows directing what is being spoken to its destination'.[41] He was fully aware of their capacity to confirm and emphasize what is being asserted. Similarly, his student, Phyllis Trible, insists that in the configuration of Hebrew rhetoric, 'particles are no small matter'.[42] Readily disposed to Muilenburg's judgment that the conjunction כי exhibits a highly varied

40. We accept the *Qere* variant that is supported by Aquila, Jerome and Targum, and followed by nearly all contemporary translations.

41. J. Muilenburg, 'The Linguistic and Rhetorical Usages of the Particle כי in the Old Testament', *HUCA* 32 (1961), p. 135.

42. P. Trible, *Rhetorical Criticism: Context, Method, and the Book of Jonah* (GBSOT; Minneapolis: Fortress Press, 1994), p. 104.

range of nuance in the Hebrew Bible, Trible avers that this 'little word harbors a multitude of meanings'.[43]

Assessed by J. Pedersen as the most comprehensive of all Hebrew particles,[44] כי commonly fulfills a demonstrative function. And as a word pointing the way forward, it is deictic in character.[45] In that capacity it can 'accent vital information and account for motivation'.[46] Due to its remarkable versatility, כי was undoubtedly a favored word among ancient Hebrew poets. Recognizing that only the paratactic ו outdistances כי in frequency as a clause connector, Anneli Aejmelaeus asks, 'How was it at all possible that one particle could be used in so many different contexts?'[47] Whereas she may be criticized for minimizing the emphatic and asseverative aspects of this conjunction, Aejmelaeus is well informed about the role performed by כי as a connective that links one clause with another. Moreover, her claim that 'the great majority of כי clauses *following* the main clause may be characterized as causal clauses' is pertinent to our own inquiry.[48] Even so, as we approach hymnic texts that yield elements of causation, we should bear in mind that 'the causal relation expressed by כי is sometimes subtle, especially in poetry, and not apparent without careful study of a passage'.[49]

Of course, specific meanings of כי vary according to context. Though it is not uncommon for this conjunction to serve the needs of Hebrew

43. Trible, *Rhetorical Criticism*, p. 145.

44. J. Pedersen, *Israel: Its Life and Culture* (2 vols.; London: Geoffrey Cumberlege, 1926), p. 118.

45. Intent on establishing that this is the case, Muilenburg ('The Particle כי in the Old Testament', p. 136) appropriates Pedersen's suggestion (*Israel*, p. 118) that the presence of כי in Hebrew discourse 'may mean that something is now coming to which we must pay attention'.

46. Trible, *Rhetorical Criticism*, p. 143.

47. Aejmelaeus, 'Function and Interpretation of כי', p. 193.

48. Aejmelaeus, 'Function and Interpretation of כי', p. 199. She uses the adjective 'causal' in the broad sense as 'cause, reason, motivation, and explanation' (p. 202). In his essay, 'Speaker-Orientated Functions of *kî* in Biblical Hebrew' (*JNSL* 11 [1983], p. 44), W.T. Claassen argues that beyond establishing causal relationships, כי regularly discloses 'the structure of an argument, the speaker's own position towards his hearer and towards factors which have influenced him'.

49. BDB, p. 473. Moreover, Aejmelaeus's own admission that 'Hebrew does not make all the distinctions that other languages make concerning the logical relationships between clauses' (*Prayer in the Psalms*, p. 77) puts interpreters on notice to exercise great care in their close reading of biblical texts.

rhetoric by signaling emphasis and lending itself to such English renderings as 'indeed' and 'surely', its use as a word of motivation where
it is perceived causally is ubiquitous.[50] Attentive to the logical relationship that ensues between clauses, Aejmelaeus observes that in
Israelite hymnody, כי performs a vital role 'in invitations to praise followed by a description of God's blessings or God's greatness as
motivation to praise'.[51] Here she cogently maintains that such usage
exhibits *indirect* causality. Indeed, in Hebrew discourse, the logical
linkage of a causative כי clause to a preceding clause can span 'from a
strictly causal and, for the main clause, necessary statement to a loose
and indirect explanation'.[52] An indirectly causal statement, therefore,
does not actually set forth the cause for what is asserted in the
antecedent main clause. Rather, it states the *reason* for saying it. This
means that 'a motivation, introduced by כי and following an imperative
petition, is typically indirect in its causality'.[53] Surely, when motive
clauses situated in the Psalter's songs of praise are perceived in that
light, the conjunction that commonly introduces them will be more
readily understood as performing a crucial causal function.[54]

Finally, some account must be taken of the position of Frank
Crüsemann, who advances a radically different understanding of the
second part of the hymn of praise that so often commences with the כי
particle once the summons to praise has run its course.[55] He insists that

50. See Muilenburg, 'The Particle כי in the Old Testament', pp. 145, 150; also
his formative essay, 'Form Criticism and Beyond', *JBL* 88 (1969), p. 14.

51. Aejmelaeus, 'Function and Interpretation of כי', p. 204.

52. Aejmelaeus, *Prayer in the Psalms*, p. 76.

53. Aejmelaeus, *Prayer in the Psalms*, p. 76.

54. Of course, to speak for the importance of recognizing כי as a connective that
effectively establishes psalmic clauses in a causal relationship is not to discount the
role it plays as an emphasizing particle. On the one hand, A. Schoors is justified in
objecting that M. Dahood overplays the importance of emphatic כי in the Psalter
(see Schoors, 'The Particle כי', in B. Albrektson [ed.], *Remembering All the Way: A
Collection of Old Testament Studies Published on the Occasion of the Fortieth
Anniversary of the Oudtestamentisch Werkgezelschap in Nederland* [OTS, 21;
Leiden: E.J. Brill, 1981], p. 253; Dahood, *Psalms III: 101-150* [AB, 17A; Garden
City, NY: Doubleday, 1970], pp. 101-50, 402-406). On the other hand, its presence
in psalmic discourse is readily evident. With regard to Ps. 147, a hymn that is
resourceful in its employment of motive clauses, Dahood rightly discerns the
twofold usage of the particle in its opening bicolon as emphatic כי intended as an
interjection: 'How good to hymn…How pleasant to laud! (p. 406).

55. Crüsemann, *Formgeschichte von Hymnus und Danklied*, pp. 32-35.

the כִּי clause should not be construed as a *reason* for praise. Rather, this crucial particle moves the hymn forward by inaugurating a clause that is part of *divine praise itself*. It is the direct fulfillment of the summons to praise with which the hymn opens. Crüsemann therefore credits כִּי with the vital role of introducing not a *motivation* for praise but rather the actual *contents* of the praise, even the words uttered or sung by those who are summoned to praise. Hence, the כִּי clause voices what is mandated in the summons to praise.

To substantiate this innovative interpretation of כִּי, Crüsemann first appeals to the logic of the imperative hymn form. He believes that something other than a motivation is needful at this juncture. Reason dictates that if a summons to praise is issued, then what is anticipated is the *act* of praise and not some *justification* that might help to evoke it. Also Crüsemann draws upon the practice of antiphonal singing that can be inferred from Psalm 118. In vv. 2-4, 'Israel', 'the house of Aaron' and 'those who fear Yahweh' are each in turn invited to praise Yahweh by declaring, 'His steadfast love is everlasting'. In this instance (and doubtlessly Crüsemann would read Psalm 136 similarly), what follows the invitation (vv. 2a, 3a, 4a) is surely not a reason but the actual response to the summons to praise (vv. 2b, 3b, 4b). And this thrice-uttered response commences with כִּי, as does the word of praise sung by the priests and Levites in Ezra 3.11, who proclaim in cultic celebration, 'For he [Yahweh] is good, his steadfast love for Israel is everlasting.' Again, what seems to be at issue is not a reason for praise but praise itself. Moreover, Crüsemann alludes to Isa. 48.20; Jer. 31.7 and Ps. 66.3 as cases in which the actual content of speaking immediately follows the summons to speak (אִמְרוּ). It is tempting to add Ps. 96.10 to his list, since in this hymn that employs motive clauses with extraordinary success we meet a tricolon that begins, 'Say [אִמְרוּ] among the nations, "Yahweh reigns!"' Nevertheless, in all four of these passages the כִּי particle is wanting, a fact that appreciably jeopardizes his argument.

Admittedly, Crüsemann's position rightly calls into question any approach that might knowingly or unknowingly turn Israelite hymnody into an excessively rationalistic phenomenon. Here Crüsemann's thinking shows some affinity with that of Carroll Stuhlmueller who advances this important clarification:

> The body of the hymn does not offer the reason for praise, as though we
> praise God after studying the reasons sufficiently. The purpose of the

central section of the hymn is more to sustain wonder and adoration in God's presence, to involve the worshipping community in God's glorious action.[56]

Even so, in his commentary Stuhlmueller assuredly gives causal clauses in biblical hymnody their due, since he openly refers to 'the motivation of praise' that is indigenous to the hymn. Also, as he spells out the structure of several songs of praise, he identifies units of motivation that span one, two or even more verses.[57] Surely Crüsemann could look to Stuhlmueller for only modest endorsement.

The same may be said with respect to the views of Patrick Miller. In his insightful analysis of hymnic form, which carefully attends to Crüsemann's assertions, Miller concedes that Psalms 113 and 146 present themselves as hymns in which the initial imperative call to praise (113.1; 146.1-2) is followed by lines that 'function more as expression of praise or the carrying out of praise than a reason for giving praise'.[58] Even so, he aptly observes that in neither hymn does the call to praise evoke a line sequence that is introduced by the כִּי particle.

What is especially problematic in Crüsemann's approach is his assumption that the כִּי constructions in the texts he examines make no sense unless they are understood as emphatic. Undoubtedly aware that this particle often heads causal clauses in Hebrew discourse, Day briefly objects that Crüsemann's perception of כִּי 'runs counter to normal Hebrew usage'.[59] Aejmelaeus's critique is more specific. Insisting that Crüsemann lacks any linguistic warrant for his claim that כִּי, following an imperative summons to praise, introduces not a motivation but the actual contents of the praise, she maintains that the particle in such contexts functions causally and not emphatically. Based on her knowledge of Hebrew linguistics, Aejmelaeus argues that

> the possible functions for כִּי after the imperatives of verbs denoting 'to praise', 'to sing', 'to declare', and 'to thank' would be to introduce either a motivation adhering to the imperative or possibly a completing

56. C. Stuhlmueller, *Psalms 1* (OTM, 21; Wilmington, DE: Michael Glazier, 1983), pp. 34-35.

57. Stuhlmueller, *Psalms 1*, p. 35; see also pp. 189 and 245, as well as *Psalms 2* (OTM, 22; Wilmington, DE: Michael Glazier, 1983), p. 95.

58. P.D. Miller, *They Cried to the Lord: The Form and Theology of Biblical Prayer* (Minneapolis: Fortress Press, 1994), Appendix 2, p. 361.

59. Day, *Psalms*, p. 40.

'that' clause adhering to the meaning of the verbs mentioned. With these
two alternatives one can hardly find any justification in adopting a third
one.[60]

Additionally, she suspects that Crüsemann has been diverted by his
misunderstanding of how כי might function in a subordinate clause that
seems to impart the 'main content' of the text in question. She submits
that the Hebrew usage of the imperative accompanied by כי constitutes
a form of expression that is triggered by 'the need of a connective other
than ו and the wide range of usage of כי from directly causal to motivating and loosely explanatory cases'.[61] She also claims that, within
diverse genres in the Hebrew Bible, to encounter a motivating כי
following the imperative is to encounter a fundamental mode of expression in a language that is not rich in 'syntactical resources'. Finally,
Aejmelaeus argues that anyone who endorses Crüsemann's notion that
כי clauses convey the contents of praise is constrained to conclude that
'Hebrew expresses these contents by means of a motivation clause'.[62]

Miller reaches a similar judgment after voicing three trenchant
objections to Crüsemann. First, Crüsemann is too inclined to dismiss a
causal reading of כי in favor of an emphatic or deictic one. Whereas the
latter usage is doubtlessly discernible in both Hebrew and Ugaritic, its
prominence in Hebrew discourse is sometimes overstated. Second, it
seems strange that ancient versions have not been more vigilant in
detecting the presence of כי as an emphasizing particle in the Hebrew
Vorlage, if its usage in the hymnic form is as widespread as Crüsemann
assumes. Third, Crüsemann's approach falters in its failure to recognize
the fact that, with the exception of the stereotypical expression, 'for his
steadfast love is everlasting' (Ps. 118.2-4), the כי particle is *absent* in
those hymns that yield a summons to praise, whereupon those so
summoned are specifically told what to say.[63] Consequently, Miller is
unwilling to abandon the view that it is customary for hymns of praise
in the Psalter to offer causal clauses engaged by the כי particle that
enumerate explicit reasons for praise. At the same time, he concedes
that such clauses may be construed as statements *of* praise that
celebrate Yahweh. Since the hymn aspires both to 'elicit' praise and to

---

60. Aejmelaeus, *Prayer in the Psalms*, p. 78.
61. Aejmelaeus, *Prayer in the Psalms*, p. 78.
62. Aejmelaeus, *Prayer in the Psalms*, p. 79.
63. Miller, *They Cried to the Lord*, p. 359.

'set forth' praise,[64] the *reason* for praise and the *act* of praise should not be bifurcated as hermetically sealed phenomena. For example, as he reflects on Ps. 96.4-6, Miller cogently insists that 'the reasons for praise indeed become expressions of praise'.[65] And this explains why such a motive clause as 'for his steadfast love is everlasting' can stand independently as a statement of praise (Ezra 3.11).

Clearly, the hymns of the Psalter are so framed that three distinctly identifiable components advance toward a common goal of praising the deity. The imperative summons to the assembled congregation that extends the invitation *to* praise, the כִּי-initiated as well as asyndetic clauses that yield motivating grounds *for* praise and those hymnic lines that are most felicitously identified as expressions *of* praise, *all three*, are mutually pledged to the act of celebrating Yahweh. Having established that the motive clause is both a legitimate and prominent feature of Israelite hymnody, we now turn our attention to specific segments of hymnic texts in the Psalter that exhibit that feature to its best advantage.

Hymns Attesting Pronounced Usage of Motive Clauses

Whereas a total of 15 hymns in the Psalter yield motive clauses, they may be said to be more prominent in eight songs of praise and less so in seven others. To the former category belong Psalms 33, 47, 95, 96, 100, 117, 136 and 148, and to the latter category Psalms 66, 98, 99, 103, 135, 147 and 149. Since space does not permit a close analysis of all passages, we shall limit our focus to the first mentioned set of psalms, in which the motivational element is more pronounced.[66] With one

---

64. These verbs are used by Miller (*Interpreting the Psalms*, p. 69) as he identifies the 'primary aim' of the song of praise.

65. Miller, *They Cried to the Lord*, p. 360.

66. The second mentioned set of psalms that manifests a more modest usage of motive clauses may be summarily described as follows: (a) Two motivations (vv. 5b, 9) present themselves in Ps. 66, an individual song of thanksgiving (vv. 13-20) prefaced by a general hymn of praise (vv. 2-12). Each opens with a participle that seeks to explicate the deity for whom praise is invoked in the cola that immediately precede them (vv. 5a, 8). (b) The first two bicola of Ps. 98 offer a succinct summons to 'sing to Yahweh a new song' that is supported by a marked motive clause directing attention to his 'marvelous deeds' (v. 1). (c) Psalm 99 hosts two refrains (vv. 5, 9) that employ similar wording. After inviting worshippers to 'exalt' Yahweh and 'pay homage' to him, they point to Yahweh's holiness as the basis for

exception we shall adhere to their canonical ordering. Since Psalms 117 and 136 have already attracted some notice in the previous section, as we sought to set in bold relief the definitive fusion of the summons *to* praise and the reason *for* praise that is foundational in the biblical paradigm of the hymn, we shall revisit these two psalms before turning to the others.

Psalms 117 and 136

As a hymn in miniature that solely consists of two bicola and a concluding monocolon, Psalm 117 first invites the Gentiles to 'praise' (הלל) and 'extol' (שבח) the deity. Engaged by the causative כי particle, the second bicolon presents the ground for these two plural imperatives. Two of Yahweh's enduring attributes, his 'steadfast love' (חסד) and his 'faithfulness' (אמת), are highlighted in a motive clause that is intended to move the nations of world history to join Israel in celebrating the deity. The reason advanced in v. 2ab directs attention to Yahweh not because he is the creator of heaven, earth and nations, but because his 'steadfast love' and 'faithfulness' have impressed themselves upon Israel by virtue of the saving deeds he has performed in his covenant people's behalf. The assertion in v. 2a, 'for great is his steadfast love *toward us*', hosts a decisive prepositional element (עלינו) that catches the attention of Miller, who astutely observes, 'Psalm 117 testifies that what prevails over "us" is not the enemy but the steadfast love of God. The singers of this song know themselves to be dominated, controlled,

---

praise. (d) Psalm 103 begins with two bicola of self-summoning discourse (vv. 1-2, 'Bless Yahweh, O my soul...') that are buttressed by three bicola of motivation (vv. 3-5). These attest a fivefold usage of participial ascriptions that enumerate Yahweh's numerous bounties. As such, these clauses tell why praise is fitting. (e) In Ps. 135, once the thrice-used plural imperative הללו (praise!) has summoned the congregation to worship Yahweh, three motive clauses follow in vv. 3-4. Each is engaged by the causal כי particle. Consisting of the statement 'for Yahweh is good', the first anticipates the initial motivation 'for he is good' in the hymn that immediately follows (Ps. 136.1). (f) Psalm 147 mounts a new strophe in v. 7 that calls worshippers to sing praises to Yahweh. Again attesting a concerted usage of participles that explicate Yahweh, motive clauses in vv. 8-9 offer the basis for praise. Another strophe opens with a renewed summons to praise (v. 12) that is supported by its motive clause (v. 13). (g) In Ps. 149 a richly expressed summons to praise (vv. 1-3) enlisting two plural imperatives and four jussive verbs is accompanied by a motive clause (v. 4) that names Yahweh's vested concern for the welfare of his people as the basis for their praise.

overwhelmed by that love'.[67] If at first glance the reason offered the Gentiles for their praising God seems ill-suited to their specific situation, we must bear in mind that this psalm projects a sure faith that in Israel's salvation 'the nations may see the revelation of God'.[68] Then in its concluding monocolon, 'Praise Yah(weh)!' (v. 2c), Psalm 117 closes an *inclusio*, as it returns to its point of origin. Structured by firmly linked imperative and motivating components, this incisive psalm integrates the summons *to* and the reason *for* praise into a compelling whole.

We return to Psalm 136. This antiphonal hymn, firmly anchored in the context of Israelite worship, presumably enlists the talents of a solo voice and the responding congregation. Each engaged by the same plural imperative, 'Give thanks' (הודו), the summoning of divine praise is the concern of the first half of the three bicola that open the psalm. Their counterparts in the remainder of this litany offer an extensive recital of Yahweh's creating and saving deeds that conveys both the congregation's understanding of the deity it worships and its rationale that is intent on justifying the praise that is commanded.

In this hymn, motive clauses are discernible in three different contexts, of which the first two yield the causative כי particle. First, v. 1a makes its all-embracing claim about Yahweh: 'for he is good'. Secondly, the stereotypical response comprising the second half of every bicolon affirms, 'for his steadfast love is everlasting'. Thirdly, with its disclosure, 'who alone has done great wonders', v. 4 initiates a series of asyndetic motivations that commence with masculine singular participles that proclaim Yahweh's attributes. The cumulative effect of these participial ascriptions, as they are interlaced with the constantly intoned formula of thankful praise, is indeed impressive. Such constructions remind us anew that in the hymns of the Psalter, the *reason* for praise may often be construed as the *expression* of praise itself. The basis and content of praise coalesce.

Psalm 33

As a 'passionate appeal to the mighty and glorious Lord',[69] this song of praise deftly employs motive clauses at three junctures, as it celebrates the deity for his creative word and sovereign control of human history.

67. Miller, 'Enthroned on the Praises of Israel', p. 13.
68. Mays, *Psalms*, p. 373.
69. Gerstenberger, *Psalms*, p. 145.

The hymn commences with a protracted invitation to praise (vv. 1-3) that is dominated by five plural imperatives: רננו (rejoice), הודו (praise), זמרו (sing praises), שירו (sing) and היטיבו נגן (play skillfully). Indeed, as the addressees of the summons, the 'righteous' (צדיקים) of the community are fervently invited to extol Yahweh. Between the first two imperative cola stands the asyndetic motivation, 'praise befits the upright' (לישרים, v. 1b). Here the psalmist reasons that for those who are right with Yahweh, praise is truly appropriate. It makes sense.

Two motive clauses immediately join this elaborate introit, inviting doxology for Yahweh (vv. 4-5). Expressing the basis as well as the content of praise, the first opens with a causative particle and the second is asyndetic:

> For [כי] the word of Yahweh is right [ישר];
> and his every deed is trustworthy [אמונה].
> He loves righteousness [צדקה] and justice [משפט];
> the earth is full of Yahweh's loving kindness [חסד].

Highlighting a rich array of enduring divine attributes, these bicola foremost remind the faithful who this God is whom they are invited to worship. Clearly, they seek to motivate divine praise. Their instruction about Yahweh is no less a naming of reasons why he is worthy of exaltation. Also their potential as genuine *expressions* of praise should not be minimized.

A third juncture of hymnic motivation is discernible in v. 9, as it buttresses a newly articulated summons. Supporting the reasonableness of two jussive verbs in v. 8 that command that all the earth 'fear' Yahweh and all its inhabitants 'stand in awe' of him, the motive clause in v. 9 declares:

> For [כי] he spoke, and it was;
> he commanded, and it stood forth.

The efficacy of Yahweh's work in creation is forcefully articulated as reason for praise. As this 'new song' (v. 3) affords Israel the occasion to sing about a world that is ever new, it speaks convincingly of Yahweh's universal sovereignty. Moreover, the motivating statements that prominently appear in the first half of this general hymn of praise make the invitation to extol the deity all the more compelling.

Psalm 47

Motive clauses are a constituent in four of the enthronement psalms that are commonly isolated as a specific subcategory of the hymn celebrating Yahweh's enthronement as king. These are Psalms 47, 96, 98 and 99. As it sets about proclaiming Yahweh's supreme sovereignty, Psalm 47 offers a dual sequence of summons to praise and reason for praise. Enlisting plural imperatives in both cases, the calls to praise span vv. 2 and 7. In the former line, the verbal summons 'clap hands' (תקעו־כף), and its companion 'raise a shout' (הריעו), are directed to foreign nations (עמים). They distinctively address *all* peoples (v. 2a), but surely foremost those who have tasted defeat in warfare against Yahweh and his people (v. 4). In the latter line (v. 7), the command 'sing praises' (זמרו) is spoken not once but four times in the hearing of the assembled worshippers. The obvious excitement surrounding it is generated by the crucial cultic moment reflected in v. 6 that immediately precedes: 'God ascends amid acclamation; / Yahweh, amid blasts of the horn.' Both vv. 2 and 7 readily confirm Gerstenberger's generalization that 'a joyful service in the ancient world was a noisy affair'.[70]

These parallel invitations to extol the deity are at once followed by motive clauses whose presence is signaled by the causative כי particle, which links them logically to what precedes.[71] In affirming Yahweh's regal nature ('a great king', v. 3; 'our king', v. 7), these motivations are scarcely terse. At v. 3 כי introduces a stirring basis for praise that ceases only at the end of v. 5. To be sure, v. 8a hosts a compact motive clause of its own: 'for [כי] God is king of the whole earth'. Yet once v. 8b, as a renewed summons, has succinctly commanded, 'Sing a *maskîl*',[72] v. 9a declares, 'God reigns over the nations.' With the goal of elaborating upon the motivation in v. 8a, this colon initiates discourse that takes up the remaining three bicola of the psalm.

As grounds for praise, vv. 3-5 refer to Yahweh's universal kingship, but they more intently focus on Yahweh's success in gaining his rule through triumphant victories over those who strove to impede Israel's taking possession of the land of promise:

70. Gerstenberger, *Psalms*, p. 18.
71. In his essay, '"Yahweh Is King over All the Earth": An Exegesis of Psalm 47', *ResQ* 17 (1974), pp. 85-98, L.G. Perdue holds that whereas the hymnic כי in v. 3 opens a statement focused on 'the attributes and deeds of Yahweh which are worthy of praise', its counterpart in v. 8 opens a statement establishing 'the reason Yahweh is to be praised' (pp. 92, 95). Since the *basis* of praise is at issue in *both* contexts, the contrast that Perdue establishes is not convincing.
72. We adhere to the Hebrew noun since the meaning of this musical term is uncertain.

> He subdues peoples [עַמִּים] beneath us,
> and nations [אֻמִּים] beneath our feet (v. 4).

Brueggemann suggests that the twofold reason offered here is

> characteristically a juxtaposition of two themes in Israel's faith. One
> reason for praise of God is his *universal sovereignty over all peoples.*
> The other reason is *God's peculiar selection of Israel* as his special focus
> of love, with the gift of special land.[73]

Additionally, the God of whom the motivation speaks is one whose
august presence is 'awesome' (נוֹרָא), who is named the Most Exalted
One (עֶלְיוֹן). Finally, as grounds for praise, v. 8a reiterates what the
motivation in v. 3 has already claimed, namely, Yahweh's kingship is
universal. It makes sense, therefore, to make this deity the object of
joyful celebration. Again, the basis of praise is itself the expression of
praise. Nevertheless, to reach that conclusion in no way marginalizes
the important role that motive clauses play in this psalm.

Psalm 95

With its dual sequence of summons to praise and reason for praise, this
imperative hymn resembles Psalm 47. Even so, in its closing verses
Psalm 95 contains a lengthy admonitory component (vv. 7c-11) that
easily distinguishes it from Psalm 47. It urges the bowing community
of worshippers not to model their conduct after their faithless ancestors,
who tested the deity during the era of wilderness wandering. The text
disclosing this earnest warning, however, does not yield data that concern us in the present essay.

This composition is enriched by two substantial calls to praise. The
first (vv. 1-2) begins with the plural imperative לְכוּ (come) and attains
closure with the plural indicative נָרִיעַ (we shall raise a shout).[74]
Between these verbs stand an impressive triad of cohortatives: נְרַנְּנָה (let
us sing joyfully), נָרִיעָה (let us raise a shout) and נְקַדְּמָה (let us come
before). Thus the faithful hear the introit to approach Yahweh. Midway
in the psalm a new strophe opens with a renewed call to praise (v. 6)
that parallels the first. Whereas it lacks a corresponding finite verb, this

73. Brueggemann, *The Message of the Psalms*, pp. 149-50.
74. By not reading this verb as a cohortative, we follow the MT that clearly
attests the indicative. This endorses the position of D.M. Howard, Jr (*The Structure
of Psalms 93–100* [BJS, 5; Winona Lake, IN: Eisenbrauns, 1997], p. 55), who
regards this as an apt way for the poet to conclude the opening summons to praise.

line likewise begins with a plural imperative, namely, באו (come), and immediately moves forward with another triad of cohortatives: נשתחוה (let us pay homage), נכרעה (let us bow down) and נברכה (let us kneel). Whereas Marvin Tate suspects that the change of verbs denotes liturgical movement from outside to inside the sanctuary,[75] that is no certainty. It is perhaps more likely that the richness of the discourse is testimony to the poet's success in framing varied lines that are no less aesthetically pleasing than they are persuasive.

Nevertheless, the invitations to engage in a song of praise stand not in isolation. Both are accompanied by motive clauses that enumerate reasons for praise. Once more, this composition resembles Psalm 47 in several ways: (1) the initial invitation to praise is supported by an extensive motivation spanning three bicola (95.3-5; cf. 47.3-5) that early on affirms Yahweh as 'a great king' (95.3; cf. 47.3); (2) the second motivation is more succinctly articulated (95.7ab; cf. 47.8a); and (3) the causal כי, a little and unpretentious word, sets the various motive clauses in motion (95.3, 7; cf. 47.3, 8).

The motivating statement in 95.3-5 first appeals to the incomparability of Israel's deity:

> For [כי] a great God is Yahweh.
> and a great king above all gods (v. 3).

It then affirms Yahweh's supreme status as creator of the world by speaking inclusively about his continuing relation to its depths and heights, its sea and dry land (vv. 4-5). The other motivation for praise (v. 7) predictably attaches itself to the renewed invitation to extol Yahweh (v. 6):

> For [כי] he is our God,
> and we are the people of his pasturage, and the sheep of his grazing plot.[76]

Just as Yahweh's special selection of Israel figures prominently as the basis for praise in Psalm 47, the motivating force in 95.7 centers on the ongoing relation between Yahweh and the people of his choice.

---

75. M.E. Tate, *Psalms 51-100* (WBC, 20; Dallas: Word Books, 1990), p. 501.

76. Our translation of v. 7b supports the claim, recently restated by Howard (*Psalms 93-100*, p. 56), that the MT requires no emendation. Also it is indebted to the insight of M. Dahood (*Psalms II: 51-100* [AB, 17; Garden City, NY: Doubleday, 1968], p. 354) that the Hebrew Bible is no stranger to the semantic transition which the noun יד, in its meaning 'portion, part', undergoes to denote 'plot, portion of ground'.

Naming Yahweh 'our maker' (v. 6), those who are in covenant connection with the deity openly confess their indebtedness to him as the great king who provides for them.[77]

If what remains in the psalm (vv. 7c-11) consists of earnest admonition for the benefit of those who have bowed the knee before Yahweh, where, then, is the praise? The answer, of course, is that in Psalm 95 the strenuous invocations to worship Yahweh and the poetic discourse establishing the grounds for that worship are themselves praise-oriented statements. The summons *to* praise honors more than its own immediate agenda. Surely no less must be claimed for those elements in the psalm that Kraus designates as 'hymnic argument',[78] namely, the motive clauses that establish the very reason *for* praise.

Psalm 96

The structural pattern that is discernible in Psalms 47 and 95 revisits Psalm 96. An invitation to praise engaging multiple verbs is followed by lines yielding the reason for praise, whereupon additional lines of invitation and reason emerge in that same sequence. As the characteristic exordium of the song of praise, Psalm 96 opens with a forthright summons (vv. 1-3) that Yahweh be made the recipient of manifestly audible praise.[79] The thrice-spoken plural imperative שירו (sing), situated early in the summons, is balanced by three other plural imperatives that follow: ברכו (bless), בשׂרו (proclaim) and ספרו (declare). Once the introit comes to rest with mention of Yahweh's נפלאות (marvelous deeds), two carefully framed clauses, each introduced by the same particle marker, present themselves:

> For [כי] great is Yahweh and most worthy of praise,
>   he is held in awe above all gods.
> For [כי] all the gods of the peoples are idols,
>   but Yahweh made the heavens (vv. 4-5).

77. G.H. Davies ('Psalm 95', *ZAW* 85 [1973], p. 191) designates v. 7ab as the psalm's 'credal and now covenantal affirmation'. Mays (*Psalms*, p. 306) cogently argues that the shepherd image is less a blissful pastoral metaphor than it is 'a royal image of the relation of a king to those he rules' as their 'leader, provider, and protector'.

78. H.-J. Kraus, *Psalms 60–150: A Commentary* (Minneapolis: Augsburg, 1989), p. 247.

79. Whereas Crüsemann (*Formgeschichte von Hymnus und Danklied*, p. 71) states that v. 3 bears a likeness to the instruction to heralds, we concur with Miller (*They Cried to the Lord*, p. 359) that it joins vv. 1-2 as 'part of the call to praise'.

In striking contrast to other deities that in fact are ciphers, Yahweh displayed his awesome power by creating the heavens. Admittedly, these lines could be interpreted as expressions of praise that promptly respond to the invitation to extol Yahweh, which is the hymn's first concern. What is more striking, however, is their potential as causal clauses spelling out reasons explaining that praise is fitting. Yahweh's high status deserves no less. Miller rightly claims, 'This is as much or more *why* praise is called for as it is *what* that praise is.'[80] Indeed, by imparting reasons, the כִּי clauses buttress the invitation to extol Yahweh with compelling warrants.

As a renewed invitation expressly directed both to humanity and to creation itself, a most extensive summons to praise brings us into the second half of the hymn. In fact, the lines spanning vv. 7-12 are concerned with little else. First enlisting plural imperatives (vv. 7-9) and then jussive verb forms (vv. 11-12) too numerous to list here, this poetic discourse mandates that the human family (v. 7) and the entire created world (vv. 11-12) come 'before Yahweh' with sweeping exaltation. Again, a reason *for* praise buttresses the summons *to* praise. Twice resorting to the causative כִּי particle, v. 13 says of Yahweh, 'for he comes, for he comes to govern [לִשְׁפֹּט] the earth'. As one whose majesty is universal, Yahweh is the God-King who comes to rule all things. This decisive disclosure is less an expression of praise than it is motivation for it. Indeed, we may infer that it is the capacity of v. 13 to establish the basis for praise that informs Mays's assertion that Psalm 96 'always places those who sing it in the presence of the LORD who has come and will rule the earth in righteousness and faithfulness'.[81] Once more, psalmic hymnody firmly endorses an item of Israelite faith that it is right that all creation glorify its sovereign Lord in song.

Psalm 100

Clearly, our text is the work of a skilled poet. Consisting of three tricola (vv. 1-2, 3 and 4) and a concluding bicolon (v. 5), Psalm 100 devotes seven of its cola to the goal of *summoning* praise (vv. 1-3a, 4) and four to the goal of providing *reasons* to justify it (vv. 3bc, 5). Despite its brevity, this song of praise does not deviate from the customary sequence: an initial summons supported by reasons (vv. 1-3) finds its

80. Miller, *They Cried to the Lord*, p. 360.
81. Mays, *Psalms*, p. 309.

counterpart in a renewed summons generating its own reasons (vv. 4-5). Although the invitations to praise avoid jussive verb forms, they employ four plural imperatives that we have previously met in similar contexts: הריעו(raise a shout, v. 1), באו (enter, vv. 2, 4), הודו (praise, v. 4) and ברכו (bless, v. 4). In two cola, 'serve [עבדו] Yahweh with gladness!' (v. 2a) and 'Know [דעו] that Yahweh is God!' (v. 3a), other crucial imperatives surface. The latter colon moves us toward the psalm's first motive clause which says of Yahweh:

> He made us [עשנו] and his we are,
> his people and the sheep of his pasturage (v. 3bc).

Yielding the only non-imperative verb in the hymn, this asyndetic motivation engages three consecutive nouns—עם (people), צאן (sheep) and מרעית (pasturage)—that appear in slightly different sequence in the marked motive clause of Ps. 95.7. What is an expression of praise is even more a justification for praise. As the people of God, whose origins and continuing existence undeniably depend on the leadership and protection of their divine king, the gathered congregation can do no other than honor Yahweh with jubilant song.

Finally, in its single concluding bicolon, Psalm 100 offers a marked motive clause that resolutely announces:

> For [כי] Yahweh is good, his steadfast love is everlasting;
> and his faithfulness to all generations (v. 5).

This causal or *Begründung* sentence highlights Yahweh's customary way with his covenant people.[82] It presents the basis of praise as well as its content.[83] This forthright reminder that Yahweh's people are upheld

---

82. Insisting that כי performs an emphatic or performance function, Crüsemann (*Formgeschichte von Hymnus und Danklied*, p. 67) offers, 'Ja, gut ist Jahwe', at the beginning of his translation of v. 5. With Tate (*Psalms 51–100*, p. 534) we find this proposal unacceptable, since the causal interpretation of כי accords well with the flow of thought in this bicolon.

83. This point is well argued by J.L. Mays, 'Worship, World, and Power: An Interpretation of Psalm 100', in Mays, *The Lord Reigns: A Theological Handbook to the Psalms* (Interpretation; Louisville, KY: Westminster / John Knox Press, 1994), pp. 74, 80. Moreover, the success of this bicolon in establishing the *basis* for praise impresses itself on A.A. Anderson (*The Book of Psalms* [2 vols.; NCB; London: Oliphants, 1972], II, p. 700): 'Here the Psalmist gives reasons why God is worthy of praise and thanks. The expression of this motivation is in general terms, well established in cultic usage.'

by divine grace serves admirably as a reason designed to motivate them to make their joyful hallelujahs heard.

Psalm 148

This imperative hymn exhibits several features that largely inform its shape and justify its location near the end of the Psalter, when an escalation of hymnic praise was prized by the editors as the most optimal means for bringing closure to this very substantial portion of the Hebrew canon. First, Psalm 148 stands midway in a series of five songs of praise (Pss. 146–50) concluding the Psalter that are framed by the liturgical exclamation הללו־יה (Hallelujah). Rendered 'Praise Yah!', it consists of a plural imperative summons to praise and an abbreviated form of the Tetragrammaton. Situated at both extremities of the psalm, this highly compressed Hebrew sentence, which is itself a hymn, both summons and expresses praise.

Secondly, Psalm 148 is bifurcated in such fashion that its main sections (vv. 1-6, 7-14) devote approximately three-quarters of their lines to language that summons praise. Lines that articulate the basis and content of praise are minimal. Thirdly, in their prolonged invitations to praise, both halves open with the plural imperative summons, הללו את־יהוה (Praise Yahweh, vv. 1, 7) and in due course shift into jussive speech that mandates, יהללו את־שם יהוה (let them praise the name of Yahweh, vv. 5a, 13a). Fourthly, in both instances the jussive clause is the harbinger of the motive clause that immediately follows (vv. 5b, 13bc). Fifthly, the plural imperative הללוהו ('praise him!'), adverbial phrases and various vocatives all play a conspicuous role in the first main section. By contrast, the imperative and the adverbial phrase each appear only once in the second section, which is heavily freighted with vocatives. Sixthly, a decisive polarity emerges when the opening half-line of the first main section is linked with its counterpart in the second. Whereas v. 1 invites Yahweh's praise מן־השמים ('from the heavens'), v. 7 invites it מן־הארץ ('from the earth').

The psalm summons the entire universe and its creatures to celebrate the deity with impassioned praise. As it recruits Yahweh's praise 'from the heavens' (v. 1), the first main section addresses the celestial choir. Angels and hosts, sun and moon and stars, as well as the highest heavens and the cosmic waters above them hear the call to praise (vv. 1-4). When this protracted invitation is completed in the summarizing jussive clause, 'Let them praise the name of Yahweh' (v. 5a), the motive clause with its causal particle marker is engaged: 'for [כִּי] it was he who commanded that they be created' (v. 5b). Its goal of setting the grounds for praising Yahweh is enhanced by the final bicolon of this first main section of the hymn. It says of the one who created all things celestial:

> He made them endure forever,
> > establishing an order that shall never change (v. 6).

The three closely linked cola moving us toward the midpoint of the psalm therefore affirm that motivation for joyful praise is to be sought in Yahweh's majestic work in creation and his mastery over the heavenly order. Here W.S. Prinsloo avers that the presence of the personal pronoun 'he' (הוּא, v. 5a) in 'a syntactically conspicuous position' ensures that Yahweh's creative work will be readily understood as 'the motive for the call to praise'.[84] And presumably, as they take their assigned positions and fulfill their calling, the diverse celestial aspects of creation are thought to be engaged in glorifying the deity whose word initially commanded their creation (v. 5b).

To be sure, the hymnic interests of Psalm 148 extend even further. On the assumption that it is crucial that praise from heavenly spheres be complemented by praise from terrestrial regions, the second half of this piece invokes a spirited magnificat 'from the earth' (v. 7). It is sought from a remarkably wide range of created beings and entities. To mention sea monsters, fruit trees, kings and maidens is merely to glean a sample of the total array. When on the brink of becoming wastefully extensive, this invitation finds rest in the jussive clause of v. 13a, which is a verbatim replica of its antecedent (v. 5a).

The poet's preoccupation with symmetry persists. The psalm concludes with a motive clause (v. 13bc) along with one further statement (v. 14) in support of its quest to justify the basis of divine praise.[85] In explaining why Yahweh merits exaltation from all terrestrial creatures, the motive clause declares:

---

84. W.S. Prinsloo, 'Structure and Cohesion of Psalm 148', *OTE* 5 (1992), p. 49.

85. Identifying them as corresponding elements, L.C. Allen (*Psalms 101–150* [WBC, 21; Waco, TX: Word Books, 1983], p. 314) rightly interprets vv. 6 and 14 as 'second motivations for praise.' This calls into question Brueggemann's assertion (*The Message of the Psalms*, p. 165) that structurally speaking, v. 14 'appears almost as an addendum to the psalm'.

for [כִּי] his name, his alone, is sublime;
his splendor is above heaven and earth.

Again, the emphasis falls on Yahweh's grandeur as creator of heaven and earth. Then with its supplementary disclosure that Yahweh 'has lifted high a horn for his people', the initial colon in v. 13 calls to mind his previous historical interventions on behalf of his covenant people that have empowered them with dignity. That, too, is basis for praise.

From first to last, Psalm 148 attests Yahweh's magnificent power as creator of all things. If the *summons* to praise is itself a celebration of Yahweh's incomparability, that same claim must be made for the succinctly articulated *basis* for praise that this hymn projects. All lines of the psalm are expressions of praise that render Yahweh the glory due him. Finally, Prinsloo argues that it is the function of Psalm 148 'to *persuade* its hearers to praise Yahweh in an all-embracing way'.[86] If this be so, those among its lines that must be classified as motivational in character are most essential to the whole.

Conclusion

With good reason, Kraus states that worship in the Hebrew Bible is 'not a natural and magical renewal of life, no dramatically engineered importation of power, but an encounter with the Lord of all of life'.[87] Surely those hymns of the Psalter that have invited our attention play a major role in facilitating that encounter. Regularly committed to the task of articulating both the summons inviting God's praise and the basis justifying it, these poems provide the assembled Israelite congregation with a felicitous means for drawing near to the God to whom it knows homage is due.

Diverse summoning statements, along with discourse advancing the corresponding grounds for praise, are most instructive as Israelite testimonies to the deity. Confessing him as maker, king and judge of all creation, these hymns do not take Yahweh's supreme power lightly. And confessing him as singularly faithful and loving, they take account of his historical interventions on Israel's behalf. Time and again, *Israel* is addressed by the numerous exhortations to praise the deity that these hymns voice. As the 'sons of Zion' (Ps. 149.2), as the 'servants' who

86. Prinsloo, 'Structure and Cohesion of Psalm 148', p. 54 (italics mine).
87. Kraus, *Psalms 1–59*, p. 70.

stand in Yahweh's temple (Ps. 135.1-2), as the 'righteous' (Ps. 33.1) whose musicians and singers are singled out (Ps. 33.1-2), the covenant people are urged to extol their God and to advise one another, 'Come, let us sing joyfully to Yahweh!' (Ps. 95.1). Nor is it unusual for the assembled congregation to be targeted by an implied vocative, since with some consistency, imperative plurals are foremost fixed on Israel (Pss. 66.5; 96.1; 98.1; 99.5, 9; 100.2, 4; 136.1; 147.7). Similarly, as the locale where the faithful gather in cultic meeting, Jerusalem/Zion is called to glorify Yahweh (Ps. 147.12). Additionally, the solicitation of Israelite praise is the goal of the self-summons in Ps. 103.1-2. At the same time, the call to glorify Yahweh extends to all nations and peoples (Pss. 47.1; 66.8; 96.1; 117.1), to 'all the earth' (Pss. 33.8; 96.1, 9; 100.1) and indeed to creation in its entirety, with its angels and heavenly hosts (Ps. 148.2), fields and forests (Ps. 96.12), and animals wild and domestic (Ps. 148.10). The entire realm of being is vulnerable to enlistment for Yahweh's praise.

To be sure, the God of Israel is studiously celebrated in the Psalter's songs of praise. 'In the hymns especially', writes Leopold Sabourin, 'God is described by what he has done and by what he is.'[88] Whereas such descriptions normatively serve as bona fide *expressions* of praise, they are not lax in pressing toward the goal of establishing the *basis* for praise. Indeed, the hymns we have inspected richly disclose *why* it is seemly for all creation to exalt Yahweh.

First, Yahweh's many *attributes* are viewed as grounds for praise. Motive clauses affirm that his sublime name (Ps. 148.13) and holiness (Ps. 99.5, 9) denote his incomparability. Thus, he is 'held in awe above all gods' (Ps. 96.4). Yahweh is the 'great king above all gods' (Ps. 95.3), whose sovereignty extends over 'the whole earth' (Ps. 47.3, 8). As a 'great' (Pss. 95.3; 96.4) and 'awesome' deity (Ps. 47.3), he is deservedly named 'the Most High' (Ps. 47.3). Moreover, Yahweh visits his covenant people as the source of upright words and trustworthy deeds (Ps. 33.4), as the one who loves 'righteousness and justice' (Ps. 33.5), as the merciful (Ps. 103.4) and faithful one (Pss. 100.5; 117.2) whose permanent attribute of 'loving kindness' extends itself toward Israel (Pss. 33.5; 100.5; 103.4; 117.2; 136.1). And Yahweh is the forgiver of sins and healer of diseases (Ps. 103.3). Then, if this were still insufficient cause to approach him with jubilant praise, one

88. Sabourin, *The Psalms*, p. 177.

all-embracing attribute is yet to be named: Yahweh is *good* (Pss. 100.5; 135.3; 136.1).

Secondly, motive clauses focusing on Yahweh's many marvelous and awe-inspiring *deeds* are further compelling warrants to praise him. Named the author of 'great wonders' (Pss. 136.4; cf. 66.5; 98.1), Yahweh merits honor as creator of the universe, as the one who brought it into being through his spoken word (Pss. 133.9; 148.5). He created the heavens (Ps. 96.5) and the earth, whose sea and dry land his hands formed (Ps. 95.5) and over whose depths and heights he holds sway (Ps. 95.4). In his sovereignty he governs the earth (Ps. 96.13) and provides for its creatures (Ps. 147.8-9). Moreover, to claim that his right hand ensures him victory (Ps. 98.1) signals his proclivity for historical intervention that upholds the people of his choice. Delighting in Israel whom he created (Ps. 100.3) as his own possession (Pss. 135.4; 149.4), he subdues their enemies (Ps. 47.5), defends them from danger (Ps. 147.13) and continuously sustains their existence (Pss. 47.9; 66.9; 103.4-5). As Israel's own king, Yahweh leads and provides for his people, 'the sheep of his grazing plot' (Ps. 95.7; cf. 100.3). And aware that they are loved by him, they address him as 'our God' (Pss. 95.7; 99.9).

Finally, the hymnic celebration of Yahweh is defended in two succinct motivations declaring that it is a 'pleasant' activity (Ps. 135.3) that 'befits the upright' (Ps. 33.1). Although a strong emotional dimension is indigenous to the divine praise that psalmic hymnody fervently encourages, the motive clauses that it regularly engages to establish the basis for that praise jointly declare that such celebration of the deity indeed makes sense. It is a proper response to what God is and what God has done. By inviting such clauses into their poetry, the hymnists of the Psalter have put a manifestly normal mode of human discourse to extremely good use. A fuller awareness of their engagement in this activity will surely enhance our understanding of the nature of worship in the Hebrew Bible.

MICAH AND A THEOLOGICAL CRITIQUE OF WORSHIP*

Rick R. Marrs

The latter half of the eighth century BCE provides a rich resource for biblical scholars interested in the history, development and nature of Israelite religion. The prophetic books of Amos, Hosea and Isaiah amply testify to the pervasiveness and vitality of cultic activities and religious life in Israel and Judah. The issue of worship is never far from the surface, even in oracles primarily treating political or ethical matters. Although manifesting somewhat different strategies and theological approaches to the conditions of their day, Amos, Hosea and Isaiah speak with a single voice regarding the inextricable relationship between worship, ethics and leadership. These prophets energetically decry the absence of ethical integrity in the lives of the worshippers and their leaders. They lament and denounce an apparently flourishing cult, but a cult devoid of any sense of social responsibility toward the powerless and disenfranchised within the community. Tragically, a fundamental element of worship, viz. the gathering together of a community as community to offer praise and prayer to Yahweh, is non-existent. Well known passages evidence such a situation (see esp. Amos 5.21-24; 8.4-6; Hos. 4.4-6; 6.1-6; Isa. 1.10-17). The oracles of these eighth-century prophets evidence their attempts to reunite worship and daily life. Significantly, Amos, Hosea and Isaiah place a major portion of the blame for the current situation at the feet of the political and religious leadership within their societies.

In the midst of these well-known prophets appears a lesser-known, but equally forceful, prophet. The prophet Micah, from the rural village

* It is a pleasure to dedicate this article to Professor John T. Willis. Professor Willis has been a faithful mentor for me both in his dedication to rigorous and careful scholarship, and in his commitment to share that scholarship with the community of faith. For his lasting influence on my professional and personal life I am truly grateful.

of Moresheth, engages the dramatic historical events and societal happenings of the eighth century with a similar flair. Like his contemporaries, he stridently challenges the divorce of worship and ethical behavior; like Amos, Hosea and Isaiah, he indicts the political and religious establishment for current social travesties.

The book of Micah has received significant scholarly attention in recent years, resulting in widely divergent interpretations.[1] Numerous recent analyses of the book of Micah take a diachronic approach.[2] The redactional history of the book appears complex and merits serious detailed study. Not surprisingly, determining the dates both for individual pericopes and for the final form of the book often rests upon crucial decisions regarding vocabulary, style, theological themes and motifs and presumed social conditions. The conclusions are often striking—the book of Micah reflects a (most likely late) postexilic product containing updatings, additions, accretions and modifications to a modest original body of Mican oracles from the eighth century.[3]

---

1.   For excellent summaries of the key issues in contemporary Micah studies, see J.T. Willis, 'Fundamental Issues in Contemporary Micah Studies', *ResQ* 13 (1970), pp. 77-90; K. Jeppesen, 'New Aspects of Micah Research', *JSOT* 8 (1978), pp. 3-32.

2.   For a sampling of diachronic analyses of the book of Micah, see J.L. Mays, *Micah: A Commentary* (OTL; Philadelphia: Westminster Press, 1976), pp. 21-33; H.W. Wolff, *Micah: A Commentary* (Minneapolis: Augsburg–Fortress, 1990), pp. 26-28; T. Lescow, 'Redaktionsgeschichtliche Analyse von Micha 1-5', *ZAW* 84 (1972), pp. 46-85; *idem*, 'Redaktionsgeschichtliche Analyse von Micha 6-7', *ZAW* 84 (1972), pp. 182-212; *idem*, 'Zur Komposition des Buches Micha', *SJOT* 9 (1995), pp. 200-22; B. Renaud, *La formation du Livre de Michée* (Paris: Gabalda, 1977); I. Willi-Plein, *Vorformen der Schriftexegese innerhalb des Alten Testaments: Untersuchungen zum literarischen Werden der auf Amos, Hosea und Micha zurückgehenden Bücher im hebräischen Zwölfprophetenbuch* (BZAW, 123; Berlin: W. de Gruyter, 1971), pp. 70-114; J. Jeremias, 'Die Bedeutung der Gerichtsworte Michas in der Exilszeit', *ZAW* 83 (1971), pp. 330-53.

3.   The conclusion of B.S. Childs (*Introduction to the Old Testament as Scripture* [Philadelphia: Fortress Press, 1979], p. 430) is apt: 'Although these scholars all agree on a complex history of redaction which passed through many stages, the analyses are so strikingly different that no common conclusions have emerged.' Numerous redactional studies begin with the assumption that authentic material from Micah appears only in chs. 1–3. (How much of these initial chapters derives from Micah is disputed.) There is disagreement about the origin and redactional history of the remaining chapters. Although most scholars regard these chapters (i.e. chs. 4–7) as decidedly later than the eighth century, a minority of scholars

Conversely, several recent analyses take a more synchronic approach to the book of Micah.[4] In these studies, issues of the form and function of the various oracles, as well as their relationship to the larger whole, are paramount. Again, not surprisingly, rather diverse arrangements and divisions of the book are suggested.[5]

Although both approaches remain valid and valuable, the approach of this study will proceed primarily against the synchronic backdrop. Since my primary focus involves determining and delineating a theological understanding of the place and role of worship in the book of Micah, articulating that understanding against the larger backdrop of the whole book is most desirable. My interest entails how subsequent Jewish communities of faith might have heard the message of the book of Micah, and how we, as contemporary listeners, may hear the work.[6]

---

continue to regard significant portions of this material as also stemming from the prophet Micah (see, e.g., E. Sellin, *Das Zwölfprophetenbuch* [KAT, 12.1; Leipzig: Deichert, 1929]; L.C. Allen, *Joel, Obadiah, Jonah, and Micah* [NICOT; Grand Rapids: Eerdmans, 1976]; J.T. Willis, 'The Structure, Setting and Interrelationship of the Pericopes in the Book of Micah', [PhD dissertation, Vanderbilt University, 1966]; D.R. Hillers, *Micah* [Hermeneia; Philadelphia: Fortress Press, 1984]). A comprehensive treatment of this discussion is beyond the scope of the present essay; for further discussion, one may consult the standard commentaries and dictionaries.

4.   For a sampling of synchronic analyses of the book, see Hillers, *Micah*; Allen, *Joel–Micah*; J.T. Willis, 'The Structure of the Book of Micah', *SEÅ* 34 (1969), pp. 5-42; *idem*, 'Fundamental Issues', pp. 77-90; *idem*, 'Thoughts on a Redactional Analysis of the Book of Micah', *SBLSP* 1 (1978), pp. 87-109; L. Luker, 'Beyond Form Criticism: The Relation of Doom and Hope Oracles in Micah 2-6', *HAR* 11 (1987), pp. 285-301.

5.   Several scholars propose a tripartite arrangement of judgment (Mic. 1–3), hope (Mic. 4–5) and further admonitions and comfort (judgment and hope [Mic. 6–7]). Others (e.g. Willis, 'Structure', pp. 5-42; Allen, *Joel–Micah*) propose a tripartite arrangement wherein each section begins with 'hear ye' (1.2; 3.1; 6.1) and judgment gives way to hope (chs. 1–2; 3–5; 6–7). Alternatively, Mays (*Micah*, pp. 2-12) suggests a bipartite division: chs. 1–5 address a universal audience of all peoples; chs. 6–7 address Israel.

6.   The perspective of Hillers (*Micah*, p. 4) is helpful here. He argues that a synchronic reading does not necessarily presume that all the material derives from the career of Micah. Rather, it may presume a recurrent social situation to which the materials, viewed as a product of the community of faith, continue to speak (see also J.L. Mays, 'The Theological Purpose of the Book of Micah', in H. Donner, R. Hanhart and R. Smend [eds.], *Beiträge zur alttestamentlichen Theologie:*

Before proceeding to an analysis of the particular passages in Micah that are germane to an understanding of the presentation of worship in the book, two recent sociological analyses of the prophet Micah and his career are relevant. Two major understandings of the prophet have emerged in the writings of Professors Hans Wolff and Delbert Hillers.

Simply put, Wolff argues that Micah originated as a prophet from the Judean countryside and traveled to metropolitan Jerusalem to speak on behalf of his rural compatriots. Utilizing insights from the larger dynamics present in the waning days of the eighth century BCE in Judah (and Israel), Wolff theorizes that the villages surrounding Jerusalem (specifically those in the Shephelah) were dramatically (and negatively) impacted by social policies implemented by the central Jerusalem authorities. These policies were not value-free; they crippled the economy and socially destabilized several of these towns. Tragically, these villagers lost any 'voice' in cosmopolitan Jerusalem. Micah became their voice. As Yahweh's spokesman on behalf of the beleaguered and despairing poor of the countryside, Micah powerfully denounced the political, social and cultic abuses of the capital city. Wolff's thesis has significant implications for reading the book of Micah.[7] Perhaps most importantly, precise identification of the various

---

Festschrift für Walther Zimmerli zum 70. Geburtstag [Göttingen: Vandenhoeck & Ruprecht, 1977], pp. 276-87).

7.   Wolff's argumentation is intriguing. He argues that Micah clearly is working 'away from home', since he is designated 'the Moreshite'. (Other prophetic cases where home towns are mentioned include Amos [from Tekoa] and Jeremiah [from Anathoth], both prophets best known for their oracles delivered away from their villages.) Jeremiah 26 is central to Wolff's thesis. Jeremiah avoids a death sentence when the 'elders of the land' arise and cite Micah as precedent for proclaiming doom against Jerusalem without receiving a judgment of death. Wolff conjectures that Micah may have belonged to the 'elders of the land' (cf. the 'elders of Judah', 1 Sam. 30.36), who possibly lost all authority to the influx of Jerusalem authorities into the Shephelah. For Wolff, this hypothesis explains many characteristics of Micah's language and appearance. Micah addresses the Jerusalem leaders as 'the heads of the house of Jacob and rulers of the iand of Israel' (3.1, 9). He reserves the designation 'my people' for his rural compatriots (1.9; 2.9; 3.3, 5). Micah forcefully decries the abuse of the Jerusalem officials who have entered towns like Moresheth and confiscated the finest properties and houses for their private use. Against such outrage, Micah stridently proclaims God's 'justice' (משפט). For a complete detailing of Wolff's thesis, see *Micah*, pp. 1-9; *idem*, 'Micah the Moreshite—The Prophet and His Background', in J.G. Gammie *et al.* (eds.), *Israelite Wisdom: Theological and Literary Essays in Honor of Samuel*

audiences and speakers in the book becomes crucial. Specifically identifying Micah's adversaries, as well as his followers, is paramount. Secondarily, passages treating Micah's credibility and authority as a divine emissary take on added meaning.

Moving in a somewhat different direction, while traveling a similar sociological highway, Hillers intriguingly reads Micah's prophetic work against the backdrop of contemporary understandings of millenarian groups. As prophet of a 'new age', Micah was instrumental in initiating and implementing a 'revitalization movement'. Hillers theorizes that Micah belonged to that group that had been disenfranchised and rendered powerless by the Jerusalem hierarchy. He became God's prophetic voice for this abandoned and excluded segment of Judean society.[8] This thesis also has important implications for reading the book of Micah. Given the apparent inability of most diachronic readings of Micah to win adherents, Hillers adopts a more synchronic approach. He compellingly argues that several oracles, typically judged post-Mican by most redaction critical analyses, may in reality derive from Micah. As God's spokesperson of a new age, Micah would have certainly voiced God's multivalent message to the various audiences in attendance. To the Jerusalem power-brokers, doom clouded the horizon; to the disaffected and deprived of the community, hope would surely follow and overwhelm the immediate debacle.

It is against the backdrop of these varied insights of Wolff and Hillers that several key passages can be read profitably. The book of Micah contains oracles addressing the religious and political leaders of Micah's day (e.g. 3.1-12 [esp. 3.5-8, 11]), as well as the religious

---

Terrien (Missoula, MT: Scholars Press, 1978), pp. 77-84; *idem, Micah the Prophet* (Philadelphia: Fortress Press, 1981), pp. 3-25.

8.   Hillers (*Micah*, pp. 4-8) defines 'revitalization' as a 'deliberate, organized, conscious effort by members of a society to construct a more satisfying culture'. He notes that in other societies leaders of such movements need not belong to the lower class. (In medieval Europe millennial movements often derived from lower clergy or nobility.) A major causal factor in the rise of millenarian groups is deprivation resulting from the refusal of the traditional authorities to maintain and regulate the social conditions necessary for meaningful and productive life. Hillers lists five elements in the book of Micah with parallels in revitalization movements: (1) the removal of foreign elements (in preparation for a coming righteous kingdom); (2) a pre-'messianic' age of distress; (3) a reversal of social classes (with the expectation of the dominance of the pariah class); (4) the idea of a righteous, peaceable ruler; (5) a new age characterized by triumph over enemies.

practices (e.g. 1.2-7; 5.9-14 [EVV, 10-15]) and symbols of his day. The book of Micah, like its eighth-century counterparts, intermingles talk of the past, the present and the future.

> For the Israelites shall remain many days without king or prince, without sacrifice or pillar, without ephod or teraphim. Afterward the Israelites shall return and seek the Lord their God, and David their king; they shall come in awe to the Lord and to his goodness in the latter days. Afterward the Israelites shall return and seek the Lord their God, and David their king; they shall come in awe to the Lord and to his goodness in the latter days (Hos. 3.4-5).[9]

> How the faithful city has become a whore! She that was full of justice, righteousness lodged in her—but now murderers! Your silver has become dross, your wine is mixed with water. Your princes are rebels and companions of thieves. Everyone loves a bribe and runs after gifts. They do not defend the orphan, and the widow's cause does not come before them. Therefore says the Sovereign, the Lord of hosts, the Mighty One of Israel: Ah, I will pour out my wrath on my enemies, and avenge myself on my foes! I will turn my hand against you; I will smelt away your dross as with lye and remove all your alloy. And I will restore your judges as at the first, and your counselors as at the beginning. Afterward you shall be called the city of righteousness, the faithful city (Isa. 1.21-26).[10]

Against the backdrop of these two passages the word of Micah regarding worship may profitably unfold. Within the book of Micah a clear vision of God's people as a worshipping community surfaces. In several passages we see the people of God as they were in Micah's day, and the prophet addresses himself forcefully to such conditions. However, radically different oracles concerning the people of God also appear. In these oracles we see God's worshipping community not as it

9. Clearly Hosea's family restoration symbolically impacts any possible national restoration. Through Hosea's proclamation, Israel hears herself stripped of her political securities ('king or prince'), her cultic securities ('sacrifice or pillar') and her divinatory securities ('ephod or teraphim'). Israel's future resides solely in the divine promise. (All quotations are taken from the NRSV, unless otherwise noted.)

10. Isaiah powerfully paints a picture of Jerusalem past, present and future. The formerly faithful city now houses lawlessness and corruption. Not content with the present, Isaiah envisions a restoration of the city to her former faithful and glorious status. However, regaining the former glory involves recapturing a vision of the Sovereign Lord, the Mighty One of Israel, and painfully removing those societal elements that thwart justice and righteousness.

was, but as it could be. Finally, we have hints within the prophetic message that delineate how Yahweh's people might move from their current condition to become what God intended them to be.

God's Worshipping Community — As It Is

Although Micah repeatedly announces that divine punishment is imminent, two passages highlight the place of worship in that judgment. In Mic. 1.2-7 and 5.9-14 (EVV, 10-15), Micah depicts scenes of devastation resulting from Yahweh's advent. The opening scene (1.2-7) is most striking. Cast in the form of a covenant lawsuit (cf. Ps. 50.1-7; Deut. 32; Isa. 1.2-20), Yahweh exits his heavenly palace and strides across the high places (במותי) of the earth. Remarkably, the opening charge addresses 'all peoples' (עמים כלם). Yahweh's zeal to establish justice is universal. Yahweh's appearance has cataclysmic consequences. Mountains melt; valleys split open (v. 4).[11] The cause of such activity is next raised; Yahweh is responding in wrath to the 'transgression' (פשע) and 'sin' (חטאות) of Israel and Judah. However, most revealing is v. 5b:

> What is the transgression of Jacob? Is it not Samaria?
> And what is the high place[12] of Judah? Is it not Jerusalem?

The oracle concludes with a final announcement of punishment (vv. 6-7):

> Therefore I will make Samaria a heap in the open country, a place for planting vineyards. I will pour down her stones into the valley, and uncover her foundations. All her images [פסיליה] shall be beaten to pieces, all her wages[אתנניה] shall be burned with fire, and all her idols [עצביה] I will lay waste; for as the wages [אתנן] of a prostitute she gathered them, and as the wages [אתנן] of a prostitute they shall again be used.

Three aspects of this opening oracle deserve comment: (1) the interplay between Israel and 'the peoples'; (2) the source of the sin; (3) the nature of the sin.

Although the opening call addresses 'all peoples', it quickly becomes clear that the true focal point of the oracle concerns the people of Israel

---

11. Cf. Judg. 5; Amos 1.2. For a striking liturgical parallel to Mic. 1.2-7, see Ps. 97.

12. MT reads 'high places'; the LXX reads 'sins of'.

(and Judah). This raises the question of the function of the peoples. Without denying a possibly complex redactional history for these verses,[13] I would suggest that Mic. 1.2-7 rhetorically functions somewhat akin to Amos 1–2. Amos opens with an abbreviated theophany and follows with indictments against several foreign nations. Charged with various war crimes (פשעים), these nations stand guilty before God and destined for punishment. However, it becomes clear that the sins of the foreign nations are really Amos's penultimate focus; the 'criminal' he considers most flagrant in action and behavior is none other than Israel (Amos 2.6-16). Similarly, one may argue that in Mic. 1.2-7 the nations are indicted, but their eventual punishment is first and foremost epitomized in the punishment rapidly enveloping Israel.[14]

Noteworthy also is the source of Israel's sin. This opening oracle of Micah presents a number of key Mican themes. Hillers states it well:

> This oracle announces a number of themes of the book, including the fundamental idea, the rule of God. This irresistible rule first appears in its destructive force, in conformity with another fundamental idea of the book: rebellion within mankind, especially the people of God, calls forth divine fury. This strikes at the central symbol of authority, the capital city.[15]

The message of Micah is consistent—the fundamental source of sin resides in the twin capitals of Samaria and Jerusalem.[16] These capital cities, symbols of power, authority and security, are for Micah symbols of sin and transgression.[17] The depiction of the punishment is graphic. Prior to the identification of the culprits, mountains melt and valleys burst open.[18] Once Samaria and Jerusalem are identified as the

13. For a redactional analysis of 1.2-7, see Wolff, *Micah*, pp. 51-53; cf. also W. McKane, 'Micah 1,2-7', *ZAW* 107 (1995), pp. 420-34; V. Fritz, 'Das Wort gegen Samaria Mi 1 2-7', *ZAW* 86 (1974), pp. 316-31.

14. It is perhaps noteworthy that Amos invites the nations to gather about Samaria and witness the atrocities within Israel against which Yahweh is bringing punishment (Amos 3.9-11). This advent of the nations is in striking contrast to their advent envisioned in Isa. 2.2-4 // Mic. 4.1-4 (see below).

15. Hillers, *Micah*, p. 18.

16. Micah regularly uses Samaria and Jerusalem where we might expect the more customary Israel and Judah.

17. Mays (*Micah*, p. 38) entitles this section well: 'Capital punishment for the capital cities.'

18. Interestingly, these capital cities, nestled atop or among mountains and hills, experience a flattening of the landscape. Later, Micah will envision a Jerusalem that

transgressors, the prophet delineates specific punishment; her (i.e. Samaria's) sources of security and protection are 'laid bare'. Appropriately, her own mountainous walls will melt as foreign invaders topple her walls and roll the stones into the valley,[19] exposing her foundations.[20]

The nature of the sin of these symbols of power resounds most eloquently in v. 7. If v. 6 elicits political securities, v. 7 envisions cultic securities. Idols and images are smashed and torched. Micah vividly articulates his contempt for such religious trappings—they are 'whore's fees'! The wordplay is evident. Although some scholars consider the first attestation of אתנן ill-suited to the context,[21] its use seems most appropriate. For Micah, these religious securities are none other than symbols of prostitution gained through illicit activities.[22] Miller captures the sense of the passage well:

> The term used previously to describe the instrument of Israel's sinfulness is now used metaphorically to characterize the manner of her acquiring these images and thus the nature of her sin. They come from hiring herself out as a harlot. That is, Israel has given herself to the worship of other gods and built altars and images out of her prosperity.[23]

experiences elevation through divine intervention (Mic. 4.1-4).

19. Cf. Josephus's (*Ant.* 8.281) account of Hyrcanus's destruction of Samaria: 'He effaced it entirely and left it to be swept away by the mountain torrents, for he dug beneath it until it fell into the beds of the torrents.'

20. Yahweh's action is better understood as a military conquest than as an earthquake. Further, the exposing of the foundation stones implies violation (cf. Pss. 79.1; 137.7; Hos. 2.10, 12; Lev. 18.6-19). The imagery of the capital city becoming a vineyard plot is puzzling. It may simply reflect Micah's animosity against the mighty urban symbols of his day. Formerly agrarian locales would return to their original state; however, that state would be cultivated. (Cf. later [3.12] where Jerusalem experiences a similar fate. The southern capital is 'plowed as a field' and becomes a 'heap of ruins' and a 'wooded height'.)

21. Several scholars emend אתנן to אשרה (or the like) (so Mays, *Micah*, p. 46 n. a; cf. J.M.P. Smith, W.H. Ward and J.A. Bewer, *Micah, Zephaniah, Nahum, Habakkuk, Obadiah and Joel* [ICC; Edinburgh: T. & T. Clark, 1911], pp. 35, 37).

22. Idolatry is elsewhere regarded as whoredom in the prophetic literature (cf. Nah. 3.4; Hos. 2). Again, the importance of the capital city to Micah is implicit. Although Bethel and Dan were key northern religious sanctuaries, Micah considers Samaria the center of idolatrous worship and the embodiment of the sins of the people (so Hillers, *Micah*, p. 21). Not surprisingly, Micah follows with a lament over the outlying villages impacted by these centers of sin (1.10-16).

23. P.D. Miller, Jr., *Sin and Judgment in the Prophets: A Stylistic and*

Clearly the reason for Israel's imminent downfall is her unfaithfulness to Yahweh.

What Mic. 1.2-7 states poetically and quickly, 5.9-14 (EVV, 10-15) elaborates and makes explicit.

> In that day, says the Lord, I will cut off your horses from among you and will destroy your chariots; and I will cut off the cities of your land and throw down all your strongholds; and I will cut off sorceries [כשפים] from your hand, and you shall have no more soothsayers [מעוננים]; and I will cut off your images [פסיליך] and your pillars [מצבותיך] from among you, and you shall bow down no more to the work of your hands; and I will uproot your sacred poles [אשיריך] from among you and destroy your towns.[24] And in anger and wrath I will execute vengeance on the nations that did not obey.

Like Mic. 1.2-7, both political (here expressed primarily in military language) and religious securities are called into question. In this judgment oracle, Micah proclaims a divine purging from Israelite society of those elements in which God's people trust. Although utilizing different language, the theological similarity to Hos. 3.4 is noteworthy. Before Israel can become what Yahweh truly intends, she must be ridded of those trappings in which she places her confidence. Israel, if she is to have a future, must first be deprived of those elements that reflect her own attempts at securing a future. Micah 5.9-10 (EVV, 10-11) echoes 1.6; 5.11-13 (EVV, 12-14) recalls 1.7. Strikingly, Mic. 1.2-7 began with mention of 'the peoples' (v. 2); Mic. 5.9-14 (EVV, 10-15) concludes with a reference to 'the nations' (v. 14 [EVV, v. 15]). The interrelationship of Israel and the nations/peoples again is key. Israel, having looked to the nations as a model for establishing national security,[25]

Theological Analysis (SBLMS, 27; Chico, CA: Scholars Press, 1982), p. 28.

24. The parallel of MT 'your cities' (עריך) with 'your Asherim' (אשיריך) is unusual. Numerous emendations have been proposed (most commonly 'your idols' [עצביך]). Although emendation is plausible, it is noteworthy that Micah considers the capital cities the center of sin (especially idolatry, 1.5).

25. Although not without problems, I would propose that the sources of security mentioned (e.g. horses, chariots, strongholds), especially the religious sources of security (e.g. sorcery, soothsaying, various forms of idolatry), implicitly suggest foreign elements within Israel's political and religious practices (cf. Isa. 2.6, 8, 15, 18; 31.1-3). If this is so, then the removal of these objects would prepare Israel to return to the true source of her security—Yahweh. For a fuller discussion of this passage and its role in the book of Micah, see J.T. Willis, 'The Structure of Micah 3-5 and the Function of Micah 5 9-14 in the Book', *ZAW* 81 (1969), pp. 191-214;

now finds in the nations a partner in punishment![26]

Suggesting the removal of cherished objects of security, whether military or religious, and attendant doom, could only produce animosity and confrontation with the political and religious establishment. At least two pericopes manifest this conflict (2.6-11; 3.5-8, 11). Micah squarely sets himself against the wisdom of his day, challenging his contemporaries' understanding of the future and the divine word regarding that future.

Micah 2.6-11 is a notoriously complex passage, fairly bristling with textual and rhetorical difficulties. Determining speakers and identifying primary and secondary audiences and the location of possible quotation marks tax the interpreter. Although the historical relationship between Mic. 2.1-5 and 2.6-11 is quite uncertain,[27] in its present literary context 2.1-5 serves as the rhetorical backdrop for vv. 6-11.

Micah 2.1-5 portrays a blatant miscarriage of justice. Simply put, the rich have found effective ways (possibly legal!) to confiscate land from the defenseless and appropriate it to themselves.[28] Micah excoriates this

idem, 'The Authenticity and Meaning of Micah 5 9-14', *ZAW* 81 (1969), pp. 353-68.

26. This judgment oracle contrasts dramatically with the vision of Jerusalem in Mic. 4.1-4. Taking these two oracles together allows us to see Micah's twofold characterization of Jerusalem's future. On the one hand, imminent punishment involves the removal of everything in which Israel trusts. Extensive devastation blankets the landscape. On the other hand, total destruction is not the final word. Arising from the rubble of ruins, Jerusalem becomes a pilgrimage city, not for judgment and war, but for instruction and peace (see the later discussion on 4.1-4). Attempting to trace the redactional history of this passage, Wolff (*Micah*, p. 154) states, 'As 5.6-7 corresponds to the saying in 4.6-7, so 5.9-12 corresponds, to a certain extent, to the universal promise in 4.1-4. For according to the original meaning of this "excommunication saying," Yahweh destroys from Israel's midst all man-made military appurtenances and heathen religious practices which would offer security; in this way Yahweh frees Israel, like the nations in 4.1-3, to seek after his instruction alone (5.12b), and to reject all that has to do with war. Whereas 4.1-4 says nothing about Israel, 5.9-12 indicates that by Yahweh's acts of purification, Israel will also be expressly equipped for the kingdom of world peace... This is the purpose of "being cut off" that is announced here.'

27. Note, however, Wolff's argument (*Micah*, pp. 75-76) that both units likely derive from the same time and place, as is clear from the close linkage of vv. 1-4 with the quotations in vv. 6-7a and accusations in vv. 8-10.

28. A. Alt's ('Micha 2,1-5. ΓΗΣ ΑΝΑΔΑΣΜΟΣ in Juda', *NorTT* 56 [1955], pp. 13-23) sharp distinction between oppressive Jerusalem nobles and oppressed

deliberate crime and pronounces Yahweh's impending judgment upon
these land-grabbers. The rhetorical power of the oracle is dramatic.
Through wordplay and thematic reversal, Micah declares that the treatment the rich have dealt the powerless will be the treatment that they
receive. While the wealthy lie awake at night 'devising wickedness
and evil deeds' (חשבי־און ופעלי רע), Yahweh is 'devising...an evil'
(חשב...רעה).[29] These powerful land-grabbers (v. 2) will find themselves robbed of their land by a more powerful foreign oppressor (v. 4);
when exploited and abused, they will immediately cry foul!

For our purposes, this passage helpfully sets the stage for the ensuing
discussion (vv. 6-11). To state the obvious, Mic. 2.1-5 clearly demonstrates that, for the prophet Micah, comment upon and evaluation of
ethical practices were within the domain of prophetic critique. Micah,
as God's spokesperson, apparently felt no hesitancy in challenging and
denouncing current business activity. More significant, however, is the
manner in which he addresses the 'problem'. Micah condemns the practices through theological critique. For Micah, these unscrupulous activities involve nothing less than 'coveting' (חמד) a neighbor's 'inheritance' (נחלה).[30] The punishment Micah foresees for these nefarious
'thieves' (גזל) involves an ironic implementation of *jus talionis*—the
land they have unethically seized will be similarly taken from them by
a more powerful oppressor!

Against this backdrop, an apparent dialogue unfolds in 2.6-11.
Although difficult, these verses seemingly contain an opening rejoinder

rural peasants lacks specific textual evidence. For a refutation of Alt's socio-his-
torical reconstruction, see Z. Kallai, 'Judah and Israel—A Study in Israelite Historiography', *IEJ* 28 (1978), pp. 251-61.

29. Further wordplays and echoes appear in the use of the term 'fields' (שדות
[cf. Isa. 5.8-10]), the interplay between the opening cry of woe (v. 1a) and the
lament of woe (v. 4), the loss of 'inheritance' (נחלה) and the interplay between 'a
man and his house' (גבר וביתו) and 'this family/clan' (המשפחה הזאת). It is also
noteworthy that the same verb (גזל) is used for land confiscation (v. 2) that is used
in the next chapter for the physical abuse of persons ('tear the skin off my people'
[3.2]).

30. 'Covet' is the only key term used twice in the Decalogue; the term 'inheritance' has no 'secular' meaning in the Hebrew Bible. By using such terminology,
we implicitly realize that these crimes are not merely secular atrocities, but crimes
against God and an attack on the basic structure of God's people (so Hillers, *Micah*,
p. 33).

to Micah by his opponents (vv. 6-7a),[31] Micah's rebuttal (vv. 7b-10) and a final caustic caricature (by Micah) of the type of prophet his audience seeks.[32] For our purposes, the theological significance of this pericope is important. Micah's vision of the scope of the prophetic task differs vastly from that of his peer prophets. Micah, using theologically laden language, savagely critiques the social behavior of influential members of the community (2.1-5). In response to the appropriateness of such critique, Micah vigorously denounces those prophetic voices that would avoid such a message.

What 2.6-11 states implicitly, Mic. 3.5-8, 11 makes explicit. In ch. 3 Micah unleashes an attack against injustice and abuse manifested among the political and religious authorities. Verses 1-4 concern the absence of justice in the courts; vv. 5-8 concern the travesty of self-serving prophets; and vv. 9-12 denounce the perverse nature of a community devoid of justice and integrity among its leadership. The language throughout is graphic and terse; gripping images (e.g. cannibalism [vv. 2b-3]) and metaphors abound. The contrast Micah draws between the prophets of 'profit' (vv. 5-7) and himself (v. 8) is most striking.[33]

In dramatic fashion, Micah declares that these prophets who primarily seek 'profit' (v. 5) will suffer extensive 'loss' (vv. 6-7). Micah graphically charges that whether these prophets proclaim weal ('peace') or woe (literally, 'sanctify war' [קדש מלחמה]) is dependent upon the

31. The precise identity of Micah's opponents is disputed. Three identifications are most common: (1) the land-grabbers denounced in 2.1-5, (2) the false prophets, and (3) the false prophets speaking on behalf of the land-grabbers. The first identification seems most plausible (cf. vv. 8-10).

32. Micah's disdain for those who would preach primarily what their audience wants to hear is reflected in his reference, 'I will preach to you of wine and strong drink' (so NRSV [MT: אטף לך ליין ולשכר]). The verb נטף may be implicitly derisive (see Amos 7.16). The reference to 'wine and strong drink' may be a metaphor for preaching only salvation (cf. Amos 9.13-14; Joel 2.24) or it may imply the self-serving nature of these prophets ('*for* wine and strong drink').

33. The issue of authority is implicitly present in the opening line ('thus says the Lord'). This is one of only two places where the messenger formula introduces an oracle (cf. 2.3). The form of vv. 5-8 resembles both judgment and disputation oracles (so Smith, *Micah*, p. 32). For a significantly different reading of this passage, see R. Carroll, 'Night without Vision: Micah and the Prophets', in F. Martinez *et al.* (eds.), *The Scripture and the Scrolls: Studies in Honour of A.S. van der Woude on the Occasion of his 65th Birthday* (VTSup, 49; Leiden: E.J. Brill, 1992), pp. 74-84.

payment they receive from the recipients of their oracles![34] Obsessed with 'profit', Micah declares the imminent extent of their 'loss'. These prophets for hire will lose their 'vision', finding themselves submerged in darkness. Blind seers, robbed of divination,[35] will experience the ultimate humiliation for a prophet—they will have no revelatory word (כי אין מענה אלהים).[36] Congruent with Mic. 2.1-5, the punishment fits the 'crime'. Just as 2.1-5 depicts landless land-barons, so here Micah depicts visionless visionaries and speechless preachers.[37]

In contrast, Micah characterizes himself and his ministry in v. 8:

> But as for me, I am filled with power [חכ], and with the spirit [רוח] of the Lord, and with justice [משפט] and might [גבורה], to declare [להגיד] to Jacob his transgression [פשעו] and to Israel his sin [חטאתו].[38]

Unique among the prophets, this self-disclosure of Micah contrasts mightily with his prophetic opponents. In contradistinction to their self-absorption, Micah's quintessential focus is justice. His polestar is declaring to God's people what they need to hear rather than what they want to hear.[39] His 'fullness' accentuates their 'emptiness'.

The closing oracle of ch. 3 depicts Jerusalem's end in language reminiscent of Samaria's end in 1.6-7. 'Micah's word of judgment

34. Again, Micah's language is graphic. His expression 'have something to eat' (v. 5), is literally 'bite with their teeth' (הנשכים בשניהם). The verb נשך occurs elsewhere of snakebite (Amos 5.19; 9.3; Prov. 23.32; Num. 21.8-9); the expression recalls the 'cannibalism' of v. 3.

35. Cf. the earlier discussion of 5.9-14 (EVV, 10-15).

36. The judges receive a similar pronouncement of punishment (3.4). Cf. a similar scenario in Amos 8.11. The reference to 'covering the lip' may intend either mourning (Ezek. 24.17, 22) or perhaps leprosy (Lev. 13.45). The thematic similarities to Hos. 3.4 are again noteworthy. These prophets become essentially non-prophets without their divinatory tools.

37. It is often noted that Micah fundamentally criticizes these opposing prophets for their pecuniary nature. These prophets, responsible for intercessory prayers, seeking oracles from God and offering counsel to leaders, have become mercenary peddlers of the word of God. For a fuller discussion, see J. Jeremias, 'Die Vollmacht des Propheten im Alten Testament', *EvT* 31 (1971), pp. 305-22; A.S. van der Woude, 'Micah in Dispute with the Pseudo-Prophets', *VT* 19 (1969), pp. 244-60.

38. 'Sin' and 'transgression' hauntingly echo Mic. 1.5.

39. Accepting such a prophetic identity may generate unavoidable confrontation. It is perhaps significant that Micah uses the term נגד (Hiph.) for himself, a term that literally means 'to stand opposite/against something'.

makes clear that a city built in sin will be destroyed in judgment.'[40] At the heart of Jerusalem's transgressions stand her judges, priests and prophets. Tragically, justice, instruction in Torah and the inspired word are for sale. Incredibly, these corrupted peddlers of God's word profess an unshakable trust in God.[41] Corruption and greed permeate the political and religious establishment. Micah 3.11 echoes Isa. 1.23.[42]

God's Worshipping Community — As It Could Be

Although one might expect a true prophet of God to retreat from society in despair, Micah eschews such an option. Not content simply to speak forcefully against the cultic and social abuses of his day, he also articulates for his listeners a vision of the divine intent for the people. God's redeemed and restored people are mentioned in several places (e.g. 2.12-13; 4.6-7; 5.6-8 [EVV, 7-9]), but nowhere is Yahweh's vision for his people more powerfully expressed than in Mic. 4.1-4.[43]

In contrast to the imminent destruction foreseen for Jerusalem (3.9-12), Mic. 4.1-4 portrays a secure and stable Jerusalem.[44] The imagery is dramatic. Mt Zion, topographically overshadowed by the Mount of Olives, is elevated in stature and grandeur.[45] In striking contrast to the

40. Miller, *Sin and Judgment*, p. 34.

41. Wolff, *Micah*, p. 108.

42. Mic. 3.11 provides a succinct commentary on 2.6-11.

43. The relationship of Mic. 4.1-4 to Isa. 2.2-4 is beyond the scope of the present essay. For a full discussion of this issue, consult the major commentaries and the literature cited therein. For a decidedly different reading of this oracle, see A. van der Woude ('Micah IV 1-5: An Instance of the Pseudo-Prophets Quoting Isaiah', in M.A. Beek, *et al.* [eds.], *Symbolae biblicae et Mesopotamicae Francisco Mario Theodoro de Liagre Bohl dedicatae* [Studia Francisci Scholten memoriae dicata, 4; Leiden: E.J. Brill, 1973], pp. 396-402), who places this oracle in the mouths of Micah's opponents.

44. The contrasts between 4.1-4 and 3.9-12 have often been noted. Jerusalem, soon to become a 'heap of ruins' swarming with animals (3.12), will ultimately become a 'house of instruction' teeming with foreign nations (4.1-2). Zion, formerly destructively 'plowed' as a field, will now be farmed with transformed war implements (4.3). Zion, formerly noted for her abhorrence of justice and perversion of equity (3.9), will become the center of equity and justice.

45. Echoes with 1.2-7 may also be implicit. Whereas Samaria experienced the meltdown of her mountains, the rupture of her valleys and the exposure of her foundation, Mt Zion rises in elevation with the temple gloriously perched atop her summit.

military devastation envisioned in Mic. 1.2-7 and 3.9-12, Jerusalem is characterized as a haven of peace and security. War implements lose functional reality; the people dwell unafraid among their vineyards and orchards.[46]

Most noteworthy is the activity of the nations in this vision. The nations flow to Jerusalem and the temple, not for war, but for instruction (תורה) and the word of the Lord (דבר־יהוה).[47] However, completely absent are the traditional brokers of those commodities: no mention is made of either priests or prophets. Instead, Yahweh himself functions as sole judge and arbiter. Not surprisingly, this vision is far from imminent reality. Strikingly, the promise concludes with a confessional affirmation (v. 5):

> For all the peoples walk, each in the name of its god, but we will walk in the name of the Lord our God forever and ever.[48]

Theologically, part of the power of this passage lies in its complete disparity with the present reality.[49] To a community battered and beset by corruption and abuse among its leaders, Mic. 4.1-4 presents a transformed Jerusalem, a city indwelt by the divine judge. To such a promise of hope, the beleaguered community responds with faithful hope (4.5).

The book of Micah depicts the community of faith both as it currently is (e.g. 1.2-7; 2.1-11; 3.1-12) and as God intends it to be (e.g. 4.1-5; 2.12-13; 5.6-8 [EVV, 7-9]). However, moving from where the people are to where God intends them to be will involve a dramatic transformation of their understanding of the cultic and socio-ethical implications of the divine–human relationship. Micah 6.1-8 presents

46. This language may reflect a 'peasant ideal' (cf. 1 Kgs 4.25; Zech. 3.10; for a fuller discussion, see Wolff, *Micah*, pp. 122-23; Hillers, *Micah*, p. 51). Such activity could only occur with the absence of war and an extensive period of agrarian productivity.

47. Just as the nations secondarily experience God's judgment and punishment (1.2; 4.11-12; 5.4b-5, 8 [EVV, 5b-6, 9]), so now they are recipients of God's salvation and blessings.

48. Although not without problems, Mic. 4.1-5 may plausibly be read within the context of a worshipping community. To the liturgical promise (vv. 1-4), the congregation affirmingly responds (v. 5). Perhaps implicit is the notion that the nations cannot learn the ways of Yahweh unless Israel is faithful to the ways of Yahweh.

49. Hillers (*Micah*, p. 52) notes that protest movements often are accompanied with visions of an ideal future, visions often appearing most unrealistic.

one scenario of that transformation. Having begun with a covenant lawsuit (1.2-7), we now conclude with a covenant lawsuit.[50] Micah 6.1-8 has been the subject of significant and extensive discussion. For our purposes, we will treat it similarly to the development of thought mentioned earlier in Isa. 1.21-26. Isaiah 1.21-26 depicts Jerusalem past, present and future. Isaiah describes a Jerusalem that in no way captures the essence of what Yahweh intended for his city. In that passage, the prophet implicitly acknowledges two key elements involved in the transformation from what God's people currently are to what they can become. The first element involves recapturing a vision of who God truly is; he is 'the Sovereign, the Lord of hosts, the Mighty One of Israel' (Isa. 1.24). The second element involves a disciplined response.[51] Although linguistically and thematically quite different, theologically Mic. 6.1-8 unfolds in a similar fashion. Verses 1-5 provide a vision of who the God of Israel truly is; his nature is captured clearly in his deeds on Israel's behalf. Following a brief interlude that epitomizes the people's fundamental misunderstanding of the divine-human relationship, v. 8 concludes with a powerfully succinct statement of the appropriate human response to Yahweh.

In vv. 1-5, Yahweh compellingly states his case and protests his innocence of any wrongdoing in his relationship with his people. Beginning with wordplay (vv. 3-4),[52] he quickly recites his redemptive deeds,

50. Although the unity and redactional history of 6.1-8 are debated, rhetorically it functions as a unit in the book. The development of thought within the verses, as well as the dialogical nature of the unit (cf. 2.1-11), clearly evinces this. A full discussion of this aspect of the passage is beyond the scope of this paper. For a fuller discussion, consult the commentaries and R. Hentschke, *Die Stellung der vorexilischen Schriftpropheten zum Kultus* (BZAW, 75; Berlin: Alfred Topelmann, 1957), pp. 104-107; cf. also T. Lescow, *Micha 6, 6-8: Studien zu Sprache, Form und Auslegung* (Arbeiten zur Theologie, 1; Stuttgart: Calwer Verlag, 1966); J.T. Willis, A Book Review of Theodor Lescow, *Micha 6,6-8: Studien zu Sprache, Form und Auslegung*, *VT* 18 (1968), pp. 273-78. Verses 1-5 present an indictment (ריב); vv. 6-8 contain a torah liturgy (rather than the expected announcement of punishment). This results in a rhetorical unit of dialogue and disputation that seems almost didactic in nature. Regarding the purpose and thrust of this passage, Wolff (*Micah*, p. 183), states, 'A didactic sermon-in-outline, the passage leads the reader from the present reality of Yahweh's great deeds of salvation, through a discussion of inappropriate cultic responses, and then on to clear statements of "what is good" for human beings.'

51. Note the smelting imagery (Isa. 1.25).

52. 'O my people...in what have I wearied [הלאתיך] you? Answer me! For I

from the exodus out of Egypt to entrance into the land.[53] Most tellingly, these 'saving acts' (צדקות) of Yahweh demonstrate his right behavior towards Israel and the essence of his being.[54]

The transition from the recitation of Yahweh's saving deeds (vv. 3-5) to the response of the people (vv. 6-7) is abrupt. However, the tendency to locate rhetorical questions strategically is well-attested in the book of Micah (cf. 1.5b; 2.7; 3.1; 4.9; 6.10-11). Here the startling 'with what shall I come before the Lord...' (במה) counters Yahweh's earlier questions ('What have I done to you? In what have I wearied you? [מה...מה]).[55] The response in vv. 6-7 seems to imply that Yahweh is in fact the problem! As a litany of possible 'adequate' offerings unfolds, the respondent moves rapidly from offerings indicating total commitment on the part of the worshipper (whole burnt offerings) to offerings of absurd proportions[56] to unthinkable offerings (child sacrifice)![57] The

brought you up [העלתיך] from the land of Egypt.'

53. A discussion of the use of cult traditions in the book of Micah is beyond the scope of this paper. For a fuller discussion, see W. Beyerlin, *Die Kulttraditionen Israels in der Verkündigung des Propheten Micha* (FRLANT, 72; Göttingen: Vandenhoeck & Ruprecht, 1959); *idem*, 'Kultische Tradition in Michas Prophetie. Ein Beitrag zum Problem Kultus und Prophet', *VoxTh* 31 (1960), pp. 2-12; B. Reicke, 'Liturgical Traditions in Micah 7', *HTR* 60 (1967), pp. 349-67.

54. The recitation is vivid and compressed. Four emphases appear: redemption from Egypt, inspired leadership (Moses, Aaron, Miriam), deliverance from the schemes of Balak and Balaam, entrance into the land. The references to the individuals are intriguing. Is the reference to Aaron a proleptic hint at the priestly language imminent in vv. 6-7, or are Aaron, Moses and Miriam highlighted simply for their (faithful) service as leaders (in contrast to the current leaders of Micah's day)? Targumic tradition highlights the prophetic nature of these three leaders: Moses taught tradition and the law; Aaron brought reconciliation to the people; Miriam instructed the women. Similarly, one wonders whether the failed attempts of Balak and Balaam to withstand God's people subtly echo other passages in the book of Micah regarding the inability of foreign nations ultimately to thwart Yahweh's purposes for his people. The futile schemes (מה־יע׳ץ) of Balaam and Balak to derail Yahweh's saving acts are suggestively echoed in reverse in the following oracle (6.9-16). Punishment engulfs the people for having followed the 'counsels' (מעצות) of Omri and Ahab (6.16).

55. Yahweh's questions in actuality function as assertions of innocence; the opening rhetorical questions of v. 6 introduce a lame defense through the use of absurdity.

56. The rapid escalation from thousands to ten thousands couples with astronomical measurements ('rivers of oil').

57. It is noteworthy that the terms 'transgression' (פשע) and 'sin' (חטאה) appear

place and purpose of sacrifice in the divine–human relationship has been completely misunderstood.

The 'offering' Yahweh truly desires is powerfully expressed in v. 8. It is neither new nor previously unheard ('he has told you').[58] The offering Yahweh 'seeks' (דרש) is 'to do justice [עשות משפט], and to love kindness [אהבת חסד], and to walk humbly [הצנע לכת] with your God'.[59] Cultic activity and worship—apart from ethical behavior pervading every facet of life—is worthless.[60] Hunter captures the theological significance of this passage well:

> The good that Yahweh seeks in every person among his people is rooted in making justice and steadfast love the controlling interests in all of life, thereby fostering a relationship with Yahweh that is characterized by paying careful and judicious attention to honoring his claim on all of life. This is the offering Yahweh accepts.[61]

Conclusion

I have attempted to demonstrate that Micah's prophetic message regarding the inseparable connection between worship and ethics is no

---

again (v. 7). Their presence is never distant for Micah; the human solution to their presence is completely irrational. The movement to the absurd comes as quickly as Yahweh's earlier recitation of his saving acts.

58. Yahweh 'declares' (נגד) his will (v. 8) just as Micah his prophet affirmed his divine commission to '"declare" [נגד] to Jacob his transgression and to Israel his sin' (3.8).

59. The first two elements of this triad (חסד/משפט) are well known and need not detain us, other than to emphasize the communal nature of both terms. Both justice and steadfast love can only occur within the context of a community. The third expression (הצנע) is best understood as 'studied attention of another'. Heeding careful attention to the ways and will of Yahweh can only result in the practice of justice and steadfast love. For a full discussion of the various nuances of this expression, see especially J.P. Hyatt, 'On the Meaning and Origin of Micah 6.8', *ATR* 34 (1952), pp. 232-39.

60. The theological and ethical similarities of Mic. 6.8 to Pss. 15 and 24 have often been noted (see, e.g., K. Koch, 'Tempeleinlassliturgien und Dekaloge', in R. Rendtorff and K. Koch [eds.], *Studien zur Theologie der alttestamentlichen Überlieferungen* [Neukirchen–Vluyn: Neukirchener Verlag, 1961], pp. 45-60).

61. A.V. Hunter, *Seek the Lord! A Study of the Meaning and Function of the Exhortations in Amos, Hosea, Isaiah, Micah, and Zephaniah* (Baltimore: St Mary's Press, 1982), p. 252.

less powerful and compelling than that of his eighth-century counter-parts Amos, Hosea and Isaiah. Utilizing Hos. 3.4-5 and Isa. 1.21-26 as conceptual and theological models, we see that the book of Micah has a similar thematic thrust. For Micah, Jerusalem (and Samaria) presently are devoid of the quintessential characteristics Yahweh seeks in a city—justice and faithfulness. Micah systematically pronounces judg-ment upon the central symbols of power and authority—Jerusalem and Samaria. Not unlike his eighth-century counterparts, Yahweh's require-ments have direct ramifications for the surrounding nations. Judgment clouds the horizon of every nation.

Like its prophetic counterparts, the book of Micah envisions a com-munity of faith beyond the immediate horizon, a community of God's people living in peace and security. However, the security is divinely fashioned and sanctioned. It lies squarely in a right relationship with Yahweh. Again, such a community becomes a source of hope and instruction for the surrounding nations.

Finally, just as becoming the faithful city and people of God involves recapturing a vision of Yahweh's mighty sovereignty and making a disciplined response (Isa. 1.24-26), so in Micah meeting the Lord's 'requirements' involves seeing his essential character in his saving deeds and mirroring those actions to every person within the commu-nity of faith (Mic. 6.1-8). Such is the community Micah calls the people of God to become; such is the inseparable nature of worship and ethics.

WHY DIDN'T DAVID BUILD THE TEMPLE?:
THE HISTORY OF A BIBLICAL TRADITION

Steven L. McKenzie

In the treatment of 2 Samuel 7 in his commentary on 1–2 Samuel, John Willis states:[1]

> The OT gives at least three reasons why Yahweh forbade David to build a temple. (1) It might leave the impression that Yahweh was limited to a particular location or structure, whereas the Israelites' relationship to him since the exodus should have demonstrated that he was constantly on the move and could work anywhere in creation (vss. 6-7). (2) David had shed so much blood that he was not spiritually qualified to build the Lord a house (1 Chron. 22.7-8; 28.2-3). (3) David was so involved in defeating Israel's enemies that he did not have time to build the temple (1 Kings 5.3-4).

I offer the following suggestions about the origin, nature and relationship of these three explanations as an *homage* to Professor Willis's work on Samuel and his interest in traditio-historical criticism. I am pleased hereby to acknowledge my debt to him for introducing me to critical scholarship on the Hebrew Bible.

2 Samuel 7

In its present form, 2 Samuel 7 is widely recognized as Deuteronomistic. While Noth, curiously, overlooked its significance,[2] McCarthy identified it in 1965 as one of the key structural passages of the

---

1. J.T. Willis, *First and Second Samuel* (LWC, 6; Austin, TX: Sweet, 1982), p. 330.
2. M. Noth, *Überlieferungsgeschichtliche Studien: Die sammelnden und bearbeitenden Geschichtswerke im Alten Testament* (Halle: Max Niemeyer, 1943). The portion dealing with the DtrH is now available in English as *The Deuteronomistic History* (JSOTSup, 15; Sheffield: Sheffield Academic Press, 2nd edn, 1991).

DtrH.[3] Nevertheless, the composition history of the chapter remains a much disputed matter, as the sense persists among many scholars that it reflects more than one hand. Since this is, in fact, one of the most controversial and frequently discussed passages in the Bible, it is impossible here to offer a survey of scholarship on 2 Samuel 7.[4] However, the discussions of the chapter by proponents of the two main compositional theories relating to the DtrH (the 'Cross' or 'Harvard' and 'Smend' or 'Göttingen' schools) will suffice as examples of the redactional approach.

In his extremely influential treatment of Judah's royal theology, Cross begins by asserting that the text of 2 Samuel 7 'is disturbed by a fundamental dichotomy', namely the opposition to the building of a temple in vv. 1-7 (esp. vv. 5-7) and the pro-temple oracle of vv. 11b-16.[5] The former also opposes Dtr's royal ideology, according to Cross. Cross explains this dichotomy by reconstructing two distinct, ancient, poetic oracles representing two different royal ideologies behind this passage. He associates what he considers anti-temple sentiments in vv. 1-7 with the (conditional) covenantal theology of the North[6] and the language of sonship in vv. 11b-16 with the 'high theology' expressed in the coronation liturgy of the Jerusalem court. The blending of these two theologies gave birth to the ideology of the royal house of Judah in which the covenant with David was interpreted as the promise or

3. D.J. McCarthy, 'II Samuel 7 and the Structure of the Deuteronomistic History', *JBL* 84 (1965), pp. 131-38.

4. Two excellent surveys of the enormous literature generated by this chapter and the specific points of dispute are available in P.K. McCarter, *II Samuel* (AB, 9; Garden City, NY: Doubleday, 1984), pp. 209-24, and most recently W. Dietrich and T. Naumann, *Die Samuelbücher* (ErFor, 287; Darmstadt: Wissenschaftliche Buchgesellschaft, 1995), pp. 143-56. As Dietrich notes in the latter (p. 143), 'In fact, this chapter is among the most discussed and most disputed chapters of the Bible' ('In der Tat gehört dieses Kapitel zu den meistdiskutierten und umstrittensten der Bibel').

5. F.M. Cross, *Canaanite Myth and Hebrew Epic: Essays in the History of the Religion of Israel* (Cambridge, MA: Harvard University Press, 1973), p. 241.

6. Even further in the background to this chapter Cross perceives in the different dwellings—tent or tabernacle and house or temple—traits belonging to entirely different Canaanite gods—El and Baal, respectively. This additional background—a hoary one indeed—suggests a reason for the suspicion of 2 Sam. 7.5-7. David's proposal of a permanent shrine was very innovative and would have been tantamount to apostasy as far as some were concerned. See esp. Cross, *Canaanite Myth*, pp. 72-73.

decree of an eternal dynasty. In combining elements of the two older oracles in 2 Samuel 7, Dtr was simply reiterating the standard Judean royal ideology, which endured until the end of the kingdom in 586 BCE.

Strikingly, Veijola's literary-critical analysis of this passage reaches conclusions that are quite similar to Cross's.[7] Like Cross, Veijola determines that two separate oracles underlie this chapter. One of them (vv. 1a, 2-5, 7) was a prophetic veto of the plan to build the temple; the other (vv. 8a, 9-10, 12, 14-15, 17), a promise given directly to David of the continuation of his house. The first Deuteronomist (DtrG) combined the two oracles and added a series of verses (vv. 11b, 13, 16, 18-21, 25-29) that effected several important changes: (1) they rendered the prohibition against temple building in the first oracle temporary; (2) they worked the combined oracle into the overall structure of the DtrG hisory; and (3) they altered the promise so as to refer to an *eternal* dynasty. A second Deuteronomist (DtrN) added vv. 1b, 6, 11a, 22-24, which made the people of Israel recipients of the promise along with David.

Subsequent scholars in both camps have continued to see 2 Samuel 7 as a layered text but have suggested significant revisions of the reconstructions of their predecessors. McCarter matches the layers to his own understanding of the literary history of Samuel.[8] In his view, the original story behind the chapter (vv. 1a, 2-3, 11b-12, 13b-15a) came from the time of Solomon and supported his construction of the temple by showing that Yahweh had approved David's intention to build and even reciprocated with the promise of a dynasty. The anti-temple strain in vv. 4-9a, 15b was added to the narrative by a prophetic writer, presumably associated with or identical to the eighth-century Prophetic Historian whom McCarter isolates as an intermediate editor elsewhere in Samuel. His additions reflect the prophetic skepticism toward monarchy, especially of the dynastic variety, and alter the message of the text so that Yahweh's promise of a dynasty (an undeniable historical reality) is a free gift rather than a response to David's proposal for a temple. The third layer in the chapter, according to McCarter, was Deuteronomistic (= Cross's seventh-century Deuteronomist [Dtr[1]]). It included 'at least' vv. [1b], 9b-11a, 13a, 16 and 22b-26 and 'was

---

7.   T. Veijola, *Die ewige Dynastie: David und die Entstehung seiner Dynastie nach der deuteronomistischen Darstellung* (AASF, B, 193; Helsinki: Suomalainen Tiedeakatemia, 1975), pp. 69-79.

8.   McCarter, *II Samuel*, pp. 220-31.

intended to incorporate David's temple plan and the dynastic promise into the larger history and to soften the negativity of the opening words of the oracle'.[9] It also identified David's 'seed' (v. 12) as an individual in anticipation of Solomon.

Finally, Dietrich agrees with Veijola in seeing two Deuteronomistic hands at work in this chapter, and he partitions most of the chapter between them: vv. 1-5a, 8aγ-9, 13, 16, 17a, 18-21, 25-29 come from DtrG, while DtrN is responsible for vv. 5b-8aαβ, 10-11a, 22-24.[10] Dietrich thus attributes the prohibition against building a temple to DtrN and not to a pre-Dtr level. He does perceive pre-Dtr material in the adoption ideology behind vv. 11b, 12, 14-15, 17b and posits that it comes from an enthronement liturgy. Like McCarter, Dietrich argues for an editorial presence between the oldest version of Nathan's oracle and its Deuteronomistic redaction. This intermediate compiler (*Bearbeiter*) used the oracle to tie together the Ark Narrative, which ends in 2 Samuel 6, with the Succession Narrative (2 Samuel 9–1 Kings 2*). Traces of his redactional work remain in 7.11bβ, 12aδb, 15b.

There is a fundamental contradiction inherent in the approaches of these scholars. They all recognize 2 Samuel 7 as it stands as a thoroughly Deuteronomistic text—crucial for the structure of the DtrH[11] and replete with Deuteronomistic language—yet they also contend that the Deuteronomistic contributions can be skimmed off in order to uncover the fundamental source material available to Dtr or the Dtrs. This contradiction is most evident in the analyses of Cross and Dietrich. Cross observes that the chapter 'fairly swarms with expressions found elsewhere in the works of the Deuteronomistic school', and he provides a detailed list of those expressions, finding them in vv. 1, 3, 5, 6, 7, 8, 9, 10, 11, 13, 16, 23, 24, 25, 27 and 29.[12] Nevertheless, he claims that remnants of older oracles are present in 2 Samuel 7, and he even goes

9. McCarter, *II Samuel*, pp. 230, 240.

10. W. Dietrich, *David, Saul und die Propheten: Das Verhältnis von Religion und Politik nach den prophetischen Überlieferungen vom frühesten Königtum in Israel* (BWANT, 122; Stuttgart: W. Kohlhammer, 2nd edn, 1992), pp. 114-36. Dietrich actually uses the symbol DtrH for Veijola's DtrG. To avoid confusion I have retained Veijola's designation.

11. For a survey of the pivotal connections between this chapter and the surrounding Dtr narrative see J. Van Seters, *In Search of History: Historiography in the Ancient World and the Origins of Biblical History* (New Haven: Yale University Press, 1983), pp. 274-76.

12. Cross, *Canaanite Myth*, pp. 252-54.

so far as to reconstruct some of their poetic couplets.[13] Dietrich states, '2 Sam. 7 is a text with heavy dtr editing' ('2. Sam 7 ist...ein stark dtr bearbeiteter Text').[14] But he is still able to find two levels of writing in a mere five verses that he determines to be non-Dtr. Veijola also refers to this chapter as a 'text with heavy dtr editing' ('stark dtr bearbeitete[r] Text') and 'the object of intensive dtr revision' ('das Gegenstand intensiver dtr Überarbeitung').[15] He admits that the title '[my] servant' in vv. 5 and 8a must be Deuteronomistic, and he regards it as a Dtr gloss. But he does not deal with other expressions in these verses nor with vv. 3 and 7 especially, which Cross and Dietrich, among others, see as Dtr. McCarter tries to downplay the extent of Deuteronomistic language in the chapter, but he is forced to admit that, in addition to occurring in 'at least' vv. 1b, 9b-11a, 13a, 16, and 22b-26, there are 'possibly, other touches here and there throughout the text'.[16]

The predominance of Deuteronomistic terminology in this chapter and the lack of agreement among redactional critics about where the older material lies, not to mention the crucial role that the chapter plays in the structure of Dtr's history as a whole, call for a careful evaluation of the arguments for multiple layers. At the risk of oversimplification, I would suggest that 2 Samuel 7 is best read as a Dtr unit. The tensions that have been perceived between the constituent parts of the chapter are more a result of the failure to understand Dtr's ideological point and literary creativity than that of the presence of different hands. This is not to deny that Dtr had sources. It seems highly unlikely that he would have invented the tradition that Solomon rather than David was the builder of the temple. The connection between temple and dynasty was well-established in the ancient Near East,[17] and the tie between David and Jerusalem specifically was extremely important to Dtr. But it is no

13. Cross, *Canaanite Myth*, pp. 255-57. For a critique of Cross's methodology see Van Seters, *In Search of History*, p. 272. Van Seters points out that word pairs are common in Deuteronomistic prose and do not necessarily indicate the presence of older poetic lines.

14. Dietrich, *David, Saul und die Propheten*, p. 124.

15. Veijola, *Die ewige Dynastie*, pp. 76, 77.

16. McCarter, *II Samuel*, p. 230. McCarter refers his reader to the Notes section of his commentary, which treats individual verses. There one finds him rather more forthcoming about the Deuteronomistic nature of many expressions.

17. On this connection especially in Mesopotamia see T. Ishida, *The Royal Dynasties: A Study on the Formation and Development of Royal-Dynastic Ideology* (BZAW, 142; Berlin: W. de Gruyter, 1977), pp. 81-99.

longer possible to determine what these sources were, much less to restore actual documents. Dtr's work in 2 Samuel 7, in short, was that of an author creating something new rather than that of an editor supplementing an inherited document.

The first problem that confronts us in 2 Samuel 7 lies in its first verse. McCarter has observed that the notice in v. 1a 'provides a narrative link to 6:20a above, sets the stage for what follows below, and introduces the key word of chap. 7, "house"'.[18] The second half of the verse, however, is difficult. Its claim that David had rest from his enemies seems contradicted by the account of his wars in the very next chapter as well as chs. 10 and 13–20. It also stands in tension with the promise in 7.11 that Yahweh will give David rest in the future.[19] In fact, Solomon would later observe in his letter to Hiram (1 Kgs 5.17-18 [EVV 3-4]) that David's occupation with warfare kept him from building a temple to Yahweh. The claim in 2 Sam. 7.1b also seems to be in tension with the theme of 'rest' in the DtrH.[20] Moses had promised that Yahweh would establish a central 'place' of worship for Israel when he had given them rest from their enemies (Deut. 12.10-11). Solomon proclaimed that Yahweh had fulfilled this promise in his (Solomon's) day, thus allowing him to complete the temple (1 Kgs 8.56). What David had been unable to accomplish because of war Solomon carried out. But 2 Samuel 7 appears to disturb this promise-fulfillment scheme when it states that David had rest.

There are basically two ways of dealing with this problem. One approach views 7.1b as a later addition, either of a redactional nature (e.g. Veijola, who assigns it to DtrN)[21] or as a result of textual corruption (so McCarter, who explains v. 1b as the accidental misplacement

18. McCarter, *II Samuel*, p. 195.

19. The tension between vv. 1 and 11 is pointed out by I. Kalimi, *Zur Geschichtsschreibung des Chronisten: Literarisch-historiographische Abweichungen der Chronik von ihren Paralleltexten in den Samuel- und Königsbüchern* (BZAW, 226; Berlin: W. de Gruyter, 1995), p. 37. On the future interpretation of the verb see McCarter, *II Samuel*, pp. 202-203 and A. Gelston, 'A Note on II Samuel 7 10', *ZAW* 84 (1972), pp. 92-94.

20. On the theme of rest in the DtrH see G. von Rad, 'There Remains Still a Rest for the People of God', in *idem*, *The Problem of the Hexateuch and Other Essays* (New York: McGraw–Hill, 1966) pp. 94-102, and R.A. Carlson, *David, the Chosen King: A Traditio-Historical Approach to the Second Book of Samuel* (Stockholm: Almqvist & Wiksell, 1964), pp. 97-106.

21. Veijola, *Die ewige Dynastie*, pp. 72-73.

of a correction to v. 11aβ).[22] The other approach explains 2 Sam. 7.1b somehow as an element in Dtr's overall scheme of rest that complements rather than contradicts the other references to the theme in the DtrH. Hence, Dietrich asserts that David's rest is temporary and does not preclude the emergence of other enemies.[23] Each of these approaches boasts some valid points in its favor. But none is completely satisfying in the full context of the Deuteronomistic passages that refer to rest.[24] Based on an assessment of those passages, I would like to suggest a new solution that borrows from both of these approaches.

Actually, 2 Samuel 7.1b is not the only time that tensions appear within the theme of rest in the DtrH. Aside from the promises of rest (הניח, מנוחה) in Deuteronomy (3.20; 12.9, 10; 25.19), their ultimate fulfillment in 1 Kings (5.18; 8.56) and the references in 2 Samuel 7 (vv. 1b, 11), the theme is mentioned in connection with the conquest of Canaan in Josh. 1.13, 15; 21.44; 22.4; 23.1.[25] The last three passages

22. McCarter, *II Samuel*, p. 191.

23. Dietrich, *David, Saul und die Propheten*, pp. 133-34. Similarly L.M. Eslinger, *House of God or House of David: The Rhetoric of 2 Samuel 7* (JSOTSup, 164; Sheffield: Sheffield Academic Press, 1994), p. 17 n. 2.

24. The distinct and provocative view of Van Seters should also be mentioned here. Van Seters (*In Search of History*, pp. 271-91 and private communication) sees 2 Sam. 7 essentially as the climax of Dtr's account of David, since he believes the 'Court History' in 2 Sam. 9–20 + 1 Kgs 1–2 (except for 2.1-4, 10-11) is a post-Dtr addition. The 'rest' given to David in 2 Sam 7.1b, therefore, came at the end of David's reign in Dtr's account and extended to Solomon's. Van Seters's literary observations are tempting, and his treatment of the Court History deserves more attention than can be afforded here. However, his conclusion for 7.1b runs into several problems. The contradiction with v. 11a remains unexplained; it is unclear whether the 'rest' has been achieved under David or still lies in the future. Also, chs. 7 and 8 continue in tension, and Van Seters must conclude that the latter is out of order and originally went with ch. 5. The content of the two chapters is similar, but there is nothing to indicate that ch. 8 ever preceded ch. 7 aside from the assumption that 7.1b presumes David's conquests. Van Seters points to 1 Kgs 5.17 as evidence that Dtr's David vanquished his enemies and thus had rest at the end of his reign. But 5.18 clearly spells out the contrast (ועתה) between David's reign as a time of war and Solomon's as the time of rest. Indeed, the current placement of 2 Sam. 8 is significant, because it is precisely the wars surrounding David according to 1 Kgs 5.17 that prevented him from building the temple that he envisioned in 2 Sam. 7.

25. R.L. Braun, 'Solomon, the Chosen Temple Builder: The Significance of

state that Yahweh has given rest to Israel in fulfillment of his promise in Deuteronomy, so that, like 2 Sam. 7.1b, they also disturb the continuity between Deut. 12.9-10 and the erection of the temple in 1 Kings. Furthermore, Josh. 18.1 describes the erection of the אהל מועד at Shiloh in compliance with the instructions of Deut. 12.9-10, and Joshua 22 recounts a story in which the transjordanian Israelites must defend themselves against the charge that they have violated the principle of centralization by building a competing sacrificial altar.

Dietrich might have appealed for support for his position to the texts in Joshua (esp. 21.44), which also refer to Yahweh's gift of rest long before the temple is built, and which are immediately followed by the conflicts narrated in Judges. On the other hand, Dietrich's contention that the rest of 2 Sam. 7.1b is temporary does not take seriously enough the contradiction that it causes within the Dtr theme of rest. This is especially odd coming from Dietrich, whose literary-critical approach frequently posits different hands at the slightest perception of narrative tension, both in 2 Samuel 7 and elsewhere. The position that 2 Sam. 7.1b is secondary is more attractive, but neither Veijola nor McCarter adequately deals with the previous disruptions of the rest theme in Joshua. Also, it is hard to see what would motivate a later editor so blatantly to contradict an important and well-known Deuteronomistic theme, as *per* Veijola's explanation.

McCarter's text-critical solution has appeal and is key to solving the puzzle of the rest theme in the DtrH. He notes that the object of Yahweh's promises changes in 2 Sam. 7.10 from David to Israel, so that the reader expects Israel also to be the benefactor of the rest promised in v. 11b rather than David as in the MT.[26] He notes further that the need for a textual change in v. 11 was recognized by older critics, even though textual support for it is lacking. Thus, he suggests that v. 1b was originally a marginal correction to v. 11b that came to be misplaced. This suggestion has the result of doing away with both references to rest under David in 2 Samuel 7. The reference to Yahweh cutting off all David's enemies in 7.9 must be taken in context to refer to those who stood in the way of David's kingship, and in any case does not use the language of rest, so that it does not undermine McCarter's proposal.

As for the Joshua materials, Noth initially contended that all of

Joshua 13–22 was a later addition to Dtr's History.[27] His argument was based in part on the fact that these chapters essentially duplicate at length the point already made by Dtr at the end of ch. 11 that Joshua conquered the land and distributed it among the tribes. He also noted the instance of narrative resumption (*Wiederaufnahme*) between 13.1a and 23.1b. The latter repeats the former verbatim: ויהושע זקן בא בימים. Since 23.1a precedes the resumptive sentence, it must be included in the addition. This means that all of the references to Yahweh having given rest to Israel in the days of Joshua occur within the section that Noth considered secondary. The author of the added section apparently wished to show that Yahweh fulfilled his promise of rest at the conquest and perhaps that the central 'place' of worship had been established in Israel before the temple was built. In any case, once the references to rest in Josh. 13.1–23.1 and 2 Sam. 7.1b, 11 are bracketed, Dtr's scheme of rest becomes clear. In Dtr's description, the land experienced quiet after Israel's wars of conquest (והארץ שקטה ממלחמה, Josh. 11.23b), but Israel did not yet have its God-given rest. The rest promised in Deuteronomy is fulfilled only in Solomon's reign, and the designated place of central worship is the temple in Jerusalem.

The establishment of 7.1b as secondary clears the way for understanding the point of 7.1-7 and the rest of the chapter. David's proposal to build a 'house' for Yahweh is implicit in his statement to Nathan in 7.2. His observation that he lives in a 'house of cedar' follows on and links well with the introduction in v. 1a that he was living in his house. Cross and McCarter are bothered by the use of the verb ישב here and especially in vv. 5-6, arguing that its use in reference to Yahweh's dwelling in a temple 'is unthinkable in an original Deuteronomistic composition'.[28] Cross contends that 'only here and in 1 Kings 8.13 (*mkwn lsbtk 'wlmym*), another quotation from poetry, does [the Deuteronomist] permit the expression to stand'.[29] Cross has overlooked 1 Kgs 8.27, which is an explanation of or response to 8.13. Solomon asks whether God could really live (ישב) on the earth—a rhetorical question to which the obvious answer is 'no'. This confirms the importance of the 'name theology' to Dtr,[30] but it does not necessarily support

27. Noth, *Deuteronomistic History*, pp. 66-67.
28. McCarter, *II Samuel*, p. 226.
29. Cross, *Canaanite Myth*, p. 255.
30. Cf. S.D. McBride, 'The Deuteronomic Name Theology' (PhD dissertation, Harvard University, 1969).

McCarter's conclusion about ישׁב being impossible in a Dtr composition. In fact, in 2 Samuel 7 ישׁב functions as a key word, binding vv. 1, 2, 5 and 6 together. As such it is a crucial part of the play that encapsulates the point of the narrative. The text avoids using Yahweh as the subject of ישׁב. It is David's 'sitting' in his house (v. 1a) that reminds him that the ark—not Yahweh—still 'sits' where he left it in the tent he pitched for it (6.17). From the outset, the ark's permanent residence is connected with David's, though Dtr is quick to point out that Yahweh himself resides on the earth in name only (v. 13).[31] The contrast between permanence and transience is then carried on through the use of ישׁב opposite התהלך in vv. 5-7.

David's observation in 7.2 merely contrasts his permanent domicile in a 'house of cedar' with the temporary and no doubt less luxurious 'curtains' of the tent where the ark resides. It is certainly not an explicit proposal, though it seems interpreted as such by both Nathan and Yahweh. Nathan's initial approval alone rules out McCarter's idea that these verses betray a Northern, prophetic, anti-temple sentiment. Those prophetic circles would hardly allow one of their own, especially one of Nathan's stature, to issue such a *carte blanche* to a king. Moreover, the reversal of his approval that Nathan receives overnight, according to this view, would be a great embarrassment in such circles, to say the least.

Yahweh's response, which begins in v. 5, is not a rejection of David's proposal, though it is often taken this way.[32] There is no hint of any anti-temple sentiment. Indeed, it must have been clear to Dtr from history that Yahweh did not disapprove of a temple per se. Solomon had built one after all, and Dtr promoted the exclusivity and centrality of the Jerusalem shrine. The pronoun in Yahweh's question of v. 5 is emphatic: 'Will *you* build a house for me to dwell in.' The question is ambiguous and not answered until v. 13 and then with another emphatic pronoun: '*He* will build a house for my name.' Though it is not spelled out, the hint, especially in light of what we have seen about 7.1, is that David's proposal did not fit Yahweh's timetable. The rest promised in Deuteronomy in which the 'place' of worship for Yahweh would be designated had not yet been bestowed. It was not time for David to

31. A point emphasized by Eslinger, *House of God or House of David*, pp. 42-43 *et passim*.
32. Van Seters (*In Search of History*, pp. 272-74) has dealt with the form critical nature of Nathan's oracle.

build a temple, just as it had not been time for any of the leaders of Israel before him to build one (vv. 6-7). Yahweh's designation of the 'place' at which the people would worship him still lay in the future (v. 10). Only then would the full promised 'rest' be given (v. 11) and the temple built (vv. 12-13).

But the matter of Yahweh's timetable is only hinted at. There is much ambiguity in the question of v. 5 and the speech that follows before its answer in v. 13. McCarter has pointed out that the issue in 2 Sam. 7.1-7 is the type of Yahweh's shrine—mobile tent versus permanent sanctuary—rather than the nature of his presence (imminence versus transcendence) there.[33] David's remark (v. 2) dealt with the resting place of the ark. It was Yahweh himself who raised the matter of *his* dwelling place (בית לשבתי, v. 5). Hence, Yahweh's words in vv. 6-7 can hardly be seen as taking up the issue of the divine transcendence. It is curious, therefore, that McCarter, as we have seen, denies these verses to Dtr based on concern for this same matter as expressed in the verb ישׁב.

Verses 6-7 provide a bridge to the change in subject that occurs in vv. 8-12. Yahweh points out that he has never had a permanent residence since the exodus but has moved around in a tent (v. 6). It has been alleged that the 'house' at Shiloh in 1 Samuel 1–4 provides a counter example and that its memory is suppressed or the reference to it as a בית is anachronistic.[34] But neither of these alternatives is very compelling if 1–2 Samuel as they stand are products of the same author/editor, Dtr. This is especially true if בני־עולה in the days of the judges in 2 Sam. 7.10-11 is an allusion to Shiloh's destruction.[35] Dtr is well aware of the Shiloh story. But to quibble about this inconsistency is to miss his point. The statement that Yahweh never stayed in a house may be taken as hyperbole. Whatever the situation at Shiloh, it was clearly one in a line of temporary stopping places for the ark rather than a permanent residence. It is that contrast between permanence and transience that is at issue here.

In v. 7 Yahweh asks whether he ever commanded any of Israel's previous leaders to build a temple. More has been made of this question (and the statement of v. 6) than is warranted. Just as there is no theological claim here about Yahweh's omnipresence transcending the

---

33. McCarter, *II Samuel*, p. 199.

34. Cf. McCarter, *II Samuel*, p. 199; Cross, *Canaanite Myth*, p. 73 n.

35. As suggested by Gelston, 'A Note on II Samuel 7 10', p. 94.

need for a temple, so there is also no claim that Yahweh prefers a tent shrine to a temple. It is not altogether clear why Yahweh has never had or commanded a permanent shrine. It may be simply a matter of timing, especially if our treatment of 7.1 is correct. But there is also a hint that something more is involved. Verse 7 makes a connection between Yahweh's shrine and Israel's leadership. The implication, especially considering what follows in vv. 8-13, is that the two go hand in hand. There was no fixed shrine because Israel's leadership was also not fixed but rather passed through a series of tribal leaders.[36]

Verse 8 announces that with David Yahweh has begun a new era. The שבטי ישראל were called shepherds (v. 7). This was a common metaphor for leaders in the ancient Near East. But Dtr has used it here to build a contrast. Yahweh took David from the pasture and made him נגיד over Israel. This is Dtr's term for 'king designate', and it also carries military connotations.[37] What marks this new era, of course, is a new permanence in leadership as Yahweh establishes David's 'house' or dynasty (v. 11b). The new permanence in leadership will be matched by a new permanence in cultic matters with the construction of a temple (v. 13). This is the situation predicted in Deuteronomy with the desig-nation of a specific 'place' for worship[38] and the bestowal of 'rest' upon Israel. This new era is imminent, for these events are 'scheduled' for the reign of David's son and successor (v. 12), who will build Yahweh's temple.

Dtr's composition in this chapter had two main objectives. The first

36. On the reading and meaning of שבטי ישראל see McCarter, *II Samuel*, pp. 192, 201. The reference is clearly to pre-monarchical individual leaders, specifi-cally the judges. However, McCarter's translation, 'staff bearers', is compelling and participates in the shepherd metaphor of the next verse.

37. The literature on נגד is voluminous. For starters, see B. Halpern, *The Con-stitution of the Monarchy in Israel* (HSM, 25; Chico, CA: Scholars Press, 1981), pp. 1-11; P.K. McCarter, *I Samuel* (AB, 8; Garden City, NY: Doubleday, 1980), pp. 178-79; and T.N.D. Mettinger, *King and Messiah: The Civil and Sacral Legiti-mation of the Israelite Kings* (ConBOT, 8; Lund: C.W.K. Gleerup, 1976), pp. 151-84. On the military connotations of the term see W. Richter, 'Die *nagid*-Formel: Ein Beitrag zur Erhellung des *nagid*-Problems', *BZ* 97 (1965), pp. 1-84. Cf. also Cross, *Canaanite Myth*, p. 220 n.

38. On the use of מקום for a cultic site and the object of the verbs in this verse see Gelston, 'A Note on II Samuel 7 10'.

was etiological.[39] Dtr sought to solve a dilemma that the traditional
attribution of the temple to Solomon posed for him. David was clearly
the hero of Dtr's work. Dtr devoted substantially more space to David
than to any other character in his history, and David's faithfulness
provided the rationale for the endurance of the nation of Judah and its
dynasty. In the thought world of the ancient Near East it was incon-
ceivable that a dynastic head like David would fail to erect a shrine to
his deity. Yet tradition ascribed the temple to Solomon rather than to
David. Dtr's solution to this problem was brilliant. He concluded that
David, being a faithful king, must have proposed building a temple to
Yahweh, as any king in his shoes would have done. Thus, David was
commended for his intentions (cf. 1 Kgs 5.18). However, it was not in
God's plan for David to build the temple. His proposal is not flatly
denied. Rather, Yahweh explains that the temple will be built by
David's son, whose reign will embody the establishment of David's
dynasty as well as the time of 'rest' anticipated in Deuteronomy. Dtr
went on to show how wars dominated the remainder of David's reign—
so much so that Solomon would later attribute the fact that David did
not build the temple to his preoccupation with war (1 Kgs 5.17). But
Solomon would go on to point out that Yahweh had given him the
promised rest in which there was neither שָׂטָן nor פֶּגַע רָע (5.18 [EVV
5.4]), an apparent allusion to 2 Sam. 7.10.

Dtr's second objective in this chapter, of course, was the introduction
of the promise of a Davidic dynasty, which was one of the key motifs
in his history. That promise also had an etiological function in that it
accounted for the duration of Judah and its royal house. Dtr combined
David's proposal to build a temple with the promise of a dynasty using
the *Leitwort*, 'house'. The crux of this combination is vv. 11b-13. The
son who would build David's house would also build Yahweh's. The
dynasty is not explicitly described as a reward for David's proposal or
for that matter as a reward for David's faithfulness; it is a gift from
Yahweh, who has in fact been 'with David' since his days in the
pasture. But Yahweh's promise to David on the occasion of his
proposal certainly cements the relationship between temple and
dynasty, two institutions that were inextricably linked in the ancient
Near East anyway.

---

39. S. Mowinckel's observation of the etiological function of 2 Sam. 7
('Natansforjettelsen 2 Sam kap 7', *SEÅ* 12 [1947], pp. 220-29) is helpful here.

Chronicles

The Chronicles version of the Nathan oracle in 1 Chronicles 17 is very close to that of 2 Samuel 7. Given the variation now widely recognized between the MT and the text of Samuel used by the Chronicler, one must be cautious not too readily to ascribe the minor differences between the synoptic accounts to the Chronicler's *Tendenz*.[40] On the other hand, a few of these differences do seem to reflect a different perspective on the part of the Chronicler and therefore deliberate change by him.[41] The most important of these for our present purposes is in 1 Chron. 17.1, which lacks the reference in 2 Sam. 7.1b to Yahweh having given David 'rest' round about. If the latter is a misplaced gloss on v. 11, as I have contended in agreement with McCarter, it is possible that the Chronicler did not find it in his Samuel *Vorlage*. However, the language about rest in 2 Sam. 7.11 is also missing from the parallel in 1 Chron. 17.10 ('I will subdue all your enemies'), which seems to reflect a deliberate change. This must mean that the Chronicler found the promise to give David rest already in his text of 2 Sam. 7.11, and he changed it because he found it problematic. He would not have objected to the promise of rest for Israel, since that is what he describes for Solomon's reign. It was only the promise of rest *in David's day* that he found troublesome. Hence, most scholars are probably correct in assuming that the Chronicler's *Vorlage* of Samuel had the same reading as the MT in 2 Sam. 7.1b, 11 and that the Chronicles parallels to those verses reflect intentional change.[42]

40. See W.E. Lemke, 'Synoptic Studies in the Chronicler's History' (ThD dissertation, Harvard University, 1963) and 'The Synoptic Problem in the Chronicler's History', *HTR* 58 (1965), pp. 349-63. Also see S.L. McKenzie, *The Chronicler's Use of the Deuteronomistic History* (HSM, 33; Atlanta: Scholars Press, 1985).

41. I accept, therefore, the common view that the Chronicler used the DtrH as his main source. As is clear from the discussion in the first half of this essay, I also accept the existence of the DtrH essentially as identified by M. Noth. Both of these theories have recently been called into question by A.G. Auld, *Kings without Privilege: David and Moses in the Story of the Bible's Kings* (Edinburgh: T. & T. Clark, 1994). My reasons for rejecting Auld's view that the authors of Samuel–Kings and Chronicles made use of a 'shared source' are detailed in my article, 'The Chronicler as Redactor', forthcoming in M.P. Graham and S.L. McKenzie (eds.), *Chronicles as Literature* (JSOTSup; Sheffield: Sheffield Academic Press).

42. See Roddy Braun, *1 Chronicles* (WBC, 14; Waco, TX: Word Books, 1986),

Even if 1 Chron. 17.1, 10 do not contain deliberate alterations of their Samuel counterparts, it still becomes obvious in reading the Chronicler's work that his explanation for David's not having built the temple differs markedly from Dtr's.[43] Chronicles does not recount the eras of Moses, Joshua or the judges and thus does not follow the Deuteronomistic time frame in which the schema of rest plays a role. His explanation, rather, has to do with the contrast he finds between David as a man of wars and Solomon as a man of peace. It was not only temporally expedient but also ritually appropriate that the temple be built during a time of peace. Accordingly, God bestowed rest on Solomon's reign and designated him, rather than David, as the temple builder.

This contrast on the part of the Chronicler is especially evident in his lengthy addition in 1 Chronicles 22–29.[44] These final eight chapters represent the climax to the Chronicler's account of David, and they bring together his three major themes in 1 Chronicles—temple, David and all Israel—in a particularly forceful way. Here David assembles all Israel in order to present his designated successor, Solomon, and to challenge him to carry out the dream that David was unable to realize: building a temple to Yahweh. The Chronicler's concern for the temple is apparent in these chapters' description of the preparation of building materials for temple construction and of Levitical divisions for the temple cult. He idealizes David by having him procure the design for

p. 198; S. Japhet, *I and II Chronicles: A Commentary* (OTL; Louisville, KY: Westminster / John Knox Press, 1993), p. 328; H.G.M. Williamson, *1 and 2 Chronicles* (NCB; Grand Rapids: Eerdmans, 1982), p. 134. J.M. Myers (*I Chronicles* [AB, 12; Garden City, NY: Doubleday, 1965], pp. 125-26) suggests that the Chronicler's reason for the omission of 2 Sam. 7.1b was that it implied a lapse in time between the bringing up of the ark to Jerusalem and David's proposal to build a temple. But as Williamson observes, this was only a contributory factor. Cf. also R. Mosis, *Untersuchungen zur Theologie des chronistischen Geschichtswerkes* (FTS, 92; Freiburg: Herder, 1973), p. 94.

43. See H.G.M. Williamson, 'The Dynastic Oracle in the Books of Cronicles [*sic*]', in A. Rofé and Y. Zakovitch (eds.), *Isac Leo Seeligmann Volume: Essays in the Bible and the Ancient World* (Jerusalem: E. Rubinstein's, 1983), pp. 305-18.

44. Many scholars consider the bulk of these chapters (esp. 23.3–27.34) to be a later addition to Chronicles. This does not greatly affect my treatment here, which focuses on David's speeches in chs. 22 and 28. Mosis (*Untersuchung zur Theologie*, pp. 91-92) contends that the latter half of ch. 22 is secondary. Even if he is right, most of my observations about David's speeches remain intact.

the temple, accumulate the materials for its erection and organize its cult in every detail. This is an expansion of Dtr's effort to credit David with the idea behind the temple. Finally, the Chronicler's vision of all Israel united emerges especially in chs. 27–29, where David assembles the heads of all the tribes of Israel to Jerusalem to present Solomon as his successor.

The material in these eight chapters evinces a remarkably different perspective from that of the DtrH. Chronicles' assignment of the entire temple cult to David is extraordinary. There is nothing about this cultic work of David in Samuel or Kings, and one assumes in reading them that the rituals for the temple originated with Moses, particularly in light of the fulfillment in the temple of Yahweh's promise to give rest to Israel. The descriptions in Chronicles and the DtrH of the transition from David's reign to Solomon's are also very different. By omitting the accounts in 2 Samuel about David's affair with Bathsheba (2 Sam. 11-12) and the subsequent revolt of Absalom (2 Sam. 13-20), the Chronicler presents an idealized picture of the unity of Israel, which is reinforced by his description of the various assemblies in 1 Chronicles 22-29. The stories in 1 Kings 1–2 about the division in David's court over who would succeed him and Solomon's eventual accession are also absent from Chronicles. The transition from David to Solomon is very smooth according to 1 Chronicles 22–29, and there is never any doubt that Solomon will be David's successor. David designates him as such before his old age (1 Chron. 22.6–23.1), and there is never any mention of a rival to Solomon for the throne.

The great burden for advancing the Chronicler's theology in 1 Chronicles 22–29 is borne by the speeches of David in these chapters, especially those in 22.6-16 and 28.2-10. These speeches are full of allusions to the Nathan oracle in both its 2 Samuel 7 and its 1 Chronicles 17 incarnations.[45] Indeed, both speeches may be described as David's summaries or retellings and hence the Chronicler's interpretations of the Nathan oracle.[46] In reinterpreting that oracle the Chronicler highlights the role of Solomon as temple builder in the history of Israel. While recent treatments of these speeches have discovered three

---

45. In at least one case (22.10) the speech relies on 2 Sam. 7 rather than 1 Chron. 17. Cf. Japhet, *I and II Chronicles*, p. 398.

46. Kalimi (*Zur Geschichtsschreibung*, p. 225) shows that the two speeches have the same structure and follow the same order as 2 Sam. 7//1 Chron. 17.

ways in which Solomon's role is highlighted,[47] they have not always
acknowledged the extent to which the Chronicler is drawing on Dtr's
own explanation for why Solomon and not David built the temple.
Moreover, I would suggest that there are not really three interpretive
moves operating in these chapters but only one. The Chronicler reinterprets the Deuteronomistic theme of rest, and he makes use of other
devices to support his reinterpretation.

To be sure, the Chronicler carries on the Deuteronomistic view of
Solomon's reign as a time of rest. But Solomon's is not the ultimate
period of rest as in Dtr's time scheme. Rest is something enjoyed by
other righteous kings in Chronicles (2 Chron. 15.15; 20.30). More
important, the Chronicler adds another element to the decline of
David's proposal to build Yahweh a house. Solomon is a man of rest
(איש מנוחה, 1 Chron. 22.9) in contrast to David, the 'man of wars'
(איש מלחמות, 28.3). But while 1 Kgs 5.17 attributes the postponement
of David's project to his preoccupation with wars in accord with the
time frame of the DtrH (2 Sam. 7.1b), 1 Chron. 22.8 and 28.3 ascribe
the delay to David's great bloodshed: 'You have shed much blood and
waged great wars; you shall not build a house for my name because you
have shed much blood on the ground before me' (22.8) and 'You are a
warrior and have shed blood' (28.3). The temple is the place of rest for
the ark (28.2) and in some way for Yahweh himself (cf. 2 Chron.
6.41).[48] Hence, it could not be built by a man of war with blood on his
hands. (This is probably another reason for the Chronicler's omission
of the account of Solomon's bloody accession in 1 Kgs 1–2). Solomon
is the appropriate one to build the temple because he is a man of peace,
as his name indicates: 'Solomon will be his name, and peace and quiet
will I give over Israel in his days' (22.9). Thus, the basis for deferring
the temple building is not the time frame for Isael's national history as
in the DtrH. Rather, in Chronicles it is inappropriate for a man of blood
and war to build a holy house of rest for Yahweh with the ark. This
should be understood as a ritual judgment not a moral one.[49] David's
bloody hands do not in any way impugn his character or detract from

    47. See especially Braun, 'Solomon, the Chosen Temple Builder', as well as the
works cited therein and in those cited below.
    48. Cf. von Rad, 'There Remains Still a Rest', pp. 97-99.
    49. See the discussion of W. Riley (*King and Cultus in Chronicles: Worship
and the Reinterpretation of History* [JSOTSup, 160; Sheffield: Sheffield Academic
Press, 1993], pp. 80-81) and the bibliography he cites on this matter.

the Chronicler's portrait of him as a model king. But the fact remains that they would have defiled the temple.

> The Chronicler's contribution to the development of the concept lies in seeing the connection between 'rest' and 'Temple building' not as circumstantial but as essential: he who is not a 'man of rest' is 'a man of war' (cf. 28.3), and as such is prevented not only in practice but *on principle* from building a house for the Lord.[50]

The Chronicler lends support to his reinterpretation of the rest motif in two ways. The first of these is the verb בחר in 1 Chr 28.6, 10 and 29.1. The use of this verb to express Yahweh's election of Solomon is unique.[51] The term is not used elsewhere for any king after David, and unlike other uses of the term in reference to individuals, Solomon's election is a matter of dynastic succession not charismatic anointing. More important for our present concerns, all the uses of בחר referring to Solomon's election in 1 Chronicles 28–29 are explicitly linked to the temple construction. Solomon is chosen specifically for the purpose of building Yahweh's temple. As David says to Solomon in 1 Chron. 28.10, 'Yahweh has chosen you to build a house for the sanctuary.'

This emphasis on the election of Solomon as temple builder is best read in the light of the Nathan oracle. As we have seen, the rhetorical question of 2 Sam. 7.5 employs the emphatic pronoun (האתה תבנה־לי בית לשבתי , 'Will *you* build a temple for me to live in?'). The question remains open until another emphatic pronoun in v. 13 reveals that someone other than David has been destined for the project ('*He* will build a temple for my name'). The Chronicler reinforces this point first by changing the question into a statement (לא אתה תבנה־לי הבית לשבת, '*You* will build me the temple to live in,' 1 Chron. 17.4). Then, David's speeches in 1 Chronicles 22 and 28 show that it is Solomon rather than David whom Yahweh has chosen for the task of building the temple.[52]

---

50. Japhet, *I and II Chronicles*, p. 397.

51. In addition to Braun ('Solomon, the Chosen Temple Builder', pp. 588-90) see V. Peterca, 'Die Verwendung des Verbes BHR für Salomo in den Büchern der Chronik', *BZ* 29 (1985), pp. 94-96.

52. Japhet (*I and II Chronicles*, pp. 329-30) contrasts Samuel and Chronicles at this point, stating, 'In Chronicles the emphasis is different. From the outset the determining factor is that of timing: not you but your successor will build a house. The days of peace and "rest" have not yet come; when they do my house shall be built.' She is followed by M.A. Throntveit ('The Idealization of Solomon as the Glorification of God in the Chronicler's Royal Speeches and Royal Prayers', in

Secondly, the Chronicler has patterned his account of the transition from David to Solomon after the Deuteronomistic account of the transition from Moses to Joshua.[53] This is clear especially from the similarity in language and concerns in David's charge to Solomon in Chronicles and the passages in Deuteronomy and Joshua that describe the transition of leadership from Moses to Joshua. Witness the following expressions: (1) 'to do the statutes and ordinances which Yahweh commanded Moses' (את־המשפטים אשר צוה יהוה את־משה לעשות את־החקים [1 Chron. 22.13; cf. 28.7; Josh. 1.7]); (2) 'be strong and courageous; do not fear and do not be discouraged' (חזק ואמץ אל־תירא ואל־תחת) [1 Chron. 22.13; cf. 28.20; Deut. 31.7, 8, 23; Josh. 1.6, 7, 9]) and (3) 'Yahweh God, my God, is with you. He will not fail you or abandon you' (יהוה אלהים אלהי עמך לא ירפך ולא יעזבך [1 Chron. 28.20; cf. 22.11, 16; Deut. 31.6; 8. 23; Josh. 1.5]). Here again, the most important aspect of the Chronicler's 'installation' of Solomon has to do with the temple. Solomon is commissioned in Chronicles specifically to complete the construction of the temple for which David has made preparation, just as Joshua is commissioned in the DtrH to lead the Israelites in the conquest of the land. By way of contrast, in 1 Kgs 2.1-5 David tells Solomon to keep the law of Moses so that Yahweh will carry out his promise to David of an eternal dynasty. Solomon is commissioned in Kings to guard the dynasty, but in Chronicles to guard the temple.

Two other minor but significant changes in the Chronicler's version of the Nathan oracle vis-à-vis 2 Samuel 7 are noteworthy in the light of his reinterpretation in 1 Chronicles 22–29. The reference in 2 Sam.

L.K. Handy [ed.], *The Age of Solomon: Scholarship at the Turn of the Millennium* [Studies in the History and Culture of the Ancient Near East, 11; Leiden: E.J. Brill, 1997], p. 416). In my view, this understanding fails to give proper credit to Dtr, who orginated the theology of rest and for whom timing is crucial. As stated, the Chronicler reinforces the dimension of timing. But he also extends his theology of rest in a different direction. In Chronicles 'rest' becomes one of the rewards for righteous kings (2 Chron. 14.5-6; 15.15; 20.30). Chronicles, therefore, dilutes the Dtr theology of rest by not limiting the 'rest' to the time of Solomon and the construction of the temple.

53. Braun, 'Solomon, the Chosen Temple Builder', pp. 586-88; Braun, *1 Chronicles*, pp. 222-23; N. Lohfink, 'Die deuteronomistische Darstellung des Übergangs der Führung Israels von Mose auf Josue: Ein Beitrag zur alttestamentliche Theologie des Amtes', *Scholastik* 37 (1962), pp. 32-44; and H.G.M. Williamson, 'The Accession of Solomon in the Books of Chronicles', *VT* 26 (1976), pp. 351-61.

7.14b to chastising David's 'seed', when he sins, 'with the rod of mortals and the stripes of humans' has been omitted from 1 Chron. 17.13. In addition, the promise in 2 Sam. 7.16, 'your house and your kingdom will be established forever before you', has been altered in 1 Chron. 17.14 to 'I will confirm him in my house and in my kingdom forever', so that the spotlight is on Solomon rather than David and on the house of Yahweh rather than the house of David. In this way, the Chronicler suggests the subordination of the king to the temple. David and Solomon are idealized because of their roles in building the temple. In this way and through his addition in 1 Chronicles 22–29, the Chronicler shifts the focus of the Nathan oracle so that the temple is no longer one element in the royal Judean theology but stands at the center of Yahweh's relationship to Israel. The king's major role in this perspective is to watch over the temple and its cult. The centrality of the temple in Chronicles has greatly enhanced the significance of Solomon (hence the change in focus in 1 Chron. 17.14). The entire function of Solomon in the Chronicler's presentation of him is to build the temple. This has also led to the idealization of Solomon in Chronicles, which is reflected in the omission of 2 Sam. 7.14b.[54]

Summary and Conclusion

There is not, perhaps surprisingly, a lengthy tradition history surrounding the question of why David did not build the temple—at least not one that can be traced in the extant literature. The first cogent explanation that we possess for the tradition that Solomon rather than David was the temple builder (2 Sam. 7) comes from Dtr, probably in the exile. The language and ideology of 2 Samuel 7 are thoroughly Deuteronomistic, and the shift in the narrative between vv. 3 and 4 accords well with Dtr's etiological objectives in the text and attests his cleverness in resolving the dilemma that the tradition of Solomon's temple presented for his portrait of David. Whether the need for an explanation of this tradition was felt earlier cannot be determined. Dtr preserved David's character by having him propose a temple. Yahweh was pleased to accept David's proposal, while also explaining that it was actually David's son who would build both houses, Yahweh's and

---

54. This dimension of the Chronicler's ideology has only recently been noted and explored by scholars. See especially R.L. Braun, 'Solomonic Apologetic in Chronicles', *JBL* 92 (1973), pp. 503-16.

David's (the former being unveiled as a gift from God). It was in the reign of this son that the time of rest Yahweh had promised would arrive. This explanation has been obscured by subsequent additions in Joshua and textual corruption in 2 Samuel 7.

A century and a half later the author of Chronicles faced the same dilemma. Reinterpreting his Deuteronomistic source, the Chronicler found the reason for Yahweh's refusal of David's proposal not in a chronological scheme of history but in the nature of the temple itself. As the most holy site it could not be erected by a man of violence whose hands were soiled with the blood of his enemies, no matter how justified his wars (and they were the wars of God). David was such a man, but Solomon was a man of peace, as was apparent from his name. Solomon was Yahweh's choice to build the temple, and Yahweh gave him rest, resulting from David's wars, to accomplish the task. By the same token, this led the Chronicler to present an idealized portrait of Solomon as the temple builder (and of David as the one who made all the preparations), as well as the unity of Israel who rallied around its construction. As the Chronicler really only makes one interpretive move in 1 Chronicles 22–29, so his overall agenda really consists of only one item. The idealization of David and Solomon and the image of all Israel are motifs that support his primary concern for the temple.

Worship in Judges 17–18

Phillip McMillion

I would like to begin by expressing my appreciation to Professor John Willis. I was fortunate to do part of my Master of Divinity work under him at Abilene Christian University. Dr Willis was always a well-organized, interesting and inspiring classroom teacher. He was also an excellent example of a diligent scholar who was constantly engaged in research and publishing the results of his inquiries. In addition, he modeled for his students how one may use scholarship in service to the community of faith. My own work, and I suspect that of many others, has been shaped in large part by the lessons I learned from his words and life.

Preliminary Remarks

The theme of this Festschrift is worship, and one may well ask what the book of Judges has to do with worship. In some ways, Judges is one of the most secular books in the Hebrew Scriptures. It is a book filled with battles, war heroes and heroines, assassinations, crimes of passion, revenge and slaughter. It sounds more like the stuff of modern action adventures than holy writ. One of the things that makes it so fascinating is that, in addition to all the human drama, it is filled with references to God, words spoken by God and people who are motivated to act by their faith in God. In Judges one sees great examples of the heights of human heroism as well as the depths of what one human can inflict on another. The motivation for much of the action, however, is linked to faith in God and even to worship.

At first glance, the world of the book of Judges appears strange and foreign to the modern reader. How could people rise to the heights and sink to the depths described in this book and believe they were all motivated by faith? Surely this is a world too ancient and primitive for modern minds to comprehend. With a bit of reflection, however, one begins to realize that the picture described in the book of Judges is not so foreign after all. It is, in fact, all too familiar. It is the same world one finds in newspapers and news reports in too many places today. Murder, brutality, greed, theft, wholesale slaughter—all in the name of religion—are hardly foreign to the modern world.

This study will focus on Judges 17–18 and the story of Micah and his idol. In this section of the book, there are numerous links to worship, including the consecration of money to God, the making of an idol and a family shrine for worship, the securing of a Levite as a priest and finally a whole tribe seizing the idol and priest for their own. After a careful look at this story, some implications for worship will be suggested.

Three Approaches to Judges 17–18

In the past two decades, biblical scholarship has experienced a dramatic increase in the variety of methods used to explore the biblical text. Methods from such fields as sociology, anthropology and various types of literary and rhetorical criticism have all been applied to the Bible. Canonical criticism is yet another critical method for the interpretation of the biblical text that has found acceptance in some quarters. Many of these methods have been applied to the study of the book of Judges, and a recent book by G.A. Yee has detailed the application of some of these methods to it.[1]

The story in Judges 17–18 raises a number of challenging questions, not the least of which is 'Why is it even here?' There is no judge and no imminent danger to Israel. The story is filled with interesting characters and surprising developments. As fascinating as the story itself, however, is the variety of ways the story has been treated in modern scholarship. Recent works have treated this material as either a late addition only secondarily related to the stories of the Judges, or, alternatively, as an integral part of the core of the book of Judges, beginning at Judg. 2.5 and continuing through 18.31.[2]

---

1.   G.A. Yee (ed.), *Judges and Method: New Approaches in Biblical Studies* (Minneapolis: Fortress Press, 1995).

2.   B.G. Webb, *The Book of Judges: An Integrated Reading* (JSOTSup, 46; Sheffield: JSOT Press, 1987), pp. 19-40, contains a survey of critical scholarship of the book of Judges.

This essay will briefly summarize three different treatments of Judges 17–18 as representative of different approaches. In conclusion, some theological observations will be made about a possible setting and message found in this material. The three representative treatments are by M. Noth, G.A. Yee and R.H. O'Connell.[3]

Martin Noth

Almost all modern work on this material either builds on or reacts to the groundbreaking work of Noth and his study of the DtrH.[4] More recently the nature—if not the very existence—of the DtrH has been the subject of considerable debate, but that discussion need not be repeated here.[5] In a later work, Noth treated Judges 17–18 in some detail, opening his discussion with the suggestion that these chapters contain many details concerning the tribal period and cultic practices that reflect 'direct knowledge of the subject matter'.[6] These details are not the focus of Noth's analysis, since he is more concerned with the purpose and the setting for the preservation of this material. Noth argues that the basic material would have been preserved by the Danites in order to relate how the tribal shrine at Dan came into existence and how it came to be located there. He states that the Danites 'took delight in telling the story of how their immigrating forefathers brought along the image from the mountains of Ephraim'.[7] In its present context, however, Noth recognizes that the story takes on a much more negative tone. From the very beginning, the silver used to produce the image is involved in controversy. Micah has stolen it from his own mother, and then she dedicates only a small portion of the silver to produce an

3. M. Noth, 'The Background of Judges 17–18', in B.W. Anderson and W. Harrelson (eds.), *Israel's Prophetic Heritage: Essays in Honor of James Muilenburg* (New York: Harper & Brothers, 1962), pp. 68-85; G.A. Yee, 'Ideological Criticism: Judges 17-21 and the Dismembered Body', in G.A. Yee (ed.), *Judges and Method: New Approaches in Biblical Studies* (Minneapolis: Fortress Press, 1995), pp. 146-70; and R.H. O'Connell, *The Rhetoric of the Book of Judges* (VTSup, 63; Leiden: E.J. Brill, 1996).

4. M. Noth, *The Deuteronomistic History* (JSOTSup, 15; Sheffield: Sheffield Academic Press, 2nd edn, 1991).

5. See S.L. McKenzie and M.P. Graham (eds.), *The History of Israel's Traditions: The Heritage of Martin Noth* (JSOTSup, 182; Sheffield: Sheffield Academic Press, 1994), and the literature cited there.

6. Noth, 'Background of Judges 17–18', p. 68.

7. Noth, 'Background of Judges 17–18', p. 69.

image. The way the Danites take possession of the image is also presented in a negative light. These more controversial elements in the
narrative transform the original story into one that reverses the positive
tone of the Danite tradition. It is at this point that the material becomes
part of a pro-monarchical theme.

Noth maintains, however, that these pro-monarchical elements are
not an argument for the acceptance of the Jerusalem kingship, but
instead a defense of the Israelite kingship. He argues that this passage
was used to justify the royal sanctuary in Dan that was established in
opposition to or perhaps in competition with the older tribal sanctuary
in Dan. In order to gain support for the royal Israelite sanctuary in Dan,
the older tribal sanctuary is cast in a negative light. The strongly pro-
monarchical statements in Judg. 17.6 and 18.1 would not have been
acceptable to DtrH, and so these chapters were not a part of his history
as envisioned by Noth.[8] They must have been added later to their
present context. Since Judg. 17.6 and 18.1 presumed the existence of
the kingship, the reference to the exile from the land in 18.30 must be a
later addition. Noth then argues that the reference to the use of the
shrine as long as the house of God was at Shiloh (18.31) was added by
someone who favored the tribal sanctuary at Dan. This final note
should be understood as meaning that 'as long as kings had not yet
interfered with the cultic traditions of Israel, everything was better than
it is today'.[9] Since this reflects such a strongly anti-monarchical tone, it
must be seen as a later addition and could not have been a part of the
original narrative of chs. 17–18.

Noth's article is a classic example of a tradition-historical analysis.
He creates possible settings for the various stages of the narrative and
shows how each new addition to the narrative adjusts the meaning to fit
a new scenario. The setting created by Noth is at the same time imaginative and perfectly logical. If one accepts Noth's presuppositions, then
his conclusions are certainly possible. But as later interpreters have
shown, this is by no means the only possible scenario to explain the
history of this passage.[10]

---

8.   Noth, 'Background of Judges 17–18', pp. 79-83. Noth saw the basic DtrH
as anti-monarchical and written after the end of the Davidic monarchy in 587 BCE.

9.   Noth, 'Background of Judges 17–18', p. 85.

10.   J. Gray, *Joshua, Judges and Ruth* (NCB; London: Thomas Nelson, 1967),
pp. 237-39, follows much of Noth's analysis.

Gale A. Yee

Yee's analysis begins with an ideological foundation, that is, that there are two different modes of production behind this text.[11] In short, there is an economic conflict at the heart of this text. The earlier tribal period is described as operating under a familial mode of production. It is characterized by strong family and village relationships. These in turn were organized by clans, which were the largest social units of this period. Highland agriculture and pastoral production were the major elements of the economy.[12] The tribes were free, self-sufficient units, and they owed no taxes or loyalties to outside rulers, so any wealth produced was retained by the tribe.

In contrast to this tribal system, Israel's monarchy developed a native tributary mode of production. Under this system, the tribal units were centralized under the control of a king. This system brought both the loss of personal freedom and the destruction of economic independence for the majority of Israel. An elite class at the top of the social structure made up the 'haves' while the great majority at the bottom were heavily taxed and became the peasant class of the 'have nots'.[13] Taxes increased to pay for elaborate building projects, costly wars and a bloated bureaucracy. Such a negative system would naturally have a devastating effect on the peasant classes.

Yee argues that the period of the reforms of Josiah is the time frame for Judges 17–21. She suggests that this material is part of the propaganda used to justify the reforms of Josiah, which were in reality only a cover for more sinister motives. According to Yee's scenario, Judah had suffered under the heavy hand of Assyria for 75 years prior to the rule of Josiah. During this period, the ruling elite of Judah were hard-pressed to pay the tribute to Assyria while still maintaining their lavish lifestyle.[14] With the decline of Assyrian power, Josiah could extend his power and tighten his grip on the economy of Judah. He could not, however, raise taxes on the already hard-pressed peasants. Instead, he destroyed the country shrines and demanded that all religious offerings and tribute flow to Jerusalem and the central sanctuary. This would stimulate the Judean economy and also increase the king's share of the

---

11. Yee, 'Ideological Criticism', p. 152.
12. Yee, 'Ideological Criticism', p. 152-53.
13. Yee, 'Ideological Criticism', p. 153.
14. Yee, 'Ideological Criticism', p. 155.

profits, since there would be no intermediaries taking a cut for their role in the collection process.[15]

Judges 17–18 is important for two elements of this process: (1) it presents the country shrines in a negative light, and (2) it denigrates the Levites, who were the major functionaries at the country shrines. By undercutting both the country shrines and the Levites, and by showing the need for a king to preserve good order, Judges 17–18 helped to justify the changes made by Josiah.

Yee has presented a clear example of an ideological interpretation, and she suggests some interesting possibilities. Several questions could be raised, however, about this scenario. First, Yee accepts some of the information in the narrative in her reconstruction of the society of Josiah's day, while leaving aside material about similar ills and reforms of earlier periods. Secondly, she is suspicious of any theological motivations behind the reforms of Josiah. Thirdly, she makes it clear that ideology—specifically Marxism—is the foundation for her analysis.[16] This ideology does provide a challenging reading of the text in Judges, but it also requires a number of assumptions that move beyond the evidence from the text itself.

Robert H. O'Connell

A third approach to these chapters is exemplified by the detailed study of R.H. O'Connell.[17] O'Connell seeks to identify the 'ostensible' situation for the writing of the book of Judges or the 'implied setting', which he also calls the *Sitz im Text*. He states that he is not concerned with the 'actual historical situation' of the compilation of Judges.[18] In his introduction O'Connell explains that for his study he understands the term rhetoric to refer to the 'ideological purpose of agenda of the Judges compiler/redactor with respect to the implied readers of the book'.[19] He intends to present a coherent reading of the present form of the book. This is significant for the study of Judges 17–18 as will be discussed below. O'Connell also states that he plans to discover the rhetorical purpose of the compiler/redactor of Judges by analyzing the 'formal structures and motivic patterns that recur throughout the

---

15. Yee, 'Ideological Criticism', p. 155.
16. Yee, 'Ideological Criticism', pp. 146-51.
17. O'Connell, *Rhetoric of the Book of Judges*, pp. 305-42.
18. O'Connell, *Rhetoric of the Book of Judges*, p. 306.
19. O'Connell, *Rhetoric of the Book of Judges*, p. 1.

narrative framework of the book as well as...patterns of plot-structure and characterization...'[20]

O'Connell presents a detailed rhetorical-critical analysis of the book of Judges, and on the basis of his analysis argues that the implied setting for the book of Judges is the early rule of David, before the capture of Jerusalem. This would correspond to the historical setting described in 2 Samuel 1–4. In this setting the purpose of the book of Judges was to present the case for the acceptance of the Davidic monarchy, which was still in its formative stages and not yet fully accepted by all the tribes.[21] Although O'Connell argues from a rhetorical-critical position, the basic view that Judges is an apology for the monarchy has been argued from various lines of evidence for well over a century.[22]

O'Connell's distinction between the implied setting and the real historical setting of the book of Judges is difficult to maintain with consistency. This is especially true if one considers O'Connell's claim to accept the present text as it stands. In Judges 17–18, the conclusion in 18.30-31 refers to events far later than the time suggested in O'Connell's implied setting. He deals with this by assigning these verses to a later redactor.[23] This is widely accepted among students of this passage, but it clearly indicates that the present text as it stands comes from a much later time than the implied setting suggested by O'Connell. If there is a text that fits O'Connell's implied setting, it is an earlier version of the text, which must be identified through historical-critical analysis. O'Connell's appendix on the compilation stratigraphy of the text of Judges indicates his awareness of this problem, although he does not specifically comment on how this relates to dealing with the 'present form of the book'.[24]

The Setting of Judges 17–18

The setting of the final edition of Judges is not the main focus of this article, but it does have some bearing on the message of chs. 17–18.

20. O'Connell, *Rhetoric of the Book of Judges*, p. 1.
21. O'Connell, *Rhetoric of the Book of Judges*, pp. 305-307.
22. P.S. Calles, *The Book of Judges* (New York: Scribner, Armstrong, 1874); D.R. Davis, 'A Proposed Life-Setting for the Book of Judges' (PhD dissertation, Southern Baptist Theological Seminary, 1978); A.E. Cundall, 'Judges—An Apology for the Monarchy', *ExpTim* 81 (1979), pp. 178-81.
23. O'Connell, *Rhetoric of the Book of Judges*, p. 424.
24. O'Connell, *Rhetoric of the Book of Judges*, p. 1.

There are two lines of internal evidence for determining the setting of the two chapters. The first is the references in 17.6 and 18.1 to a time when 'there was no king in Israel'. Judges 17.6 adds the phrase, 'Every man did what was right in his own eyes.' This is missing from 18.1, but, following so closely after the initial reference, it may well be that the audience is expected to remember the whole phrase.[25] In any case, it clearly indicates that the setting is after the time when there is/was a monarchy in Israel. The problem is that these references give no indication of how long after the establishment of the monarchy the writer is viewing these events. Here 18.30 provides additional information. The sanctuary established is said to continue until 'the day of the captivity of the land'.

Since the sanctuary in Judges 18 is established in the northern territory, the most immediate reference to the captivity of the land would fit the captivity of Israel under Assyria. It is significant, however, that this same root for 'captivity' (גלה) is also found in references to the captivity of Judah in 2 Kgs. 25.21 ('So Judah went into exile out of its land') and in 2 Chron. 36.20 ('He took into exile in Babylon those who had escaped from the sword'). The root גלה occurs regularly in the Hebrew Bible, and so one must not press these occurrences too far. It appears likely, nevertheless, that the reference to exile in Judg. 18.30 could be intended to point beyond the immediate context of the northern kingdom and suggest a reference to the exile of Judah as well.[26] The echo of this term at the end of both the books of Kings and Chronicles would support this reading.

The Message of Judges 17–18

Discussion will no doubt continue over the setting and audience for this passage, but of equal concern is the message of Judges 17–18. What is the purpose of this material and what does it intend to teach? It is assumed by this essay that this material is theological in nature and was intended at some level to provide instruction to a community of faith.[27]

25. Y. Amit, 'Hidden Polemic in the Conquest of Dan: Judges xvii-xviii', *VT* 60 (1990), pp. 4-20.

26. W.J. Dumbrell, '"In Those Days There Was No King in Israel; Every Man Did What Was Right in His Own Eyes". The Purpose of the Book of Judges Reconsidered', *JSOT* 25 (1983), pp. 21-33.

27. R. Rendtorff, '"Covenant" as a Structuring Concept in Genesis and Exodus',

One could also read this material in light of various political agendas.[28] As has been noted above, one can also analyze this literature in terms of its sociological and economic context.[29] Since the material was ultimately preserved and transmitted in a community of faith, however, the theological elements should not be ignored.

The narrative in Judges 17 divides itself into two nearly equal parts in vv. 1-6 and 7-13. The two sections begin with almost identical openings. In v. 1 the phrase ויהי איש ('there was a man') is followed by a the preposition 'from' and a geographical location. In v. 7 the opening phrase ויהי נער ('there was a young man') is followed by the preposition 'from' and a geographical location. This twofold opening links the stories stylistically just as the appearance of the character Micah in both stories links the content of the stories.

At the same time there are significant differences in the two stories. The mother is missing in vv. 7-13. Micah's son, whom he installed as priest, is also ignored in vv. 7-13. The sanctuary is assumed in vv. 7-13, since the Levite is invited to serve as priest, but there is no specific mention of the idol, the graven image, the ephod or the teraphim. There has been considerable discussion over these four articles of worship mentioned in vv. 4 and 5. Moore argued that the 'graven image' (פסל) was the original term, and 'molten image' (מסכה) was added as a later expansion.[30] More recent commentators have suggested that the two terms are an example of hendiadys, and so no distinctions should be sought between them.[31] The additional terms 'ephod' and 'teraphim' are also found in 17.5 and appear later in the narrative in 18.14, 17 and

---

JBL 108 (1989), pp. 385-93, makes a similar point, although dealing with a different set of texts, when he writes that he is 'assuming that the OT texts in their present form are theological by nature, and that, therefore, the texts themselves contain the—or at least a—theological message' (p. 386).

28. M. Brettler, 'The Book of Judges: Literature as Politics', *JBL* 108 (1989), pp. 395-418.

29. Yee, 'Ideological Criticism'.

30. G.F. Moore, *A Critical and Exegetical Commentary on the Book of Judges* (ICC, 7; New York: Charles Scribner's Sons, 1895), p. 375; so also C.F. Burney, *The Book of Judges* (New York: Ktav, 1970, repr. of 1918 original), p. 419.

31. R.G. Boling, *Judges* (AB, 6A; Garden City, NY: Doubleday, 1975), p. 256; J.A. Soggin, *Judges* (OTL; Philadelphia: Westminster Press, 1981), p. 265; H.W. Hertzberg, *Die Bücher Josua, Richter, Ruth* (ATD, 9; Göttingen: Vandenhoek & Ruprecht, 1965), p. 240; so also an earlier article by J.A. Bewer, 'The Composition of Judges, Chapters 17–18', *AJSL* 29 (1913), pp. 261-83.

18. This second pair of terms have also been seen as additional idols,[32] as cultic equipment needed for the sanctuary[33] or as an ironic narrative device ridiculing the senseless multiplying of cultic objects.[34] The resolution of this issue is not crucial for the present discussion, although it may well be that historical references have come to be used in a stylized way by the narrator.

When Judges 17–18 is considered in terms of the prohibitions against idols and the requirements of centralized worship, the graven image, the molten image, the ephod and the teraphim may all be seen as collectively representing the corruption of proper worship in this period. It is interesting that all four terms are repeated in 18.14, 17 and 18. In 18.20, however, only three terms are repeated, and the graven image is missing from the list. Later, in v. 24 Micah complains that they have taken away 'my gods' using only the collective term אלהי. When 18.30-31 relates the establishment of the sanctuary in Dan, the term פסל (graven image) is used twice without any of the other terminology found previously. This could be seen as an indication that the narrator was not primarily interested in the historical details of the individual items. Through a gradual elimination of details, the narrative sharpens the focus on the real issue. The four items are, in fact, seen as a group and symbolize the general corruption of worship during the time described in the narrative.

The physical elements and the existence of sanctuaries outside Jerusalem represent only part of the picture. The attitudes of the people involved are also used to develop the negative picture presented here. That the narrator is using the characters to emphasize this problem may be seen in the fact that every character exhibits some questionable behavior or motive.[35] This begins in 17.1-3 with the mother, who had placed a curse on the 1100 pieces of silver that had been stolen. As any mother might, she immediately forgets the theft when she learns that the guilty party was her own son. She and her son then devise a way to dedicate the money to God in order to remove any negative

32. Burney, *Book of Judges*, p. 420.

33. A. Malamat, 'The Danite Migration and the Pan-Israelite Exodus—Conquest: A Biblical Narrative Pattern', *Bib* 51 (1970), p. 12.

34. J.C. Exum, 'The Centre Cannot Hold: Thematic and Textual Instabilities in Judges', *CBQ* 52 (1990), p. 426.

35. D.R. Davis, 'Comic Literature—Tragic Theology: A Study of Judges 17–18', *WTJ* 46 (1984), pp. 156-63.

consequences of the curse. The motivation here appears to be more self-preservation and the avoidance of disaster than any genuine concern for an offering to God. Micah insures that the shrine and any benefits from it will stay in the family by appointing one of his own sons as the officiating priest.

The use of an entire paragraph to detail the origin of this image is significant.[36] It shows the corrupt nature of this sanctuary and its image from the very start, and this is important for the remainder of the narrative in chs. 17–18. The opening narrative sets the stage for what follows by indicating that no good will come out of this bad beginning.

The impropriety of this entire scene is emphasized by the words of 18.6, 'Every man did what was right in his own eyes.' The unspoken contrast may be to 'that which is evil in God's eyes', a phrase that is found throughout Judges (3.12; 4.1; 6.1; 10.6; 13.1), as well as in the theologically powerful passage of 2 Sam. 11.27. There David does as he pleases with Bathsheba, but the entire scene is evil in God's eyes. So here in Judges 17, people do what is right in their own eyes, but how does it appear in God's eyes? That is the question that the narrator encourages the audience to consider throughout this section.

Judges 17.7 opens the second scene in this section with another introduction. An unnamed Levite from Bethlehem is introduced as the second major character. Only at the end of the narrative in Judg. 18.30 is the name of Jonathan given with a brief genealogy connecting the Levite to the family of Moses. Not only is the Levite initially without a name, but he is also evidently without a permanent dwelling place. After relating that he is from Bethlehem, Judg. 17.7 states that 'he sojourned there' (גר שם). This would suggest that his status there was not as solid as that of other citizens.[37]

This picture of the Levite is further developed with additional references in v. 8. The narrative states that he left Bethlehem in order 'to live wherever he might find' (לגור באשר ימצא). This could certainly suggest that he was not concerned with the place, since it could be 'wherever'. באשר carries a similar indefinite meaning in 1 Sam. 23.13

36. P. Satterwhite, '"No King in Israel": Narrative Criticism and Judges 17–21', *TynBul* 44 (1993), pp. 75-88.

37. Soggin, *Judges*, p. 266, although he notes that some have suggested this phrase should be read as Gershom from the geneology in Judg. 18.30. This is unnecessary, esp. if this phrase is seen as contributing to the unstable commitment of the Levite to either place or duty.

and 2 Kgs 8.1. It is also interesting that the text does not specify what he hopes to find, although English translations such as the RSV supply the term 'place'. Is he going wherever he finds a 'place' or perhaps a 'livelihood'? If this is the case, it would contribute to another negative element of the picture, which is that he is primarily concerned with making his living rather than with any deep conviction about what he is doing. This would fit with other parts of the picture in the following section. This same phrase is also repeated in the following verse, when the Levite responds to the question from Micah. The Levite says he is going 'to live wherever I may find'. Again, he does not explain what he hopes to find. One further element of this picture is the phrase at the end of v. 8. The Levite came to the hill country of Ephraim as far as the house of Micah 'in order to make his way' (לעשות דרכו). A literal translation is given here in order to emphasize the sense of the Hebrew. The RSV translation 'as he journeyed' misses the point. This phrase is not used in the Hebrew Bible in the sense of making a journey.[38] The point of the phrase is not the journey itself, but the purpose of the journey, which was to find his 'way' or his livelihood.

When Micah questions the Levite in v. 9, the Levite replies that he is going 'to live wherever I may find'. Then Micah immediately responds with his offer. If the Levite will become his priest, he will provide a salary, clothing and a living. When the Levite agrees, Micah is sure that his problems are solved. He is quite sure that the Lord will make him prosper since he has the proper kind of priest to officiate at his sanctuary. The narrator has presented a picture of two individuals who are both out for their own gain. Micah has built a sanctuary and an idol from questionable funds, and is primarily interested in securing his own prosperity. The Levite sees his work as a profession, that is, as a way of making his living in the world, rather than as a calling from the Lord. Both parties appear to have achieved their goals. This convenient arrangement would appear to be ideal for both sides.

At the end of ch. 17, all the problems of the major participants are solved, at least for the moment. The curse on the stolen money has been disarmed, a sanctuary has been built to secure blessings for its owner, and the Levite has found the living he sought. The tension within the narrative has been resolved, and all is at rest. In the concluding statement of the chapter, Micah proclaims his confidence that the Lord

38. Burney, *Book of Judges*, p. 423, argues that the use of the infinitive + ל makes the translation 'as he traveled' unlikely if not precluded altogether.

will surely make him prosper because of this wonderful arrangement. Is
this simply confidence in the Lord's blessings, or does Micah's certainty rest on an even more sinister belief? If the ephod and teraphim
are elements of divination, as Boling suggests,[39] then Micah may
believe that he is now able to manipulate the blessings of the Lord. One
cannot be certain of this, but it is an intriguing suggestion. What is
striking, however, is the omission of any word of confirmation from the
Lord. To the human participants, all appears well, but is it? The problem was that all were doing what was right in their own eyes. The real
issue is how this situation looks in the Lord's eyes. The narrative never
answers that question, and in fact God is not present in chs. 17–18. This
absence of the Lord is all the more striking, since God was an active
participant in the earlier part of the book of Judges.[40]

Chapter 18 begins with the second occurrence of the phrase, 'In those
days, there was no king in Israel.' This repetition clearly links the
chapter with what has gone before. Even though the second part of
17.6, 'every man did what was right in his own eyes', is not repeated, it
would be understood by the reader or listener.[41] This transitional statement serves as both summary of what has gone before and as introduction to what is to come. It also calls into question the statement of
Micah at the end of Judges 17. If, in fact, the people are doing only
what is right in their own eyes, perhaps they should not be so certain
that the Lord will cause them to prosper.

The parallel between 17.6 and 18.1 suggests that one consider other
similarities in these two episodes. There are few exact linguistic parallels, but just as the Levite was a sojourner with no permanent place,
who went abroad seeking his living, so too did the Danites. They had
no inheritance among the tribes, and so they were seeking a place for
themselves. The fact that the Danites were seeking an inheritance
would not in itself be negative, but in the context it gradually becomes
clear that this is indeed another negative example from a time when
people did what was right in their own eyes.

When the spies come to the house of Micah, they recognize the voice
of the Levite. Did they know him previously,[42] or did they simply

39. *Judges*, pp. 256-57.
40. Exum, 'The Centre Cannot Hold', p. 426.
41. Amit, 'Hidden Polemic', p. 6.
42. Burney, *Book of Judges*, p. 425.

recognize his southern accent as not being from Ephraim?[43] In any case, they stop to speak with him. When they learn that he is a priest, they immediately ask him for an oracle concerning the success of their mission.

The narrative then relates that the Levite gave them an answer, but it does not report that he had in fact inquired of God. Is the reader to assume that the inquiry has been duly made? If so, it will be just that— an assumption, since nothing is said in the text. Boling suggests that the priest glibly give a pronouncement without even consulting his instruments of divination.[44] The Danites have heard the reassurance that they sought and are satisfied, even though the oracle is open to both positive and negative interpretations. Is their mission under the eye of God for success, or for destruction?[45] Either is possible, although the Danites certainly understand it as a promise of success for their mission.

This episode gives two statements that express God's view of this plan to gain new territory. As noted above, the first comes from the priest in Judg. 18.6. The second is expressed by the spies in their report in 18.10, when they announce that God has given the land into the hand of the Danites. In both cases, these words about God's view of the plan succeed in inspiring the listeners to press on with their intentions. In the end, the Danites are successful in capturing new territory, and one could argue that this indicates that the oracles should be accepted at face value. Since both the priest and the spies are cast in a negative light, however, one has some reason to question the validity of their statements. Adding to this uncertainty is the fact that the narrator never gives any word of confirmation from the Lord. Arguments from silence must always be handled with caution, but in this case, what the narrator does not say may be significant. Did God, in fact, approve this mission? Is success a sufficient guarantee of God's approval? The audience cannot be sure and has reason to question this, especially in light of the later developments in ch. 18.

There is another term used twice in this passage that also casts some doubt on the claims that God is with this venture. The term is found in vv. 7 and 27 as a part of a hendiadys used to describe the city of Laish. The city is characterized as 'quiet and unsuspecting' (ובטח שקט). The key term here is שקט, which is usually translated 'quiet' or 'peaceful'.

43. Boling, *Judges*, p. 263.
44. *Judges*, p. 263.
45. Yee, 'Ideological Criticism', p. 159.

This is the same term used previously at four important junctures in the book of Judges to describe the 'rest' for the land that is secured by God's work through a judge. It occurs in the summary of the work of Othniel in Judg. 3.11, where the land 'rested' (תשקט) for 40 years. In this case, the narrative is quite specific and says that the Lord was with Othniel, and the Spirit of the Lord came upon him to bring about this rest.

The second case is equally decisive and is found in Judg. 3.30, when Ehud delivered Israel and the land 'rested' (תשקט) for 80 years. The narrative is clear about the source of this rest, since in 3.15 it is the Lord who raised up the deliverer. The third passage is found in Judg. 5.30. At the end of the poetic description of the victory of Deborah and Barak, the land 'rested' (תשקט) for 40 years. In the Deborah story as well, it is clear that God is the source of this rest (Judg. 4.23). The Gideon story (Judg. 8.28) provides the fourth occurrence of this key term, where the land 'rested' (תשקט) for 40 years. In the Gideon story, it is also clear from the narrative that God is the source of this rest. In Judg. 6.14-16, God confirms that he will be with Gideon and will deliver Israel. These four passages (Judg. 3.11, 30; 5.31; 8.28) are all important summary statements that contribute to the overall theme of the book. The point in all these passages is that God is the source of this special rest.

When the narrative of Judg. 18.7 and 30 echoes this term, how is it to be understood? God has given 'rest' to Israel, and now the Danites claim they have God's blessing as they plan to sweep down and destroy this same 'rest' that characterizes Laish. This repetition of a crucial term is another clear indication that all is not as it appears on the surface of the narrative. Neither the fact that the Danites claim to have God's approval, nor even the success of their mission, can be taken as proof that God did actually look with favor on this adventure. In fact, the clear indication of the narrative is just the opposite: God did not approve of what was done here. This reversal is important, because normally one would expect Israel's forces to be supported by God and the enemy city to be presented in a negative light. In this case, however, it is just the opposite that is true.

The Levite who was presented in a less than ideal light in Judges 17 fares no better in ch. 18. His primary concern was to make his living wherever he could, and this continues in his meeting with the Danites. When the Danites come to take the idol, the image, the ephod and the teraphim in 18.16-20, the Levite questions them about this, but is quickly silenced. One could argue that the presence of the 600 armed men at the gate would be enough to prevent any vigorous protest. The narrative, however, tells us that the Levite is given the option of becoming a priest to the entire tribe, and that he found this too attractive to turn down. Judges 18.20 says, 'The priest's heart was glad.' This supplements the earlier picture of the Levite as concerned primarily with his work as a source of livelihood. His salary will surely increase as the priest for an entire tribe. There is no indication of any strong commitment on his part to the house of God built by Micah or to the agreement that he had made to serve as priest for the family.

The characterization of the Danites contributes to the picture of corruption in this period. When they learn from the spies of the existence of a shrine and its implements, they turn aside from their journey to take the shrine for themselves. They convince the priest to come with them, although this is not too difficult. When Micah protests over their taking of his property, their reaction is swift and overwhelming. They threaten him and his entire household with destruction. Violence is their answer to any protest. Their capture of Laish is also striking for its violence. The city is described as peaceful, at rest, without concern for defense. It should have been an easy target and one that could be captured with a minimum of force. That was not the way of the Danites. They fell upon the city, struck it with the edge of the sword and burned all that remained. Violent destruction was their solution.

One could protest that such destruction was commanded by God on other occasions and so was justified here. The problem is that it is not commanded here, and in fact Laish is outside the territory allotted to the Danites. This adventure was at their own initiative and is presented as typical of what happens when one 'does what is right in his own eyes'.

One final element of this story deserves attention, and that is the appropriation of the shine of Micah by the Danites.[46] As they pass by the territory of Micah, they steal the elements of the shrine and take them on their journey. After the conquest of Laish, they establish a new sanctuary with the stolen elements from the shrine of Micah. This new sanctuary and its priest have a troubled history that has been presented in detail by the narrative in Judges 17–18. The image had its origin in

46. Malamat ('Danite Migration', p. 11) argues that 'the presence of a priest and cult objects was thus essential to underwrite the campaign of inheritance'.

tainted funds, stolen from Micah's mother and then dedicated to God in order to salvage them from the curse of the mother. Micah's sanctuary was set up so he could maintain control of the funds and perhaps control of the deity, as well. The Levite accepted the role as priest in order to make his living rather than through a call from the Lord. The Danites compound the problem by hiring the priest, who is happy to go with the highest bidder. They steal the corrupt images, and then set up a sanctuary that results from a whole series of corrupt actions. It is difficult to imagine a more negative scenario for the establishment of a place of worship. The narrative never states that this is evil in the eyes of the Lord, but it need not do so. The narrative makes it obvious that the series of events started wrong in 17.1 and became more tangled and corrupt as the story unfolded.

This story can be read as an indictment of the shrine at Dan that was set up by the northern monarchy, or in a more general sense as a condemnation of the northern kingdom as a whole. It has often been seen as a part of an apology for the monarchy either in the time of David, the divided kingdom or later in the time of Josiah. One appealing suggestion is that this could reflect a time after the destruction of the monarchy and the fall of Jerusalem to the Babylonians.[47] In this case, it could be seen as a lesson to those who once again find themselves in a setting where 'there is no king in Israel'. The challenge is for them to learn from these negative examples from the past.[48] Now that they again face a period without kingship, will they choose a better course, or will they again do what is right in their own eyes? That is the issue that the narrative forces the audience to confront.

Theological Implications of Judges 17–18

Whatever the historical setting for the final text, there are important theological implications for the community of faith in any age. There are principles of worship and commitment that are valid at any time.

The first and perhaps most obvious point in the narrative is the

47. Dumbrell, 'In Those Days', p. 29.
48. R.G. Boling ('In Those Days There Was No King In Israel', in H.N. Bream, R.D. Heim and C.A. Moore [eds.], *A Light Unto my Path: Old Testament Studies in Honor of Jacob M. Myers* [GTS, 4; Philadelphia: Temple University, 1974], p. 37) states, 'An exilic edition had to be relevant to the educated leadership of folk who were once again living in a period like that of the judges—with no king in Israel.'

condemnation of Micah's image. As was often the case in the Hebrew Scriptures, the issue here was not one of pure paganism. The worship of other deities is a problem in some texts, but that is not the problem here. Judges 17.2, 3 and 13 specifically mention the name YHWH in connection with the image that was installed at the sanctuary. The real issue was syncretism and the corruption of true worship.[49] This should serve as a warning to believers in any age. One of the great dangers to the community of faith is an insidious, creeping syncretism, where the power of this age infiltrates and corrupts genuine faith and worship. That danger always looms large and demands constant vigilance.

The three major characters of Micah, the Levite and the Danites may also serve as illustrations. Micah established a family shrine and a place of worship that could certainly be a worthy accomplishment. The motivation, however, was problematic from the start. He did it, not out of any deep sense of reverence and awe toward the Lord and not out of any desire to promote worship of God. He did it to maintain control over his inheritance, which he feared might be lost, and perhaps even in an attempt to manipulate God through divination. Here it is not the actions that are most important, but the motivation behind the actions. In any age, why does a community build a place to worship? Is it out of a sincere desire to worship and praise God, or is it a shrine to their own power and importance? At its worst, worship can become an attempt to manipulate and control the Lord through the proper rituals rather than a recognition of the Lord's sovereignty. The history of the community of faith indicates that this problem has not been limited to ancient times.

The Levite officiates at the sanctuary and performs his duties with ease. When the Danites ask for an oracle, he delivers on the spot without hesitation. The text makes clear, however, that he is available to the highest bidder. He is a functionary, a hireling who is simply interested in making his living. He exhibits no sense of a higher calling from the Lord. He shows no commitment to a duty to serve. He is doing his job in order to make his way in the world. This should serve as a powerful reminder to all those who lead in the community of faith. Those who profess, either in the classroom or the sanctuary, must be constantly vigilant. There is always a danger that one may become too familiar and too comfortable with the sacred and allow it to become mundane and secular.

In the present setting at the end of the twentieth century, this is a

49. Davis, 'Comic Literature', p. 163.

special danger that can affect not only those who speak but also those who hear. One of the greatest threats to worship in the modern world is the loss of a sense of awe. Much of modern society has no awareness of what Rudolf Otto described as the 'wholly other'.[50] All that is high and majestic has been leveled. The holy has become profane. How can one worship in such a setting?

Finally, the Danites took matters into their own hands. Through sheer force, they wanted to control their own destiny. By their own power, they carved out a place for themselves in the land. Here too, a warning to Israel still sounds relevant. The exilic community had seen the devastation brought about by self-reliance. Dependence on military power, alliances and power politics had brought them to ruin. Perhaps the example of the Danites was a warning of the danger of that seductive path. So too today the temptation is to rely on human resources and abilities. This can be true even in communities of faith that claim to depend on God. There is an idea accepted in some circles that if one simply uses the right techniques and follows the right formulas, success will be inevitable. This is not the message of Scripture. The warning there is to beware of these human tendencies, which are all too natural but which will ultimately lead to destruction.

The warning of Judges 17–18 highlights the dangers of a lack of commitment and wrong worship. By focusing on these negatives, the narrative attempts to turn its readers to a better way. True worship should flow out of right motives. Pure worship should be selfless. Genuine worship will have power—the power that flows from the worshipped Lord.

---

50. *The Idea of the Holy: An Inquiry into the Non-rational Factor in the Idea of the Divine and its Relation to the Rational* (London: Oxford University Press, 1923, 2nd edn, 1950).

ISAIAH IN THE WORSHIPPING COMMUNITY

Roy F. Melugin

I am delighted to have an opportunity to write an essay for the purpose of honoring John Willis. I have known him for nearly a quarter of a century or perhaps even longer, and I am deeply indebted to him as scholarly colleague and friend. I have profited from his writings and from many oral discussions. I have worked with him in discussion groups and committees related to the Society of Biblical Literature, both at the national and the regional levels. His scholarship has stimulated me, his loyal service has inspired me, and his abiding friendship has enriched my life.

My friend John has long been interested in worship in ancient Israel. His interest in reconstructing Israelite worship practices and his concern for comprehending the Israelites' understanding of worship are indeed worthy of scholarly attention. But there is another side to John Willis which also has to do with worship: John Willis is himself a devoted worshipper. His interest in Israelite worship is undoubtedly related to a conviction on his part that the biblical traditions are of supreme importance in present-day communities of faith.

Limitations of an Enlightenment Hermeneutic

I have chosen to center this essay upon the use of biblical traditions in present-day communities of faith. There have been many historical-critical studies that have dealt with the practice of worship in Israel and the early church. And these studies are indeed of importance. Yet biblical scholars have tended to be so singularly concerned with exploring biblical texts to reconstruct worship in the early period of Judaeo-Christian history that the potential contributions of the Bible to worshipping communities of our own time have been given much less attention.

It is strange that this is so. If Scripture is deemed to be of paramount importance for shaping the life of ongoing communities of faith, why are religiously faithful biblical scholars so overwhelmingly devoted to the reconstruction of past historical reality and so seldom concerned with how to use Scripture to inform the life and worship of present-day worshipping communities—communities whose cultural context is markedly different from the societies in which the biblical traditions were first produced and used? The neglect described above is not the result of bad faith on the part of biblical scholars. It is rather the consequence of a prevailing paradigm—a paradigm that locates the meaning of biblical texts in the ancient contexts in which they arose and were first used. Such a paradigm, whatever benefits it may offer, cannot suffice as the only paradigm for the interpretation and use of Scripture in communities of worship.[1]

Every year in the season of preparation for Christmas, anyone who participates in Christian worship is likely to hear the following words:

> For to us a child is born,
>   to us a son is given;
> and the government will be upon his shoulder,
> and his name will be called
>   'Wonderful Counselor, Mighty God,
>   Everlasting Father, Prince of Peace.'
> Of the increase of his government and of peace
>   there will be no end,
> upon the throne of David, and over his kingdom,
>   to establish it, and to uphold it
> with justice and with righteousness
>   from this time forth and forevermore.
> The zeal of the LORD of hosts will do this.
>
> Isa. 9.6-7 [RSV; Hebrew: 9.5-6]

Does not almost every well-educated, modern biblical scholar know that this text was not created with a figure like Jesus in its original horizon?[2] Modern Christian scholars who interpret Isaiah are by no

---

1.   See also my essay, 'Scripture and the *Sitz im Leben* of the Interpreter', in R. Kessler *et al.* (eds.), *'Ihr Völker alle, klatscht in die Hände': Festschrift für Erhard S. Gerstenberger zum 65. Geburtstag* (Munster: LIT Verlag, 1997), pp. 226-37.

2.   See, e.g., H. Wildberger, *Isaiah 1–12: A Commentary* (Continental Commentaries; Minneapolis: Fortress Press, 1991), pp. 398-410; M.A. Sweeney, *Isaiah*

means naive about the differences between the original meaning of Isaiah 9 and its usage in the Christian community. But why have they been so preoccupied with its meaning in ancient Israel that they typically do little with its use in Christian context? Surely they do not believe that the Christian church's typical use of it is illegitimate. But do they think that its most important meaning resides in its ancient Israelite context? I suspect that many Christian biblical scholars would be reluctant to put it quite this way, especially since such a claim would seem to relegate the text's connection with Jesus Christ to a status of secondary importance. Perhaps many of them would argue instead that its meaning in ancient Israel is of primary *scholarly* importance. But why should this necessarily be so? Why should *original* meaning necessarily be the most important meaning for scholarly purposes? Why might it not be of equal importance, or perhaps even of greater importance, for Isaiah scholars to examine the significance of this text as presently existing religious communities construe its meaning for shaping their faith and life in *their* history and social context?[3]

A number of conversations with scholarly colleagues in biblical studies have left me with the impression that there is widespread lack of clarity in our ranks regarding such questions as those that I have raised above. Most with whom I have spoken seem quite aware that original meaning by itself is insufficient for the Christian worshipping community. But they also usually appear to be persuaded that original meaning is somehow *bedrock*—a kind of foundation upon which later Christian meanings supposedly can securely rest. But when I ask *why* original meanings are so critically important for Christian usage, a clear answer generally seems lacking as to precisely how the two meanings are related or why original meaning is necessary in legitimating later Christian meanings.

Our discipline's rootage in the Enlightenment has obviously engendered among us habituated behavior that tends to program us to look for original meaning. But what seems equally obvious is that our field's predilection for original meaning is inconsistent with what redactors of books like Isaiah actually did. Isaianic redactors juxtaposed materials

1-39, with an Introduction to Prophetic Literature (FOTL, 16; Grand Rapids: Eerdmans, 1996), pp. 180-87.

3. See R.B. Hays, *Echoes of Scripture in the Letters of Paul* (New Haven: Yale University Press, 1989), p. 105; Melugin, 'Scripture and the *Sitz im Leben* of the Interpreter', pp. 226-27.

from various periods and added their own words, thus giving older traditions new meaning without feeling compelled to distinguish explicitly between older and newer meanings.[4]

O.H. Steck's redaction-historical proposals regarding Isaiah 60 illustrate superbly how redaction-historical critics often proceed. According to Steck, the early kernel of Isaiah 60 is limited to vv. 1-9 and 13-16.[5] This text begins with an exhortation to 'arise' and 'shine' because their light has come and YHWH's glory will come upon them. Indeed, nations will come to their light (Isa. 60.1-3). Then comes an exhortation, 'Lift up your eyes round about and see', plus an announcement that Zion's sons will come from afar and that her daughters will be carried in the arms (v. 4). The abundance of the sea and the wealth of the nations will come to Zion. Camels and gold and frankincense, and also 'flocks of Kedar' and 'rams of Nebaioth' will come to YHWH's altar and glorify YHWH's house (vv. 5-7). Even ships of Tarshish will come bringing Zion's children back home, and bringing with them silver and gold, for the sake of the name of YHWH who has glorified Zion (vv. 8-9). Furthermore, in vv.13-16 Zion is promised that the glory of Lebanon will come to her, with that country's trees employed to glorify YHWH's sanctuary. And 'the sons of those who oppressed you shall come bending low to you...and they shall call you City of YHWH, the Zion of the Holy One of Israel'.[6]

Steck considers vv. 10-12 to be later additions. Verses 10-11, which promise that foreigners will build up Zion's walls, that their kings will minister to Zion and that Zion's gates will be open perpetually, represent an internally coherent saying that does not belong to vv. 8-9's development of the theme of 'riches of the sea' first introduced in v. 5b nor to the identically structured two-part unity of vv. 6-7 and 8-9.[7] Moreover, the interest of vv. 10-11 in walls seems to Steck superfluous in a text that is otherwise concerned with city and temple.[8]

Steck considers v. 12 to be secondary also, partly because it falls

---

4. Melugin, 'Figurative Speech and the Reading of Isaiah 1 as Scripture', in R.F. Melugin and M.A. Sweeney (eds.), *New Visions of Isaiah* (JSOTSup, 214; Sheffield: Sheffield Academic Press, 1996), pp. 284-85.

5. O.H. Steck, *Studien zu Tritojesaja* (BZAW, 203; Berlin: W. de Gruyter, 1991), p. 119.

6. See Steck, *Studien*, pp. 49-71, for a discussion of Isa. 60 as a whole.

7. Steck, *Studien*, p. 65; see also p. 60.

8. Steck, *Studien*, p. 66.

outside the metrical patterns of its surrounding context. Furthermore, the contention that 'the nation and the kingdom which will not serve you shall perish' (v. 12a) is verbally dependent upon Jeremiah 27.8-10.[9] Verse 12b ('and the nations will be utterly laid to waste') is a gloss even later than v. 12a.[10]

Steck further argues that vv. 17-22 are later than vv. 1-9 and 13-16. In vv. 1-3, for example, it is *nations* who do the coming, whereas in vv. 17-22 the coming is done by YHWH, who makes gold and silver to 'come'. In vv. 4-9, Zion's sons and daughters 'come' (v. 4); the nations' wealth will 'come' (v. 5); the coastlands will make their sons 'come' from afar (v. 9). Indeed, Steck argues, others do the coming or bringing in vv. 1-9 and 13-16, while in vv. 17-22 it is YHWH who does this.[11] Furthermore, vv. 1-3 speak of light as 'coming' and of YHWH and YHWH's glory arising upon Zion, *so that the nations will come to Zion's light*. But vv. 1-3 do not say that YHWH is the light, as in vv. 17-22.[12] Moreover, according to Steck, vv. 17-22 are the only verses in Isaiah 60 that have intertextual connections with passages in 'Proto-Isaiah' (e.g. cf. 60.17b with 3.12 and 32.16-17).[13]

A question as to the probability of Steck's redaction-historical reconstruction of Isaiah 60 would undoubtedly precipitate a lively debate in almost any gathering of Isaiah specialists, but that question is not the primary concern of this essay. My point is this: even if Isaiah 60 did experience growth in two or more stages of redaction, those who constructed Isaiah 60 apparently were not concerned that the worshipping community making use of this text distinguish between earlier and later textual materials or distinguish between original meanings and redactional reinterpretations. Indeed, the various parts of the chapter have been placed side by side with no signals that explicitly direct readers to distinguish the redactional strata that may underlie the text and its growth.[14] The redactors who produced this and other texts in the book of Isaiah seem to have employed a hermeneutic that is markedly different from the Enlightenment-sponsored association of meaning with their significance for the contexts in which they were generated. Those

9.   Steck, *Studien*, pp. 49-50.
10. Steck, *Studien*, p. 50.
11. Steck, *Studien*, p. 51.
12. Steck, *Studien*, p. 52.
13. Steck, *Studien*, p. 56.
14. Melugin, 'Figurative Speech', pp. 284-85.

who gave Isaiah its canonical shape readily filled with new meaning any earlier materials that they used.[15]

If shapers of the book of Isaiah so readily reinterpreted earlier meanings to guide their communities of YHWH-worshippers, why should modern biblical scholars who serve communities of faith be so often committed to a hermeneutic that is so different from that employed by the shapers and early users of books like Isaiah? Why should modern biblical interpretation be so inconsistent with what redactors of prophetic books did in *their* use of sacred texts?

Performative Language

The traditions originating in Greek philosophy have had a powerful influence upon the understanding and use of language in Western culture. Indeed, biblical interpreters themselves have often been thoroughly shaped by that philosophical heritage. Pervasive in much of the philosophical tradition that began among the Greeks is the conviction that reliable language is language that adequately represents an object or an idea. Language adequately representing reality is said to communicate truth.[16] Theology in the West has commonly understood itself to be articulating the truth about what is ultimately real. Biblical interpretation has frequently seen its task as enabling readers to comprehend texts that represent what is ultimately real.

The history of biblical interpretation conceived in this way is long and complex. Sometimes it has been expressed in Platonic categories; on other occasions the characterization is more Aristotelian. Indeed, many philosophical systems have been influential in shaping biblical interpretation over the past two millennia. Even in our own time one sees the concern for adequately representing reality, for example, in such diverse forms as biblical interpretation that makes use of process philosophy[17] and in fundamentalist biblical interpretation.[18]

---

15. B.S. Childs, *Introduction to the Old Testament as Scripture* (Philadelphia: Fortress Press, 1979), p. 326.

16. J.H. Ware, Jr, *Not With Words of Wisdom: Performative Language and Liturgy* (Lanham, MD: University Press of America, 1981), p. 9.

17. See, for example, R. Pregeant, *Christology beyond Dogma: Matthew's Christ in Process Hermeneutic* (Philadelphia: Fortress Press, 1978).

18. See the discussion by J. Barr, *Fundamentalism* (London: SCM Press, 2nd edn, 1981).

Historical criticism of the Bible, as most contemporary biblical scholars practice it, generally seems to exhibit a modification of the traditional task of a metaphysical representation of reality in favor of promoting accurate representation of *historical* reality—representation of historical events and social institutions in Israel and early Christianity, representation of past meanings contained in biblical texts and the like. The shift from the metaphysical to the historical has by no means left behind the goal of representing reality.

Those who shaped the book of Isaiah (and other prophetic books as well) were not primarily interested in representing historical reality or depicting accurately the original meanings of earlier traditions that they used, but were fundamentally concerned with using language *performatively* or *transformationally*, namely, to shape or transform the life of the faith community. They used language much more to *do* something than to explain or represent reality.[19] They could take utterances originally designed with the Assyrian threat in mind and use them to shape the life of the worshipping community in the context of the Babylonian exile without explaining the differences between original meanings and later reinterpretations, precisely because they were fundamentally more interested in using language to shape their community's life than to represent what the language they borrowed originally meant.

Performative language theory in contemporary philosophy has taught us that many utterances, both ancient and modern, are used primarily to *do* something rather than to explain reality.[20] The words, 'I pronounce you husband and wife', create a marriage rather than explain a marriage. The exhortation, 'Defend the orphan, plead for the widow' (Isa. 1.17), seeks to transform behavior rather than explain something.[21]

It is admittedly the case that language in the Bible is often in some sense representational. The Abraham story is *about* something. It refers

19. Melugin, 'Scripture and the *Sitz im Leben* of the Interpreter', pp. 228-29. See also the essays in *Semeia* 41 (1988).

20. J.L. Austin, *How to Do Things with Words* (Oxford: Clarendon Press, 1962); J.R. Searle, *Speech Acts: An Essay in the Philosophy of Language* (Cambridge: Cambridge University Press, 1970).

21. See Melugin, 'Scripture and the Formation of Christian Identity', in E.E. Carpenter (ed.), *A Biblical Itinerary: In Search of Method, Form and Content: Essays in Honor of George W. Coats* (JSOTSup, 240; Sheffield: Sheffield Academic Press, 1997), pp. 168-70.

to certain characters and purports to describe a 'reality' beyond its words, however historical or fictive the events described may be. But the purpose of the narrative is more to shape the life of the community using it than it is to represent reality accurately. When the story tells us that God tested Abraham by commanding him to sacrifice his only son, the primary purpose of the story is not to lead us to ask, 'Did this event actually happen? Was this story first used to legitimate the end of child sacrifice in Israel?' The story itself seems to be a legend,[22] the story of a pious and faithful man—a story that was surely used paradigmatically over the centuries primarily performatively or transformationally to shape Israel's way of relating to God. Although the story does use language to refer to the 'reality' that it depicts, the representational character of the narrative is subservient to its function of shaping the life of the community of faith that uses it.

Prophetic promises are more fundamentally performative in function than they are representational in function.[23] A promise does of course manifest *some* representational use of language. A promise does say something representational about the future. The book of Isaiah does contain promises about the judgment of Judah and Jerusalem at the hands of the Assyrians (Isa. 5.26-30; 7.20; 10.27b-24) as well as promises of the demise of Assyria (Isa. 10.5-19; 14.24-27). But promises are not predictions. A weather forecaster predicts the weather, and the prediction is either true or false. The prediction has either accurately represented future reality or it has not. A promise, however, is neither true nor false; it is instead fulfilled or unfulfilled. What constitutes the fulfillment of a promise may or may not correspond completely to the reality that the language of the promise appears to represent. When my daughter Cynthia was about six or seven years of age, I promised her that the tooth fairy would bring her 25 cents for each baby tooth that she lost. For some time she received 25 cents in US currency. But then we went to Europe for a sabbatical, and the tooth fairy began to dispense tooth loss compensation in German marks, Italian lira and Austrian schillings. The promise continued to be fulfilled, but not in the terms that the language of the promise had depicted.

22. G.W. Coats, 'Abraham's Sacrifice of Faith: A Form-Critical Study of Genesis 22', *Int* 27 (1973), pp. 389-400.

23. W. Zimmerli, 'Promise and Fulfillment', in C. Westermann (ed.), *Essays on Old Testament Hermeneutics* (Richmond, VA: John Knox Press, 1963), pp. 89-122; Searle, *Speech Acts*, pp. 54-71.

In biblical traditions promises function in analogous ways.[24] For example, the promise of the land could be said to have been fulfilled in the conquest led by Joshua. But it could also be understood as having been fulfilled in the return of exiles from Babylon.[25] Or it might be construed as fulfilled in the creation of the modern state of Israel or even in the Six Day War of 1967 and the restoration of the ancient holy sites in the old city of Jerusalem into Israeli hands.[26]

Obviously the promise of the land was not originally made with the return from Babylon in mind. Nor were the land promises in the Pentateuch and in exilic and postexilic texts, such as Isaiah 40–66, made with the modern state of Israel in mind. But, just as my promises about the tooth fairy could legitimately be understood as fulfilled by payments in European currencies instead of the US currency (as the language of the promise had originally stated the terms of payment), Israelite promises of the land, which articulated a future reality as represented in ancient Israelite conceptualization, can *properly* be construed as fulfilled in a context that no ancient Israelite would have been able to imagine or to express in language. Promises are by nature performative utterances that need not be confined to the rules governing predictions.

In his use of promises Isaiah employs language in analogous ways. In Isaiah 1, for example, an oracle of judgment against the faithful-bride-turned-harlot proclaims a judgment against YHWH's enemies who take bribes and oppress the poor (Isa. 1.21-26)—an oracle of judgment that construes the judgment as a process of purification that will remove the impurities of the community and that will therefore culminate in a promised new day in which the city's once-corrupt officials will be restored and the harlotrous wife will once again be a faithful bride.[27] What appears to be a third-person literary supplement (vv. 27-28) reinterprets a first-person speech of YHWH (vv. 21-26) by promising that

24. Zimmerli, 'Promise and Fulfillment', pp. 101-108.

25. Zimmerli ('Promise and Fulfillment', p. 105) indicates that in the time of Deutero–Isaiah the promise of land was seen as fulfilled but that this understanding of the fulfillment of the promise is not the only time in which that promise could be seen as fulfilled.

26. See A.J. Heschel, *Israel: An Echo of Eternity* (New York: Farrar, Straus & Giroux, 1969), pp. 5-38.

27. See K.P. Darr, *Isaiah's Vision and the Family of God* (Louisville, KY: Westminster / John Knox Press, 1994), pp. 137-40.

'Zion will be redeemed by justice and her returners in righteousness.'
Verses 21-26 seem to portray the judgment and restoration of Jerusalem
as something happening to the community as a whole, but vv. 27-28
reinterpret that promise by distinguishing between the good fortune of
those who 'return' and the fate of sinners.[28] Verses 29-31, probably
also a redactional supplement, reinterpret the preceding announcement
of judgment and promise of restoration by elaborating on the fate of
sinners.[29] These additions to vv. 21-26 indeed take an earlier announcement of judgment and promise of restoration and reinterpret it for a new
context in the book of Isaiah as a whole—a book that is concerned with
the different destinies of the faithful and the disobedient.[30] The
language of promise functions here in a performative way to reshape
the worshipping community's expectation of promise and fulfillment.

Other speeches in Isaiah underwent reinterpretation as the book took
its shape. The pronouncement of woe upon the 'sinful nation' that is
'heavy with iniquity' (Isa. 1.4) is a pronouncement upon a nation that is
said on the one hand to have a few survivors (1.9) but on the other
(30.14) is depicted as a nation whose iniquity is compared to a collap-
sing wall so broken that not a single fragment remains.[31] The texts,
undoubtedly originally formulated with the future imagined in the context of the Assyrian threat, underwent reinterpretation as fulfillment
was understood in terms of the Babylonian exile and beyond. Isaiah 39
tells us that the exile, in which nothing is left (see Isa. 30.14), will not
come in Hezekiah's days (39.6-8). Indeed, the redactor who produced
Isaiah 39 reinterpreted earlier Isaianic traditions as speech finding fulfillment in the Babylonian exile and its aftermath.[32] Indeed, many,
many speeches in Isaiah underwent analogous reinterpretations for the
performative purposes of shaping and reshaping the life of the worshipping community.

28. Sweeney, *Isaiah 1–39*, pp. 86-87; Melugin, 'Figurative Speech', p. 293.

29. Sweeney, *Isaiah 1–39*, pp. 68, 86.

30. See Isaiah 65–66 and the discussion by D.M. Carr, 'Reading for Unity in
Isaiah', *JSOT* 57 (1993), pp. 61-80, esp. pp. 73-75.

31. R.F. Melugin, *The Formation of Isaiah 40–55* (BZAW, 141; Berlin: W. de
Gruyter, 1976), pp. 178-79.

32. C.R. Seitz, 'Isaiah 1–66: Making Sense of the Whole', in C.R. Seitz (ed.),
Reading and Preaching the Book of Isaiah (Philadelphia: Fortress Press, 1988),
pp. 110-11.

Use of Scripture by Modern Worshipping Communities

If a worshipping community cannot limit itself to original meaning in the use of scriptures for the shaping of its own life, what concrete guidance can be given to that community for Scripture's felicitous performative or transformational use in its activity of worship? What can scholarly interpretation contribute to the use of that ancient text's use to illumine and shape a modern community's life and worship? No complete and comprehensive discussion is possible here, but I hope I can begin the task in a fruitful way.

a. *Shaping a Symbolic World*

One of the most important functions of the use of Scripture in the worshipping community is the shaping of a symbolic world in which the community can live and through whose use the community may be transformed. No one achieves identity apart from a symbolic world shaping that identity.[33] Americans often live in a symbolic world that is shaped by the telling of stories about persons such as George Washington, Benjamin Franklin, Thomas Jefferson and Patrick Henry. Sexual identity is constructed through living in a particular symbolic world. Ethnic identity also is shaped by the symbolic world in which the ethnic group lives.

Jewish and Christian communities achieve their identity in relationship with God through a symbolic world that is constructed through the communities' scriptures and other sacred traditions. Stories of Abraham, Isaac, Jacob, Joseph and Moses, for example, constitute part of the communities' sacred story-world. For Christians the Gospel narratives are also important in the construction of a symbolic world.

1. *Isaiah 1*. A brief study of Isaiah 1 can illustrate for us how a text could be used to construct a symbolic world for ancient Israel.[34] Israel is invited by this text (Isa. 1.2-3) to hear itself summoned to trial as YHWH's stubborn and rebellious children who, unlike ox and ass, who know their owner and their master's crib, do not 'know' or

---

33. P. Ricoeur, *Interpretation Theory: Discourse and the Surplus of Meaning* (Fort Worth: Texas Christian University Press, 1976), pp. 25-44, esp. pp. 36-37.

34. See Melugin, 'Figurative Speech', pp. 282-305, for a more complete discussion.

'understand'.[35] They continue to be depicted as stupid children who lack the good sense to cease rebelling (vv. 4-9). They learned nothing from the stripes inflicted upon them; indeed, they keep returning for further blows (v. 5). Thus their wounds from head to foot remain, continuing to fester (v. 6). The figurative speech about YHWH's stupid and rebellious children is succeeded by different imagery: aliens 'eat' their land, with the result that they are left like a booth in a vineyard, a lodge in a cucumber patch (vv. 7-8). The theme of foolishness appears to persist, however; YHWH's children seem not to recognize how close they have come to total annihilation: 'If YHWH of hosts had not left us a few survivors, we would have been like Sodom, like Gomorrah we would have become' (v. 9).

In a prophetic torah speech that follows (vv. 10-17),[36] YHWH claims to be utterly sated with their sacrifices. YHWH hates the cultic meals brought by the stupid children who failed to know the One who feeds them (vv. 2-3)—indeed, these same stupid and rebellious children whose land aliens feed upon (v. 7)! What YHWH wants instead is for them to become clean and, in so doing, to behave responsibly in the legal sphere by 'judging' the orphan and 'pleading' for the widow.[37]

The metaphor of lawsuit, which began with the trial of YHWH's stupid and rebellious children (vv. 2-3) and continued with the exhortation to uphold the legal case of orphan and widow (v. 17), comes to a close with vv. 18-20, which begins with a summons to a legal proceeding: 'Come, let us plead together' (v. 18a). The legal dispute begins with a rhetorical question: 'If your sins be as scarlet, can they be as white as snow? If they are red as crimson, can they be as wool?'[38] Absolutely not! Therefore, there are but two choices: 'If you are willing and obedient, you will eat the good of the land, but if you refuse and rebel, you will be eaten by the sword.'

The symbolic world in which Israel is encouraged to live is this:

35. See J.W. Whedbee, *Isaiah and Wisdom* (Nashville: Abingdon Press, 1971), p. 21.

36. Sweeney, *Isaiah 1–39*, p. 80.

37. Melugin, 'Figurative Speech', p. 290.

38. Translating v. 18b as questions suggests that scarlet and white, crimson and wool are to be understood as incompatible and cannot be changed from one to the other. Such an understanding seems consistent with the alternatives between being willing and obedient and eating the good of the land on the one hand and rebelling and being eaten by the sword on the other (vv. 19-20).

They are stupid and rebellious children whom YHWH has put on trial. Their rebellion brings about a punishment in which they are bruised from head to foot, and they are so stupid that they keep coming back for future beatings. Furthermore, YHWH will not eat their cultic meals, will not listen to their prayers, but instead exhorts attention to the legal case of orphan and widow. Finally, a legal dispute shows that 'scarlet sins cannot be white, just as their reddened bloody hands will not be ignored'.[39] The only choices are obedience and 'eating' the good of the land or rebellion and being 'eaten' by the sword.

2. A Symbolic World. The world that Israel was invited to construct and inhabit, based on their reading of this text, is clearly a *symbolic* world—a figurative world by means of which Israel's self-identity could be molded. That it is a figurative world rather than a literal world is of the greatest importance. This means that the ancient Israelites who used this text could not possibly have used it to depict reality in any literal sense. To be sure, the *text* constructs a figurative reality—a figurative reality appearing to point beyond itself to an actual historical reality about which the prophet is greatly concerned. But the picture the text presents is so thoroughly figurative that we cannot penetrate it to reconstruct a literal reality that may have occasioned it. Besides, the text does not seem to prompt Israel primarily to describe things but rather to *respond*. The people are accused, asked why they are 'still smitten' that they 'continue to rebel', criticized for their sacrifices and prayers, exhorted to do justice to orphan and widow, and to choose to obey rather than to rebel. The language of this text is thoroughly performative; its primary aim is to transform the behavior of Israel. Representation of reality—even a figurative reality—is subservient to a transformational purpose.

What should modern biblical scholars do with this text, especially those whose vocation is the service of a community of faith? We should not eschew historical interpretation, for both Judaism and Christianity bear witness to God's relationship with Israel in ancient times. But constructing a picture of how this text might have functioned in creating a symbolic world for ancient Israel is only a limited part of our task. Our larger task is to prepare the way for worshipping communities to use the text in a transformational way.

What we must do, I contend, is to propose models for usage of the

39. Melugin, 'Figurative Speech', p. 291.

ancient text to construct symbolic worlds for communities of faith in modern settings. A symbolic world constructed for a present-day worshipping community must necessarily be a hybrid; it must include both the language that comes from the past *and* a construal of a symbolic world in which a modern worshipping community can be shaped *in the context in which it lives.*

Elsewhere I began this task in a primitive and sketchy way.[40] Here I will use the scenario that I employed there but in a more fully developed form. For heuristic purposes, let us create an imaginary church, which could be in the inner city of Atlanta or Chicago or Dallas. It is an all-white congregation in an area that is now almost entirely African-American and where most people live in poverty. Many of the members of the congregation have moved from the inner city to the suburbs. A large number are interested only in middle-class ministries, and more than a few prefer that the membership remain largely white. Several members of the congregation are slum landlords who profit significantly from renting substandard dwellings to persons who live in the area. Yet there is a relatively small but fairly well-organized group within the congregation that lives to a large extent in a symbolic world constructed through the use of Isaiah in their worship and study. Thus they are committed to a ministry of compassion and justice for the ghetto in which the church is located.

What might their symbolic world be? They might see themselves as a remnant group in a larger body that they see as God's stubborn and rebellious children in a declining and ailing community of faith whose wounds continue to fester because the ongoing division within the church congregation leads to a series of blows to congregational unity. Their part of the city (their 'land') is after all being 'eaten' by outsiders who move into the neighborhood. If no remnant had remained, the church might well have become extinct.

The remnant in the church might well see their congregation as standing under judgment, with YHWH despising their eucharistic meals and their prayers because they have not addressed the circumstances of the poor within their midst. But they could see themselves as exhorted to become clean through looking to the cause of 'orphan and widow'.

Some scholars might be inclined to see this church's construal of

40. Melugin, 'The Book of Isaiah and the Construction of Meaning', in C.C. Broyles and C.A. Evans (eds.), *Writing and Reading the Scroll of Isaiah: Studies of an Interpretive Tradition* (VTSup, 70.1; Leiden: E.J. Brill, 1997), I, pp. 51-54.

Isaiah 1 as subjective and arbitrary and as a kind of interpretation that has no place in the scholarly world. There is of course much in this congregation's symbolic world that is constructed from its own life in the particular context in which it finds itself. But its symbolic world is by no means arbitrary. It is deeply rooted in the language of the text itself and is guided by a close reading of the text that makes use of disciplined literary analysis. If one argues that biblical scholarship should be limited exclusively to meanings in antiquity, one fails to take seriously the performative interpretation that redactors themselves created. Indeed, if biblical scholarship committed to serve the worshipping community fails to include the work of the Spirit as a part of its interpretive work, it has not been fully responsible to its hermeneutical and theological task.

3. *The Nature of Interpretation.* It is furthermore the case that a supposition that historical scholarship can reproduce past meanings with full objectivity is quite misguided. Scholars who have immersed themselves in hermeneutical discussions outside the field of biblical studies are usually aware that what we call textual meaning is to no small degree the result of what interpreters do.[41] So much of the activity of interpretation is shaped by the questions that interpreters put to the text, and no interpretation is a truly neutral enterprise untainted by the interpreter's presuppositions and activities. Even historical reconstruction is to a considerable extent a construct created by the historian, because the historian must select from the 'record' what to consider and what to leave out, must create a 'plot' to connect the various individual parts of the 'record' that the historian has selected and must necessarily be influenced by his or her own world-view and other biases in the reconstruction of the past.[42]

41. S. Fish, *Is There a Text in This Class? The Authority of Interpretive Communities* (Cambridge, MA: Harvard University Press, 1980), pp. 1-17, 303-21; E.W. Conrad, *Reading Isaiah* (OBT, 27; Minneapolis: Fortress Press, 1991), p. 31; K.P. Darr, *Isaiah's Vision and the Family of God*, pp. 13-32; G.T. Sheppard, 'The "Scope" of Isaiah as a Book of Jewish and Christian Scriptures', in R.F. Melugin and M.A. Sweeney (eds.), *New Visions of Isaiah* (JSOTSup, 214; Sheffield: Sheffield Academic Press, 1996), pp. 257-68; R.F. Melugin, 'The Book of Isaiah and the Construction of Meaning', in Melugin and Sweeney, (eds.), *New Visions of Isaiah*, pp. 39-50.

42. H. White, *Topics of Discourse: Essays in Cultural Criticism* (Baltimore: The Johns Hopkins University Press, 1978), pp. 51, 61-75; E.W. Conrad, 'Prophet,

Although good interpretation is not capricious and must be shown to 'fit' the text, more than one interpretation might conceivably 'fit' a given text.[43] Moreover, a reinterpretation of a text for performative purposes might well 'fit' that text as appropriate usage. My hypothetical white congregation's usage of Isaiah 1 might 'fit' as a responsible usage of the text. And, I would argue, a scholarly interpretation that is both well-grounded in the text and skillful in articulating a hermeneutic for a present-day worshipping community's appropriate reinterpretation of the text for transformation of its life is an interpretation that 'fits' the text and its potential usage. Precisely what 'rules' or 'conventions' might be fruitful for this task cannot yet be clearly seen, but in a time when Enlightenment culture is turning into a postmodern age, it is time to explore the possibilities.

b. *Typological Use of Scripture*

Another issue regarding the use of the Hebrew Bible in Christian worshipping communities has to do with the need for such methods as typology. The book of Isaiah, even in its final and canonical form, promotes the expectation that Israel is to live once again in the land of Palestine (Isa. 49.8-12, 19-23; 60.4-9, 21) with a full population (49.19-21). Moreover, the text fosters the hope that Jerusalem as a concrete geographical entity will be rebuilt (49.15-17; 54.11-12; 60.10-13). Even though Israel's return to Jerusalem and the rebuilding of Zion is sometimes depicted metaphorically in Isaiah, there is nonetheless an expectation of an actual return to Jerusalem and of a physical restoration of Zion.

Such expectations were obviously important for shaping faith and hope in ancient Israel. Even in present-day Judaism, especially in Zionism, the hope of living in the 'promised land' and hope for the security and prosperity of Jerusalem continues to be of importance. For the Christian community, however, living in that land and rejoicing in Jerusalem's physical reconstruction are not of central importance. To

Redactor and Audience: Reforming the Notion of Isaiah's Formation', in Melugin and Sweeney (eds.), *New Visions of Isaiah*, pp. 311-24; R.F. Melugin, 'Prophetic Books and the Problem of Historical Reconstruction', in S.B. Reid (ed.), *Prophets and Paradigms: Essays in Honor of Gene M. Tucker* (JSOTSup, 229; Sheffield: Sheffield Academic Press, 1996), pp. 74-77.

43. See Melugin, 'The Book of Isaiah and the Construction of Meaning', pp. 50-51.

be sure, ancient Israel's hopes in this regard are part of the story
Christians tell. The activity of God prior to the beginnings of the Christian community is an important part of the Christian church's confession. Nevertheless, the primary significance of the book of Isaiah for
the Christian community surely cannot be in the hope of returning to
Palestine and living there. The historic Christian practice of typological
interpretation therefore needs to be revived. Walter Brueggemann's
construal of the church as living in spiritual exile represents a typological interpretation of a text that originally envisaged an actual return
of exiles to dwell once again in the land of Palestine.[44] Or, to use
another example, the construal of the messianic promise in Isaiah 9 as
fulfilled in Jesus represents a reinterpretation of a text envisioning an
actual political ruler in the Davidic line in such a way that Jesus, who
was a king only in symbolic terms, is typologically related to a real
Davidic monarch. If typological interpretations such as these do not
have an important place in the church's interpretive repertoire, the use
of Isaiah in Christian worship will surely be significantly impoverished.

Typological usage of Isaiah is clearly performative in function, for its
use in Christian worship is clearly not primarily to represent original
meanings but to shape and transform the life of the church. Even
though recovery of Isaianic meanings in ancient Israel can help the
church articulate its convictions about God's relationships with ancient
Israelites, it seems unlikely that ancient Israelite meanings can be the
most important meanings for the church in its transformational usage of
Isaiah. If interpreters of Isaiah who are concerned with its usage in the
church do not concern themselves with hermeneutical questions as to
how to reconstrue Isaiah figuratively for performative uses in the
Christian community, they will have failed to undertake a critically
important interpretive task. Indeed, to limit themselves to the meaning
of Isaiah in ancient Israel would be to focus upon what is an admittedly
important but yet relatively limited part of the larger interpretive enterprise.

c. *Use of Scripture as Precedent*
The use of Scripture as precedent is still another valuable performative
use of the Bible in worshipping communities. Using a text or other

---

44. W. Brueggemann, 'Second Isaiah: An Evangelical Rereading of Communal
Experience', in C.R. Seitz (ed.), *Reading and Preaching the Book of Isaiah* (Philadelphia: Fortress Press, 1988), pp. 73-74.

tradition as precedent involves the employment of something that arose in one situation for usage in another. The statement in Thomas Jefferson's Declaration of Independence that 'all men are created equal', written in the eighteenth century, when women's suffrage and the abolishment of slavery were surely not envisioned by all those who signed it, is often used as precedent in twentieth-century contexts in order to support equality of *all* persons. Or, to cite another example, a former law school professor once proposed in my presence that the Fourteenth Amendment to the US Constitution could be used as a precedent for a legal argument that resident aliens should be given the right to vote. The shapers of the Fourteenth Amendment undoubtedly did not envision that the text they wrote in *their* historical context might be interpreted (and perhaps even become law) as proposed by a law professor in the last half of the twentieth century.

In analogous ways Jewish rabbis used *torah* as precedent as they considered, for example, what kind of behavior would be in keeping with the commandment prohibiting work on the Sabbath. Knots tied by sailors or by camel drivers would not be permissible, the rabbis reasoned, presumably because they considered knots of this kind to be connected with work, whereas knots that one ties in one's clothing were not seen as work related (see *Shabbat* 15.1-2 in the *Mishnah*). Jesus is also portrayed as wrestling with the use of biblical prohibitions concerning the Sabbath as precedents for behavior in concrete situations. In response to criticisms that Jesus' disciples were violating *torah* by picking grain on the Sabbath (Mk 2.23-28), Jesus first cites a precedent in which David ate food unlawfully because he was hungry (Mk 2.25-26). Then, by contending that the Sabbath was made for humans rather than humans for the Sabbath (Mk 2.27), Jesus seems to be relying on Deut. 5.14's assertion that cessation from work was decreed for humane reasons, namely, that servants would be entitled to rest from their labors. Picking grain, normally understood as work, is construed as humane in this particular context. Behavior normally prohibited can here be permitted when the purpose of the precedent text is considered.

Precedents can sometimes be set aside in favor of other precedents. When Jesus is asked whether a man can divorce his wife for any cause (Matt. 19.3), he chooses a precedent from Genesis 1–2, arguing that God created humans male and female and joined them together as one (Matt. 19.4-5). When asked why Moses allowed divorce, Jesus claims that it was Moses' concession to the people's hardness of heart, but that 'from the beginning it was not so' (Matt. 19.7-8). One biblical precedent (Gen. 1–2) is judged here to outweigh another (Deut. 24.1-4).

1. *Use of Isaiah as Precedent*. Use of Isaiah as Scripture in the worshipping community can involve using Isaiah as precedent. If one were to imagine oneself as having been pastor of a leading white Christian church in Selma, Alabama, in the turbulent days when a great civil rights march was about to take place in that normally tranquil southern town, one might ask what strategy that pastor should have used. Should that pastor have denounced segregation as unjust? Even though such a denunciation would have surely been morally justified, would it have led to repentance? Or would the pastor's congregation have been hardened in their hearts and less inclined to repent *because* of their pastor's condemnation of segregation? Is hardening the congregation's heart a part of that pastor's calling? Or would another course of action have been more responsible?

Isaiah 6 could obviously be weighed as a precedent in this situation. The prophet is commissioned to harden hearts, lest the people 'turn and be healed' (Isa. 6.10). When he asks, 'How long?' he is told that the judgment will last until cities 'lie waste without inhabitant' and no one is left in the land (Isa. 6.11-12). Even if a tenth is left, like a stump that remains after a tree is felled, that remnant will be burned again (6.13). Yet that remnant is a 'holy seed'.

Careful interpretation of Isaiah would show that YHWH is ready to judge the once-faithful city now turned harlot, a city whose high officials oppress widow and orphan (Isa. 1.21-26). YHWH will clearly punish (Isa. 1.24-25aα) but the purpose of the judgment is purification (vv. 25aβ-26a), with the intent that a just and righteous *social order* will be restored (v. 26). YHWH further judges the haughty daughters of Zion, stripping them of their finery and bringing about a military defeat so calamitous that there will be only one man left for seven women (3.16-4.1). But YHWH also plans a purification of Zion and the glorification of a remnant (4.2-6). In Isaiah 5, YHWH's vineyard is accused of injustice and punishment is decreed (5.1-7); woe is pronounced upon those who unjustly 'join house to house' (5.8-10), followed by a punishment by exile (5.13), presumably at the hand of a powerful invader (5.26-30). YHWH's plan for judgment and salvation includes hardening of hearts and decimation of cities, including the suffering of a remnant

(Isa. 6). Yet the remnant is a 'holy seed' that appears to be the basis of a new future.

Should our imaginary pastor in Selma use these precedents as warrants for preaching a message of judgment against segregation? Should that pastor recognize that such a message would harden the hearts of most of the church's members but nevertheless feel a calling to harden hearts as a participant in God's judging and saving purposes for America and the South? Surely that pastor would also need to consider precedents proclaiming love as greater than any other calling (Matt. 22.34-40; Rom. 13.8-10). Would these precedents about the primacy of love suggest more of a strategy of forgiveness and acceptance, much the way Jesus treated tax collectors and sinners, instead of emphasizing a message of judgment? Or is judgment against injustice necessarily a prominent aspect of a gospel of love?

I know of no unambiguous resolution of our imaginary pastor's dilemma. But careful interpretation of relevant biblical precedents and weighing their significance in relation to one another is of utmost importance. Even if conscientious theological interpreters are not always in agreement, the task of interpretation and comparison of precedents is still necessary.

2. *Effects on the Church.* Comparison and weighing of biblical precedents having to do with Isaianic messianic texts can be of critical importance for their use in shaping and transforming the life of Christian worshipping communities. Messianic passages in Isaiah 9, 11 and 32 express hope that a new king will bring about justice in the social and political order (Isa. 9.5-6; 11.3-4; 32.1). Indeed, these messianic texts manifest a concern for a just political order that may be found in other Isaianic texts as well (1.10-17, 21-31; 3.13-15; 5.1-7, 8-10; 10.1-4; 33.13-16; also 58.6-12; 59.1-21; 61.1). If one calls these Isaianic messianic texts 'eschatological', they are eschatological in the sense that they reflect a hope for a transformation of the body politic after a significantly catastrophic judgment (1.21-26; 6.9-13). The age of the new messianic ruler in these Isaianic texts appears to envisage a rule within history rather than after a final judgment at the end of history, as seems to be the case within some early Christian texts (see Mk 13 and parallels).

Our imaginary Christian community in the inner city of Atlanta, Chicago or Dallas might responsibly, in some ways at least, give special weight to the Isaianic messianic hope with its focus on social and political justice and less emphasis to the less political portrayals of Jesus as Messiah that are common in the New Testament. To be sure, Jesus is sometimes presented as one who is concerned about the poor and the oppressed (Lk. 4.16-30; Mt. 25.31-46), but a concern for the transformation of political realities (as in Martin Luther King and among liberation theologians) is not as prominent in most New Testament understandings of messiahship as it is in the messianic texts in Isaiah. The setting in which our imaginary church worships and conducts its ministry might lead it to give special prominence to Isaiah in its understanding of messianic mission. Although this church would by no means ignore New Testament portrayals of messianic rule, it would have good reason to give the Isaianic precedents special significance in the particularity of its life and worship.

A Beginning

A Christian worshipping community's use of Isaiah should employ the book primarily performatively, for the transformation of the community's life is its most important task in its use of Scripture. Indeed, as I have argued above, interpretive paradigms generated in the Enlightenment are insufficient for the task. Although historical criticism will certainly continue to be of value, there is nonetheless a great need for reconceptualizing biblical hermeneutics for the sake of better preparing the church for the use of Scripture in a transformational way.

What I have proposed here (and in other essays noted above) can be considered at best a modest beginning. The application of performative language theory to biblical studies is in its infancy; indeed, few biblical scholars are conversant with this understanding of the function of language. Moreover, the consciousness of the majority of biblical scholars is so deeply embedded in historical criticism that a more fully articulated alternative paradigm must surely be developed if a significant dent in the prevailing paradigm is to be made. Furthermore, because I do not envision a rejection of historical criticism, a more complete exploration of the relationship of historical-critical approaches to other relevant interpretive strategies needs to be undertaken. Finally, the transition from an Enlightenment-dominated thought world to a postmodern intellectual environment requires a sophisticated rethinking of biblical hermeneutics, most of which remains to be done, especially as it applies to the use of the Hebrew Bible as Christian Scripture.

Contemporary Worship in the Light of Isaiah's Ancient Critique[*]

J.J.M. Roberts

The contemporary American church is racked by an often acrimonious and divisive debate about appropriate worship that appears to cut across denominational lines. The issues are complex, and they play out in quite different ways in different religious groups, but one feature that recurs with disturbing regularity is the degree to which congregational worship is increasingly shaped by music programs that introduce elements alien to and even in conflict with the group's traditional theology of worship. To cite but one minor example, in many Reformed and Presbyterian churches it has become a tradition to follow the charge and benediction with a musical response that at best seems redundant and often appears downright contradictory. After the minister has pronounced the benediction over the congregation, it seems unnecessary for the choir to sing or the organist to play a second benediction. But when the congregation, having stood to receive the minister's charge to go forth and serve the Lord and having been blessed to this end, is then expected to sit back down and listen to a musical performance, something is definitely skewed. What is the theological rationale for such a bizarre, illogical pattern?[1]

---

[*]   John Willis, a friend of many years, has been both an active churchman and a scholar who has devoted much of his work to the elucidation of the prophetic literature, and it is with appreciation for his contributions in both these areas that I offer this attempt to apply Isaiah's ancient critique of worship to the contemporary church debate.

1.   I puzzled over this practice for a long time before Paul Rorem, one of my church history colleagues at Princeton Theological Seminary, pointed out its historical background to me. After the Reformation had swept through Holland and the Reformed had taken over the big cathedrals in Holland from the Catholics, the Reformers would not allow the great organs in these cathedrals to be played during the worship services. But the populace missed their organ music, and to keep the

Another recurring feature, again focused especially in the musical part of the worship, is a conflict between those who favor a more 'contemporary' form of music in worship and the defenders of traditional church music. The same basic conflict can be seen across denominational lines, but the particular contours of the struggle vary from group to group. Within the Churches of Christ the proponents of more contemporary music have introduced the so-called praise songs, usually short, repetitive, easily learned songs with very simple, happy lyrics, which are often projected, without any accompanying musical notations, upon a screen set up in the front of the auditorium. Against the objections of traditionalists that many of these songs are vacuous, the lyrics theologically inane—songs your pet could have written, as one student put it—the defenders of contemporary music argue that traditional church music no longer speaks to the current generation. If the church wants to keep its own young people and attract and hold the increasing masses of the unchurched, they argue that it must adopt such contemporary music. Moreover, the almost exclusive emphasis on praise songs to the exclusion of songs of lament, songs that give serious attention to the afflictions of life, is justified on the basis that attendance will drop off if the services are not kept upbeat and happy. Theology must be kept simple and packaged in positive and entertaining ways if the church is to grow.

It is easy to charge the traditionalists with being opposed to anything new and thus guilty of hindering the proclamation of the Gospel by straitjacketing it in earlier, outmoded cultural expressions. It is also true that many of the older hymns in traditional Church of Christ hymnals, to mention only my own tradition, are just as vacuous and theologically suspect as the praise songs the traditionalists critique. This criticism does cut across denominational boundaries, however. A modern praise song's sheer repetition of 'Praise God! Praise God! Praise God!',

populace happy while still prohibiting such music during the worship, the Reformers, following the final benediction and a clear end of the religious service, allowed a secular official to play an organ concert to any who wished to remain for it. I have heard more theological rationales for the organ piece following the benediction, but all appear to be secondary rationalizations. Any practice, if it lasts long enough, can be cloaked in a theological justification, but there is a profound difference between a theology that shapes a congruent pattern of worship and a theology that simply adapts itself to patterns of worship forced on it willy-nilly by quite untheological forces and concerns.

without any articulation of the content and thus the reason for this praise is vacuous, but the same repetitive words do not become less vacuous when sung in a traditional hymn in Latin or Hebrew instead of English. Nonetheless, the conflict between the traditionalists and the proponents of contemporary music should not be dismissed as simply a generational dispute. There are theological issues at stake that need to be examined in the light of the witness of Scripture, and the words of the prophet Isaiah have something to contribute to such reflection.

Though Isaiah left no extended discourse on the nature of appropriate worship, it is clear from several passages that he was very critical of what passed for worship in his day. Isaiah 29.13-14 contains a particularly sharp critique of the piety of his day, and it is worth extended analysis.

> And my Lord said:
> Because this people draws near with its mouth,
> And with its lip they honor me,
> But its heart has gone far from me,
> And their worship of me is a human commandment, learned by rote;
> Therefore I am again about to show this people an astounding miracle—
> The wisdom of its wise shall perish,
> And the insight of its insightful ones will disappear.[2]

According to the New Testament, Jesus cited this passage in his debate with the Pharisees and some of the scribes when they accused his disciples of breaking the traditions of the elders (Mt. 15.1-9; Mk 7.1-13). Jesus retorted that his accusers, like Isaiah's contemporaries, kept the human traditions of the elders at the expense of nullifying the word of God:

> But answering he said to them, 'Why do you transgress the commandment of God because of your tradition? For God said, "Honor your father and mother!" and, "Let anyone who curses father or mother be put to death!" But you say, "Whoever may say to his father or mother, 'Whatever you were due from me is a gift [to the temple]', need not honor his father." So you nullify the word of God because of your tradition. Hypocrites, well did Isaiah prophesy concerning you, saying, "This people honors me with the lips, but their heart is far removed from me; and in vain they worship me, teaching as doctrines human commandments"' (Mt. 15.3-9).

In traditional preaching within the Churches of Christ, the Isaiah

---

2.   Unless otherwise indicated, all the translations are my own.

passage has usually been refracted through this lens, sometimes supplemented with Col. 2.21-22, where the teaching of heretical rigorists, 'Don't touch! Don't taste! Don't handle!' is characterized as 'according to human commandments and teachings'. The passage thus refracted is then used in such preaching to critique other Christian groups for alleged rejections of the clear word of God in favor of human traditions. The appropriateness of Jesus' use of the passage is not in question, and despite widespread abuse in slipshod, arrogant, insensitive and often ignorant polemic, even the contemporary homiletical use of the passage in intra- or interdenominational religious debate may sometimes be intellectually appropriate. This essay, however, is more interested in looking at the Isaiah passage in its original context to see if that context may yield any useful insights for the current discussion about worship.

The first thing to note about the Isaiah passage is that it reflects a situation in which the people showed all the outward signs of great religiosity. They drew near to God with their mouth and honored God with their lips. The problem in Isaiah's time had nothing to do with a lack of church attendance. There is no indication that significant portions of the population of Judah were avoiding worship in the late eighth century BCE. The evidence we possess would suggest that even the most rabid proponents of church growth would have been happy with temple attendance in Isaiah's day. Moreover, the contributions appear to have been quite generous, unlike the situation in the time of the much later Malachi (Mal. 1.6-14; 3.8-10), when the people were withholding their tithes or defrauding God by offering only sick, lame or other defective animals that they could not use themselves. If anything, in Isaiah's time the very abundance of the people's gifts seems to have irritated God. The racket created by the tramping of the worshipping crowds and the bellowing, bleating and clattering of their sacrificial animals being dragged across the temple courtyards to the altar appears to have given God a headache.

> Hear the word of Yahweh, O rulers of Sodom,
> Listen to the instruction of our God, O people of Gomorrah.
> 'What to me is the multitude of your sacrifices?' says Yahweh.
> 'I have had enough of burnt offerings of rams and the fat of fatlings.
> The blood of bulls, and lambs, and goats I do not desire.
> When you come to see my face,
> Who asked this from your hand?

Trample my courts no more.[3]
Bringing offerings is futile.
Incense is an abomination to me.
New moon and sabbath, the calling of assembly—
I cannot stand iniquity and solemn assembly.
Your new moons and festivals my soul hates.
They have become a burden to me;
I am weary from bearing (them).
When you spread your palms (in supplication),
I will hide my eyes from you.
Even when you make your prayer many times,
I will not listen (Isa. 1.10-15b).

Despite record breaking attendance and offerings, God, like many contemporary Christians, found the whole experience of public worship a tedious, unbearable burden. In Isaiah's day the human crowds were still present for worship; it was God who had opted out. The problem for religious leaders then was not how to get the people to come back to attending worship; it was how to get God to attend. It might be wise even in the present to look at worship from that perspective. Perhaps we are spending far too much energy trying to figure out how to adapt worship so as to interest and attract a disinterested public. Perhaps we might better spend our time trying to attract and please a potentially disinterested and increasingly irritated God.

God's objection to Israel's piety in Isa. 29.13 is characterized by two expressions. Despite Israel's public affirmations of devotion, God asserts that 'its heart is far from me'. God also complains that 'their fear of me', that is, 'their piety' or 'their worship of me', 'has become (only) a learned human commandment'. Both of these expressions need unpacking; the precise meaning of neither is immediately self-evident. It is clear that Israel's outward expressions of religion following learned conventions did not satisfy God's desire for the people's wholehearted commitment, but what precisely was lacking?

The parallel in Isaiah 1 is suggestive. According to Isa. 1.15c-17, God found Israel's worship unacceptable because the rest of Israel's life was characterized by sin, oppression and injustice:

3. The translation of this and the two following lines depends on a redivision of the Hebrew lines and a correction of *minḥat-šāwʾ* to *minḥōt šāwʾ*. It is suggested by the LXX reading of the text and appears to offer a better poetic division of the lines.

> Your hands are full of blood.
> Wash yourselves! Cleanse yourselves!
> Remove the evil of your deeds from before my eyes!
> Cease to do evil! Learn to do good!
> Seek justice! Right the wronged!
> Give justice to the orphan! Vindicate the widow!

One should be careful how one characterizes this contrast between the conspicuous display of public piety and the lack of ethical behavior. It is not unusual for scholars to characterize Israel's attitude toward the cult as magical. Thus Eichrodt claims:

> It is because of their experience of the divine Thou, that the prophets put up such a passionate resistance against anything that tends to deperson-alize this relationship and, this is just what happens when the fear of God is misprized in the relations between man and man, and God himself is sought only in the cultus. God becomes an impersonal source of magical power, which can be manipulated with no feeling of reverence whatso-ever simply by means of a meticulous routine; for, so far as his will, the core of his personality, is concerned, man by such an attitude declines to recognize the claims of his divine Lord.[4]

Whatever truth there may be in Eichrodt's statement, it seems to me deficient in two respects. In the first place, the reference to magic makes it too easy for any contemporary audience to dismiss the proph-etic criticism as irrelevant for the modern worshipping community. Hardly any modern community could be convinced that they regarded God as an impersonal source of magical power. Secondly, the assertion that the worship critiqued by the prophets involved 'no feeling of rever-ence whatsoever' is probably untrue, and in any case places too much significance on the subjective feelings of the worshipper. Anyone with even a limited experience in the modern church will have encountered pious Christians who both claim and appear to be deeply moved by their participation in worship, and yet who seem to be oddly blind to the ethical and moral demands of the God they so reverently worship. Something far more important than a feeling, even a feeling of rever-ence, is at stake here. Israel's worship was rejected, whatever feelings of reverence may have accompanied it, because it was unaccompanied by obedience to God's other commands.

In this connection, it is worth looking at the judgment in Isa. 29.14 in

4. W. Eichrodt, *Theology of the Old Testament* (2 vols.; OTL; Philadelphia: Westminster Press, 1961), I, p. 365.

light of the larger context. Isaiah 29.9-12, the verses immediately before Isa. 29.13-14, threaten an end to any prophetic vision, a judgment probably associated with the royal court's desire to pursue its political goals without submitting its plans to prophetic inquiry.[5] Isaiah 29.15-16, the verses immediately following, speak of the royal counselors who wanted to keep their counsel secret from Yahweh, again presumably to avoid negative prophetic reaction to their political plans. Such bracketing suggests that, while these royal officials participated in the official Jerusalem cult that celebrated the kingship of God and God's choice and protection of both the Davidic dynasty and Jerusalem, they wanted to make their political plans without regard to such religious traditions. Like Ahaz in Isa. 7.10-13, they did not want their political freedom of action compromised by theology or prophetic promises from God, no matter how miraculous the signs that confirmed them. In response to their refusal to revere the divine king truly, that is, their refusal to follow a policy based on confidence in the divine promises,[6] God threatens to show Israel another negative miracle.[7] Just

5.   See my study, 'Blindfolding the Prophet: Political Resistance to First Isaiah's Oracles in the Light of Ancient Near Eastern Attitudes toward Oracles', in J.-G. Heintz (ed.), *Oracles et prophéties dans l'antiquité, Actes du Colloque de Strasbourg 15–17 juin 1995* (Université des Sciences Humaines de Strasbourg, Travaux du Centre de Recherche sur le Proche-Orient et la Grèce Antiques, 15; Paris: de Boccard, 1997), pp. 135-46.

6.   Cf. the warning using plural verb forms addressed to the royal court in Isa. 7.9b, 'If you do not stand firm in faith, you will not be firmly established.'

7.   The motif of the negative miracle is most clearly spelled out in Jer. 21.1-10. There King Zedekiah, who knew Israel's religious tradition and was familiar with its accounts of the mighty acts of salvation God had performed for Israel in the past, sent to Jeremiah asking the prophet to inquire of the LORD on Israel's behalf, hoping that God would once again intervene on Israel's behalf with a miracle of deliverance. This was the same Zedekiah, however, who had continuously refused to follow the demands of God as they were spelled out in Israel's religious tradition, though the king knew the demands of the tradition quite as well as he knew the miracle stories. Under the pressure of the Babylonian siege, for example, Zedekiah even led the people in a renewal of the Mosaic covenant, making a firm commitment with all the people to follow the covenant by releasing their illegally retained Hebrew slaves. But as soon as there was a brief respite from the siege, Zedekiah and the people reneged on their commitment, and those who had just been released were again enslaved (Jer. 34.8-22). God apparently thought that divine deliverance and human obedience were more integrally connected than Zedekiah wished. In any case, Jeremiah responded that the divine warrior would

as God had threatened to do a strange work by rising up to attack Jerusalem instead of defending it (Isa. 28.21; 29.1-4), so now instead of endowing Jerusalem's rulers with the wisdom celebrated and idealized in the royal Zion Tradition (Isa. 11.2-4), God threatens to destroy the wisdom of the royal counselors (Isa. 29.14).

What links Isaiah's critique of the cult in Isa. 1.10-17 and 29.13-14, then, is not a concern about the absence of feeling, spirit or emotion in Israel's worship; it is rather a concern about the absence of a true knowledge of God. Isaiah complained more than once that Israel was perishing for lack of knowledge (Isa. 1.3; 5.13).

Such knowledge of God clearly involves knowing the intellectual content of Israel's long religious tradition. Isaiah assumes his audience is familiar with the Mosaic covenant and its demands (Isa. 1.2-20; 3.13-15),[8] and his repeated confrontations with the Davidic court clearly presuppose that the members of the royal entourage were as familiar with the Zion Tradition[9] as the prophet was.[10] One may well wonder

---

indeed appear to fight with his outstretched hand and his mighty arm, only God would fight against Israel to hand Zedekiah and his people over to the king of Babylon. Zedekiah would see God's miracle, but it would be a negative miracle of judgment rather than a miracle of deliverance.

8. See my study, 'Form, Syntax, and Redaction in Isaiah 1.2-20', *PSB* 3 (1982), pp. 293-306.

9. For a discussion of the content of the Zion Tradition, see my articles, 'The Davidic Origin of the Zion Tradition', *JBL* 92 (1973), pp. 329-44; and 'Zion in the Theology of the Davidic–Solomonic Empire', in T. Ishida (ed.), *Studies in the Period of David and Solomon and Other Essays* (Tokyo: Yamakawa-Shuppansha, 1982), pp. 93-108. For its use in Isaiah, see my discussions in, 'Isaiah 33: An Isaianic Elaboration of the Zion Tradition', in C.L. Meyers and M. O'Connor (eds.), *The Word of the Lord Shall Go Forth: Essays in Honor of David Noel Freedman in Celebration of his Sixtieth Birthday* (Winona Lake: Eisenbrauns, 1983), pp. 15-25; 'The Divine King and the Human Community in Isaiah's Vision of the Future', in H.B. Huffmon, F.A. Spina and A.R.W. Green (eds.), *The Quest for the Kingdom of God: Studies in Honor of George E. Mendenhall* (Winona Lake, IN: Eisenbrauns, 1983), pp. 127-36; 'Isaiah 2 and the Prophet's Message to the North', *JQR* 75 (1985), pp. 290-308; and 'Yahweh's Foundation in Zion (Isa. 28.16)', *JBL* 106 (1987), pp. 27-45.

10. See my study, 'Isaiah and his Children', in A. Kort and S. Morschauser (eds.), *Biblical and Related Studies Presented to Samuel Iwry* (Winona Lake, IN: Eisenbrauns, 1985), pp. 193-203. The logic of Isa. 7.7-9 (see my reconstruction, 'Isaiah and his Children', pp. 95-96 n. 2) seems to be as follows: the plans of Syria and Ephraim will not not come to pass because the royal city of Syria is only

whether even that level of knowledge of the religious tradition can be presupposed in the typical Christian congregation today. It is certainly worth asking whether our worship contributes to a coherent knowledge of our religious tradition.[11]

A saving knowledge of God, however, involves more than just a passing and passive intellectual assent to traditional formulations of the faith. It means actively interpreting the world, evaluating the events around oneself and ordering one's life in accordance with what the tradition claims about God. This point is particularly clear in the prophet Jeremiah's comments about knowing God. When he complains that the people do not know God, God's way or God's judgment (Jer. 2.8; 4.22; 5.4; 8.7), Jeremiah is not talking about a mere cognitive awareness of the content of God's law; he is talking about a volitive acknowledgment of God's will expressed by obedience. Not knowing God is equivalent to rebellion (Jer. 2.8), to doing evil (Jer. 4.22), to breaking God's yoke (Jer. 5.5), to rejecting God's word (Jer. 8.9); and Jeremiah charged even the theological experts of the time, the 'handlers of the law', with this volitive ignorance (Jer. 2.8). Indeed, he claimed that the theological experts used their interpretive expertise to turn God's law into a lie, thus using their theological knowledge to reject God's word (Jer. 8.8-9).

Isaiah has a very similar understanding of what it means to know God.[12] What Isaiah means by the knowledge of God involves

Damascus, and its king is only Rezin; and the royal city of Ephraim is only Samaria, and its king is only the son of Remaliah; but Yahweh has chosen Zion for God's imperial city and has appointed David and his dynasty to be God's earthly regent there, and the ancient promises associated with this double choice (see Ps. 132.11-14) will stand firm if only Ahaz and his royal court will stand firm in faith.

11. The importance of this question was brought home to me recently when, in a discussion with a middle-aged woman who had spent all her life faithfully worshipping in Churches of Christ, it suddenly dawned on me that her understanding of the Christian faith and even the religious language she used to articulate that understanding were totally foreign to the theological tradition of the Churches of Christ.

12. To Jeremiah's comment about the 'lying pen of the scribe' one may perhaps compare Isaiah's remarks about those who issue decrees of iniquity and trouble in order to deprive the poor and needy of justice (Isa. 10.1-3). There must have been collusion between the political administration and important religious officials, a positive theological spin put on public policy, for Judean society of the late eighth century so easily to have embraced the widespread confiscation of the property of the poor (Isa. 5.8-10; Mic. 2.1-2).

perceiving God's work in the ongoing events around oneself (Isa. 5.12-13). It means sanctifying God and making God the only object of ultimate fear in one's life, so that, no matter what the external situation may be, no matter how terrifying the circumstances, one fears God more and thus continues to live by the promises and commandments of God even in midst of such other terrors (Isa. 8.12-13). It means observing the covenant and treating other members of the covenant community with justice and respect because they too are God's people (Isa. 1.16-20; 3.15). In relating to outsiders, it means rejecting oppression and deceit as the means to security (Isa. 30.12), opting instead to trust God for security while pursuing justice and righteousness (Isa. 28.12, 16-17; 30.15).[13]

True worship is in part a response to such knowledge of God. One praises God or approaches God in prayer because one knows and believes the tradition of what God has done in the past. But worship itself can, in the best of circumstances, give the worshipper a clearer knowledge of this God, which in turn gives the worshipper a clearer understanding of him- or herself and a clearer vision of what God demands of the worshipper.[14] It is no accident that Isaiah's awesome vision of God as exalted king, a vision that probably began and certainly gave direction to Isaiah's prophetic ministry, occurred in the temple in the context of sacrificial worship (Isa. 6.1-13). Eichrodt was right about the personal nature of this knowledge of God. A communal knowledge of God unappropriated by the individual is not a saving knowledge. Each individual must appropriate this knowledge of God for him- or herself. Such an appropriated personal knowledge of God is one of the ideals of the New Covenant (Jer. 31.34; cf. Jn 17.3) and more to be valued than wisdom, strength or riches (Jer. 9.22-23).

But if one wants worship to contribute to the individual's appropriation of a saving knowledge of God, as it did in Isaiah's case, perhaps one should rethink some of the current wisdom about how to improve

13. Cf. my studies, 'A Note on Isaiah 28.12', *HTR* 73 (1980), pp. 49-51, and 'Yahweh's Foundation in Zion', pp. 27-45.

14. Calvin stresses this connection between the knowledge of God and the knowledge of oneself quite strongly, but he is anticipated in this by earlier Christian writers, such as Clement of Alexandria and Augustine, to mention only two. Cf. J.T. McNeill (ed.) and F.L. Battles (trans.), *Calvin: Institutes of the Christian Religion* (2 vols.; LCC, 20; Philadelphia: Westminster Press, 1960), I, pp. 35-39, esp. p. 36 n. 3.

worship services. The trend to simplify worship—by removing theological complexity, to make it more popular by emphasizing entertainment at the expense of education and to increase its appeal by stressing only happy thoughts and ignoring the bitter and painful aspects of religious experience—has little in common with the ideal of worship envisioned by Isaiah. Isaiah does not appear to have been entertained by the worship service in which he experienced his vision of God, and, at least in the short run, it does not seem to have made him feel better about himself or his neighbors. 'Woe is me! I am undone, for I am a man of unclean lips, and I dwell in the midst of a people of unclean lips...' (Isa. 6.5) is not an expression of the positive feelings that are supposed to be engendered by the modern 'praise' service. The dumbing down of contemporary worship with its almost total loss of articulate theological depth, particularly in the singing but increasingly in the preaching as well, does not bode well for the knowledge of God. The vacuous repetition and infantile thought of many popular contemporary hymns is hardly a good medium through which to encounter the real God and the complexity of that God's dealing with the universe. The real God is a God of love, but even our hymns should remind us that God's love sometimes finds expression in negative miracles and strange works, including the scandal of the crucifixion.

If one used Isaiah's thought as a basis for reforming contemporary worship, one would try to make worship *more* theological rather than less so. Beginning with the inherited tradition, it would celebrate what God has already done for the community of faith, but in the process worship would try to express who God is, what God's goals are and what God demands of his followers in articulate enough fashion that the individual worshipper could come to know this God personally, recognizing God's directions for his or her life in all of life's complexity. In short, an Isaianic reformation of worship would focus on God and what pleases God, not on the masses of the unchurched and what is purported to attract them.

'EAT AND REJOICE BEFORE THE LORD':
THE OPTIMISM OF WORSHIP IN THE DEUTERONOMIC CODE

Timothy M. Willis

The nature of worship in the book of Deuteronomy has been extensively mined in previous studies.[1] These have exposed the richness and
depth of ancient Israel's ideas about worship in ways that, sadly, are
surprising to many Christian readers, who often assume that worship in
ancient Israel was little more than repetitive ritual that missed the 'true
meaning' of worship. My goal is to highlight a few common components of the Deuteronomic laws prescribing occasions of worship that
reveal some of the true spiritual richness of Israelite worship. This richness has been a major theme in my father's teaching and personal life
for many years now, and so it is especially gratifying for me to be able
to make this contribution to the volume honoring him.

Worship Laws in Deuteronomy

There are seven passages in the main law code (chs. 12–26) of the early
core of Deuteronomy (chs. 5–28)[2] that prescribe sacral (worship)

1.   See especially the extensive work of G. Braulik, 'The Joy of the Feast', in
The Theology of Deuteronomy: Collected Essays of Georg Braulik, O.S.B. (BIBAL
Collected Essays, 2; N. Richland Hills, TX: BIBAL, 1994), pp. 27-65; *idem*, 'Com-
memoration of Passion and Feast of Joy', in *Theology of Deuteronomy*, pp. 67-85;
M. Weinfeld, *Deuteronomy and the Deuteronomic School* (Oxford: Clarendon
Press, 1972), pp. 210-24; and R.E. Clements, *God's Chosen People: A Theological
Interpretation of the Book of Deuteronomy* (Naperville, IL: SCM Press, 1968),
pp. 70-88; *idem*, *Deuteronomy* (OTG; Sheffield: JSOT Press, 1989), pp. 60-63.
2.   The question of the composition history of Deuteronomy is very complex,
having been discussed at length in numerous studies (see the following note). My
own conclusions are consistent with the 'general agreement' among scholars that
the original book consisted of Deut. 4.44–28.68, in some form. See M. Weinfeld,
Deuteronomy 1–11 (AB, 5; Garden City, NY: Doubleday, 1991), p. 10. As for the

gatherings at 'the place which the Lord your God will choose' and the performance of specified acts of worship, often stipulated as acts to be performed 'before the Lord your God' (Deut. 12.2-28; 14.22-27; 15.19-23; 16.1-8, 9-12, 13-15; 26.1-11).[3] Also, Deut. 27.1-8 contains worship instructions that match those in these seven passages, while diverging

date of this early composition, my own opinion is that it occurred no later than the period of Assyrian domination. Subsequent expansions and redactions were made in conjunction with the redactions of the Deuteronomistic History (Dtr1, Dtr2).

3. This enumeration of passages is fraught with difficulties. First, I have chosen not to include passages detailing what worship practices are forbidden (Deut. 12.29-13.1; 16.21-17.1; cf. 23.1-8). This would require a completely different sort of study. Other concerns more directly related to the passages discussed are those raised by redaction critics. On the one hand, there are questions regarding the unity of each of these laws individually. For example, Deut. 12.2-28 'is conventionally divided into four originally independent laws, each concerned with cultic centralization (vv. 2-7, 8-12, 13-19, 20-28)' (B.M. Levinson, *Deuteronomy and the Hermeneutics of Legal Innovation* [New York: Oxford University Press, 1997], p. 24). The alternation between singular and plural addressees is the springboard for the numerous theories about the history of the passage's composition. The standard critical commentaries provide the basic proposals, but several more detailed investigations have also been produced. See G. Braulik, *Deuteronomium 1-16,17* (Würzburg: Echter Verlag, 1986); N. Lohfink, 'Zur deuteronomischen Zentralisationsformel', *Bib* 65 (1984), pp. 297-329.

For redaction-critical studies of these passages, see R.P. Merendino, *Das deuteronomische Gesetz: Eine literarkritische, gattungs- und überlieferungsgeschichtliche Untersuchung zu Dt 12–26* (BBB, 31; Bonn: Peter Hanstein, 1969); G. Nebeling, 'Die Schichten des deuteronomischen Gesetzeskorpus: Eine traditions- und redaktionsgeschichtliche Analyse von Dtn 12–26' (PhD dissertation, Münster, 1970); G. Seitz, *Redaktionsgeschichtliche Studien zum Deuteronomium* (BWANT, 93; Stuttgart: W. Kohlhammer, 1971). For an innovative approach and solid bibliography on the redaction of several of these laws, see W.S. Morrow, *Scribing the Center: Organization and Redaction in Deuteronomy 14.1–17.13* (SBLMS, 49; Atlanta: Scholars Press, 1995). For a recent survey of studies of Deut. 26.1-11, see D.R. Daniels, 'The Creed of Deuteronomy XXVI Revisited', in J.A. Emerton (ed.), *Studies in the Pentateuch* (VTSup, 41; Leiden: E.J. Brill, 1990), pp. 231-34.

Finally, one might wish to include Deut. 26.12-15 in this list (see n. 79, below). While not mentioning 'the place...', it does call for one to swear 'before the Lord your God' that one has properly handled his tithes. I have omitted it from this study, simply because it prescribes only what the worshipper will say, not what acts he will perform in association with the oath. Nevertheless, it is interesting (in the light of the present investigation) that one of the (apparently non-Yahwistic) acts of worship to be avoided is eating tithes while in mourning.

from descriptions of similar settings in later passages (see 29.9-10; 31.9-13); so, it will be examined in conjunction with the seven.[4] Some of these laws involve gatherings of the families of the entire nation at once (16.1-8, 9-12, 13-15; 27.1-8);[5] others are to be observed by the entire nation, but according to the 'schedules' of individual family units (14.22-27; 15.19-23; 26.1-11).[6] The main centralization laws (12.2-28) apply to both types.

Not surprisingly, the main scholarly interest in these laws has been their call for or presumption of the centralization of worship. Interpretations of this feature have clustered primarily around two foci: (1) those who say that the calls for centralization were originally 'distributive', propounded by groups in the North;[7] and (2) those who say centralization originated in the South, always carrying an 'exclusivistic' (to Jerusalem) sense.[8] While that discussion is significant for the study of worship in Deuteronomy, the focus of the present investigation is on

4. Except for the unusual and syntactically awkward inclusion of 'the elders of Israel' in the introduction (on which, see the critical commentaries), Deut. 27.1-8 appears to be a Deuteronomic redaction of an older instruction regarding a Shechemite sanctuary (see Weinfeld, *Deuteronomy 1–11*, p. 13; contra Braulik, *Theology*, p. 223 n. 128). If this impression is correct, it would support the view that the main redaction of the D Code is pre-Josianic, perhaps even pre-Hezekian.

5. The fact that Deut. 21.1-9 calls for a sacrificial ceremony away from the central sanctuary has caused no small consternation among those studying the question of centralization. See, e.g., Weinfeld, *Deuteronomy and the Deuteronomic School*, pp. 210-11; Braulik, *Theology*, p. 223 n. 124. Perhaps the explanation is in the fact that the situation envisioned there is so isolated, both temporally and spatially. The activities in which one participates at the central sanctuary are temporally regular and/or common to the whole nation.

6. 'Deuteronomy founds the festival community on the families and the individuals, so that the community is structured from below, so to speak, instead of being organized from above' (Braulik, 'Joy', p. 57; see also 'Commemoration', p. 80).

7. E.g., J.G. McConville, *Law and Theology in Deuteronomy* (JSOTSup, 33; Sheffield: JSOT Press, 1984); A.D.H. Mayes, *Deuteronomy* (NCB; Grand Rapids: Eerdmans, 1979), pp. 60-71; B. Halpern, 'The Centralization Formula in Deuteronomy', *VT* 31 (1981), pp. 20-38; A. Rofé, 'The Strata of Law about the Centralization of Worship in Deuteronomy and the History of the Deuteronomic Movement', in *Congress Volume: Uppsala 1971* (VTSup, 22; Leiden: E.J. Brill, 1972), pp. 221-26.

8. See Levinson, *Deuteronomy*, pp. 23-24 n. 1, for proponents of this view and the main arguments.

the worship activities specifically mentioned in Deuteronomy and on the groups who are called upon to participate in that worship.

In some ways, this line of investigation follows a path set out by Weinfeld.[9] He appropriately highlighted the humanitarian aspect of the laws on worship, as well as the private, internal understanding of repentance and gratitude, which downplays the significance of ritual and the atoning aspect of sacrifice. The only additional aspect of these laws that I would suggest is that they function as inducements to obedience of all the Deuteronomic laws.

The Expectation of Heartfelt Celebration

Weinfeld begins his discussion of worship in Deuteronomy by noting that there are no explicit references to 'sin offering' or 'guilt offering' in any Deuteronomic law.[10] This is not to be taken, however, as the writer's denial of the need for sacrifice, nor does he envision an Israel in which sin and guilt offerings would never be required. It is difficult to imagine that the writer could speak of Israel as 'a stubborn people' (9.6) or that he would exhort them repeatedly to keep Yahweh's laws, if he looked upon them as a people who would never need to seek forgiveness in the years to come. Further, 'sacrifices' and 'burnt offerings' are occasionally mentioned elsewhere alongside 'sin offerings' or 'guilt offerings' (e.g. Lev. 4.1-12; 7.37-38; 2 Chron. 29.24). Therefore, it is possible (probable?) that the former are being used here more broadly, as terms that encompass the latter as well.[11] Nevertheless, the more penitent, somber side of worship is very muted in the D Code.

Weinfeld concludes from the omission of explicit references to sin and guilt offerings that 'the author's view seems to be that spiritual

9. Weinfeld, *Deuteronomy and the Deuteronomic School*, pp. 210-24.

10. In fact, the terms are rare in the Deuteronomistic History, being used only in 1 Sam. 6.1-9 and 2 Kgs 12.17. On this, see Weinfeld, *Deuteronomy and the Deuteronomic School*, pp. 210-11; Braulik, 'Joy', p. 47.

11. Ps. 51 illustrates that 'sacrifices' and 'burnt offerings' could accompany a petition for forgiveness. The same is probably implied in such passages as Hos. 6.6, where 'love' and 'knowledge of God' (see Jer. 22.16) are desired above 'burnt offerings' and 'sacrifice'. The implication is that Hosea's audience had been offering sacrifices, asking Yahweh to forgive them of injustices committed against their neighbors. Hosea's words tell them that true repentance does not find its realization in animal sacrifice alone, however, but in the changing of one's behavior. Cf. Isa. 1.11-17; Mic. 6.6-8.

purification and repentance—consisting of confession and prayer—and not sacrificial offerings expiate sin'.[12] The possibility that sin and guilt offerings might actually be implied in the terms 'sacrifices' and 'burnt offerings' does not undermine this conclusion. This view of expiation—widely recognized in prophetic writings—permeates the book of Deuteronomy. This can be missed by readers who focus on the numerous calls to worship in a particular place or the repeated commands to be careful to keep Yahweh's 'statutes, his ordinances, and his commandments always' (11.1; *et passim*). What is sometimes overlooked is the writer's assumption that words and actions—including the offering of sacrifices—are manifestations of what is in one's heart.

External acts of obedience—both cultic (ceremonial) and non-cultic—are ultimately manifestations of heartfelt devotion for Yahweh; therefore, calls to obedience in Deuteronomy are generally prefaced by appeals for obedient hearts and exhortations to love Yahweh. The writer holds up the people's initial respectful acceptance of the Decalogue as a praiseworthy example. Their acceptance occurs prior to any ceremonial oath of confirmation (such as one finds in Exod. 24.1-11), and it is lauded by Yahweh because it reveals 'a heart...to fear me and to keep all my commandments' (Deut. 5.28-29). The lengthy parenetic section that follows this story begins with the command to 'love the Lord your God with all your heart' (Deut 6.5), followed by the instruction to put 'these words which I command you...upon your heart' (6.6; cf. 11.18).[13] A bit later, the writer reminds his audience that their sojourn in the wilderness was a time when Yahweh was 'testing you to know what was in your heart, whether you would keep his commandments, or not' (8.2).

Conversely, acts of disobedience are manifestations of an unfaithful heart. Doubt, pride and self-righteousness are attributes of the heart against which the writer warns his audience (7.17-19; 8.17-18; 9.4-5). The refusal to 'open your hand' to the poor is attributed to the 'highness' of one's heart (15.7-8). Further, when the writer spells out the appropriate lessons to be learned from the nation's previous acts of disobedience, he couples together the command to 'love...the Lord your God with all your heart' with the command 'to keep the com-

12. Weinfeld, *Deuteronomy and the Deuteronomic School*, p. 210; cf. Clements, *God's Chosen People*, pp. 82-88.
13. Similarly, if the people 'lay it to heart' that Yahweh alone is God, then they will 'keep his statutes and his ordinances' (4.39-40).

mandments and the statutes of the Lord' (10.12-13; 11.1).

This expectation that heartfelt devotion to Yahweh is the foundation (and true test) of obedience applies to all spheres of Israelite life. Concerning prescribed times for worship in particular, the reader is to remember that it is the heart (the 'spiritual' side) of the offerant, not the mere performance of the ritual, that determines a sacrifice's ultimate acceptability before Yahweh (cf. Ps. 51.17).[14] As Clements says, 'It was not the gifts [in the form of sacrifices] themselves which were holy, but the attitude of the offerer, and it is this right attitude of thankfulness that was pleasing to God.'[15] The same criterion would be used for evaluating all other (non-sacrificial) worship activities.

Clements's reference to an 'attitude of thankfulness' steers our attention toward the fact that celebration dominates the descriptions of worship gatherings in Deuteronomy.[16] One sees this by isolating the acts that are specifically prescribed in these laws.

The initial centralization law, with its plural addressees (Deut. 12.2-12), instructs the people to 'seek' Yahweh's chosen place (12.5) and 'bring' their sacrifices there (12.5, 11). As noted above, these might include sacrifices of penitence, but that is not brought out in any way. Rather, the other activities specifically prescribed here for the people are that they shall 'eat...' and/or 'rejoice before the Lord your God' (12.7, 12).[17] The subsequent double stipulations regarding 'profane slaughter', with their singular addressee, allow for the eating of meat in

14. Weinfeld, *Deuteronomy and the Deuteronomic School*, p. 210.

15. Clements, *God's Chosen People*, p. 88. 'Deuteronomy made "rejoicing" its basic liturgical attitude' (Braulik, 'Commemoration', p. 77). Many Christians, familiar only with the stories of Jesus' criticisms of one strand of interpretation current in his day, are unaware that this perspective on worship permeates Deuteronomic legislation. Thus, his teachings constitute worship renewal more than worship reform (see Braulik, 'Joy', p. 63).

16. See also Braulik, 'Joy', pp. 27-28, 40-44, 60-63. For a discussion of festival in the Priestly materials, see E. Otto and T. Schramm, *Festival and Joy* (Biblical Encounters Series; Nashville: Abingdon Press, 1980).

17. The law presupposes a setting of plenty. This does not eliminate the ambiguity that has plagued the debate regarding the date of the composition of the D Code (see nn. 2 and 3 above). The author could be living at a time of plenty (the reign of Josiah? of Uzziah?), exhorting the people to initiate or perpetuate their joyful worship so that Yahweh might continue to bless them. Or, the author could be living in a time of poverty (the reign of Manasseh?), using the possibility of divine blessings as an inducement for reform.

any Israelite town (12.15, 20-22; the prohibition against eating blood is also duplicated—12.16, 23-25), unless it is part of one's tithes, first-lings, votive offerings or freewill offerings (12.17-18, 26-27). Those sacral items are always to be brought to the central sanctuary, again with the consequent expectation that 'you shall eat them before the Lord your God…and you shall rejoice before the Lord your God (12.17-18).[18]

This prescription to 'eat…and rejoice' is reiterated in some form in every other law concerning worship in Deuteronomy 12–26 (and 27.1-8). The law concerning tithes (14.22-27; cf. 26.12-15) instructs those distant from the central sanctuary to exchange goods for money so that they can buy food at 'the place which the Lord your God chooses, and…eat there before the Lord your God and rejoice'. Firstlings are to be consecrated from work and then are to be eaten 'before the Lord your God…at the place which the Lord will choose' (15.19-20). The Passover/Unleavened Bread observance (16.1-8) concludes with a 'solemn assembly' (עצרת) and stands as the only 'non-festive' worship prescribed for the entire nation in the D Code; yet even here, the only activities mentioned in connection with it are the offering of sacrifices and eating.[19] The other two annual gatherings (16.9-12, 13-15) are 'festivals', during which 'you shall rejoice (before the Lord your God)' (16.11, 14), '…so that you will be altogether joyful' (16.15).[20] Sim-ilarly, the conclusion of the law prescribing the offering of firstfruits calls for the offerant to 'worship before the Lord your God…and rejoice' (26.10-11). Finally, the site of the altar of unhewn stones is, naturally, to be a place where sacrifices are offered; but also, 'you shall eat there, and you shall rejoice before the Lord your God' (27.7). So, while the more solemn side of worship is perhaps implicit in the sacri-fices prescribed in these laws, the only worship-related activities (besides offering sacrifices) that are explicitly mentioned are those that are celebrative.

Granted, it is not the acts of 'eating' and 'rejoicing' in and of them-selves that are so significant. These activities are mentioned fairly often

---

18. Clements, *Deuteronomy*, p. 61.

19. Braulik, 'Joy', p. 43.

20. On the redaction of these laws, see E. Auerbach, 'Die Feste im alte Israel', *VT* 8 (1958), pp. 1-18; Levinson, *Deuteronomy*, pp. 53-97. Braulik speaks of this as '*the* feast' ('Joy', pp. 50-51; see also p. 232 n. 24; 'Commemoration', p. 85).

outside a cultic setting.[21] What is significant is (1) that these activities, along with sacrificing, always occupy a central place in the worship prescribed in the D Code; and (2) the writer's insistence that all these activities are to be carried out 'before the Lord' (12.7, 12, 18; 14.23, 26; 15.20; 16.11; 26.10; 27.7), 'at the place which the Lord your God will choose' (12.5-7, 18; 14.23; 15.20; 16.7, 11, 15).

The overwhelmingly celebrative tone of worship in these laws is quite striking. Whatever the reason for the gathering—whether the accompanying sacrifice is one of penitence or gratitude—it inevitably turns into a time of festival. This seems overly optimistic—considering the precarious climate[22] and political vulnerability of the region—but purposefully so, in my opinion. The author could have presented a more 'balanced' picture, as in Deut. 27.9–28.68, where opposing potentialities are laid out for the reader;[23] or as in Deut. 15.1-11, where the idealistic 'there will be no poor among you' (15.4) is offset by the more realistic 'the poor will never cease out of the land' (15.11). He could have continued in the same vein as Deuteronomy 5–11, interjecting warnings against apostasy and exhortations for obedience, 'that it may go well with you'. Instead, in most of these laws concerning worship gatherings, he optimistically assumes fidelity and blessing.[24]

The purpose behind such optimism is not immediately clear. One strong possibility is that the author is 'painting a rosy picture' in association with worship to suggest to the reader that obedience has its rewards. These worship laws assume abundant agricultural blessings; those blessings, in turn, assume a faithful people.

21. Conversely, fasting and mourning are commonly linked together (e.g. 2 Sam. 12.20-23).

22. The contrast made between the agricultural climates of Egypt and Israel (Deut. 11.10-12) points to the precariousness of Israel's economy. On the interplay between economy and ecosystem in Israel, see L. Marfoe, 'The Integrative Transformation: Patterns of Sociopolitical Organization in Southern Syria', *BASOR* 234 (1979), pp. 3-10; D.C. Hopkins, *The Highlands of Canaan: Agricultural Life in the Early Iron Age* (Social World of Biblical Antiquity, 3; Sheffield: Almond Press, 1985); O. Borowski, *Agriculture in Iron Age Israel* (Winona Lake, IN: Eisenbrauns, 1987).

23. One aspect of these 'opposing potentialities' involves eating. The curses that disobedient Israelites would face include famine (28.31, 33, 39, 51). The only references to eating here are to eating the flesh of children (28.53, 55, 57).

24. The only exceptions to this are found in Deut. 12.13, 19, 25 (cf. vv. 28-32).

Worship as Grateful Response to Yahweh

In these particular laws it is assumed that Israel will be blessed in the days to come, and it is because of such blessings that the Israelites will regularly 'eat and rejoice'. The danger inherent in such a situation is that the people will misinterpret the cause or means of the blessings they enjoy. Therefore, the worship laws seek to set up worship as a time when the people are reminded that Yahweh alone—not some other deity (6.10-15), and not they themselves (8.17-18)—has provided them with their blessings.[25]

The author achieves this goal not only (1) by presuming prosperity as the occasion for each time of worship, but also (2) by envisioning 'exceptions' that would arise due to increased prosperity and (3) by reminding his readers in these laws that that prosperity has been provided by Yahweh prior to the occasion for worship. This means that worship of Yahweh alone will always be understood as an act of natural response, that it will be the 'natural' thing to do in a time of prosperity. By extension, faithful observance of *all* the laws in the D Code should be the 'natural' thing to do in a time of prosperity.

The author inserts characteristic Deuteronomic phrases in these laws as reminders to the reader of Yahweh's prior acts to which the people are to respond with obedience (in these cases, in the prescribed worship). First, there are the general instructions to worship at the central sanctuary (12.2-7); but this worship will only be possible after the people 'come to the rest and the inheritance which the Lord your God gives you... when he gives you rest from all your enemies round about' (12.8-10; cf. 27.2, which prefaces the altar law with the reminder that they are in 'the land which the Lord your God gives you'). When they slaughter and eat meat, even outside a ceremonial setting, they do so 'according to the blessing of the Lord your God which he has given you' (12.15). If the people eat meat in their towns, it first of all assumes that they have enough of a surplus to allow for such a feast.[26] Further, if they eat meat in their towns because the journey to the central sanctuary is too long, they are here reminded that this is the case solely because

25. Braulik, 'Joy', pp. 27-28; 'Commemoration', p. 83.

26. On the consumption of meat in recent agrarian Middle Eastern society, see L. Holy, *Neighbours and Kinsmen: A Study of the Berti People of Darfur* (New York: St Martin's Press, 1974).

Yahweh has expanded their territory (12.20).[27] Similarly, the supplementary tithe-stipulation (to convert the tithe to money to be taken to the sanctuary) will become necessary 'when the Lord your God blesses you' (14.24).[28] Firstlings are 'consecrated to the Lord' (15.19), likewise pointing to the fact that Yahweh alone has provided these livestock.[29] The worshippers will provide offerings 'as the Lord your God blesses you' during the Feast of Weeks (16.10). The Feast of Booths will last a week, 'because the Lord your God will bless you in all your produce and in all the work of your hands' (16.15; cf. v. 17). The ceremony for the offering of firstfruits concludes with the instruction to 'rejoice in all the good which the Lord your God has given to you' (26.11).

The references to Yahweh's blessings in these passages remind the readers that those blessings come prior to the times of worship. The blessings are already received when the worshippers come to the chosen place. This is thought to be in marked contrast to non-Israelite worship, which was conducted as a way of winning a deity's favor so that the deity would bless the worshippers. In Israel's case, worship does not instigate divine blessings; at the most, worship contributes to the preservation and perpetuation of blessings by fostering an ongoing recognition of dependence on Yahweh for those blessings.[30]

27. Braulik ('Joy', p. 49) says, 'It was in consequence of the cult centralization that it became necessary to allow profane slaughtering.' This might be true, but the lawgiver attributes the need to the 'future' expansion of Israelite territory. Whatever the reality of the situation, the worshippers' capability to set aside significant foods through tithing, to provide unblemished firstlings without ruining themselves economically and to pay off vows (12.17) should in their minds be directly related to Yahweh's blessings on their behalf. Instructing them to bring such offerings to Yahweh's chosen sanctuary would obviously reinforce in their minds the notion that he is to be credited with their abundance (see below).

28. In a sense, these laws envision a 'nice problem' to have—Yahweh will bless the people so much for their obedience that the previously stated centralization laws will not be feasible for some (who, of course, will want nothing more than to show their gratitude to Yahweh). The purpose of the laws then is to provide a solution to this 'problem'.

29. See Braulik, 'Joy', p. 55. The strict instruction that sacrificial animals be without blemish (15.21-22; 17.1) is similarly dependent on prosperity.

30. Cf. 12.29–13.1; 16.21-22. D.W. Harvey, '"Rejoice Not, O Israel"', in B.W. Anderson and W. Harrelson (eds.), *Israel's Prophetic Heritage: Essays in Honor of James Muilenberg* (New York: Harper & Brothers, 1962), pp. 123-27; Braulik, 'Joy', pp. 34-52, 56; *idem*, 'Commemoration', pp. 77, 81-82; R.L. Christensen, 'Deuteronomy 26.1-11', *Int* 49 (1995), pp. 59-60.

Thus, the Deuteronomic laws are in some sense prophetic. First, they promise what Yahweh will do for his people so that, when the promise is fulfilled, the people will naturally respond with gratitude toward the promise-giver who has faithfully provided. Then they take the next step by prescribing what forms that grateful response should take: uncompromised worship and obedience to Yahweh's will.

Worship is fundamentally, then, to be a grateful demonstration of one's reliance on Yahweh.[31] The shrines and altars of the other gods will be destroyed (12.2-3), insuring that no one will give them credit for the good things the people receive, because those gods have in fact given no blessings. Instead, the entire nation will worship together only 'at the place which the Lord will choose' (12.4). When they 'eat and rejoice' together—when they are 'altogether joyful' (16.15)—they will do so 'before the Lord', thereby realizing that their joy is possible because of what Yahweh alone has done for them.[32]

In this light, one can see more clearly the significance of the repeated call for worship 'before the Lord (your God)'.[33] It is more than a spatially exclusive prescription, limiting worship to a single locale. The singularity of place—indicated in the phrase 'at the place which the Lord your God will choose'—is conceptually linked to this phrase, which points to a singular object of worship.[34] This infuses an attitudinal element into worship, which is to linger with the worshippers when they have returned to their homes.[35] By repeatedly stating that worship is to be 'before the Lord', the writer is reinforcing the idea that

31. Clements, *God's Chosen People*, pp. 71, 84-88; and *Deuteronomy*, pp. 60-63; Braulik, 'Joy', pp. 43-44.

32. This notion is stated most clearly in Deut. 6.10-15. Yahweh is acting first by giving the people cities, houses, cisterns, vineyards and olive trees that they did not build or plant. The response called for then is to 'fear the Lord...' and 'not go after other gods', 'for the Lord...is a jealous god'.

33. For a welcome corrective in the discussion over the transcendence/presence of Yahweh in the D Code, see I. Wilson, *Out of the Midst of the Fire: Divine Presence in Deuteronomy* (SBLDS, 151; Atlanta: Scholars Press, 1995).

34. Wilson (*Out of the Midst*, pp. 154-56) argues persuasively that 'before the Lord your God' is not a mere circumlocution for the central sanctuary, because the former is usually found in the same context as the phrase 'at the place which the Lord your God will choose'. Using such a less precise circumlocution would be needlessly redundant. As he recognizes, this phrase must point beyond the place of worship to 'a personal referent'.

35. Braulik, 'Joy', pp. 61-63; *idem*, 'Commemoration', p. 82.

worship is to be a time when one is reminded that Yahweh is the sole provider of all that is enjoyed at the time of worship and beyond.[36] The meal comprised of tithe-gatherings eaten 'before the Lord your God' demonstrates that the people enjoy an overabundance that Yahweh has provided (14.22-27); the eating of firstlings (15.19-23) and the offering of firstfruits (26.1-11) 'before the Lord your God' remind the people that these are but the first of many meals provided by Yahweh. One is blessed throughout the year, but a few particular days are set aside as times to remember that those everyday blessings come from Yahweh, 'before' whom the worshippers gather.[37]

Humanitarianism a Natural Result of Worship

A well-known aspect of Israelite thought is that Yahweh's gracious actions toward the Israelites are to be reflected by them in gracious actions toward dependent persons in their midst. So, it is not surprising that the Deuteronomic laws are not solely concerned with the vertical aspects of worship; they also point to consequent horizontal ('humanitarian')[38] obligations. This consequence of worship should be seen as an integral part of an Israelite's celebrative response to Yahweh's prior actions.[39] Because Yahweh alone blesses his people, he can be a

36. 'Forms of worship can and must be clarified by sharp concentration on the faith realities they are intended to celebrate' (J.A. Wharton, 'Deuteronomy 16.1-8', *Int* 41 [1987], p. 288).

37. The corollary centralization phrases carry at least this significance as well. 'The place which the Lord your God will choose, to make his name dwell there' is to be distinguished from places chosen for the worship of other gods (see 12.2). It is the place where Yahweh alone is called to remembrance, where Yahweh alone is praised for the blessings enjoyed by the people. See Clements, *God's Chosen People*, pp. 74-81.

38. Weinfeld, *Deuteronomy and the Deuteronomic School*, p. 212. M. Cohen, 'Ségrégationnisme et intégrationisme comme mobiles sous-jacents à l'antinomie de Dt 14,21 et Lv 17,15-16', *RHPR* 73 (1993), pp. 128-29, takes issue with Weinfeld on this point, saying that these laws allow for a condescending attitude. On the contrary, while these laws might assume that Israelites are currently looking down on those in their midst, the most natural result of observing such laws would seem to be the undermining of such an attitude.

39. For a look at this as an aspect of worship more generally, see D.E. Miller, 'Worship and Moral Reflection: A Phenomenological Analysis', *ATR* 62 (1980), pp. 307-20; E. LaVerdiere, 'Worship and Ethical Responsibility in the Bible', in M.E. Stamps (ed.), *To Do Justice and Right upon the Earth: Papers from the Virgil*

'jealous God' (6.10-15) who demands that all worship be carried out 'before' him (see above). For the same reason, he can command his people to show justice and mercy toward the dependent members of their family groups.[40] Since their material possessions come from Yahweh, he can prescribe how they are to use them.

The Deuteronomist brings out this notion in two ways. First, he tries to get the people to identify with their dependents by speaking of those with property as Yahweh's dependents. To this end, he repeatedly reminds his audience that they were 'sojourners' and 'slaves' whom Yahweh rescued from the land of Egypt (5.15; 16.12; 24.18, 22).[41] Secondly, the writer sets out Yahweh himself as an example of how one is to treat dependent persons:

> For the Lord your God is God of gods and Lord of lords, the great, the mighty, and the terrible God, who is not partial and takes no bribe. He executes justice for the fatherless and the widow, and loves the sojourner, giving him food and clothing (10.17-18).[42]

Michel Symposium on Liturgy and Social Justice (Collegeville, MN: Liturgical Press, 1993), pp. 16-32; Braulik, 'Joy', p. 35; *idem*, 'Commemoration', p. 83.

40. The sense of corporate unity is quite marked in these laws. The inclusion of dependent persons is not viewed as a forcing of one's beliefs on another. Rather, those directly addressed ('you') look upon their dependents as parts of themselves. See D. Patrick, 'The Rhetoric of Collective Responsibility in Deuteronomic Law', in D.P. Wright, D.N. Freedman and A. Hurvitz (eds.), *Pomegranates and Golden Bells: Studies in Biblical, Jewish, and Near Eastern Ritual, Law, and Literature in Honor of Jacob Milgrom* (Winona Lake, IN: Eisenbrauns, 1995), pp. 421-36.

41. C. de Groot van Houten, 'Remember That You Were Aliens: A Traditio-Historical Study', in E. Ulrich *et al.* (eds.), *Priests, Prophets and Scribes: Essays on the Formation and Heritage of Second Temple Judaism in Honour of Joseph Blenkinsopp* (JSOTSup, 149; Sheffield: Sheffield Academic Press, 1992), pp. 224-40; C. Hardmeier, 'Die Erinnerung an die Knechtschaft in Ägypten', in F. Crüsemann, C. Hardmeier and R. Kessler (eds.), *Was ist der Mensch...? Beiträge zur Anthropologie des Alten Testaments. Hans Walter Wolff zum 80. Geburtstag* (Munich: Chr. Kaiser Verlag, 1992), pp. 133-52; G.C. Moucarry, 'The Alien According to the Torah', *Themelios* 14 (Oct.-Nov., 1988), pp. 17-20.

42. Several have placed the composition of this passage in the exile. See, e.g., P.-E. Dion, 'Israël et l'étranger dans le Deutéronome', in M. Gourgues and G.-D. Mailhiot (eds.), *L'Altérité, vivre ensemble différents: approches pluridisciplinaires: Actes du Colloque pluridisciplinaire tenu à l'occasion du 75e anniversaire du Collège dominicain de philosophie et de théologie; Ottawa, 4-5-6 octobre 1984* (Paris: Cerf, 1986), p. 232; Mayes, *Deuteronomy*, pp. 207-208. I would place it earlier because it addresses concerns about 'justice for the fatherless and the

Many of these laws bring out this humanitarian aspect of worship by delineating the various dependent groups who shall attend the worship gatherings with the landowners whom all the laws address.[43] Two passages generalize about the attendees, specifying those summoned as 'you and your household' (12.7; 14.26). Others spell out in greater detail who would be intended by 'household'. In 12.18, the writer calls for the participation of 'you and your son and your daughter, your manservant and your maidservant, and the Levite who is in your gates'. Verse 12 contains the same list but in the plural. A more expanded list of celebrants is found in 16.11, 14, where 'the sojourner, the fatherless, and the widow who are among you' are included as well.[44] Deuteronomy 26.11 appears to be conflated, mentioning Yahweh's blessings

widow'. It seems more likely to assume that a writer would address problems with judicial corruption when Israelite officials were actually abusing their judicial powers in their own land, rather than while the Israelites were living as a conquered people in another land under a foreign judiciary.

43. The author appears to be addressing adult male landowners throughout the book of Deuteronomy. It is curious, though, that some of these lists include 'daughters' and 'maidservants', but not 'wives'. This implies that wives are actually implied in the term 'you' here and perhaps throughout the book. This could mean that the writer envisions a legal equality between husband and wife or that because they are 'one flesh', one refers to them in a legal context as if they were indivisible. In either case, this would imply a greater legal status for wives in these laws than is sometimes realized. See Weinfeld, *Deuteronomy and the Deuteronomic School*, p. 291-92; Braulik, 'Joy', p. 52-53; *idem*, 'Commemoration', pp. 80-81.

44. On these groups, see A. Causse, 'L'idéal politique et social du Deutéronome. La fraternité d'Israël', *RHPR* 13 (1933), pp. 304-13; F.C. Fensham, 'Widow, Orphan, and the Poor in Ancient Near Eastern Legal and Wisdom Literature', *JNES* 21 (1962), pp. 129-39; T. Krapf, 'Traditionsgeschichtliches zum deuteronomischen Fremdling-Waise-Witwe-Gebot', *VT* 34 (1984), pp. 87-91; and N. Lohfink, 'The Laws of Deuteronomy: A Utopian Project for a World without Any Poor', *ScrB* 26 (1996), pp. 7-13. This triad is found in scattered references throughout the Hebrew Bible (Deut. 10.18; 24.17-22; 27.19; Ps. 94.6; Jer. 7.6; Ezek. 22.7; Zech. 7.10; Mal. 3.5). In one passage, the Levite is added to this group (Deut. 14.29).

Braulik ('Commemoration', pp. 75-76) makes too much, in my opinion, of the omission of 'aliens' or 'Levites' from some of these lists, saying that these festivals do not concern those groups not mentioned. For example, to say that 'aliens' (= 'sojourners') would not 'fit in' at a festival commemorating the exodus (16.1-8) runs counter to the sentiment of 26.5, which reminds the worshippers that their ancestor 'sojourned' in Egypt.

on 'you and your house, you, and the Levite, and the sojourner who is among you'.[45]

These dependent groups are mentioned elsewhere in Deuteronomy in two contexts besides worship. First, the addressees are responsible in part for overseeing the religious integrity of their dependents. Sons and daughters are to be taught Yahweh's laws by the addressees (6.20-25). It is the responsibility of the addressees to eliminate apostate members from their house, because they threaten the integrity of the entire nation (13.6-11). The 'stubborn and rebellious son' (21.18-21) and the promiscuous daughter (22.20-21) likewise threaten the moral reputation and integrity of their household and the broader community; so, the addressees are instructed to 'purge the evil from your midst' in these cases through the actions of the offenders' parents and the 'men' of their community.[46]

The other non-worship context in which these dependent persons are mentioned is that of humanitarian obligations. Sons in a polygamous household are mentioned as persons deserving fair treatment regarding inheritance (21.15-17). The physical and judicial needs of the other groups (Levites, sojourners, widows, orphans) are mentioned as of special concern to Yahweh (10.18-19), and specific instructions are given to the addressees to imitate Yahweh in their own treatment of these groups (14.28-29; 24.17-22; 27.19; cf. 26.12-13).[47]

45. Curiously, 'you' is given twice; 'the Levite' is one of those mentioned in the lists in 12.12, 18; 'the sojourner' is in the expanded lists of 16.11, 14.

46. The fact that the D Code looks to the 'laity' to maintain justice in these passages raises interesting questions about the provenance of the laws. Fensham ('Widow, Orphan, and the Poor', p. 138) remarks that the responsibility for protecting these needy groups traditionally fell to the king in the ancient Near East (see 2 Sam. 12.1-5; 15.1-6; Ps. 72). This suggests that D was composed at a time when Israel's kings were not fulfilling this responsibility. Therefore, there is some plausibility to Cohen's proposal ('Ségrégationnisme', pp. 128-29) that Shilonite priests of the North, displaced by Jeroboam's reforms, are responsible for D. However, it seems just as likely to suppose that southern Yahwists, disgruntled by the corruptions of Manasseh's day, could turn to the local populations for maintaining justice. Likewise, the repeated attacks by Isaiah (Isa. 1.10-17; 5.1-7; 10.1-4) against judicial corruption during the reigns of Ahaz and Hezekiah leave open the same possibility for the law code's composition during Isaiah's career.

47. On the tithe laws, see R.B. Herron, 'The Land, the Law, and the Poor', *Word and World* 6 (1986), p. 79. On the conceptual unity of 26.1-15, see F.C. Holmgren, 'The Pharisee and the Tax Collector: Luke 18.9-14 and Deuteronomy 26.1-15', *Int* 48 (1994), pp. 257, 260.

The writer accomplishes complementary goals by calling for the inclusion of these dependent groups in his laws on worship. On the one hand, he refers to these dependents to remind the addressees of their own dependence on Yahweh in the past.[48] This is part of the writer's goal of reminding the people that their prosperity is dependent solely on Yahweh, discussed earlier. At the same time, the goal of the laws is to spur the addressees to fulfill their obligations to those who in turn are dependent on them.[49]

The law of centralization calls for the addressees and their dependents to 'eat…and rejoice before the Lord your God' (12.12, 18). This suggests that the landowners are not to view the blessings of Yahweh as theirs solely. Those who are landless have 'no portion' of their own in the land, because Yahweh has not given them a portion. But this is not to be taken as a sign that they are ignored or excluded by Yahweh. To the contrary, Yahweh is providing for them through the landowners. This is highlighted in 14.27, where the landlessness of the Levites is the very reason given for not forsaking them (cf. 26.12-13). The landowners are blessed by Yahweh with more than they need so that they can provide for the needs of the landless. The reminder of the Egyptian slavery in the law of the Feast of Weeks (16.9-12) suggests to the addressees that Yahweh brought slaves out of Egypt in order to provide them with a feast; so, those former slaves should likewise provide a feast for their own slaves (and other dependents). Finally, the offering of firstfruits (26.1-11) is a time to 'rejoice in all the good which the Lord your God has given to you and to your house'. 'The good' that the landowner receives from the land is not for him alone.[50] His portion of

48. See Causse, 'L'idéal politique', p. 309; de Groot van Houten, 'Remember That You Were Aliens', pp. 228-33.

49. Holmgren, 'The Pharisee and the Tax Collector', p. 258; Lohfink, 'Laws of Deuteronomy', p. 15. '[Psalm 95] makes clear that parenesis did have a place in Israel's formal liturgy. Thus we cannot avoid inferring that liturgy was the proper setting for parenesis whenever and wherever it occurred'. S.J. de Vries, 'Deuteronomy: Exemplar of a Non-Sacerdotal Appropriation of Sacred History', in J.I. Cook (ed.), *Grace upon Grace: Essays in Honor of Lester J. Kuyper* (Grand Rapids: Eerdmans, 1975), p. 101.

50. 'There is acknowledgement [in Deut. 26.1-11] that God expects something from one who worships (e.g., regarding "the Levite, the sojourner, the fatherless, and the widow"), something more than a warm heart. Religion that comes from the heart is something other than religion that remains in the heart. Covenant faith

'the land which the Lord your God gives you for an inheritance' is to be enjoyed by his entire 'house', which includes sons and daughters, slaves and sojourners, widows and orphans, and Levites.[51]

So, in the laws that call for the prosperous landowner to come 'before the Lord' to celebrate his prosperity, he is reminded of the expectations that Yahweh has placed upon him regarding the landless around him. Similar instructions are given elsewhere to motivate the addressees to provide food and clothing to these dependent persons, to respect their properties and persons, and to defend them in court (10.17-19; 24.10-22). These two types of laws should be viewed as complementary, with the worship laws prescribing specific and regular contexts in which the landowners will be reminded of their obligations to the landless among them.

Final Reflections

It should be obvious that the various aspects of worship described here are inseparable, being indelibly intertwined in the lawgiver's mind; they 'come as a package'. His message is this: those who prosper should recognize that they are dependent on Yahweh alone for their economic livelihood. They should naturally 'love the Lord with all their heart', responding as if by instinct with celebrative worship that acknowledges their dependence on him. This 'celebrative' response is not limited, however, to occasions of worship. Rather, it spills over into the everyday lives of the worshippers, being manifested in their obedience to Yahweh's instructions. In particular, they should 'celebrate' their blessings by imitating the way Yahweh provides for them in the way they provide for those who depend on them. The 'bridge' linking worship and general obedience together as celebrative response is founded on the inclusion of those dependent groups in the prescribed worship gatherings in the D Code.[52]

moves beyond good-heart feeling and emotion to action' (Holmgren, 'The Pharisee and the Tax Collector', p. 259).

51. Herron, 'The Land, the Law, and the Poor', pp. 78-84.

52. Again, it is intriguing to consider when such a message might have been composed and propagated in the nation of Israel. Unfortunately, no clear answer emerges. The assumed point of view of the writer is that prosperity will come in the future (when the Israelites have taken possession of the land), so that these laws are designed to instruct them on how to worship once they have 'arrived' (in more ways than one). This could support the view that the D Code was composed during

These overlapping ideas provide us with an understanding of worship that is far richer spiritually than the supposed 'repetitive ritual' that so many today assume for ancient Israelite worship. In fact, the spiritual richness revealed in these laws poses several challenges to the authenticity of worship among worshippers in Western culture. First, these laws declare Yahweh to be the sole source of blessings and personal well-being. Such talk is in direct opposition to the rhetoric of 'self-made millionaires' and numerous 'self-help' programs that abound in our culture. It is a challenge for worshippers today to know how to perpetuate meaningfully the same sense of daily dependence on God through worship as these laws intend. Further, perpetuating the authentic sense of gratitude in worship called for in these laws presents a serious challenge to those who enjoy prosperity in a technological age. It is relatively easy to see a connection between eating in a worship setting and a recognition of Yahweh as provider of agricultural prosperity. It is more difficult to see a connection between traditional worship and God as provider of prosperity based on technology. Similarly, vast changes have occurred in socio-economic structures that distance providers from dependents today much more than in ancient Israel. The Deuteronomic laws challenge providers to fulfill their obligations to dependents by bringing the two groups together in worship. Such a situation was relatively natural in ancient Israel owing to the domestic proximity of the groups. Those socio-economic conditions no longer exist, though. Nevertheless, similar theologically based, humanitarian obligations do exist. Thus, the Deuteronomic laws challenge contemporary worshippers to find ways to structure worship so

a time of economic hardship, such as the reign of Manasseh. In such an environment, the repeated references to rejoicing would most naturally be something of an inducement to obedience. In other words, if the Israelites will serve Yahweh, then he will provide for them so that they can come and eat and rejoice before him. On the other hand, one could argue that these laws were composed in an environment of prosperity. The author's goal in this case would be to convince his audience that their prosperity is to be attributed to Yahweh's blessings, and that they should share their blessings with dependent groups. Statements referring to Israel's 'future' prosperity would thus be interpreted as *ex eventu* prophecies. In either case, the eventual outcome should be the same. Worship serves as a reminder of one's dependence on Yahweh. During periods of want and need, the Israelites would see in Deuteronomy a motivation to rely on Yahweh, because people 'eat and rejoice' when Yahweh cares for them. In times of prosperity, worship would serve as a reminder to maintain one's focus on Yahweh.

that it reminds them of their obligations to their fellow human beings, just as they challenged the ancient Israelite.

The worship laws of Deuteronomy show that worship should be genuine, from the heart. The 'natural' tone of worship in times of prosperity should be celebratory, as worshippers respond to the perceived beneficence of God and acknowledge their dependence on him alone for their well-being. Finally, worship should provide ways of reminding participants that they are obligated to provide for others as God has provided for them.

SELECT BIBLIOGRAPHY OF THE WRITINGS OF JOHN T. WILLIS

Timothy M. Willis

Dissertation

'The Structure, Setting, and Interrelationships of the Pericopes in the Book of Micah' (PhD dissertation, Vanderbilt Divinity School, 1966).

Books

Engnell, I., *A Rigid Scrutiny: Critical Essays on the Old Testament* (ed. and trans. J.T. Willis and H. Ringgren; Nashville: Vanderbilt University Press, 1969).

Crenshaw, J.L., and J.T. Willis (eds.), *Essays in Old Testament Ethics: J. Philip Hyatt, In Memoriam* (New York: Ktav, 1974).

Botterweck, G.J., and H. Ringgren, *Theological Dictionary of the Old Testament* (vols. I–II, trans. J.T. Willis; vol. III, trans. J.T. Willis, G.W. Bromiley and D.E. Green; Grand Rapids: Eerdmans, 1974-1978).

Willis, J.T. (ed.), *The World and Literature of the Old Testament* (LWC, 1; Austin, TX: Sweet, 1979).

—*Genesis* (LWC, 2; Austin, TX: Sweet, 1979).

—*Isaiah* (LWC, 12; Austin, TX: Sweet, 1980).

—*First and Second Samuel* (LWC, 6; Austin, TX: Sweet, 1982).

Articles and Essays

Willis, J.T., 'On the Text of Micah 2.1aα-β', *Bib* 48 (1967), pp. 534-41.

—'ממך לי יצא in Micah 5.1', *JQR* 58 (1968), pp. 317-22.

—'A Note on ואמר in Micah 3.1', *ZAW* 80 (1968), pp. 50-54.

—'Micah IV 14-V 5—A Unit', *VT* 18 (1968), pp. 529-47.

—'Some Suggestions on the Interpretation of Micah I 2', *VT* 18 (1968), pp. 372-79.

—'The Authenticity and Meaning of Micah 5.9-14', *ZAW* 81 (1969), pp. 353-68.

—'The Structure of Micah 3–5 and the Function of Micah 5.9-14 in the Book', *ZAW* 81 (1969), pp. 191-214.

—'The Structure of the Book of Micah', *SEÅ* 34 (1969), pp. 5-42.

—'Fundamental Issues in Contemporary Micah Studies', *ResQ* 13 (1970), pp. 77-90.

—'Ivan Engnell's Contributions to Old Testament Scholarship', *TZ* 26 (1970), pp. 385-94.

—'Micah 2.6-8 and the People of God in Micah', *BZ* NS 14 (1970), pp. 72-87.

—'An Anti-Elide Narrative Tradition from a Prophetic Circle at the Ramah Sanctuary', *JBL* 90 (1971), pp. 288-308.

—'Cultic Elements in the Story of Samuel's Birth and Dedication', *ST* 26 (1972), pp. 33-61.
—'The Function of Comprehensive Anticipatory Redactional Joints in 1 Samuel 16–18', *ZAW* 85 (1973), pp. 294-314.
—'The Song of Hannah and Psalm 113', *CBQ* 35 (1973), pp. 139-54.
—'A Reapplied Prophetic Oracle', in D. Lys *et al.* (eds.), *Studies on Prophecy: A Collection of Twelve Papers* (VTSup, 26; Leiden: E.J. Brill, 1974), pp. 64-76.
—'Ethics in a Cultic Setting', in J.L. Crenshaw and J.T. Willis (eds.), *Essays in Old Testament Ethics: J. Philip Hyatt, In Memoriam* (New York: Ktav, 1974), pp. 145-69.
—'Old Testament Foundations of Social Justice', in P.C. Cotham (ed.), *Christian Social Ethics* (Grand Rapids: Baker Book House, 1979), pp. 21-43.
—'Psalm 1: An Entity', *ZAW* 91 (1979), pp. 381-401.
—'Redaction Criticism and Historical Reconstruction', in M.J. Buss (ed.), *Encounter with the Text: Form and History in the Hebrew Bible* (Philadelphia: Fortress Press, 1979), pp. 93-89.
—'Samuel Versus Eli: I Sam. 1–7', *TZ* 35 (1979), pp. 201-12.
—'The Genre of Isaiah 5.1-7', *JBL* 96 (1977), pp. 337-62.
—'The Juxtaposition of Synonymous and Chiastic Parallelism in Tricola in Old Testament Hebrew Psalm Poetry', *VT* 29 (1979), pp. 465-80.
—'Thoughts on a Redactional Analysis of the Book of Micah', *SBLSP* 13 (1978), pp. 87-107.
—'Some Recent Studies on Genesis and the Literary-Historical Approach', *ResQ* 23 (1980), pp. 193-200.
—'On the Interpretation of Isaiah 1.18', *JSOT* 25 (1983), pp. 35-54.
—'The First Pericope in the Book of Isaiah', *VT* 34 (1984), pp. 63-77.
—'An Important Passage for Determining the Historical Setting of a Prophetic Oracle— Isaiah 1.7-8', *ST* 39 (1985), pp. 151-69.
—'Dialogue between Prophet and Audience as a Rhetorical Device in the Book of Jeremiah', *JSOT* 33 (1985), pp. 63-82. Reprinted in R.P. Gordon (ed.), *'The Place Is Too Small for Us': The Israelite Prophets in Recent Scholarship* (Winona Lake, IN: Eisenbrauns, 1995), pp. 205-22.
—'God and his Chosen People', *The Seminary Review* (Cincinnati Christian Seminary 31/1985), pp. 1-30.
—'God and the Nations', *The Seminary Review* (Cincinnati Christian Seminary 31/1985), pp. 31-49.
—'The Nature of God', *The Seminary Review* (Cincinnati Christian Seminary 31/1985), pp. 51-68.
—'Interpreting Hebrew Syntax', in F.F. Kearley, E.P. Myers and T.D. Hadley (eds.), *Biblical Interpretation: Principles and Practices: Studies in Honor of Jack Pearl Lewis* (Grand Rapids: Baker Book House, 1986), pp. 138-45.
—'Lament Reversed—Isaiah 1.21ff.', *ZAW* 98 (1986), pp. 236-48.
—'Alternating (ABA′B′) Parallelism in the Old Testament Psalms and Prophetic Literature', in E.R. Follis (ed.), *Directions in Biblical Hebrew Poetry* (JSOTSup, 40; Sheffield: JSOT Press, 1987), pp. 49-76.
—'Psalm 121 as a Wisdom Poem', *HAR* 11 (1987), pp. 435-51.

—'The Old Testament and the Book of Revelation', in J.E. Priest (ed.), *Johannine Studies: Essays in Honor of Frank Pack* (Malibu, CA: Pepperdine University Press, 1989), pp. 231-39.

—'A Cry of Defiance—Psalm 2', *JSOT* 47 (1990), pp. 33-50. Reprinted in D.J.A. Clines (ed.), *The Poetical Books* (The Biblical Seminar, 41; Sheffield: Sheffield Academic Press, 1997), pp. 117-34.

—'An Attempt to Decipher Psalm 121.1b', *CBQ* 52 (1990), pp. 241-51.

—'Prophetic Hermeneutics', *ResQ* 32 (1990), pp. 193-207.

—'Qûmah YHWH ["Arise, O Yahweh"]', *JNSL* 16 (1990), pp. 207-21.

—' "Rod" and "Staff" in Isaiah 1–39', *OTE* 3 (1990), pp. 93-106.

—'Historical Issues in Isaiah 22,15-25', *Bib* 74 (1993), pp. 60-70.

—'Huldah and Other Biblical Prophetesses', in C.D. Osburn (ed.), *Essays on Women in Earliest Christianity* (2 vols.; Joplin, MO: College Press, 1993), II, pp. 105-23.

—'Women in the Old Testament', in C.D. Osburn (ed.), *Essays on Women in Earliest Christianity* (2 vols.; Joplin, MO: College Press, 1993), I, pp. 25-39.

—' "I Am your God" and "You Are my People" in Hosea and Jeremiah', *ResQ* 36 (1994), pp. 291-303.

—'Textual and Linguistic Issues in Isaiah 22,15-25', *ZAW* 105 (1994), pp. 377-99.

—'The "Repentance" of God in the Books of Samuel, Jeremiah, and Jonah', *HBT* 16 (1994), pp. 156-75.

—'The Newly Discovered Fragmentary Aramaic Inscription from Tel Dan', *ResQ* 37 (1995), pp. 219-26.

—'אב as an Official Term', *SJOT* 10 (1996), pp. 115-36.

—'An Interpretation of Isaiah 22.15-25 and its Function in the New Testament', in C.A. Evans and J.A. Sanders (eds.), *Early Christian Interpretation of the Scriptures of Israel: Investigations and Proposals* (JSNTSup, 148; Studies in Scripture in Early Judaism and Christianity, 5; Sheffield: Sheffield Academic Press, 1997), pp. 334-51.

INDEXES

INDEX OF REFERENCES

OLD TESTAMENT

Reference	Pages
33.1-3	172
33.1-2	182
33.1	159, 163, 172, 182, 183
33.3	172
33.4-5	172
33.4	155, 182
33.5	162, 182
33.8	172, 182
33.9	162, 172
34	64, 158
34.10-11	158
35.13-14	66
35.14	62, 63
37	64, 158
37.1-2	158
37.4	158, 161
37.5-6	158
37.6	161
37.8-9	158
37.27-28	158
37.27	161
37.34	158, 161
37.37-38	158
39.14	121
41.11	157
42.5	32
44.1-26	64
44.10-17	65
45–48	64
46	67
47	169, 172, 173, 174-76
47.1-2	174
47.1	182
47.2	173
47.3-5	173, 175
47.3	162, 173-75, 182
47.4	173, 174
47.5	173, 183
47.6	173, 174
47.7-11	174
47.7	173
47.8	162, 173-75, 182
47.9	183
48	33, 67
50.1-7	190
50.14	69
51	279
51.17	281
61.4-8	69
66	169
66.1-20	69
66.1-12	70
66.1-5	70, 71
66.2-12	169
66.3	166
66.5	162, 169, 182, 183
66.6-7	70
66.6	70, 72
66.7-12	70
66.7	70, 72
66.8	70, 169, 182
66.9	162, 183
66.10	72
66.13-20	70, 71, 169
66.13-17	69, 71, 72
66.13-15	25
66.13	72
66.16	72
66.18-19	71, 72
66.20	71, 72
68.2	75
68.25-28	32
68.30	39
71.20	65
72	64, 290
73.24	111
76	64, 67
76.12	39
79.1	192
84	64, 67
86.13	65
87	64
93	64
95	169, 176, 291
95.1	182
95.3-5	175
95.3	162, 175, 182
95.4	183
95.5	183
95.6	175, 176
95.7-11	176
95.7	162, 175, 176, 178, 183
96	169, 173, 176, 177, 182
96.1-3	176
96.1-2	176
96.1	182
96.3	176
96.4-6	169
96.4-5	176
96.4	155, 162, 182
96.5	162, 183
96.7-12	177
96.7-9	177
96.7	177
96.9	182
96.10	166
96.11-12	177
96.13	162, 177, 183
97–99	64
97.5	75
98	159, 169, 173
98.1	162, 182, 183
99	169, 173
99.5	163, 169, 182
99.9	162, 169, 182, 183
100	159, 169, 177, 178
100.1-3	177
100.1-2	177
100.1	159, 178, 182
100.2	178, 182
100.3	163, 177, 178, 183
100.4-5	178
100.4	177
100.5	162, 177, 178, 182, 183
101	64
102.17	19
103	162, 169, 170
103.1-2	170, 182

Worship and the Hebrew Bible

Reference	Pages
Isaiah (cont.)	
29.14	270, 272
29.15-16	271
30.12	274
30.14	253
30.15	274
31.1-3	193
32	263
32.1	263
32.16-17	248
33.13-16	263
33.14-16	87
36.7	45
36.10	45
37.28-29	45
39	253
39.6-8	253
40–66	54, 252
40–55	37, 45, 48, 49
40.1-11	45
40.1	46
40.2	113
40.3	25, 47
40.4	46
40.5	45, 46, 52, 54
40.6-8	117
40.6	46
41.8-13	74
42.1-9	45, 46
42.3	47
42.4	46, 48, 53
42.6	47, 48
42.10-12	46, 50
42.10	46, 50
42.11	46
42.12	46, 50
44.1-5	46
44.5	46
44.28	46
45	47
45.1-3	46
45.4-5	46
45.4	46
45.6	47
45.14	47, 51, 54, 55
45.20-25	47
45.20-21	47
45.20	47
45.22	47
45.23	47
45.24	47
45.25	47
48.20	166
49–55	47
49.1-6	47
49.3	45
49.6	47, 48
49.8-12	259
49.15-17	259
49.19-23	259
49.19-21	259
51.4-5	47
51.4	47
51.5	51, 53
52.1	48, 49, 54
52.11-12	25
52.11	48
52.13–53.12	48
52.15	48
53.1-10	48
54.11-12	259
56–66	37, 48, 49
56.1-8	48-50
56.2	49
56.3-8	49, 50
56.3	49
56.4-5	49, 50
56.4	49
56.6-7	49, 50, 54
56.6	49, 50, 53-55
56.7	49, 50, 53, 55
56.8	50, 52
58.6-12	263
59.1-21	263
60–62	51
60	51, 55, 247, 248
60.1-22	50
60.1-9	247, 248
60.1-3	247, 248
60.4-9	248, 259
60.4	53, 247, 248
60.5-7	247
60.5	51, 248
60.6-7	247
60.6	50, 51
60.7	50, 51, 53-55
60.8-9	247
60.9	50, 53, 54, 248
60.10-13	259
60.10-12	247
60.10-11	247
60.12	247, 248
60.13-16	247, 248
60.13	51
60.14	51
60.17-22	248
60.17	248
60.21	42, 259
61.1	263
61.5-7	51
61.5	53
61.6	51, 55
63.1-6	51
63.7–64.11	51
63.8	54
63.18	51, 52
63.19–64.1	52
64.7	42
64.10	51, 52
64.12	54
65–66	253
65.17	54
66	35
66.15-16	53
66.18-24	54
66.18-23	35, 52, 54
66.18-20	53
66.18-19	52
66.18	52, 53, 55
66.19	52, 54, 55
66.20	53, 54
66.21	54, 55
66.22	54
66.23	54, 55
66.24	122
Jeremiah	
1.5	75
2.8	273
4.22	273

NEW TESTAMENT

OTHER ANCIENT REFERENCES

INDEX OF AUTHORS

JOURNAL FOR THE STUDY OF THE OLD TESTAMENT
SUPPLEMENT SERIES